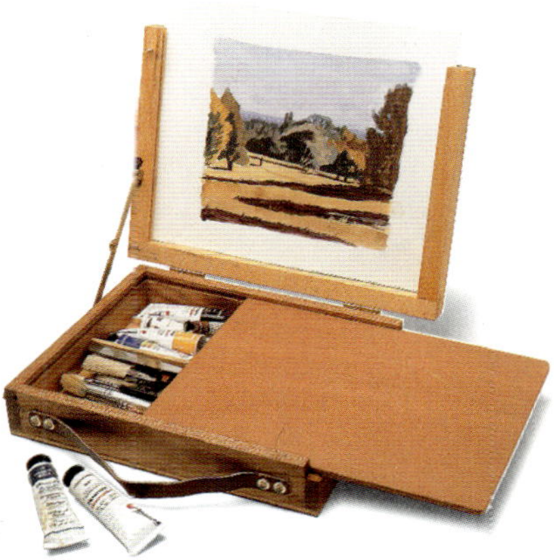

THE ARTIST'S BIBLE

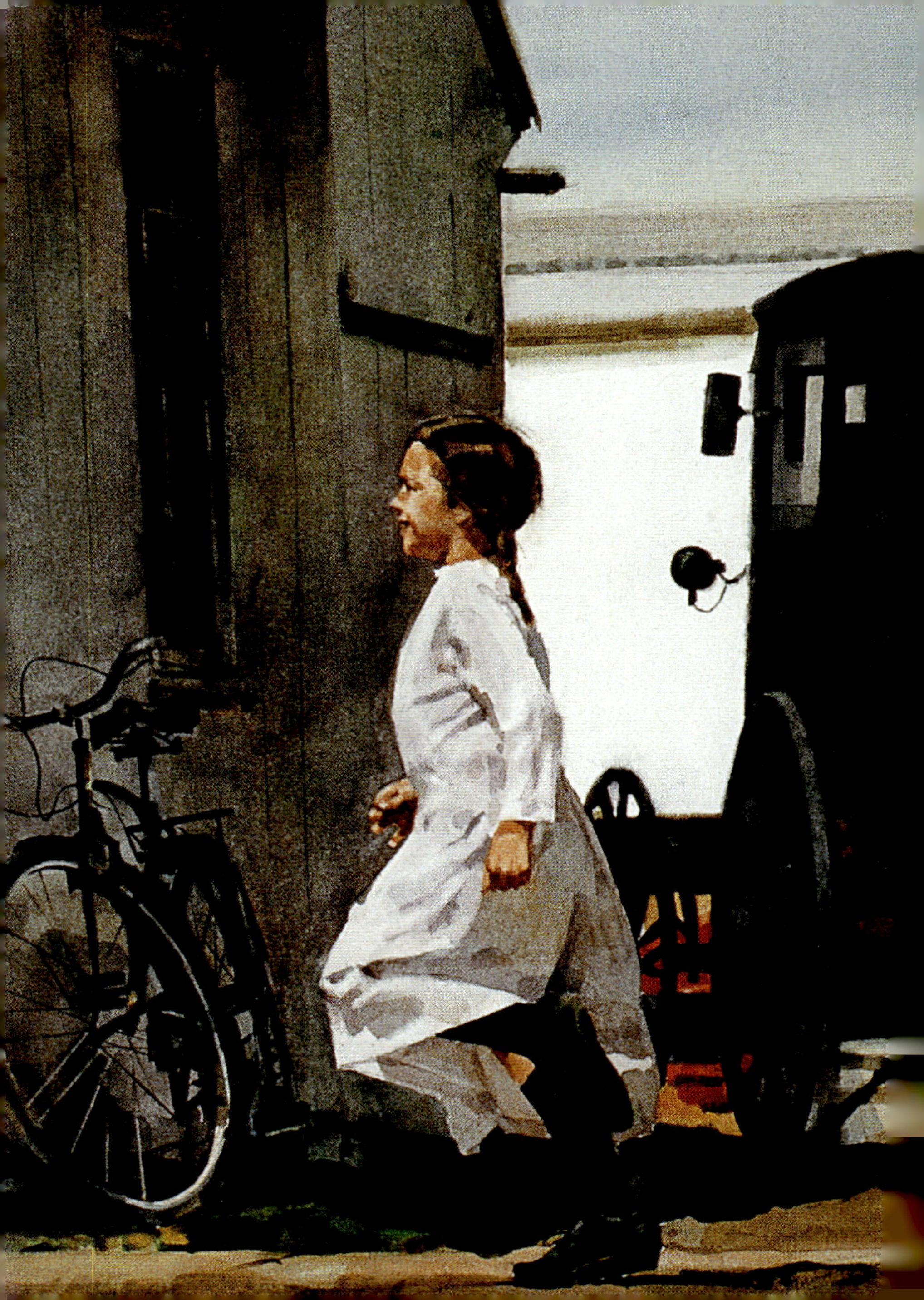

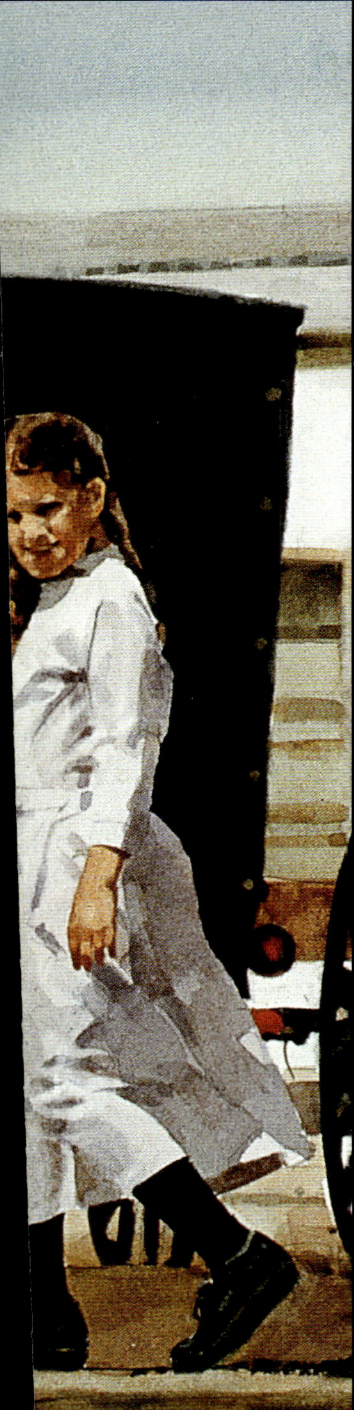

THE ARTIST'S BIBLE

Consultant Editor
Helen Douglas-Cooper

BARNES & NOBLE
BOOKS
NEW YORK

This edition published by Barnes & Noble, Inc.,
by arrangement with Quarto Publishing

2004 Barnes & Noble Books

M 10 9 8 7 6 5 4 3 2 1

ISBN 0-7607-5067-X

QUAR.TBU

Project Editor: Jocelyn Guttery
Art Editor and Designer: Jill Mumford
Assistant Art Director: Penny Cobb
Photographers: Colin Bowling, Paul Forrester, Laura Wickenden, Chas Wilder
Proofreader: Claire Waite Brown
Indexer: Rosemary Anderson
Art Director: Moira Clinch
Publisher: Piers Spence

Manufactured by PICA Digital Singapore
Printed in China by Midas Printing International Limited

Preceding page: "Double Dutch" by Frank Nofer (detail).

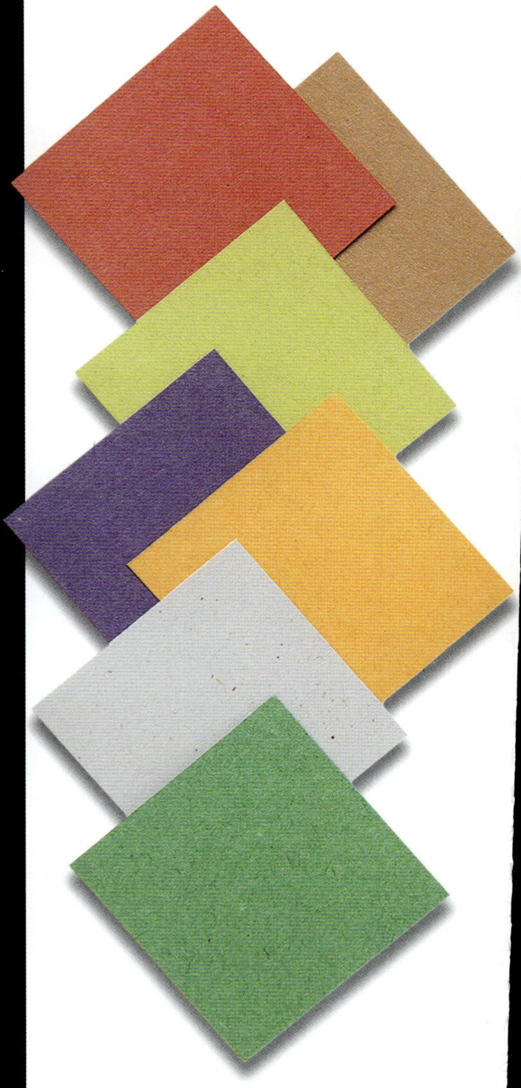

CONTENTS

INTRODUCTION

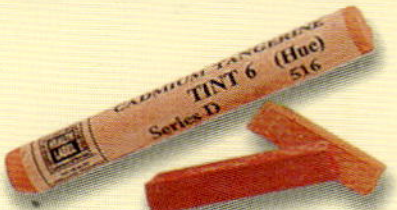

THE SUN IS HIGH, and the scene you are painting is a patchwork of sparkling colors and deep shadows. Your watercolor painting is looking good, but it's drying too fast. Or you are working in oils and you want to layer one color over another, leaving flecks of the first color showing through. You have seen this in other paintings, but you are not sure how to do it. Or do you wonder which medium to mix into your acrylic paints to get the effect you want?

Even professional artists have frustrations and near-disasters, but they learn to overcome them, and so will you with the help of this book. Unlike other books, this is not a painting course, but a source of advice for working in watercolors, oils, pastels, and acrylics.

Each type of paint has its own special qualities, and each also has its problems and pitfalls This book is therefore divided up into four sections, each devoted to one medium. To help you find the advice you need quickly, each section is divided up into topics such as materials and equipment, color mixing, painting techniques and special effects, working out of doors, and tips for individual subjects, such as foliage, water, and portraits. As a whole, the book tackles many of the problems that you may come across in your work, and suggests a wealth of ideas across the different media to inspire you to experiment with different materials and ways or working.

In Joe Anna Arnett's "Magnolias with Cherries," the curved forms of the flowers, vase, and fruit have been modeled by blending adjacent areas of light and shadow to create smooth, rounded surfaces.

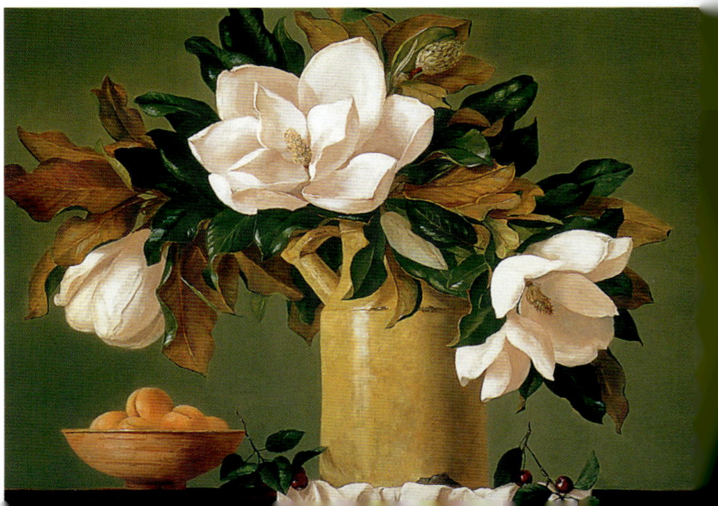

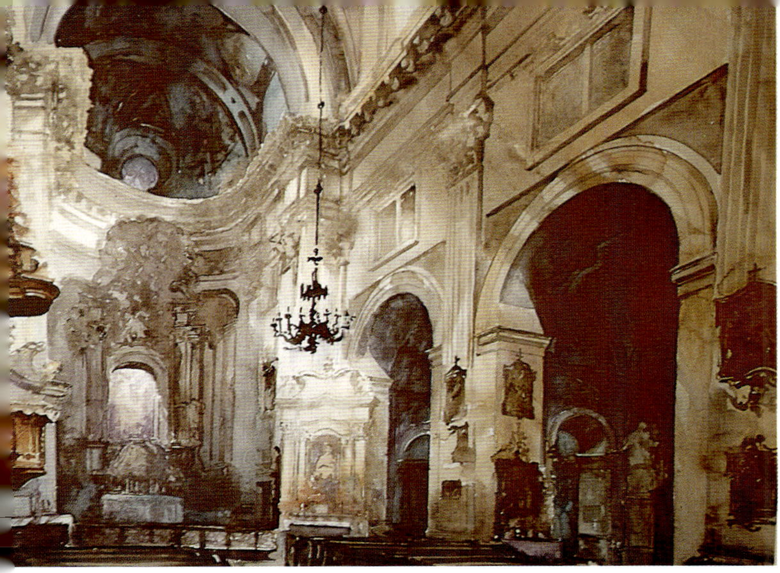

Paul Dmoch's complex interior has been captured through careful use of light, medium, and dark watercolor washes, the darkest tone creating deeply recessed areas.

WORKING IN WATERCOLOR

WATERCOLOR is notoriously difficult to control. And even experienced artists can find it frustrating. This section starts with the basics, with advice on selecting paints from the huge range available, and ways of making the paint easier to use and apply. Paper types are described with tips on selecting and treating the right type of paper for the effects you want to create. Brushes are also covered, with advice on how to judge a brush's quality, and which type to use for different effects. The basis of all watercolor painting—laying a wash—gets a whole section, with tips on how to achieve a flat, even tone and how to perfect graduated and variegated washes, without the associated problems.

This section goes on to cover more advanced and unusual techniques, including sponging and spattering, and ways of turning accidents such as blots and runs to creative advantage for interpreting landscapes, skies, and trees in unusual ways. This part encourages you to experiment with new techniques, and to give yourself the chance of unleashing a whole torrent of creative ideas.

Finally, there are tips for painting problem subjects, including reflections on water, color for trees and foliage, techniques for capturing details of leaves and flowers, and adding people into landscapes.

MANY PEOPLE think that oil paints are more difficult to use than other media. But with a little knowledge about the best materials to use, and the different ways of applying paint and building up the image, you may find it easier than you imagined to get good results. Tips are included on the selection of paints and other equipment, and on the re-use and recycling of materials. The different types of canvases and boards are described, with advice on stretching canvas, and sizing and priming your painting surface. The different types and shapes of brushes and the types of marks each make are illustrated, and there are tips on cleaning and looking after brushes to ensure their longevity. The section on color covers choice of colors and laying out a palette, and different ways of mixing colors and achieving color effects with oil paints.

Oil paint can be applied into wet paint or over dry paint, it can be built up using thin, transparent glazes or by applying thicker, opaque layers. It can be applied with a brush or a knife, and it can be scraped or wiped off. These techniques are described in detail, together with advice on how you can avoid the accompanying problems, such as paint cracking or sinking.

Oil paints can be cumbersome to take on location, but with careful selection of equipment and materials you can lighten the load. There are also various strategies to help with the other problems—such as constantly changing conditions and limited time—associated with working out of doors. And then there is the problem of transporting wet paintings home again. All are covered here. And special tips are included to help you tackle tricky subjects such as clouds, light on water, foliage, moving figures, and groups.

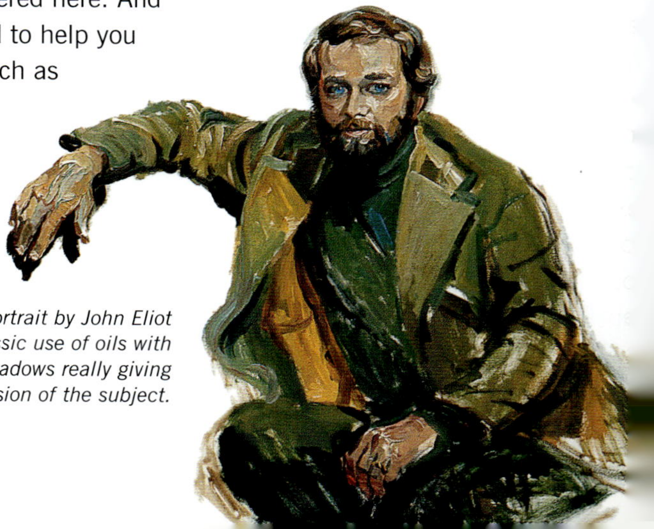

This informal portrait by John Eliot demonstrates a classic use of oils with subtle tones and shadows really giving an impression of the subject.

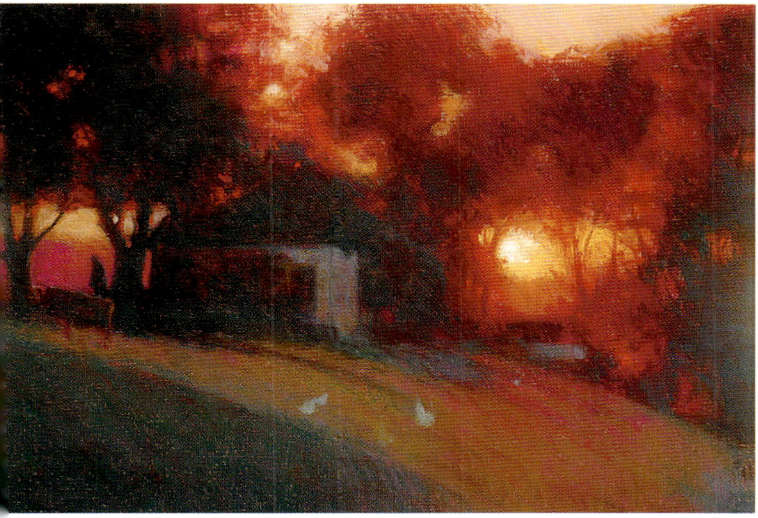

In "Country Sunset" by Doug Dawson, the intensity, texture, and depth of color are captured perfectly using a very limited range of colors.

PASTEL COMBINES vibrant color with the immediacy of drawing. With a pastel stick you can draw as you would with a stick of charcoal, but you can also spread, blend, and overlay colors to build up thick, painterly effects. There are no set rules or ways of working, but once you know what can be done, you will be halfway to finding your own style.

The section begins with general advice on types of soft and oil pastels and how to look after them. This is followed by tips on selecting from the wide range of paper types according to the effect you want to create. Ideas are included on ways to tint paper for working on, how to create textured effects by working over an acrylic ground, how to turn oil pastel into paint, and how to combine pastel with other media, such as paint and charcoal. Tips are given for special techniques, such as dragging and crosshatching as ways of creating texture and mixing color, and for reviving an overworked painting or toning down colors that are too bright, together with tips for creating solid forms, space, and depth, and adding fine details. Special tips are also included on capturing colors and shadow detail in landscapes, skin tones in portraits, and the delicacy of flowers—a subject to which pastels are especially well suited.

Pastel is a fragile medium, and your pictures won't last unless you look after them, and there are hints on framing and caring for your work in this section.

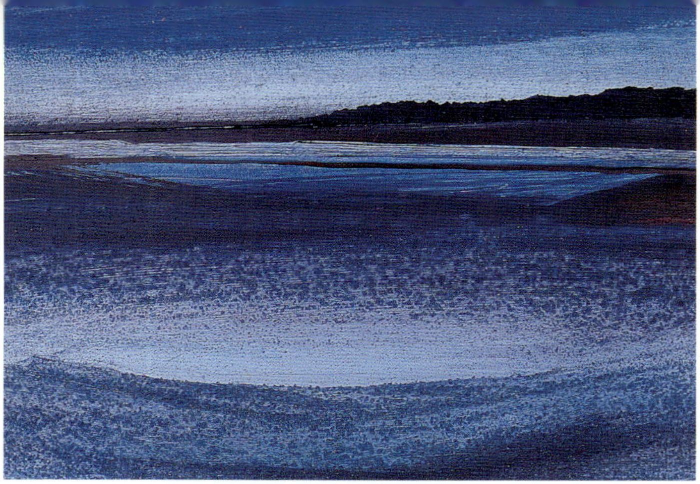

In "Night Sea" Robert Tilling has used acrylics to paint alternating bands of warm and cool color that recede into the distance. The textural detail in the foreground heightens the sense of space.

WORKING IN ACRYLICS

ACRYLIC PAINT is a relatively new medium, so there is no well-established body of techniques associated with it, nor should there be as you can do more or less anything you like with it. You can paint on paper, canvas, or board, use the paint thin or thick, apply it with knives or brushes, combine it with other media, use it for collage—the list is virtually endless.

This section begins with practical advice about selecting paints and preparing surfaces to paint on. There are tips on selecting and looking after brushes and palettes, advice on choosing colors and how to mix colors you see accurately, and how to modify colors in a painting. And should you want to thin the paint down or make it thicker, speed up or slow down the drying time, create textured grounds or even-toned washes, the different mediums for mixing with acrylic paint are described, with tips on how to use them. Ways of using special effects are covered, such as spattering and scraping, combing and collage, and ways of combining acrylics with other media such as charcoal and pastel. Advice is included for capturing subjects such as foliage and glass, and on different ways of making corrections without damaging the picture surface. Finally, there is a section on using acrylics for craft applications, such as painting on wood, fabrics, and terra-cotta pots.

HOW TO USE THIS BOOK

Throughout the book, there are tips that tell you how you can save money by choosing materials wisely or using alternatives to purchased materials; tips that will save you time while you are working; and tips that will help you avoid disasters. Some tips will be of particular help to beginners; others let you in on trade secrets for getting the most out of your chosen medium.

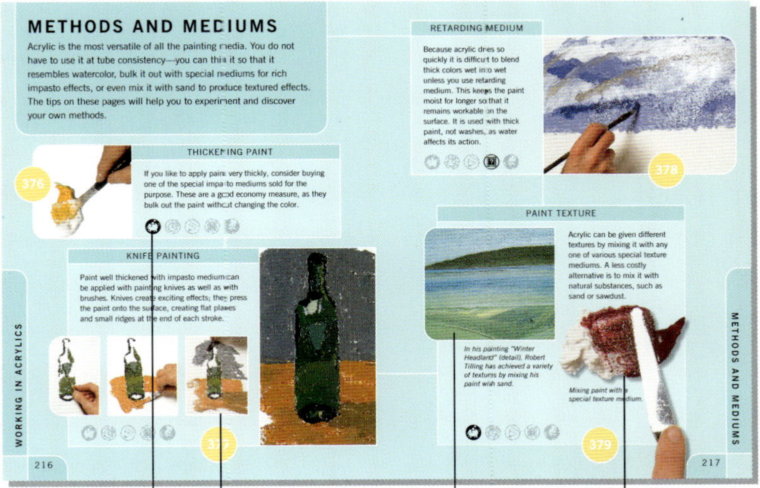

METHODS AND MEDIUMS

Acrylic is the most versatile of all the painting media. You do not have to use it at tube consistency—you can thin it so that it resembles watercolor, bulk it out with special mediums for rich impasto effects, or even mix it with sand to produce textured effects. The tips on these pages will help you to experiment and discover your own methods.

376 THICKENING PAINT

If you like to apply paint very thickly, consider buying one of the special impasto mediums sold for the purpose. These are a good economy measure, as they bulk out the paint without changing the color.

377 KNIFE PAINTING

Paint well thickened with impasto medium can be applied with painting knives as well as with brushes. Knives create exciting effects; they press the paint onto the surface, creating flat planes and small ridges at the end of each stroke.

378 RETARDING MEDIUM

Because acrylic dries so quickly it is difficult to blend thick colors wet into wet unless you use retarding medium. This keeps the paint moist for longer so that it remains workable on the surface. It is used with thick paint, not washes, as water affects its action.

379 PAINT TEXTURE

Acrylic can be given different textures by mixing it with any one of various special texture mediums. A less costly alternative is to mix it with natural substances, such as sand or sawdust.

In his painting "Winter Headland" (detail), Robert Tilling has achieved a variety of textures by mixing his paint with sand.

Mixing paint with a special texture medium.

WORKING IN ACRYLICS 216

METHODS AND MEDIUMS 217

At-a-glance icons that, when highlighted, indicate the specific areas covered by each particular tip.

Step-by-step sequences guide you through the techniques.

Examples show you the effects you will be able to achieve.

Most tips have an explanatory illustration.

GUIDE TO ICONS

Money saving	*Time saving*	*Beginner artists*	*Trade secrets*	*Correcting mistakes and avoiding disaster*

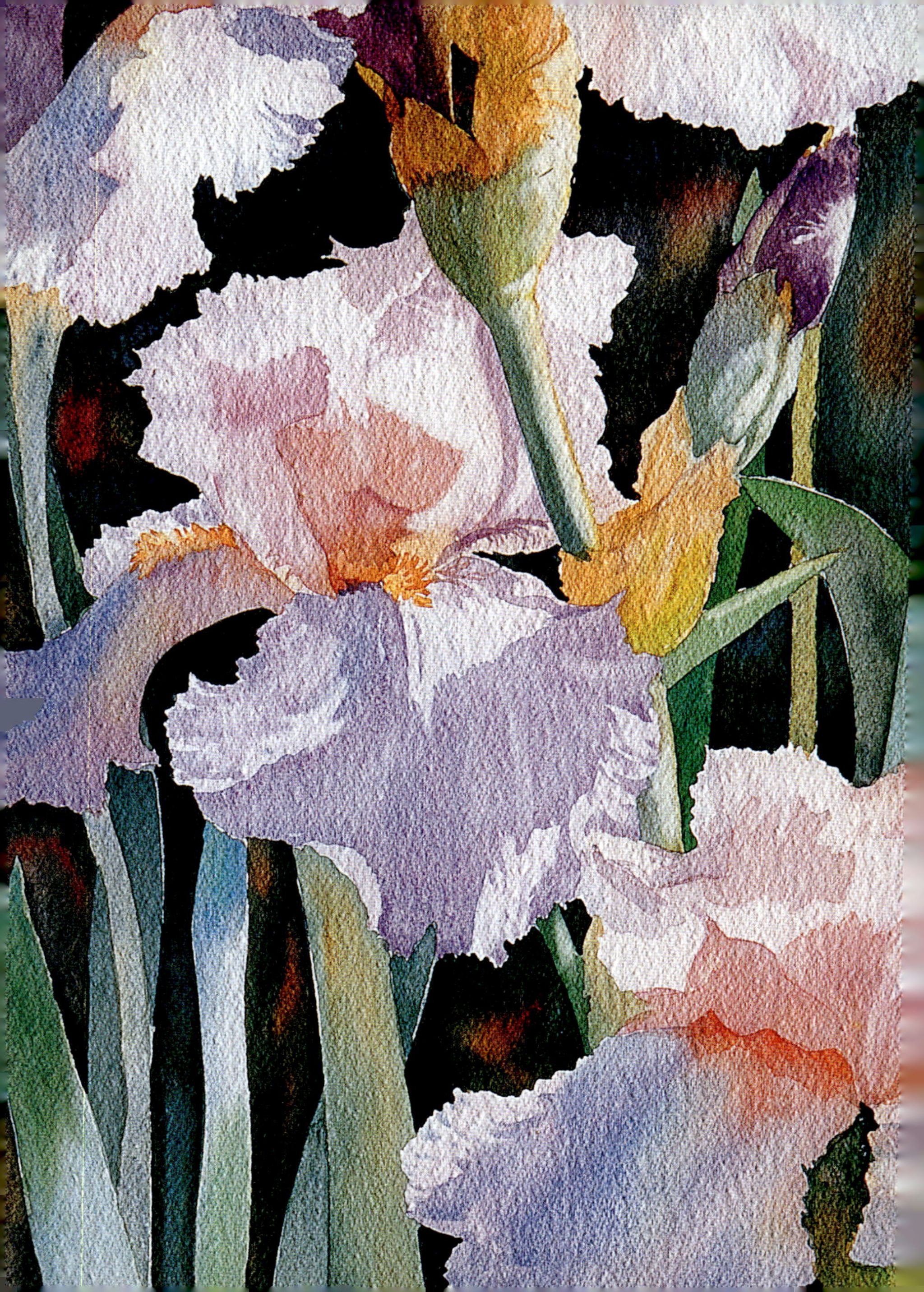

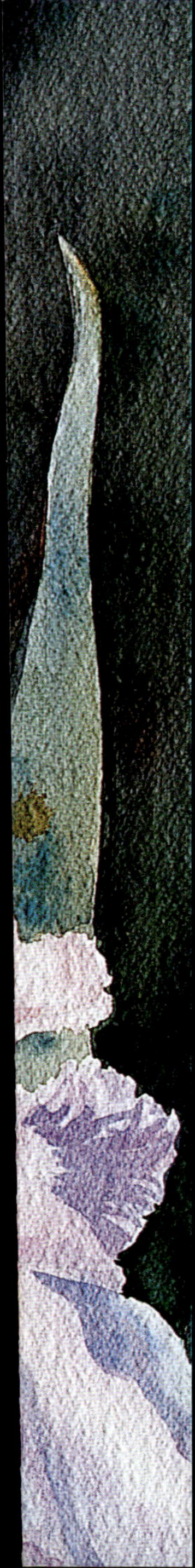

1

WATERCOLOR

Whether you want to gain more confidence in your watercolor painting, or look up a quick remedy for a problem, or find a source of new ideas and techniques, you will find the advice you need in the following pages. This section covers selecting paints and watercolor papers, types of brushes and brushstrokes, applying different kinds of washes, using special effects, creating highlights, making alterations, opacity, how to travel light, and painting landscapes, trees and foliage, buildings and people.

Nancy Baldrica, "Three Irises" (detail).

INTRODUCTION TO WATERCOLORS

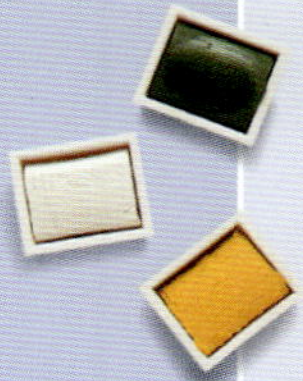

THE SUN IS at its zenith, the dazzling noon light creates short, exciting shadows—your watercolor is looking good, but it's drying too fast. Painting the delightful debris of a picnic lunch, the crumbs of freshly baked French bread scattered over the gingham cloth—you want to erase your pencil lines and lighten the background, but you've left your putty eraser behind in the hotel room. These are a couple of the problems that as a watercolor painter you may find yourself faced with.

Watercolor is an exciting and challenging medium, but beginners, in particular, can feel bewildered by a host of supposed rules. Even those artists who paint in watercolor regularly and have acquired the confidence of practice find themselves locked into habits that they would benefit from breaking. One word of advice from another artist can release a whole torrent of ideas, or one seemingly simple tip can unleash a whole wave of creativity.

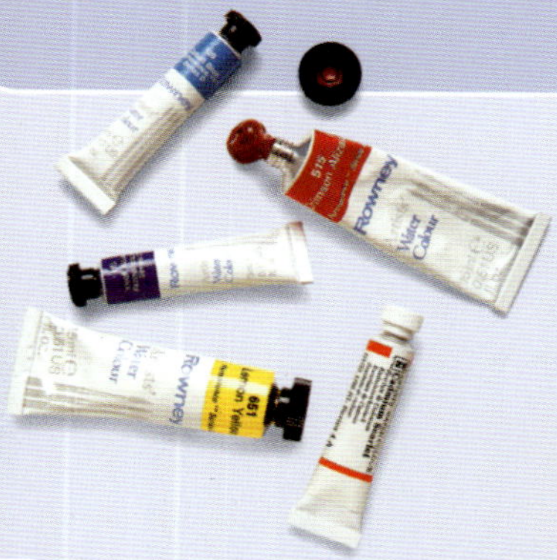

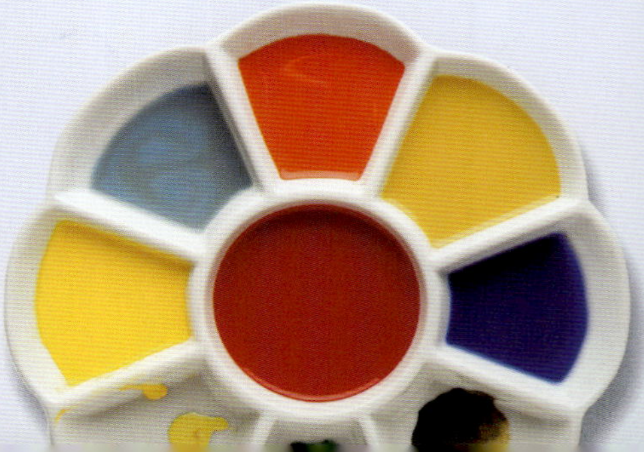

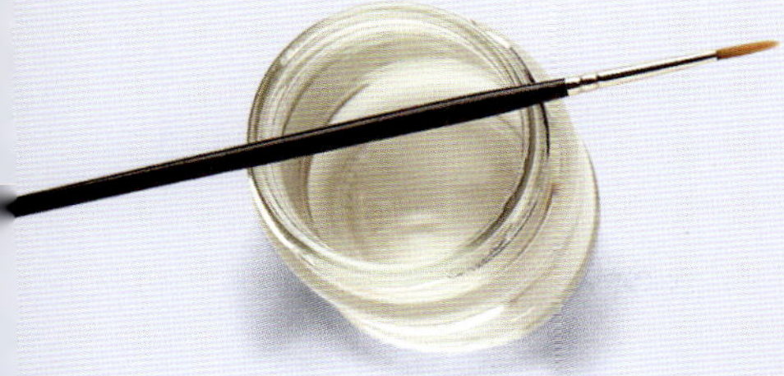

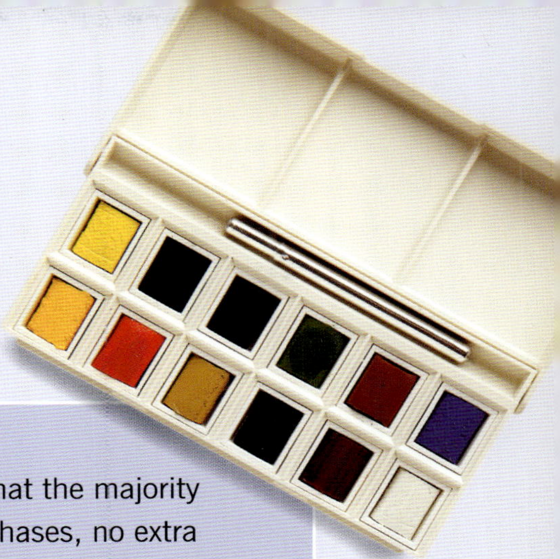

The beauty of this section is that the majority of the ideas require no extra purchases, no extra space, and no heavy reading. The tips are divided into sections highlighting the most common problem areas for watercolor artists. They cover the materials used and the painting in progress, running through washes, special effects, and highlighting and masking, with small sections on altering and erasing, body color and colored grounds, and brief hints on traveling light.

You can have a lot of fun just trying out some of the hints. Plenty of new ideas result from simply playing with watercolor rather than trying to make finished paintings. This is true both for the beginner and for the seasoned artist. I have enjoyed experimenting with ideas in the Special Effects section, making quick, tiny watercolors just to try out the effect. Some of these "dispensable" paintings have more vibrancy than a finished painting because they were done in such a relaxed manner.

CONTROLLING THE PAINT

One of the disadvantages of watercolor is that you don't always know what it is going to do. One color has a way of running into another just when you don't want it to, and refusing to do so when you do. The tips in this section provide some useful hints on how to make the paint "behave itself," as well as giving practical basic advice on colors.

PRESERVING PAINT

1

To prevent your watercolor pans from drying or cracking up, mix them with gum arabic. If you don't have any gum arabic, put a blob of honey or glycerin onto the dried-out pan instead. Allow the glycerin or honey to soak into the paint before you start using it. This will make the paint more soluble, while retaining some of the moisture in its composition.

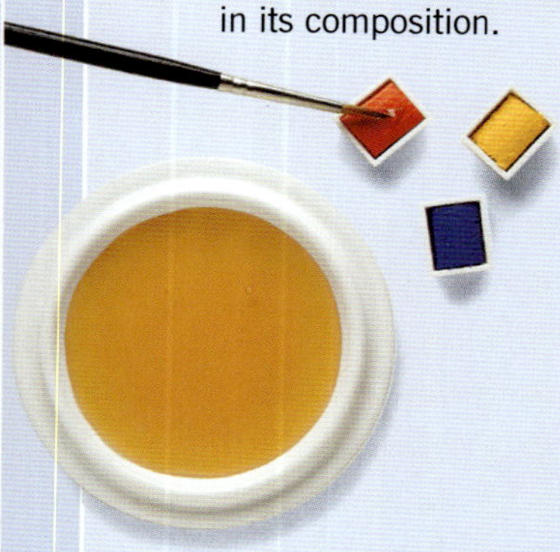

FASTER DRYING

If you are working in damp weather and find that your watercolor is not drying quickly enough, use a hairdryer to accelerate the process. However, be careful when working across very wet pools of color, as the dryer can easily blow and smudge your work.

2

3 ALCOHOL MEDIUM

If you do not have a hairdryer for speeding up slow-drying washes, try adding alcohol to your paint as an alternative. In the days before the invention of hairdryers, gin added to the paint water was a popular choice for accelerating the drying process because it evaporates more quickly than water.

4 SLOWER DRYING

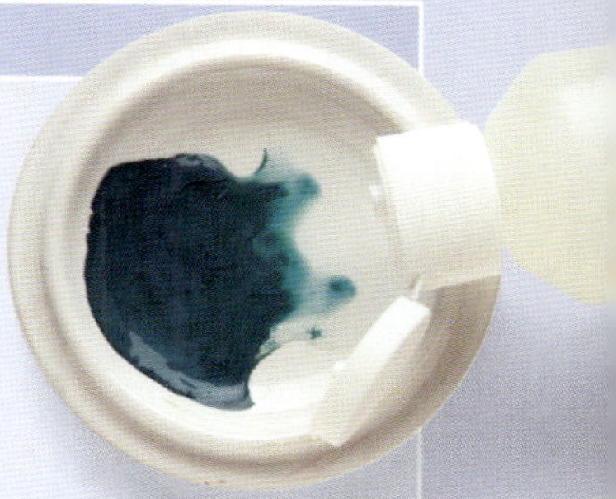

If you want to work with watercolor over a long period and so need to prevent it from drying out, mix it with ox-gall or a similar flow-medium that will retard the drying process. There are three ways of using flow-medium: you can prime the paper with it and then paint over it when dry; you can mix it with water and use the water to mix the paint; or you can mix the flow-medium directly into the paint on the palette. An added advantage is that flow-medium increases the vibrancy of your watercolors.

5 SOAKING THE PAPER

If you work slowly and watercolor seems to dry too fast for your requirements, soak the paper in water for at least 15–20 minutes before you stretch it and start painting. This will mean that it stays wet for longer.

THE BEST PAINT

Although it may seem expensive to buy artist's quality watercolors, they are worth the extra cost. Because there is a higher proportion of pigment to binder, the colors are purer and more intense. The paints are also available in a wider choice of colors, and many are more lightfast than their cheaper equivalents.

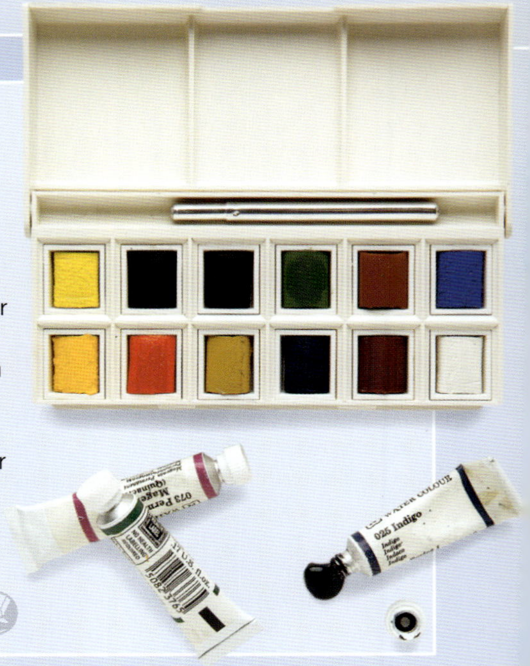

6

WATER

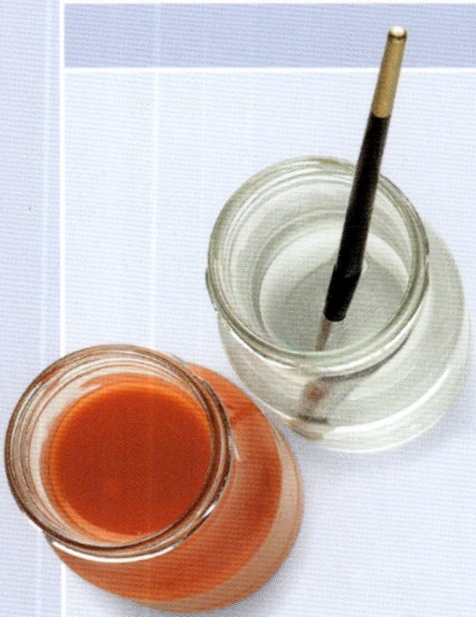

Always have three pots of water ready when you paint: one of clean water for loading brushes and wetting the paper; one of constantly replaced clean water for mixing with the paint to produce clean, clear colors; and one for rinsing brushes while you work.

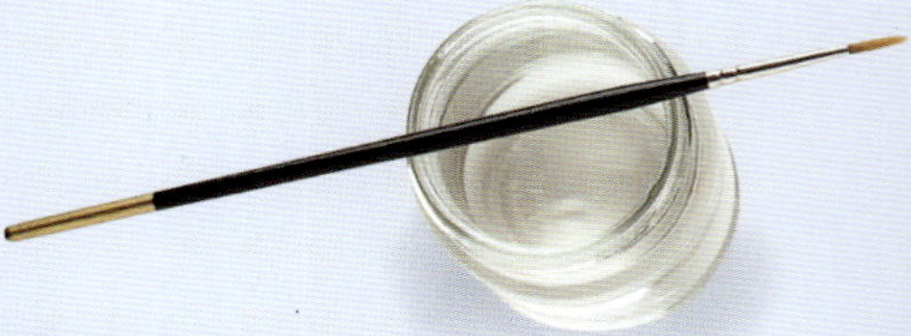

7

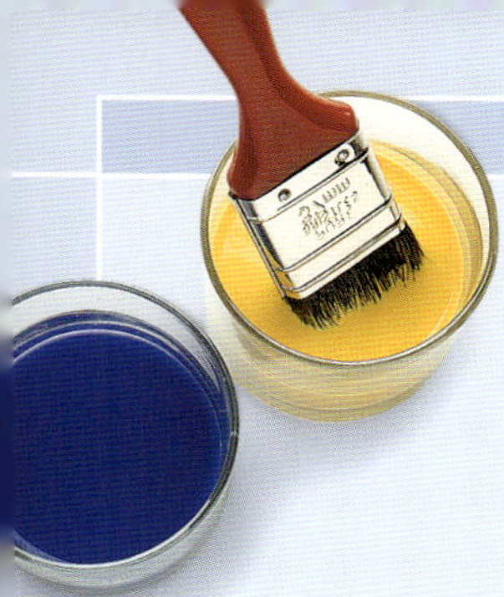

8 WORKING BIG

When you work on a large scale, try mixing watercolors in containers, rather than in your paint box. This means you can paint quickly and smoothly without having to stop to mix more colors, and you will be able to store the fluid for following sessions, retaining the exact color mix required.

9 DECEPTIVE COLOR

Do your watercolors always look washed out when you have finished? This may be because you have used too little pigment with too much water. Very wet color looks deceptively strong and will dry lighter.

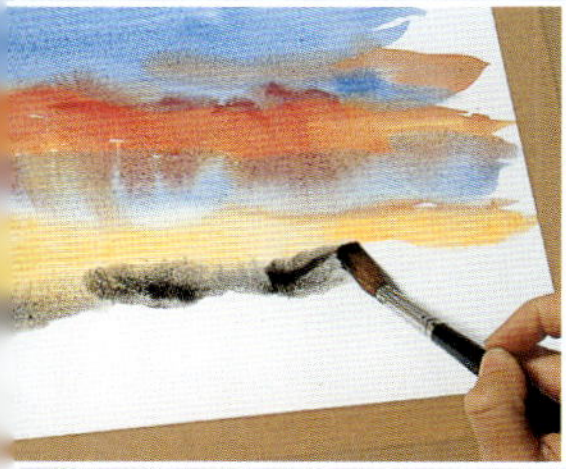

The colors in this variegated wash are still wet and appear bright and vibrant.

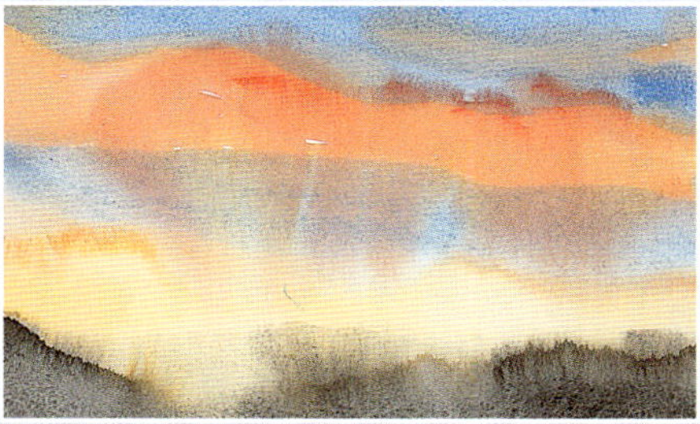

Once dry, they have paled considerably.

10 TESTING COLOR

Always keep a small piece of watercolor paper beside you to test the mixtures and strengths of colors before you use them on your painting. If you note the color mix beside each test mark, you will always be able to remix any color for further applications.

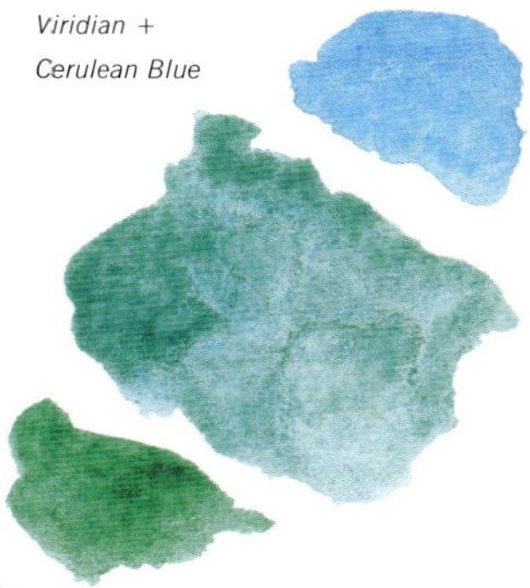

KEEPING PAPER DAMP

If you want your paper to retain dampness throughout the painting process, place a cloth soaked in water underneath it and leave it there while you paint. To stop the paper from cockling, press it tightly over the cloth and attach the edges to the board with gummed-paper tape.

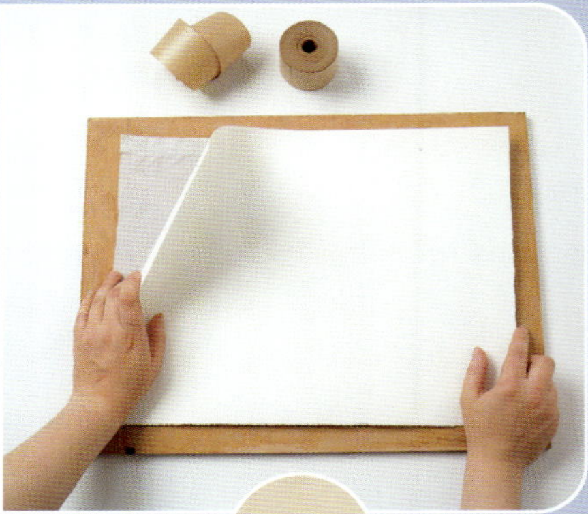

11

TESTING FOR DRYNESS

12

Touching the surface of your watercolor with your fingers to test how dry it is can easily leave grease marks on the paper, to which paint will not adhere. To test for dryness, try using the back of your hand instead. It is a more sensitive receptor than the fingers and will quickly detect any remaining dampness.

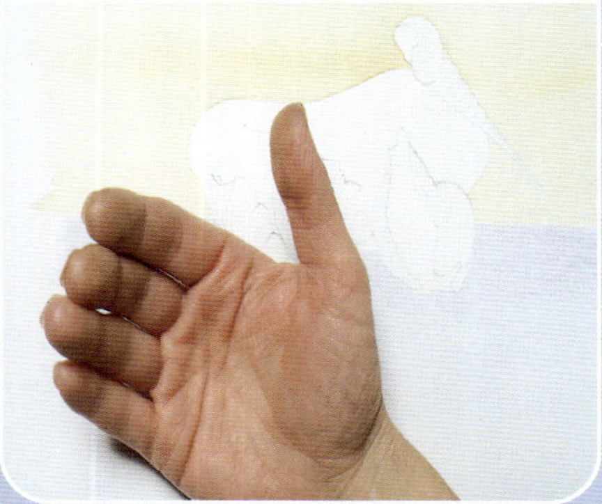

WATER QUANTITIES

If you have trouble measuring the right amount of water to mix with your watercolor, try adding the water to the paint with a pipette tube. This way, you won't overwater or spill water, and the device is also useful for sucking paint from a palette and storing it in a bottle for later use.

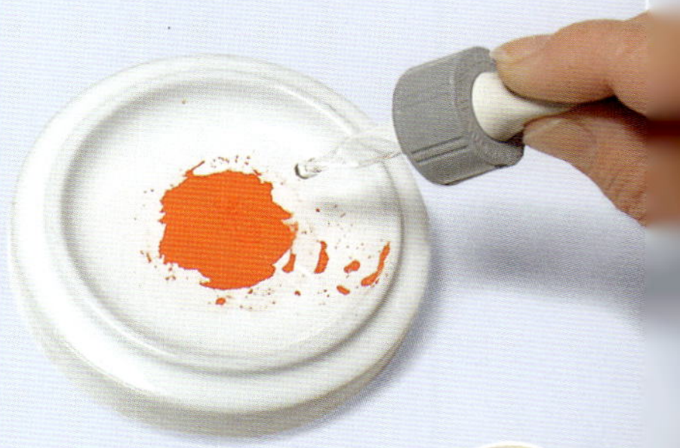

13

BETTER BLENDING

If you add a little gum arabic to your water when mixing paint, it becomes less runny and easier to blend. This is particularly useful if you are building up a painting in a series of small brushstrokes, because they will remain separate rather than flowing together.

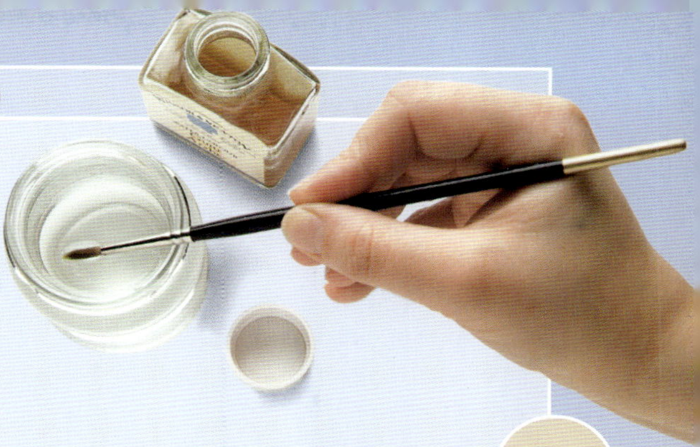

14

REFLECTED LIGHT

If your watercolors look dull you may not be taking full advantage of the whiteness of your paper. The brightness of watercolor paint comes from the reflection of light from the white paper back through the paint. Think of the paper as an extra color on your palette, and let it do some of the work for you.

15

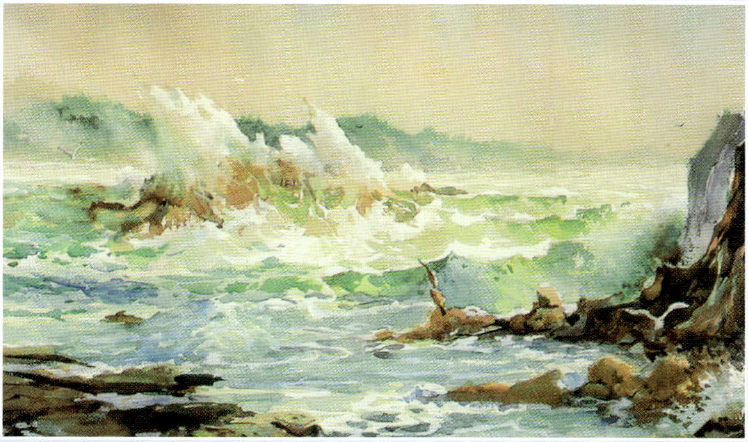

In La Vere Hutchings' painting, "Monterey Bay," the sparkling effect of the breaking waves is created by reserving white paper.

16

DRIED-UP PAINT

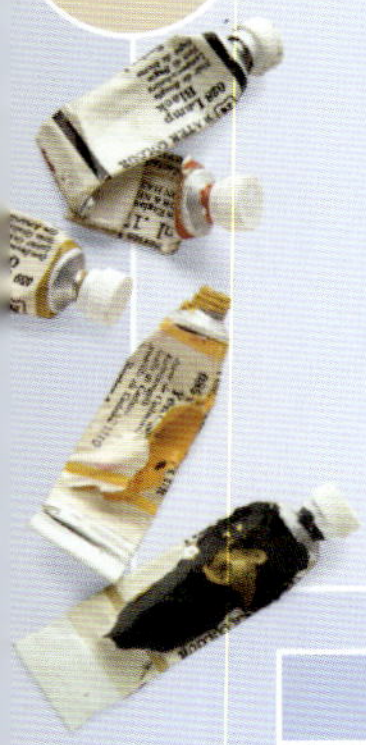

Rather than throwing dried-out tubes of paint away, split them open and use the remains as pan watercolor. But be careful: some tube colors become less insoluble when dry and will create a flaky solution, so always test them before use.

BLENDING TONES

To prevent harsh edges from forming between light and dark tones, dampen the paper in both the light and dark areas to allow the paint to spread. Then lay the light tones down first, and allow the paint to flow into areas that will then be colored with darker tones.

Elizabeth Apgar Smith, "Lilies" (detail).

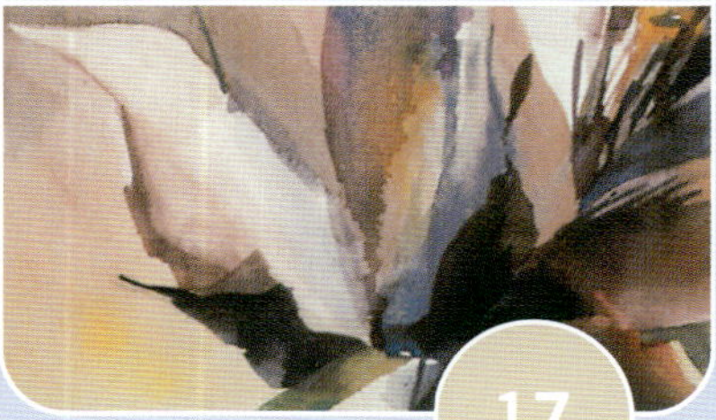

17

BACKRUNS

If you place wet paint next to an area that appears to be dry but isn't, the fresh watercolor will suddenly bloom into the semi-dry area, usually creating unplanned effects. This is called a backrun. To avoid them, always check that areas you want to remain untouched are completely dry before adding fresh paint next to them. However, backruns can create interesting effects that enhance your work, and some artists exploit them deliberately.

In John Lidzey's painting, backruns on the wall and window create attractive effects.

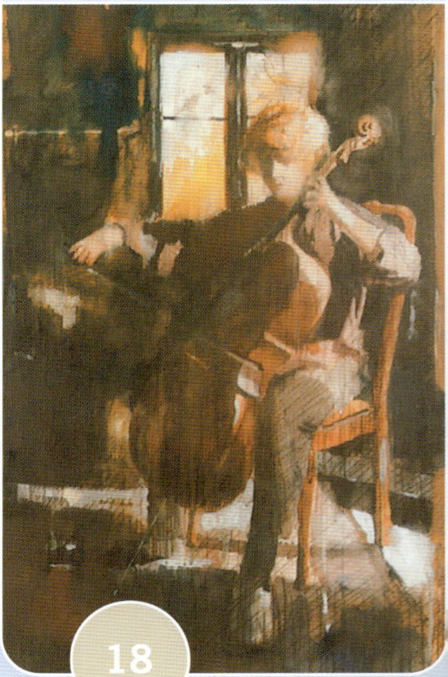

18

WATERCOLOR PAPERS

If you visit a specialist supplier, you will find a bewildering variety of handmade watercolor papers, but most artists use machine-made papers available from all art stores. This section will help you make an initial choice, and you can experiment with more exotic papers later if you wish. There are also tips on stretching paper and dealing with problems such as creasing.

AN ALL-ROUND PAPER

19

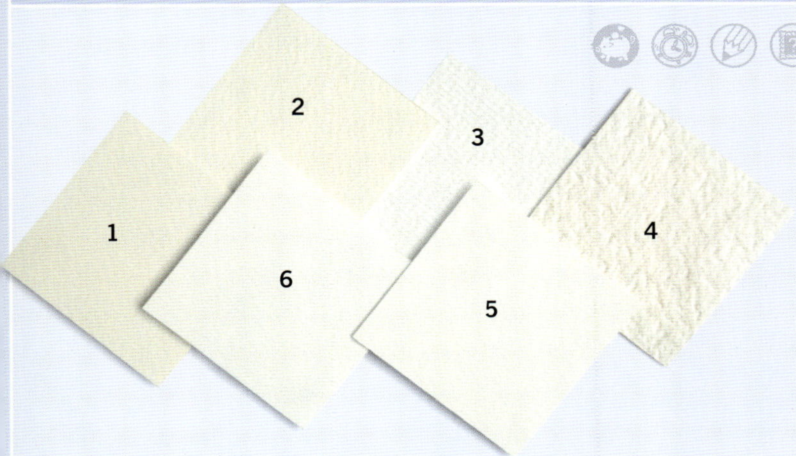

Most watercolor paper is made by machine, though you can also buy handmade papers, **4**, that have a high rag content. They are expensive and not usually available in ordinary art stores. Machine-made papers come in different surfaces, of which there are three main categories: **6** smooth (otherwise known as hot-pressed or HP for short); **1 & 5** medium (sometimes called cold-pressed or CP, but most commonly known as Not); and **2 & 3** rough (also cold-pressed, but with a much more pronounced texture). Although some artists choose smooth or rough paper for special effects, the all-round favorite is Not, which has enough texture to hold the paint but not enough to interfere with color and detail.

HEAVY PAPER

20

If you want to experiment with textures and effects on watercolor paper, use a good, heavy paper or watercolor board, which will take real punishment. A heavyweight paper or board will not need stretching and should soak up a lot of water without disintegrating. This helps to retain the transparent quality of the watercolor paint. You can also use a sponge to remove or add color.

STRETCHING PAPER

21

Thinner watercolor papers need to be stretched so that they don't buckle when paint is applied. When stretching paper, sponging the painting side can sometimes stir up the surface. To avoid this, smooth some dry paper towels over a board. Place the top side of the paper face down on the paper towels and sponge the back of the paper. The paper towels will absorb any residual water that seeps through to the top side. Turn the paper over and remove the towels. Then tape down the paper with gummed-paper tape. Using this method, the painting surface remains undisturbed, no dust or specks are picked up from the board, and any prior drawing remains intact.

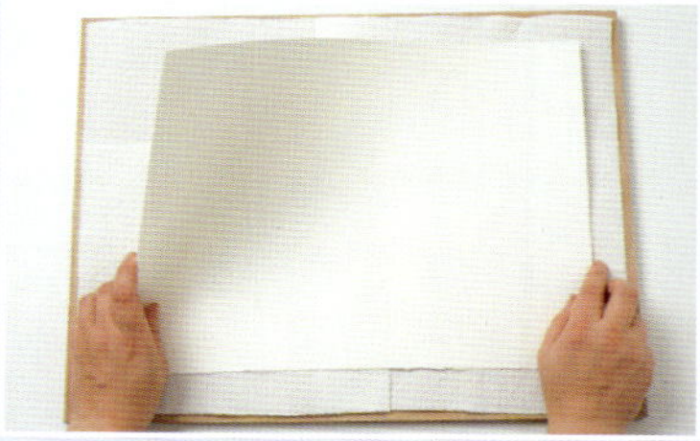

Place the paper over paper towels.

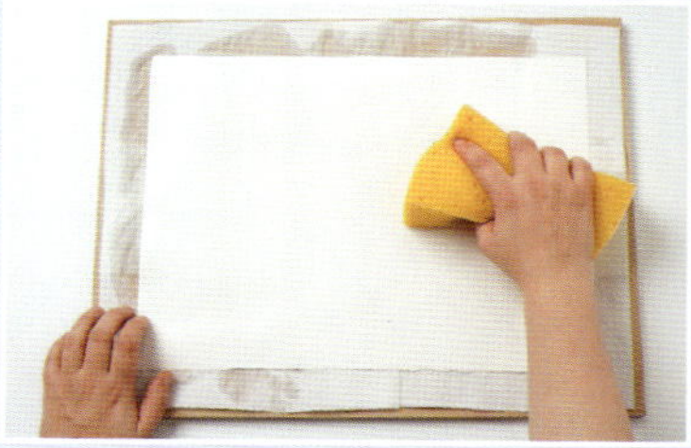

Lightly sponge the back of the paper.

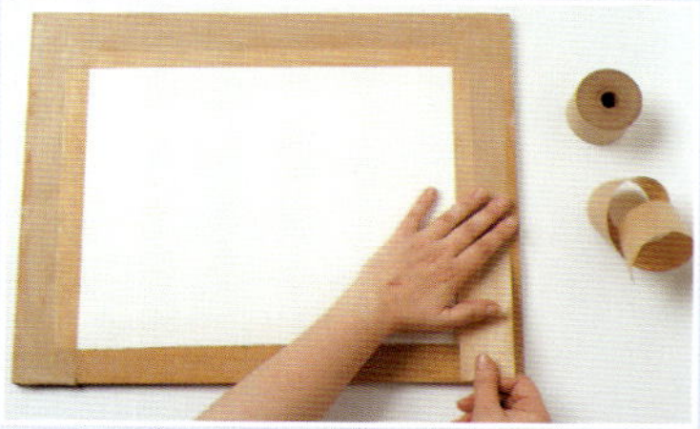

Secure the paper to the board with gummed-paper tape.

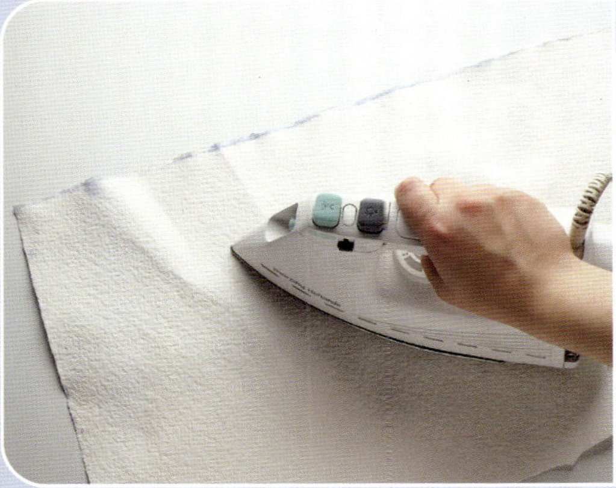

REMOVING CREASES

22

If you have accidentally creased your paper while stretching or painting, it can often be smoothed out when dry by ironing the back with a warm iron. Lay it face down on clean white paper to protect the painting.

BUCKLED PAPER

If your paper has buckled, it is often possible to stretch it after you have finished the painting, unless there is a heavy buildup of paint. However, be very gentle with the painted surface. Allow the painting to dry out completely, place it between two sheets of blotting paper, and put weights over the top.

23

BRUSHES AND BRUSHSTROKES

Most people will know that the best brushes for watercolor work are sables, and that they are very expensive. But there are many other brushes you can use, such as household brushes that are ideal for large washes. This section will help you to make wise choices, as well as learn to exploit the marks of the brush so that they play a part in your work.

LOOSENING UP

24

To loosen your painting style and add a sense of spontaneity to your painting, try holding the brush at the top end, so you are forced to make quick dashes of color. This will prevent you from working too lightly.

Holding the brush at the top encourages a looser, freer approach and more expressive strokes.

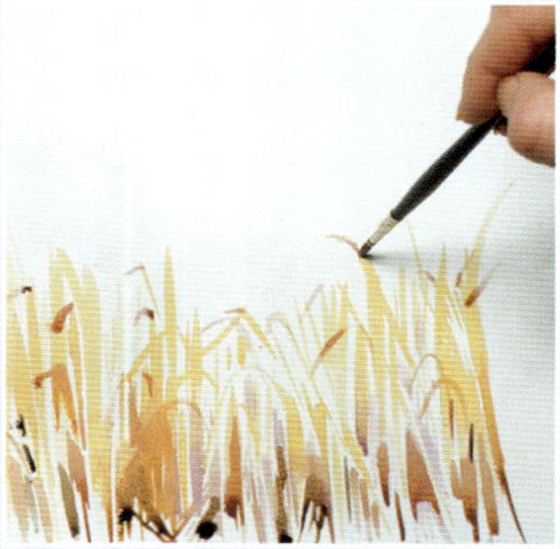

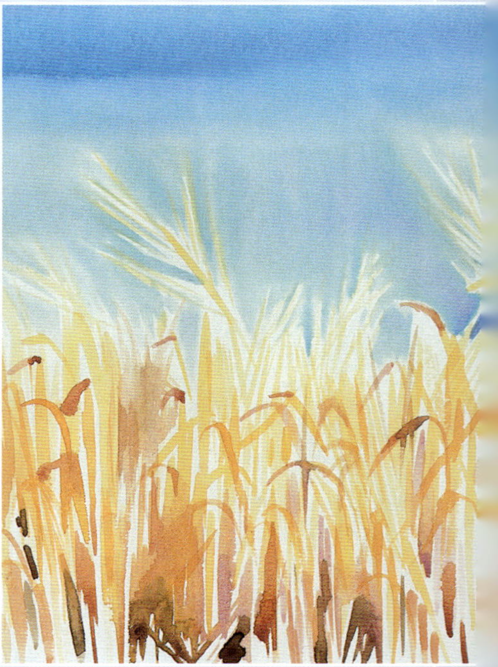

CHINESE BRUSHES

25

If you can only afford a few brushes, Chinese brushes are a wise choice. They can create both very broad and very fine marks, and large, round, Chinese brushes are not as expensive as the equivalent sable ones.

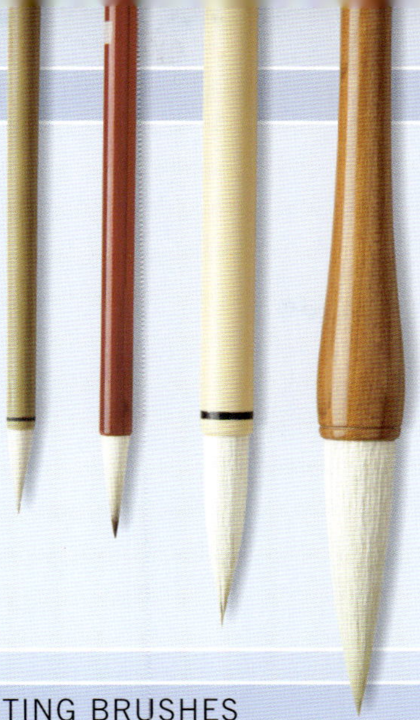

TESTING BRUSHES

26

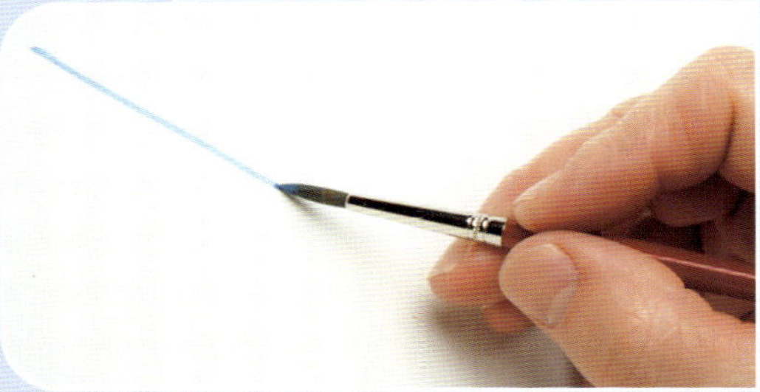

With a pointed brush, the line created is delicate.

The better the quality of brushes, the better your brushmarks are going to be, so check the quality of any round or pointed brush by painting a fine line with it. The point of a good brush should give a fine line whatever its size.

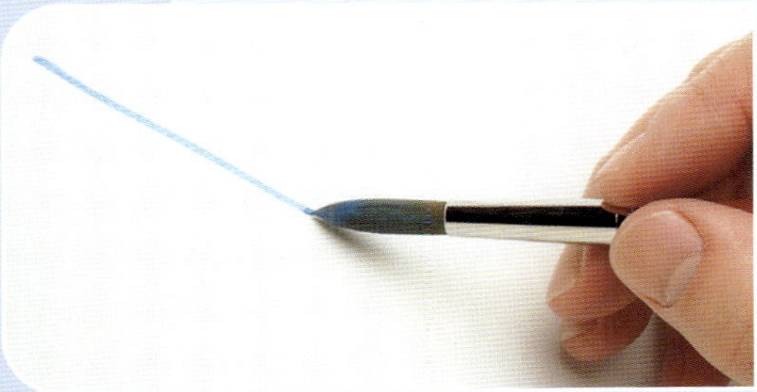

With a rounded brush, the line created is equally clean.

27

BRUSH QUALITY

A good brush should have a certain resilience. You can test the spring of a brush by wetting it into a point and dragging it lightly over your thumbnail. It should not droop but spring back.

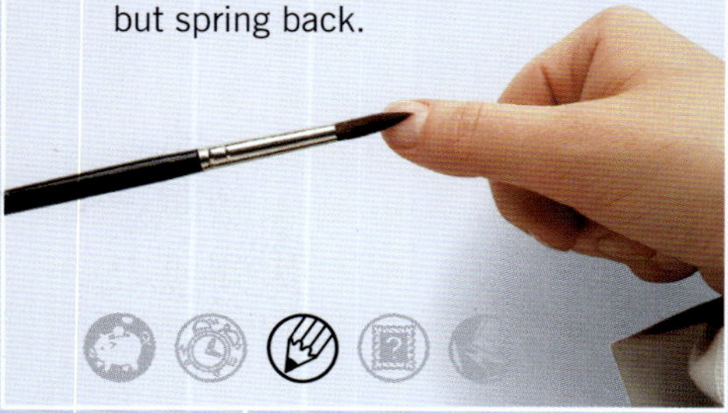

WATER RETENTION

To test whether a brush will hold a suitable amount of water, try moistening it with your mouth. Do not try this with a paint-loaded brush, however, as trace elements from the paint can be retained in the body.

28

STRAIGHT LINES

Although long, straight lines can be made using a round brush, for variety try a "writer" or a "striper," which were traditionally used for this role. Writers are long-haired sables that taper to a point. They are also called riggers, as they were used to paint the rigging on ships. Stripers are long-haired sables that form a chisel edge. Different sizes of brush produce different line thicknesses.

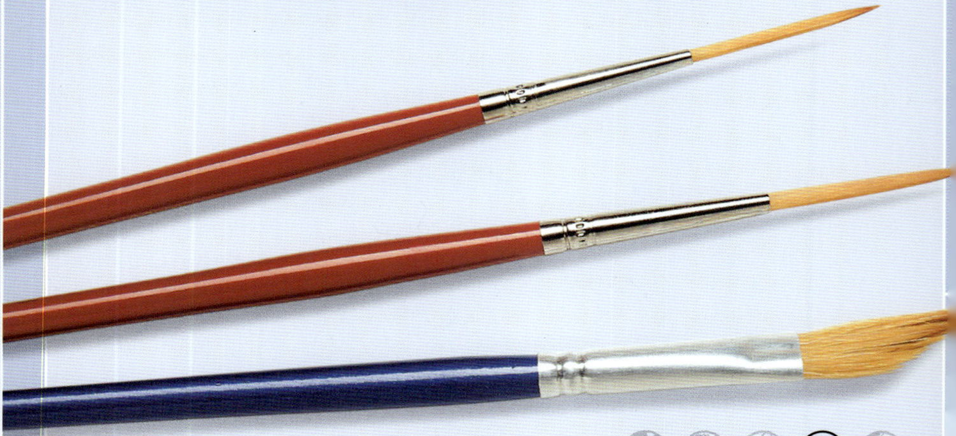

29

30

BROAD LINES

One-stroke brushes, commonly made from synthetics, or ox-hair, are good for creating broad lines. Short flats and long flats can also be used. They are all chisel-edged and held in flat ferrules. Short flats are particularly suitable for applying short dabs of color, while long flats hold enough paint for you to make one stroke across the paper.

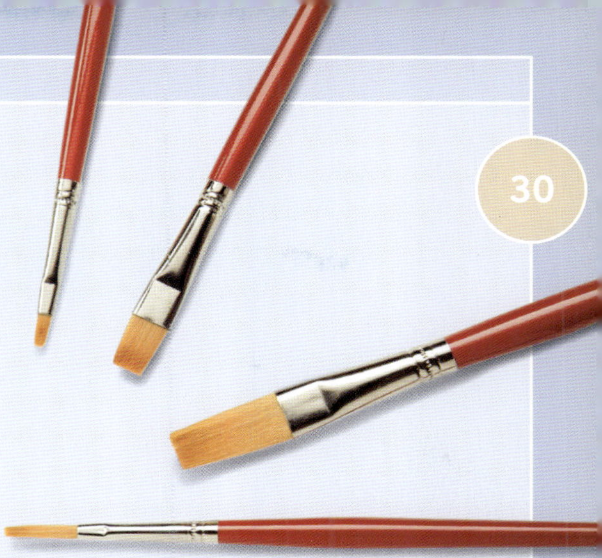

31

DIFFERENT BRUSHES

Remember that the larger the brush head, the more paint it will hold, so make sure you have a choice of brush sizes for different applications.

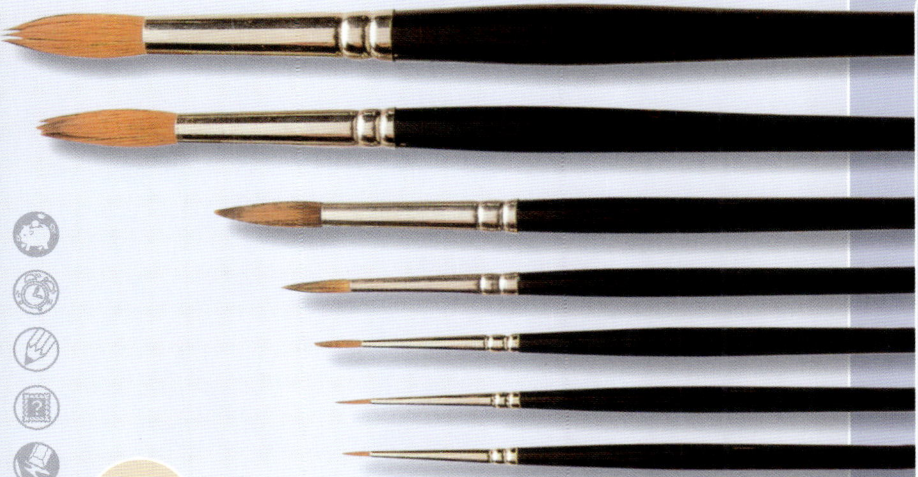

WASHES

The first skill the watercolorist must master is that of laying a perfect flat wash. This takes a little practice. However, as this section demonstrates, there are many ways of guaranteeing success, and you can then move on to more ambitious projects, such as graduated and variegated washes and working wet into wet.

DAMPENING THE PAPER

For a really even flat wash, dampen the paper with a sponge or large brush to help each "band" of color flow into the adjacent one.

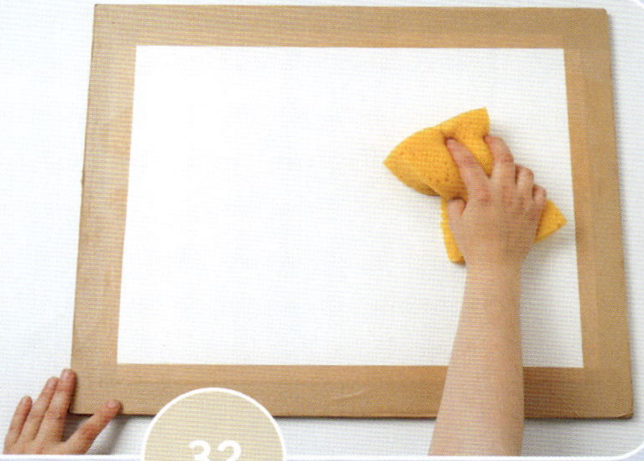

32

SPREADING COLOR

If the paint "furs"downward (spreads in little, feathery lines) when you are painting a wash on wet paper, tilt the board sideways or diagonally to disperse the color in all directions.

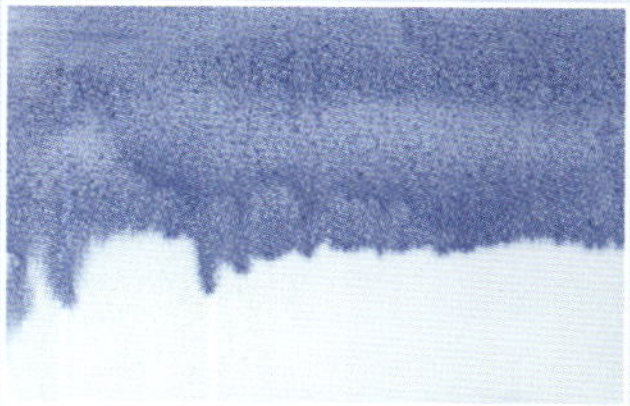

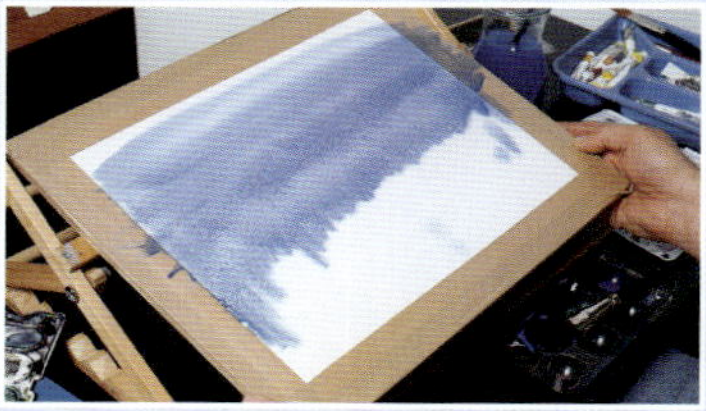

33

ALTERNATIVE WASH BRUSH

An old, worn-down shaving brush or a household paintbrush are both very effective for creating really large washes.

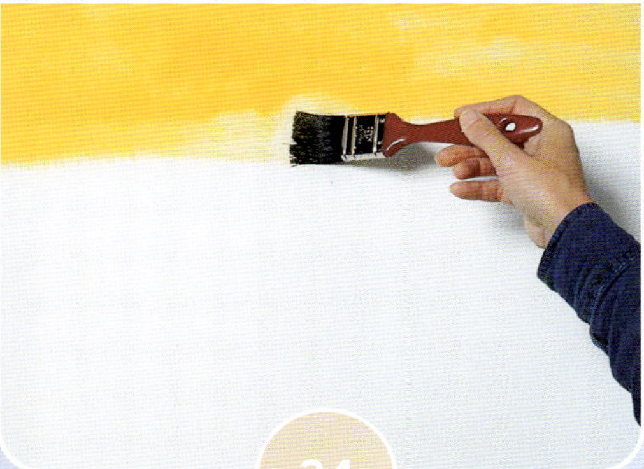

34

EVEN TONE

If a flat wash is uneven in tone, you may not be charging your brush fully enough. Do not press too hard with the brush, and do not overcharge it with paint or you will create unwanted streaks. Once you have laid down a wash, avoid going over it again, because this will definitely result in streaking.

35

FLAT WASHES

When painting flat washes (washes that are the same color and tone all over), always mix more paint than you think you will need. The wash will be spoiled if you have to stop and mix more paint.

36

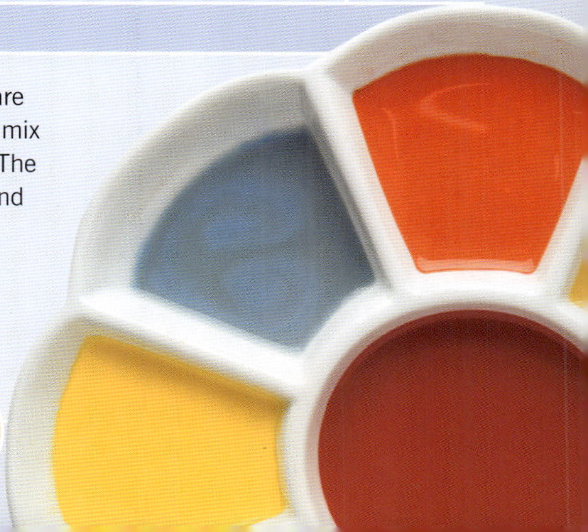

GRADUATED WASHES

When creating a wash that blends from dark to light in the same color, lay the first band at full strength, then dip your brush first into the water and then into the paint for each successive band. This guarantees that the wash mixture becomes lighter by the same amount.

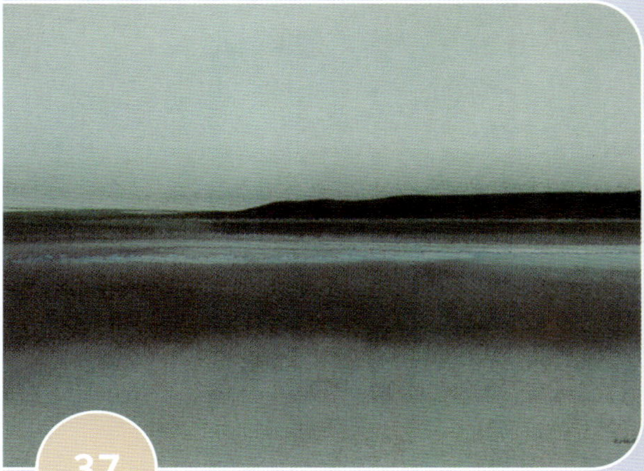

Robert Tilling makes expressive use of washes in "Grauville Bay, Jersey."

37

UPSIDE-DOWN WASH

If a graduated wash needs to appear more concentrated in color toward the bottom of the paper, turn the board upside down and start from what will be the bottom, working toward the top.

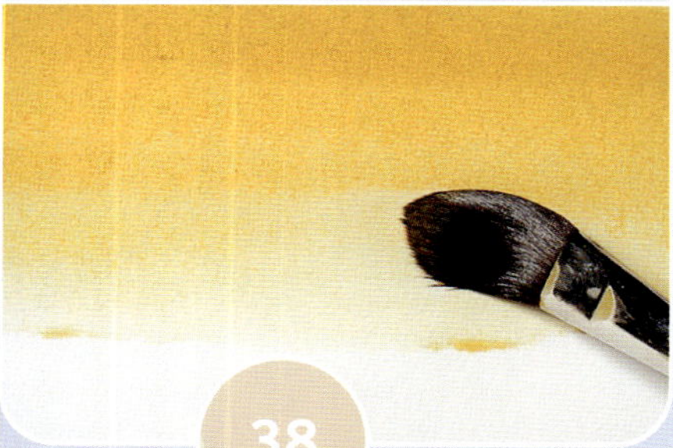

38

MERGING TONES

When you have completed a graduated wash, work over it gently with a clean, damp, one-stroke brush to merge the change in tones.

39

VARIEGATED WASHES

To create successful variegated washes (ones in which different colors are blended), apply each color side by side and let them bleed into each other.

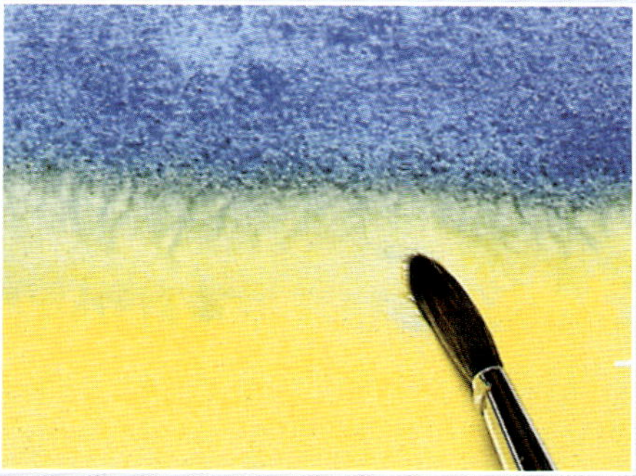

Yellow applied next to wet blue.

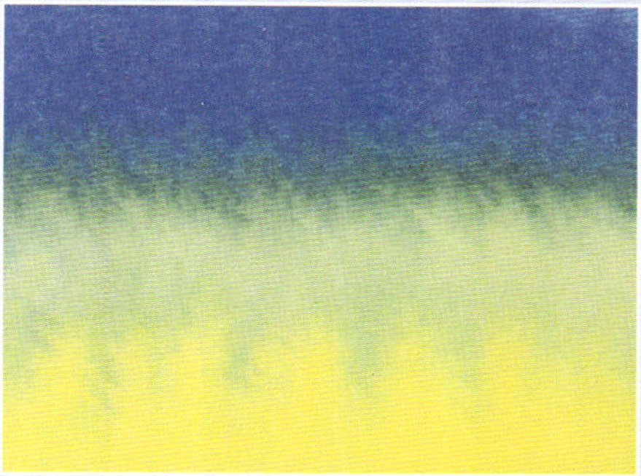

Where the two washes merge, they create a third color, green.

40

MUDDY COLORS

If you often achieve muddy results with variegated washes, you could be working too fast, with the result that the colors bleed into each other too much. To avoid this, apply your first color, then let it start to dry before adding the next. Use only one stroke of the brush to apply each line of wash. Work methodically in this way until you have applied all of the washes. Judging when to add the next color is a matter of practice and experience.

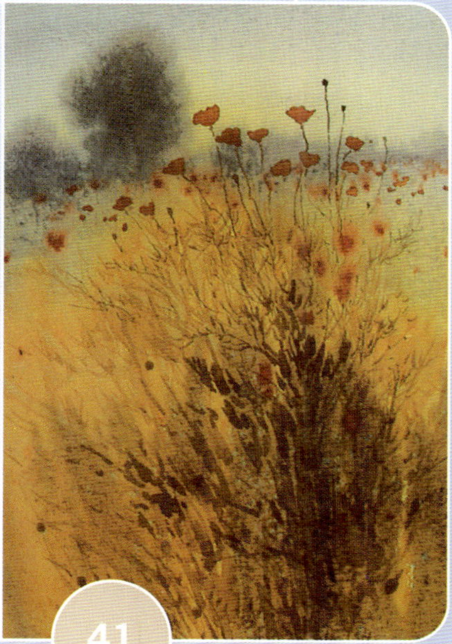

In Alan Oliver's "Poppy Field," the colors are fresh and clear.

41

DROPPED-IN COLOR

If you want to add special effects, like light-colored clouds, try dropping clear water into semi-dry paint. To create denser effects, drop Chinese White or White Gouache onto a damp wash. A very liquid, darker color will bleed into the surrounding wash and produce more dramatic effects. Experimental washes such as these might form an attractive background for a still life, suggest clouds, storms, or distant trees, or provide an abstract quality.

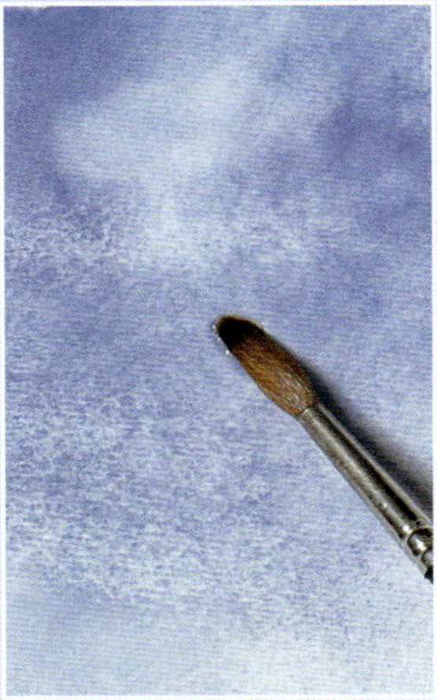

Water is dropped onto still-damp blue paint.

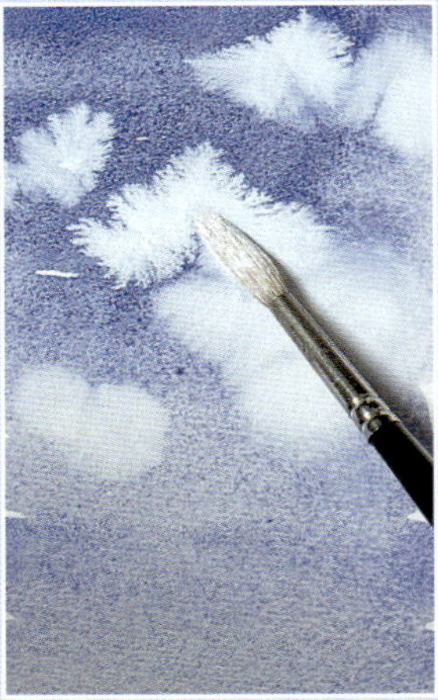

Adding Chinese White creates denser effects.

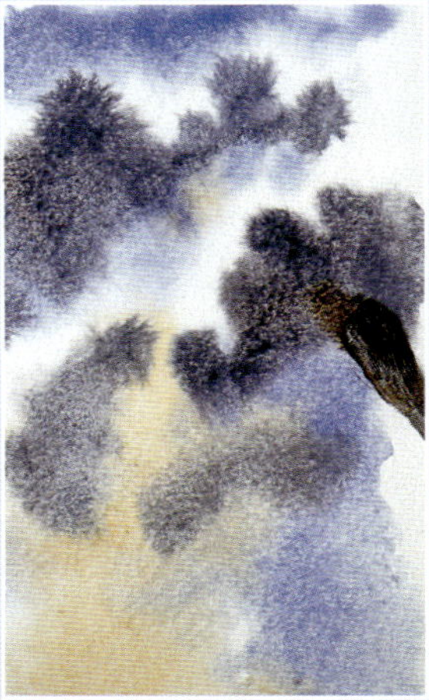

A darker liquid color creates dramatic effects.

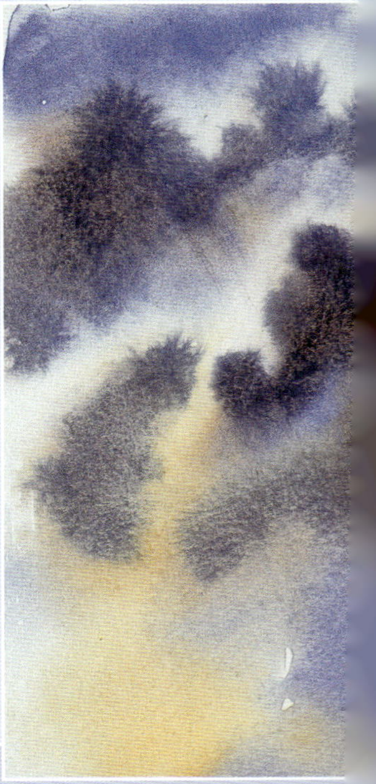

The colors have merged to create abstract patterns.

42

43 MEETING AN EDGE

If you only want your wash to cover part of the paper—for example, when painting a sand around ojects such as shells—start laying the wash from the edge of the shells, rather than having to meet this intricate edge when finishing the wash. Tilt the wash away from the shell edges to prevent pools of paint from gathering there unless desired.

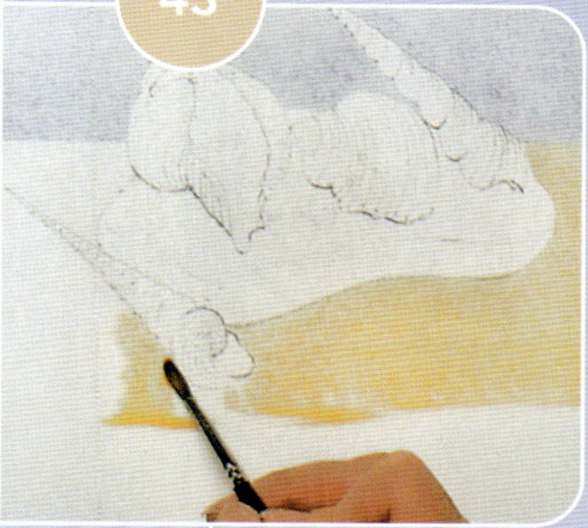

44 MASKING OUT

If you do not seem able to create clean washes over areas that you have blocked out with masking fluid, try to create the color density and effect you want with only one stroke. If you work over the wash with further strokes, the effect will be less successful.

45 IMPROVED COVERAGE

If white pinpricks appear on the surface of your watercolor paper when you are painting a wash, mixing a drop of ox-gall into the paint will both increase its flow and help its coverage.

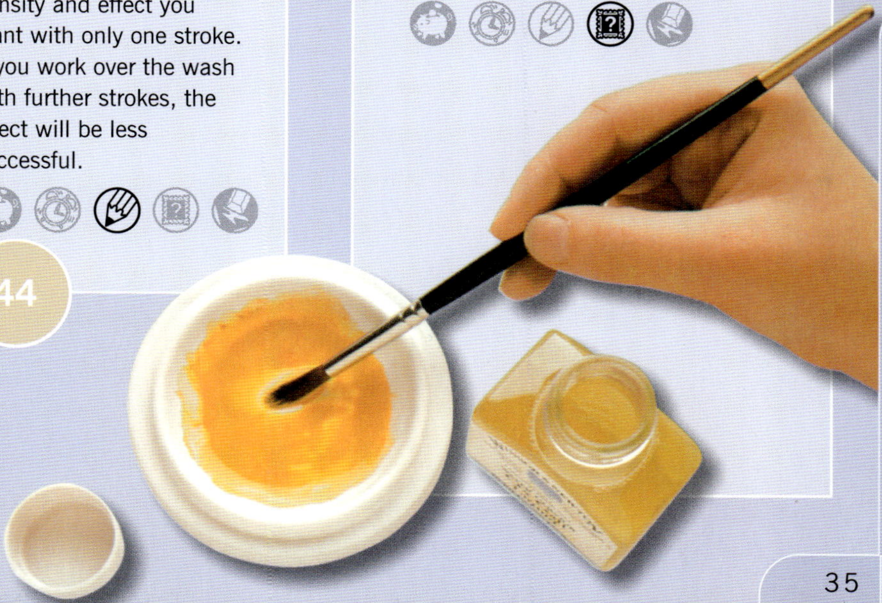

PENCIL WASHES

46

You may have problems creating broad washes if you use watercolor pencils. One method, on pre-wetted paper, is to scrape dry pigment with a mat knife from the pencil point onto the wet paper. Brush this in to dissolve the scrapings. Alternatively, scrape pigment into a dish of water until the desired density of color is reached and then brush it onto the paper as if it were watercolor paint.

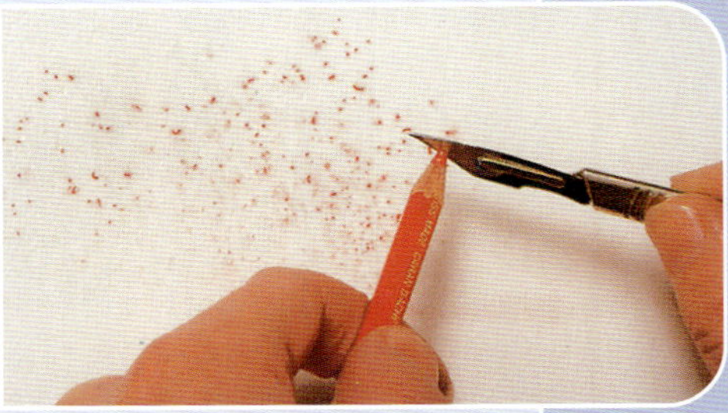

Scrape the pencil pigment onto wet paper with a mat knife.

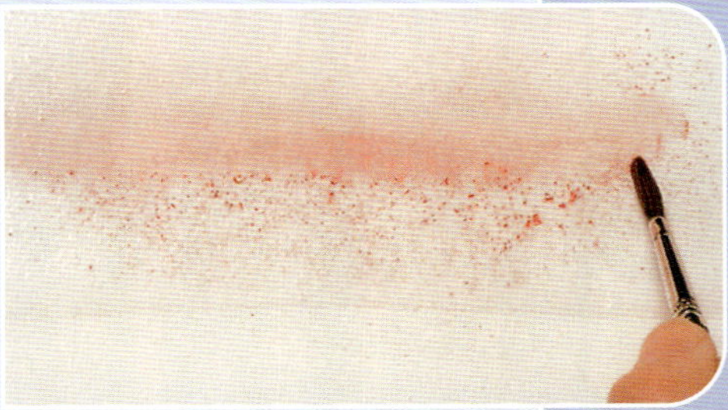

Brush the scrapings into the wet paper until they dissolve.

SOAKING UP DRIPS

47

If you find that drips collect at the bottom of your paper when you are painting a wash, place soft facial tissues across the area where the wash is intended to finish, and it will soak up all the drips.

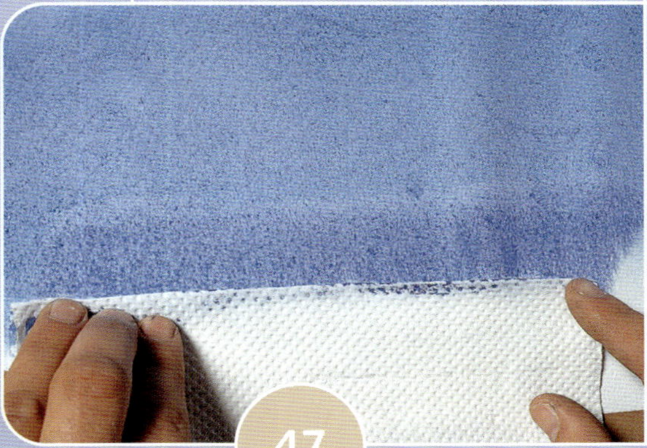

EXCESS WATER

48

To avoid leaving a thick pool of paint at the bottom of the paper, pick up the paint from the previous stroke as you work your way down the paper, mopping up the edge of the paint as you progress. When you reach the bottom of the paper, carefully pick up the pool of color that has accumulated there with a barely damp brush.

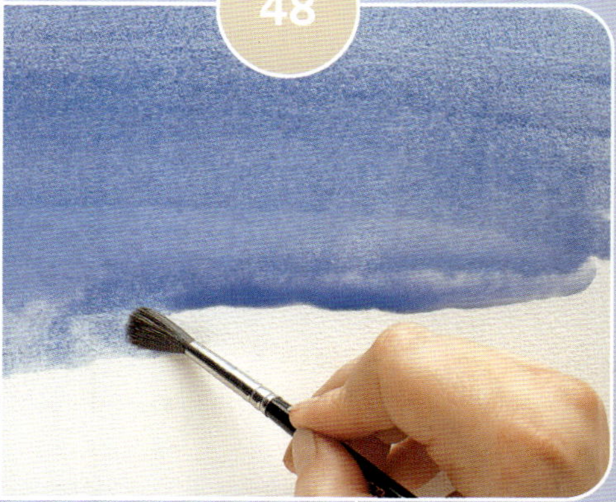

WET INTO WET

If you always seem to be left with pools of water when creating wet-into-wet washes (painting into an area that is still wet), you might be applying the second layer of paint before you have allowed the paper to soak up enough of the first wash. As water soaks into paper, it begins to lose its shine. Once a lot of the water has been soaked up, a brushload of paint will still flow freely, but you will have more control over it. When the paper loses its shine completely, but is not yet dry, you can control the paint you apply even more, while still being able to achieve soft-edge effects for such subjects as bushes or trees against a horizon.

49

50

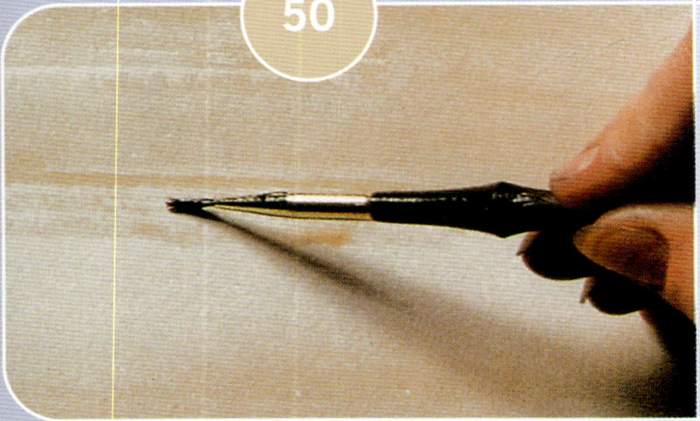

RETOUCHING

If you try to retouch a semi-dry wash, you will be left with blotches. Let it dry completely first, then dampen around the area and touch in gaps with the point of a brush.

51

REMOVING A WASH

If a wash is developing in patches, stripes, backruns, or with any other unwanted effect, flood the paper with water immediately, lay blotting paper over the area, and lift it all out. Repeat if necessary. If part of the wash has already dried, wait until it is completely dry, then brush clean water over the entire area. The paint should then spread out evenly.

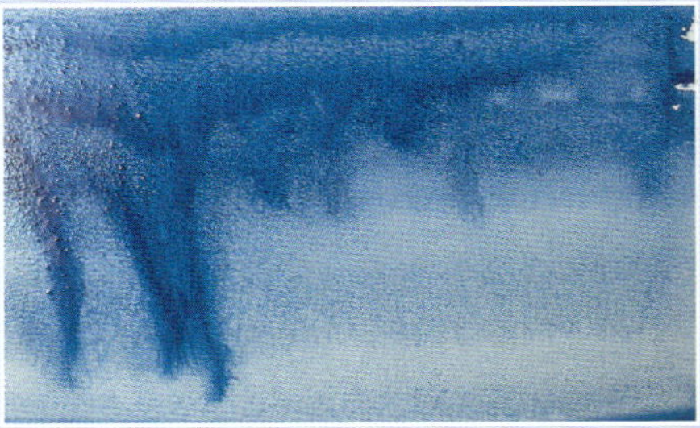

The wash is first flooded with water.

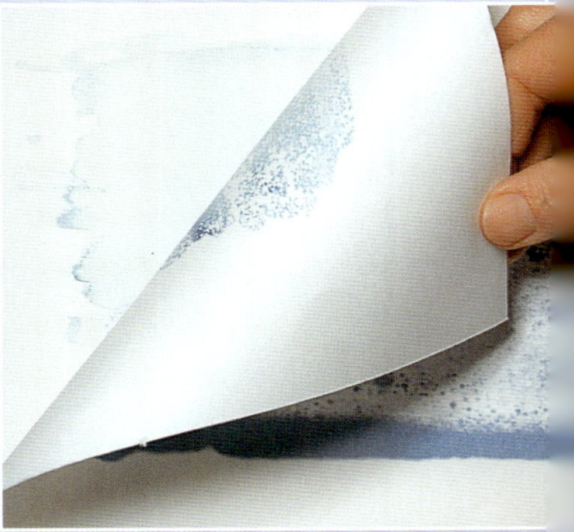

Blotting paper is pressed onto the wet paint and then removed, lifting the color away.

SPECIAL EFFECTS

One of the joys of painting is discovering what the medium can do, and through the decades, watercolor painters have invented and perfected many different methods and "tricks of the trade." Some of them derive from exploiting the "happy accidents" that occur in watercolor work—for example, a wash that has gone wrong and formed blotches and runs can suggest a whole new approach. With practice you will find your own watercolor tricks and techniques, but why not benefit from the experience of others initially, and try out some of the fascinating methods shown in this section?

SOFT GLAZE

52

To create a soft glaze over dry work and to vary the surface colors, use a diffuser to blow out a fine spray. For the best results, make sure that the watercolor is completely dry before you add the spray. You can use a mouth diffuser—sold for applying fixative in pastel work—or experiment using a plant sprayer, which is also useful for redampening watercolor paper while you are working. Do not hold the diffuser too close to the work while spraying, or you will make areas of the paint run into pools.

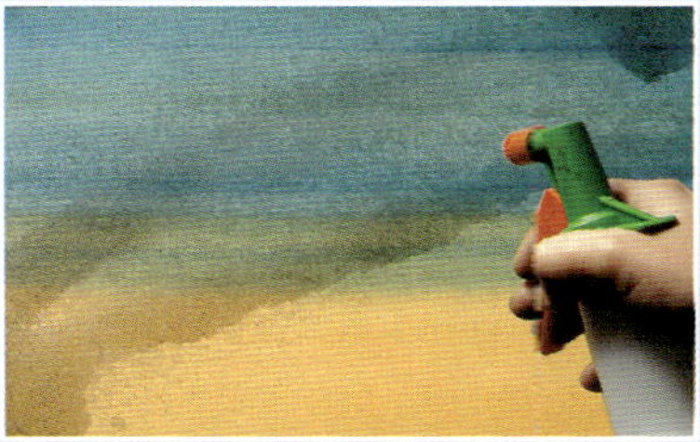

A quantity of paint is mixed and applied with a plant sprayer.

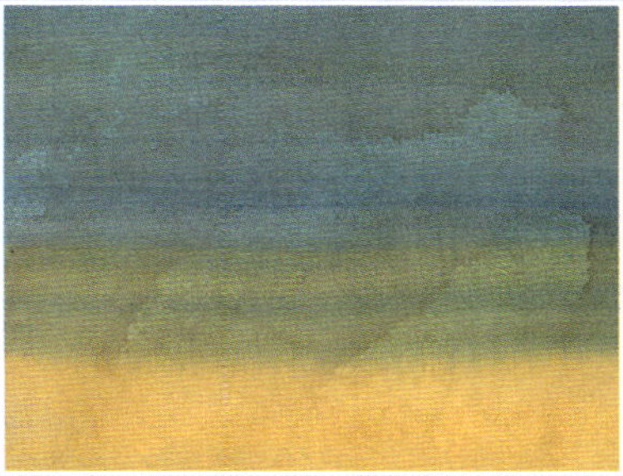

This creates an uneven "wash," adding surface texture.

53

PAINT RUNS

If you want to create an unusual wash while the work is still damp, direct a soft spray of water onto the surface. It will dislodge the damp pigment, causing it to run into surrounding areas. If the area sprayed is very wet, most of the color will run. If it is fairly dry, only a little will run, leaving a light coloration in its path. Once you have sprayed the surface, you can direct the water's run by guiding it with a brush or by tipping the painting slightly. Alternatively, allow the paint to run freely. Using this technique, you can blend one color into the background or bring a background color into the foreground. Spraying an area of more than one color will produce a more interesting run than a single color.

INK BLOTS

You can use watercolor inks experimentally to free up your technique and also as a novel way of suggesting the texture of foliage, flowers, or pebbles. If you drop ink from a height, it will form a blot. You can produce different effects by changing the height, diluting the ink, tilting the paper, flicking the wet ink to form spatters or blowing on the wet ink so it makes tendrils. Sometimes the random effects formed will suggest a subject that can be developed more representationally; at other times, the effects will simply make a pleasing background.

54

SOFTENED EDGES

If soft features such as clouds look too strong against a wash, use a cotton swab to blend the edges into the wash while the paint is still wet.

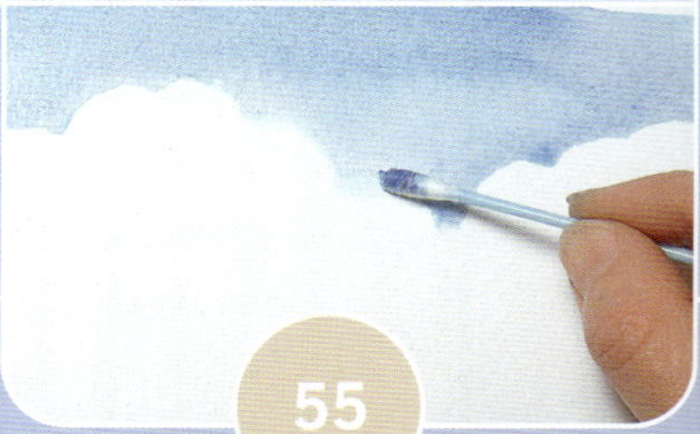

55

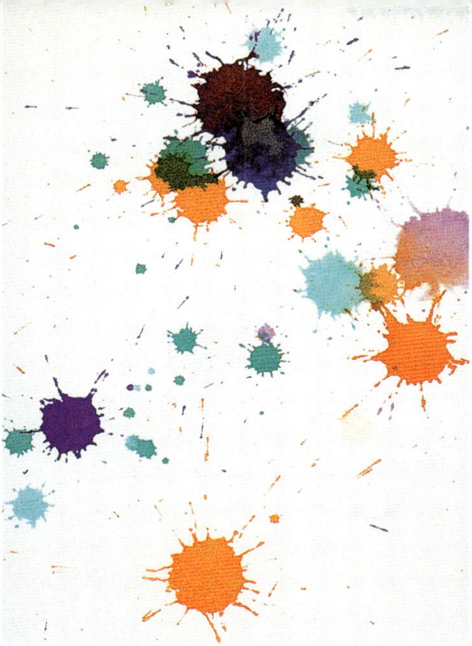

Ink dropped from a height blots and spatters.

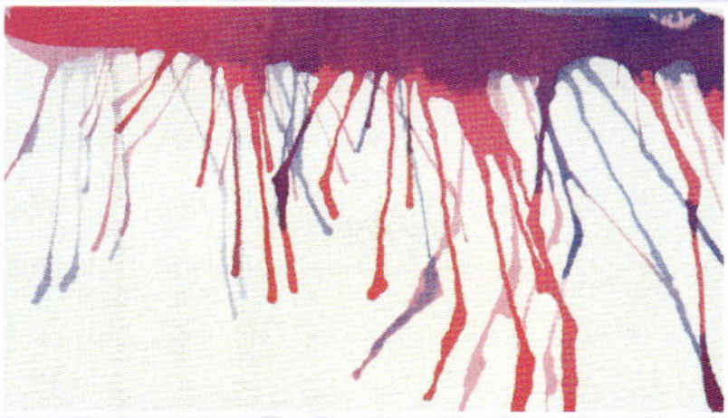

Blowing on wet ink creates tendrils.

Experiment with different random effects.

EXPERIMENTAL TEXTURES

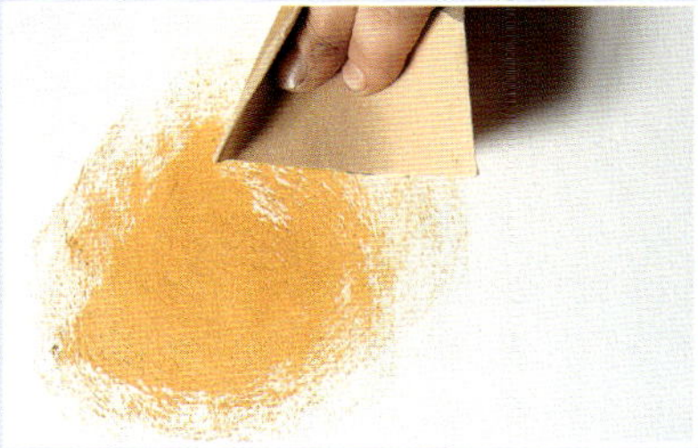

Rubbing into paint with sandpaper.

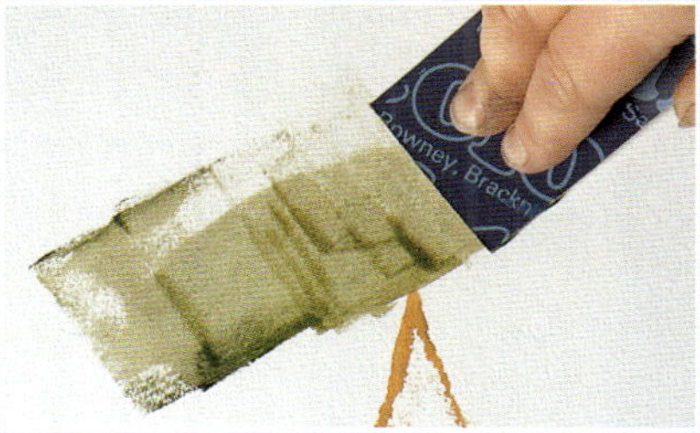

Spreading paint with card.

Don't be afraid to experiment with texture. Try applying paint with a variety of household items, including potatoes, card, rags, razor blades, sandpaper, rubber spatulas, and credit cards. Rub or scratch them over the paper.

56

57 PENCIL TRICKS

To create interesting textures with watercolor pencils, take two different-colored pencils and scrape pigment off them. Then wet a large round brush and pick up traces of the pigment scrapings. Paint directly onto the paper or the watercolor to create unusual blends and textures.

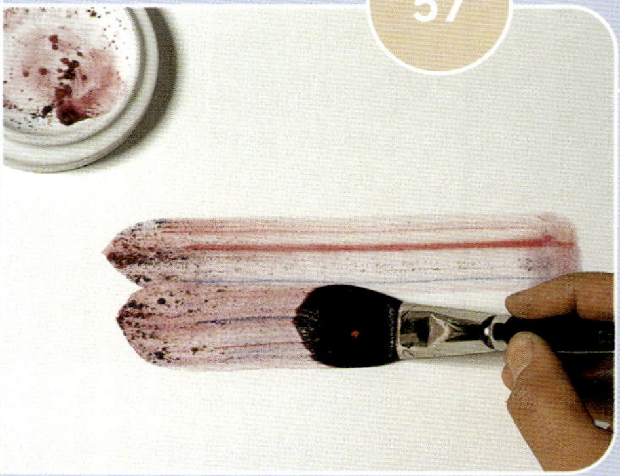

58 SPATTERING

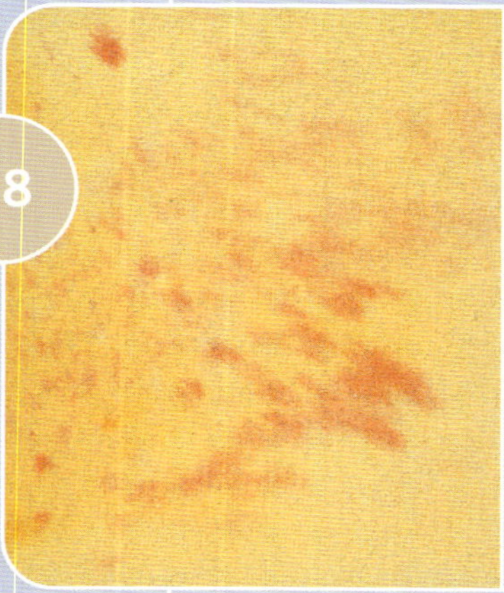

Rather than following the normal practice of using a toothbrush for spattering, flick a pre-wetted brush across the tip of a pencil. A moist, thin brush will give a fine effect, while a large, very wet brush will give a more generous, random result. This effect can be achieved on wet or dry paper.

Large wet brush with wet paper.

59 SPECKLED EFFECT

To add interesting texture to your work, try scraping dry pigment from a watercolor pencil over wet work. As the pigment flakes, it will stick to wet areas in the painting. You can then blow any excess away when the paint has dried.

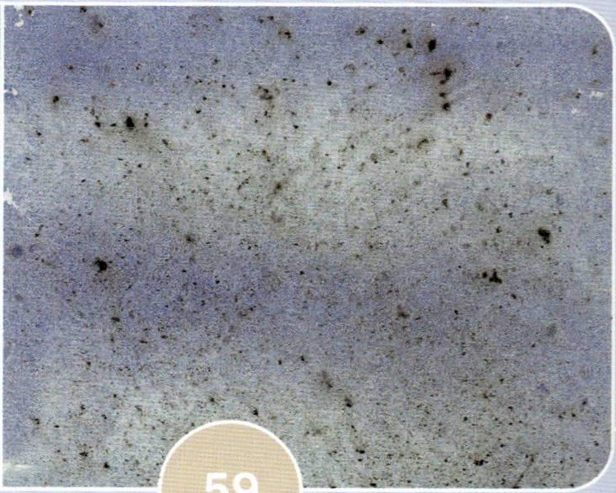

BLOWN TEXTURE

60

Allow a variegated wash tc dry completely, then blow paint down a straw, following the line of the paper upward to create interesting textural effects.

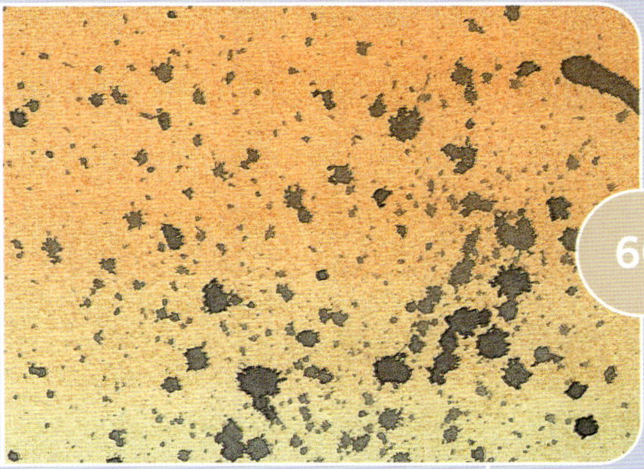

SPONGING

61

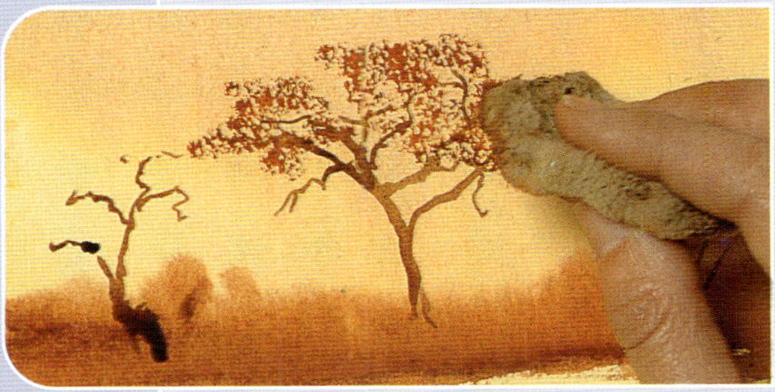

A small, natural sponge dipped in a pool of watercolor and dabbed on the paper will create interesting effects for such features as foliage, rocks, or sand.

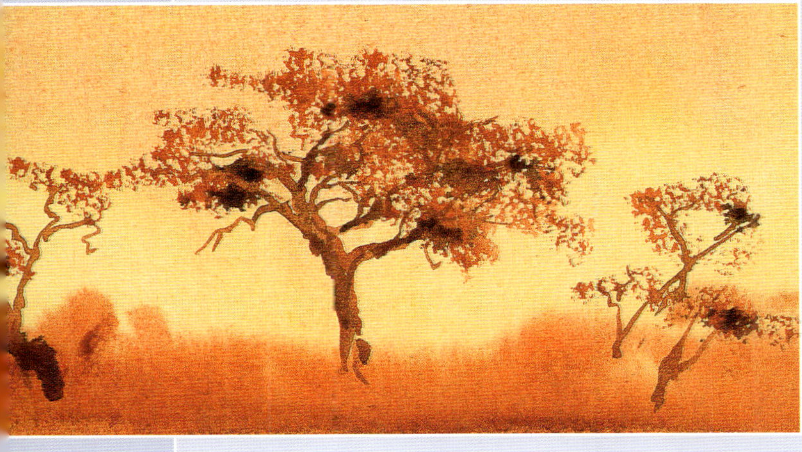

GRAINY TEXTURE

To create a texture that gives the impression of sand or snowflakes, try sprinkling grains of coarse salt into wet paint and then brushing them off once it is dry.

La Vere Hutchings has used salt spatter in her painting "After Frost," of which a detail is shown here.

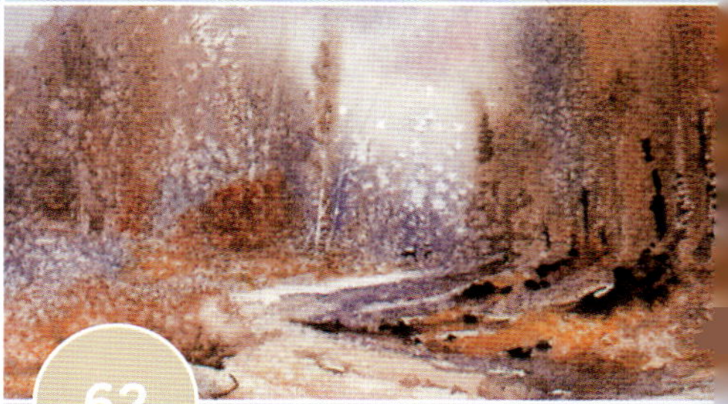

62

ROLLED-ON COLOR

63

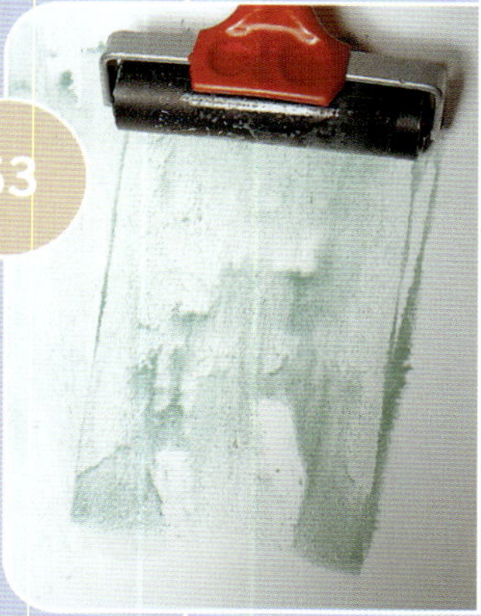

To apply a textured wash of color, squeeze some color from a tube onto a piece of glass or plastic, then mix it with a small amount of water and apply it with a roller on unevenly dampened paper. The roller will disperse the color in blotches over the driest areas of the work, creating interesting textures. In the more heavily dampened areas, the paint will spread evenly onto the paper, leaving soft edges.

ADDING SHINE

A brushful of gum arabic mixed with the paint makes it slightly shiny and more viscous. It allows the paint to dry on the surface of the paper instead of sinking in. This makes lifting off the paint very easy. Interesting wet-into-wet and textural effects can be achieved with this slightly slower-moving paint, especially if you spatter it with water or another color when dry or half-dry. A drop of gum arabic mixed with strong colors will not prevent them from looking dull and flat—any more than a drop will cause the paint to become shiny, and it may crack in time.

64

MIXED MEDIA

65

Watercolor washed over wax crayon, pastel, or oil pastel creates exciting textures and has the added advantage of binding the medium underneath.

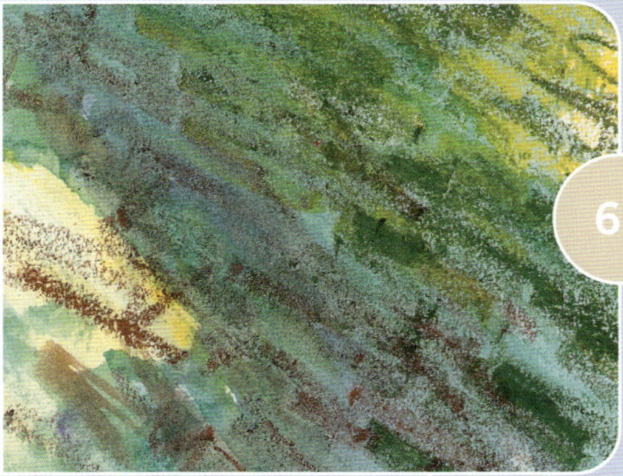

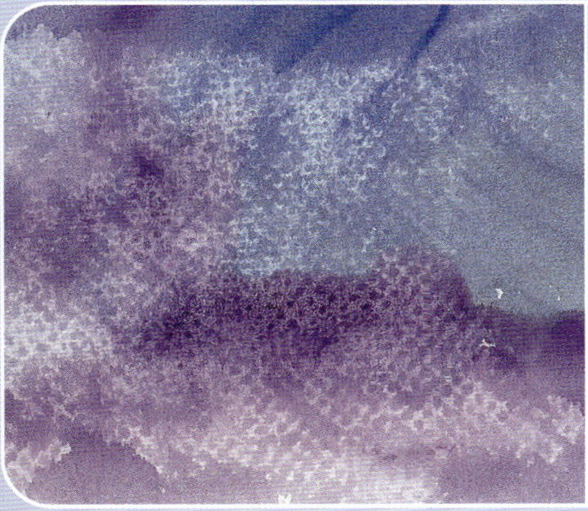

LIFTING OFF

66

Blot out unwanted runs, bleeds, or blocks with highly textured paper towels. This is particularly effective on medium-surfaced (Not) paper. It will not leave a smooth mark, as blotting paper does, but the imprint of the rough surface of the paper.

USING MASKING FLUID

67

If a particular color on a dry painting is too strong and needs lightening, try using masking fluid as an alternative to blotting paper or a damp sponge. Apply the fluid over the area to be lightened, allow it to dry, then remove it.

Masking fluid has been used to create a soft, broken highlight.

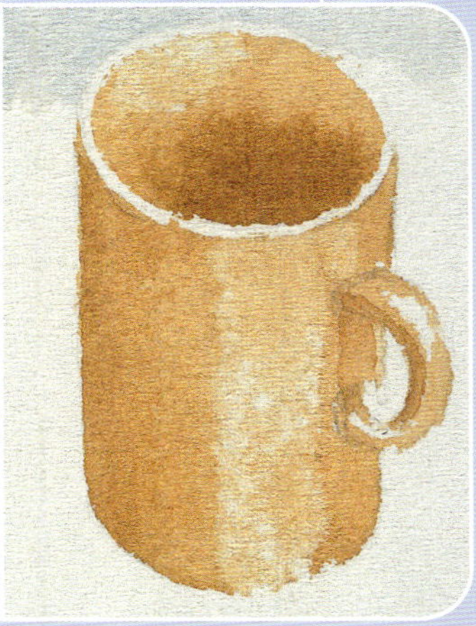

68

Unusual effects can be achieved by running hot or cold water over your painting at various stages of its development.

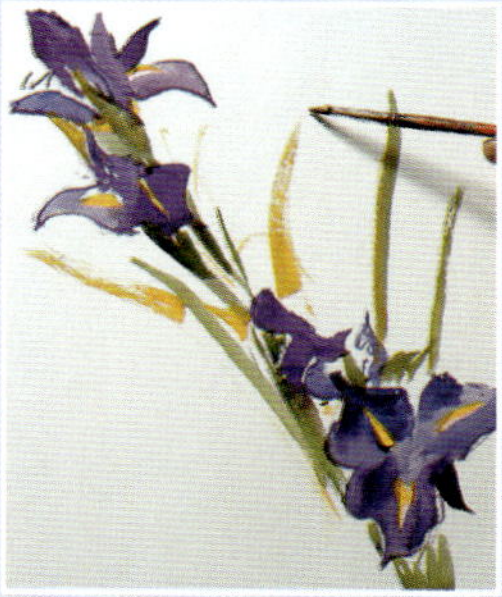

Flowers are painted strongly.

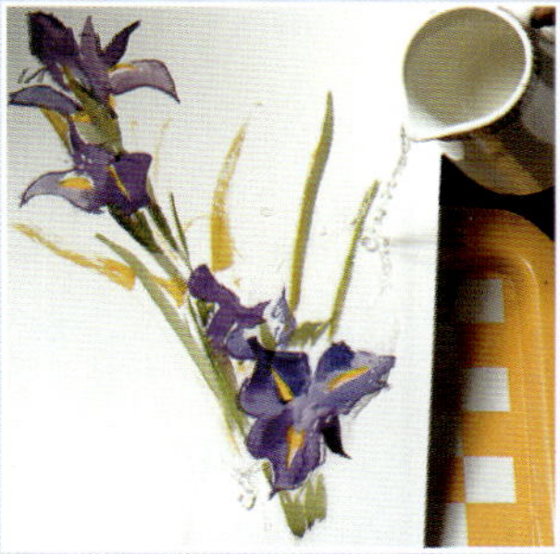

Cold water is poured on paper.

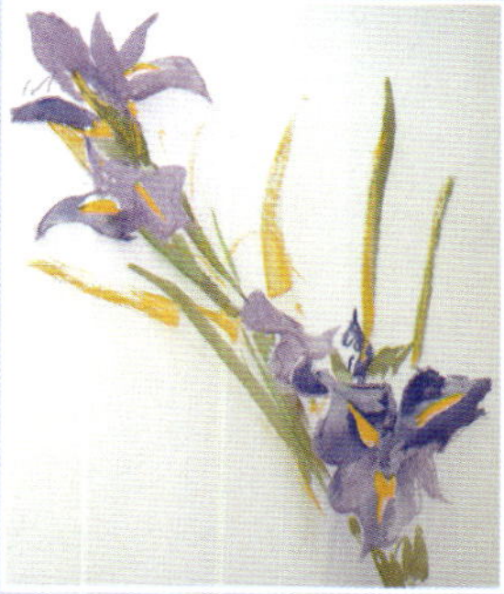

Paint spreads, blurring lines.

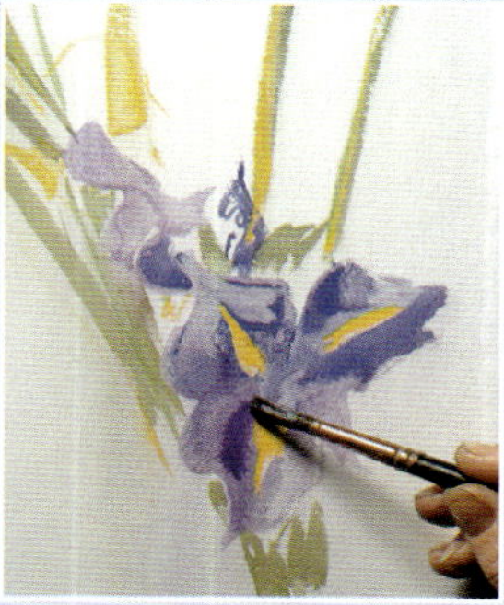

More paint is applied.

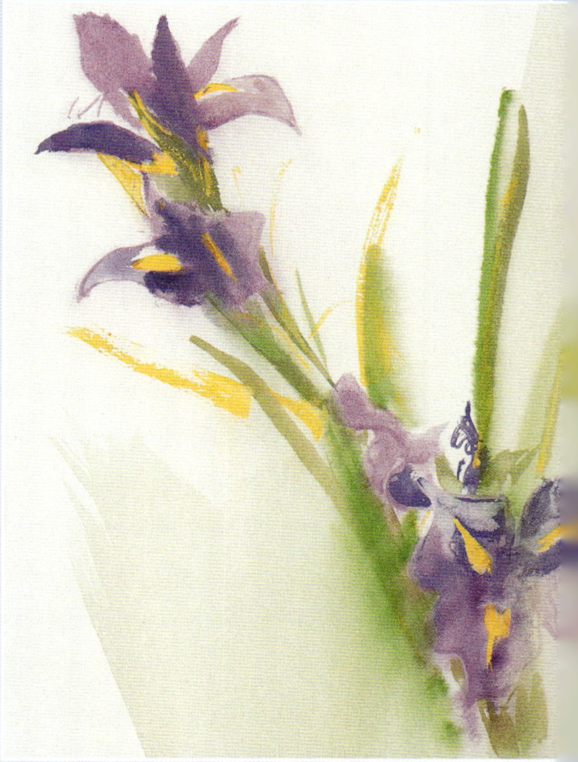

The final effect is delicate and interestingly textured.

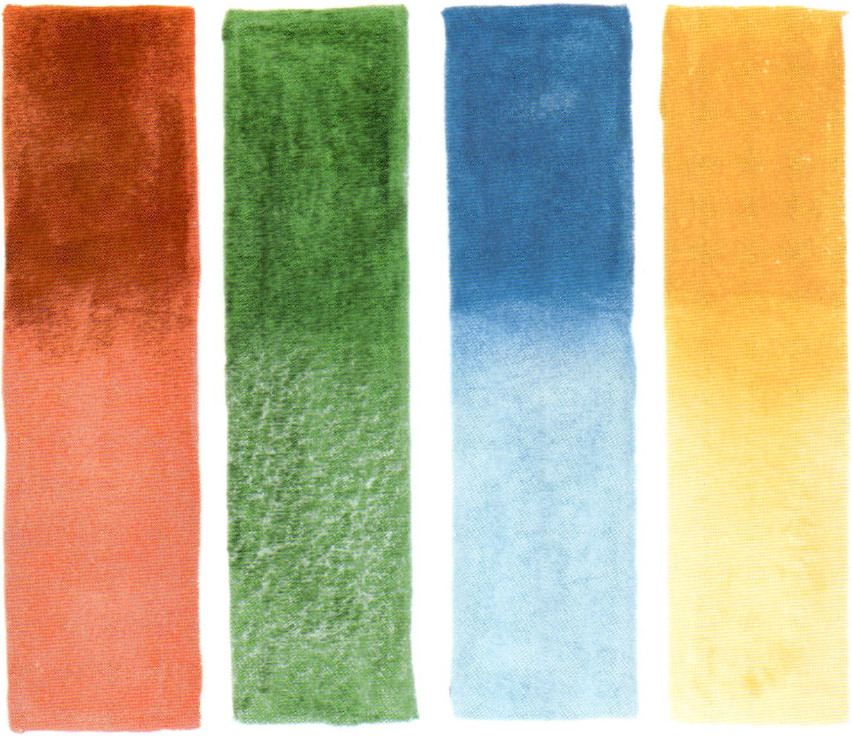

WASHING OFF

If you are using a heavy or pre-stretched watercolor paper, you can create a texture effect by laying washes, allowing them to dry, and then washing them off. Place your work at a slight angle, then wash the pigment away carefully with a hose. The harder the spray, the more pigment it will remove. Any very thin applications of watercolor will have been almost totally absorbed by the paper's surface, and very little of the color will wash away. Heavily painted areas, however, can be cleanly washed away and may leave an interesting texture. Remember that staining pigments, like Alizarin Crimson and Viridian, leave more color behind. Sedimentary pigments, like Cerulean Blue and Naples Yellow, tend to sit on top of the paper and lift off more cleanly.

69

HIGHLIGHTS AND MASKING

Because watercolors are transparent, white highlights are achieved by reserving, or painting around the shapes to leave bare paper. Aids such as masking fluid make this once-tricky process much easier. And even if a highlight has become "lost," there are many ways of saving the situation.

LIGHTENED HIGHLIGHTS

70

Once a painting is dry, highlights can be emphasized by rubbing over them gently with a typewriter eraser, sharpened to a point for accuracy. This removes some of the top layers of paint, occasionally rubbing down the surface of the paper, and enhances the brightness of shafts of light. The nature of the eraser makes it easier to enhance very specific details.

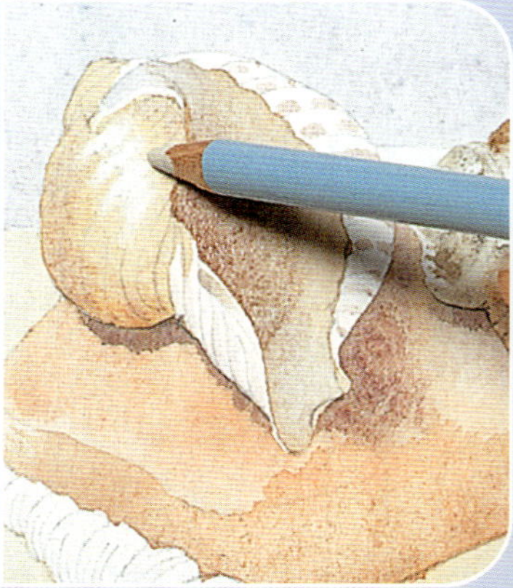

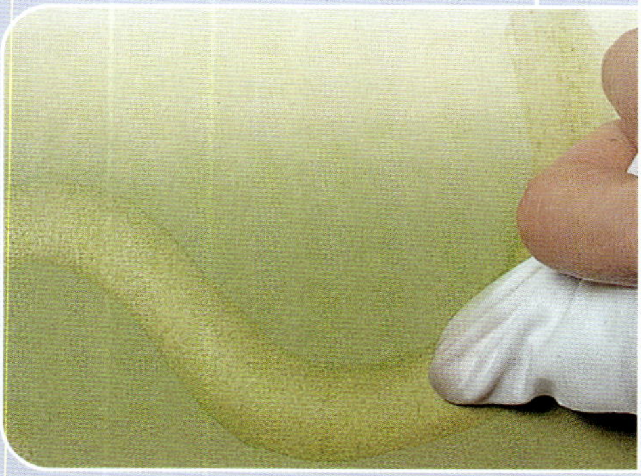

WIPED HIGHLIGHTS

While a wash is still wet, use a piece of cotton rag to wipe out highlight lines. If the wash has dried, use a dampened tissue to do the same. This technique is particularly effective for light clouds or shafts of sunlight.

71

SCRATCHED HIGHLIGHTS

Use a mat knife to scratch out color to create detailed highlights. Make sure that the watercolor is completely dry before doing this—not just touch-dry.

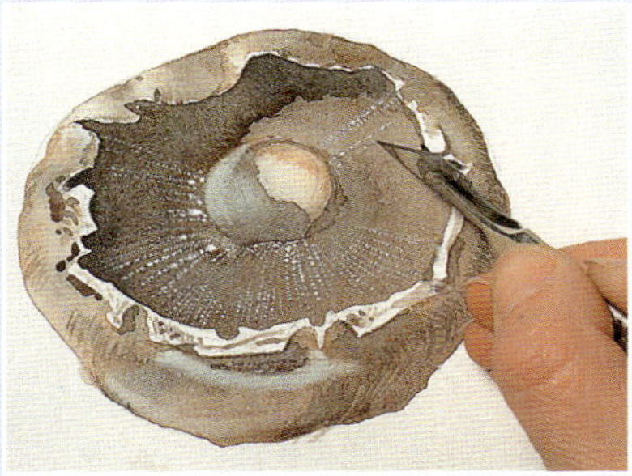

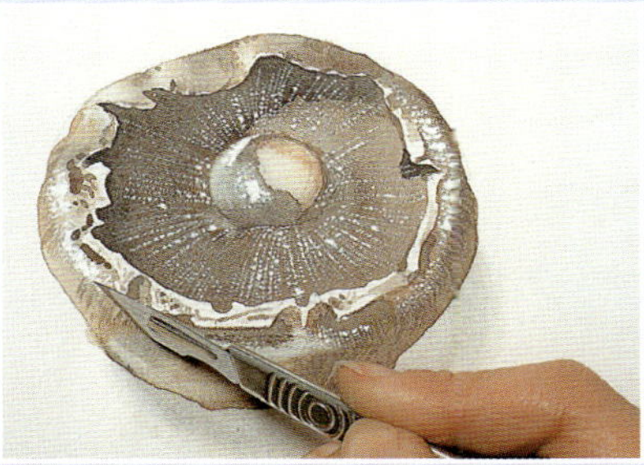

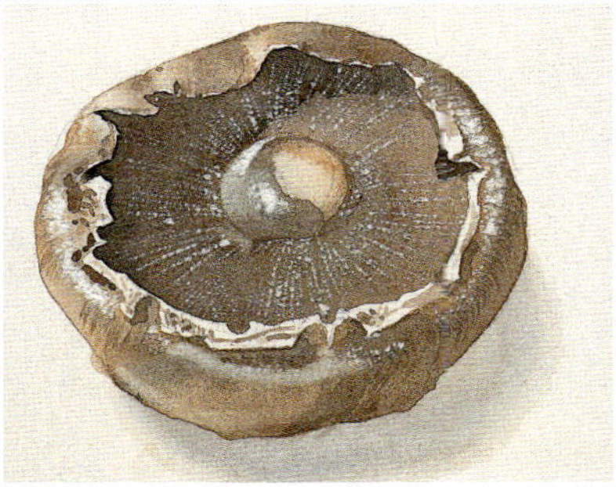

72

ERASER SUBSTITUTE

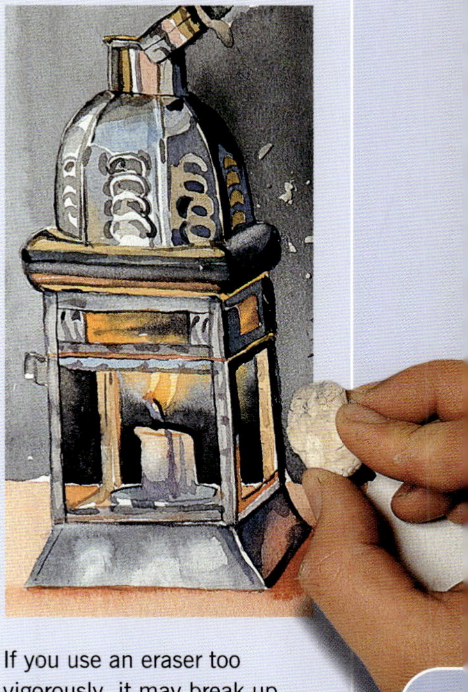

If you use an eraser too vigorously, it may break up the texture of both the paper and the paint. Crumbs of bread make a gentler eraser to clean up highlights. Knead the bread until it is soft, then use it in the same way as you would a conventional eraser. Do not apply too much pressure, however, or the bread will crumble.

73

LIFTED HIGHLIGHTS

74

To create highlights while a wash is drying, use a dry brush to lift the color out of the area. You will need to repeat this several times because the color will continue to seep into the highlighted areas until the wash is nearly dry.

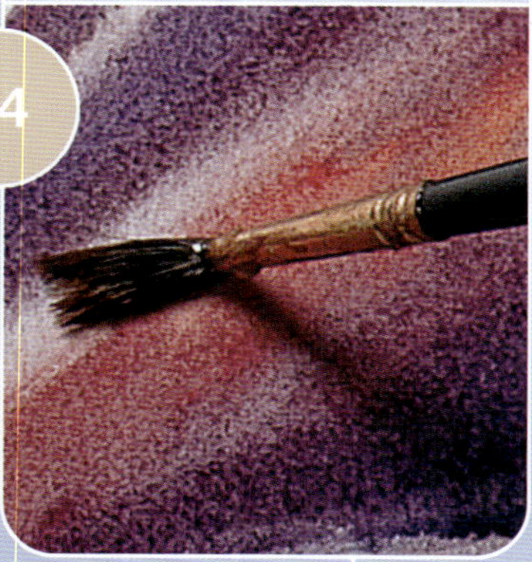

PASTEL HIGHLIGHTS

75

If a lost highlight cannot be regained by any standard method, soft, pale pastel tints used over the area and lightly rubbed in will retrieve the highlight.

GILDED HIGHLIGHTS

76

An unusual way to pick out highlights in a watercolor painting is to apply gold leaf to areas to be lightened. This is an effect that the painter Samuel Palmer often employed.

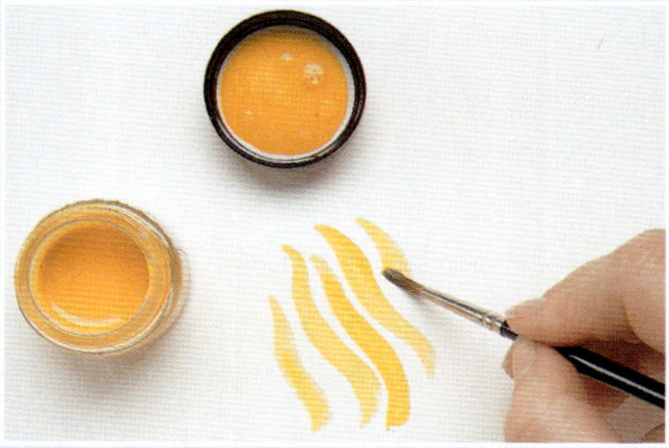

First apply size to the areas you wish to highlight and allow to dry for 20–25 minutes.

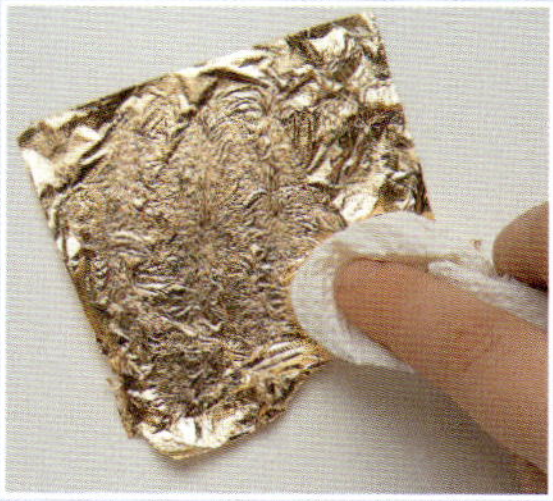

Use paper towels to apply gold leaf to the sized areas.

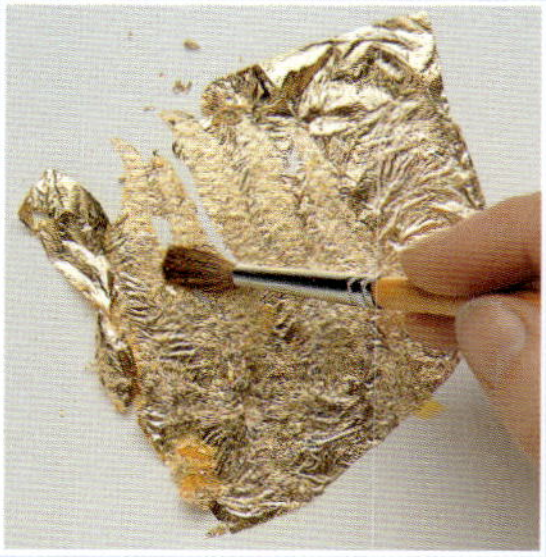

Leave for 2–4 hours, then brush excess leaf away and burnish.

MASKING WITH PAPER

To create random white areas, mask the paper with torn pieces of newspaper before applying your initial washes. For crisp effects, do not remove the newspaper until the wash is dry.

77

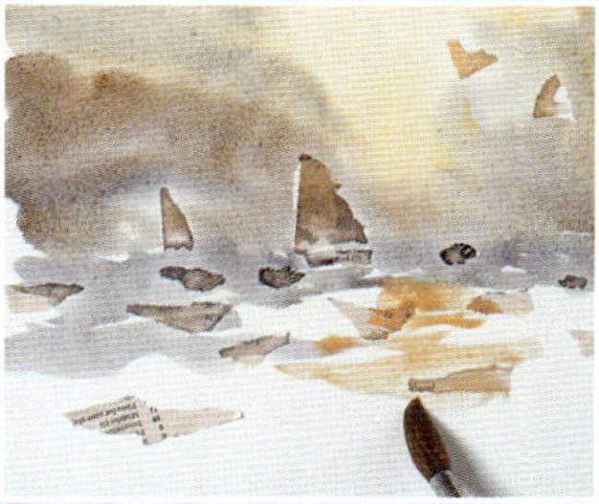

Washes applied over random pieces of paper.

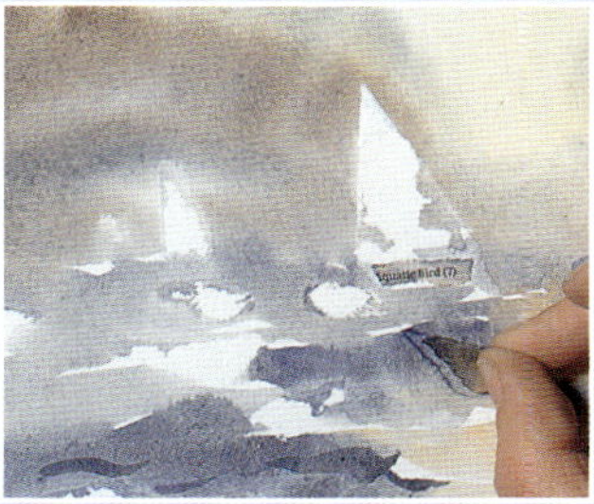

The paper is removed, leaving white shapes.

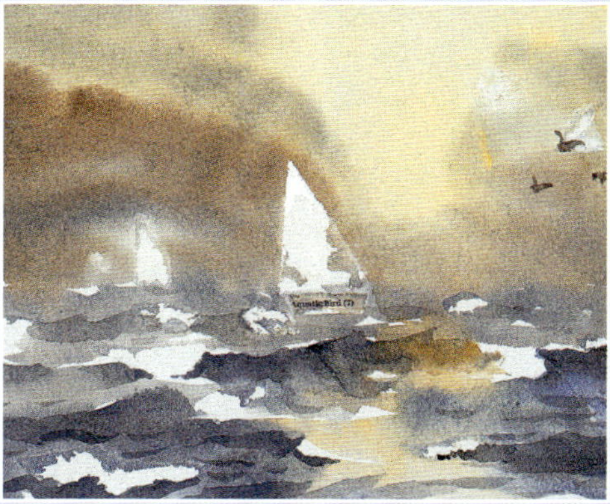

Final touches of paint complete the work.

MASKING-FLUID HIGHLIGHTS

A series of small highlights can be difficult to achieve by reserving white areas of paper. It is far easier and more effective to paint the required shapes with masking fluid.

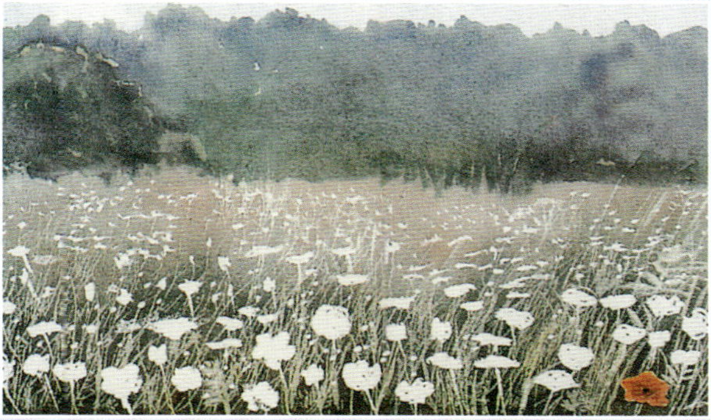

Doreen Bartlett, "Poppy Field."

78

REMOVING MASKING FLUID

79

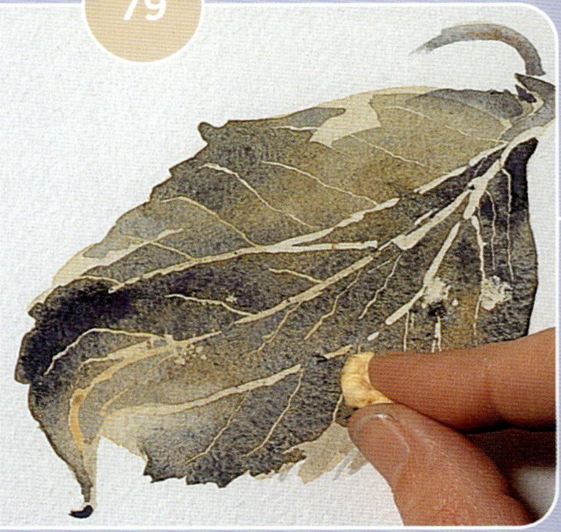

If you find it difficult to remove masking fluid cleanly, you may be leaving it on the paper for too long. Once dry, the fluid should be removed as quickly as possible. The prevailing temperature and humidity will affect its drying time. It may help to keep a ball of used fluid, like an eraser, and when you are ready to rub your masking fluid off, roll the ball across it, always starting at the edge. Rolling is also less likely to tear the paper.

ALTERNATIVE MASKING FLUID

A good alternative to using masking fluid is white fabric glue, mixed with an equal amount of water and a little nonstaining pigment so that you can see where you have placed it. Nonstaining pigment will also help you to see masking fluid.

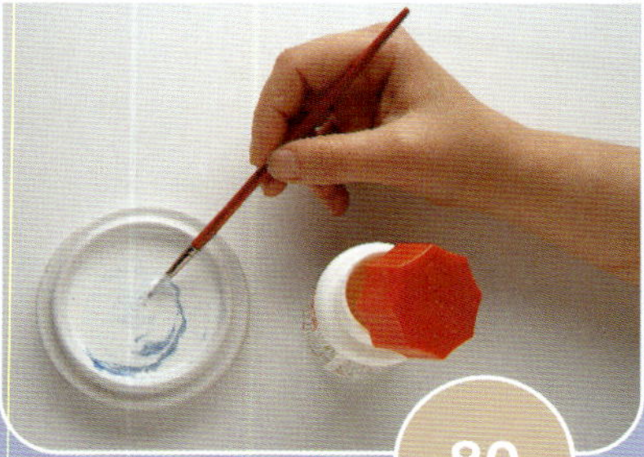

80

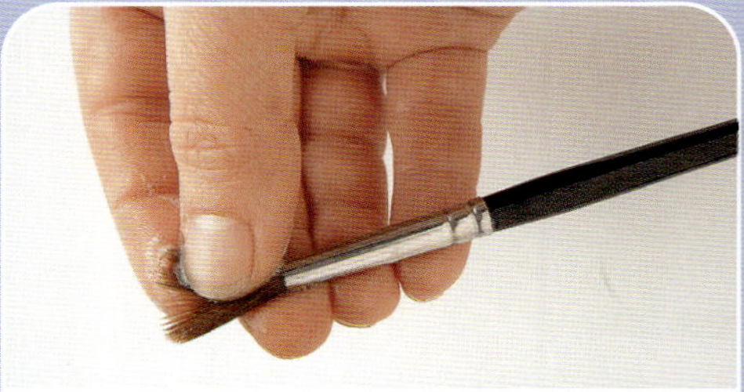

PROTECTING BRUSHES

To avoid ruining your brush when using it to apply masking fluid, work very quickly and clean the brush out as soon as you have finished. You can protect the brush by coating the bristles with some soap lather before dipping it into the masking fluid. The soap will not affect the application of the fluid, but will make it much easier to remove once you have finished.

81

BRUSH SUBSTITUTES

Instead of applying masking fluid with a brush, try using a pen for masking out fine lines, and cotton swabs for larger areas.

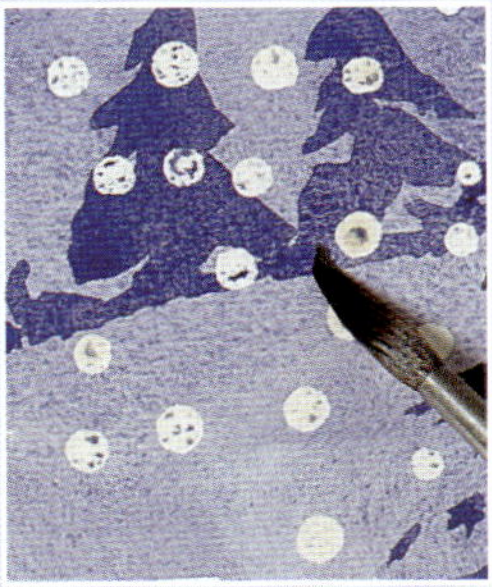

Washes are laid over masking fluid applied with a cotton swab.

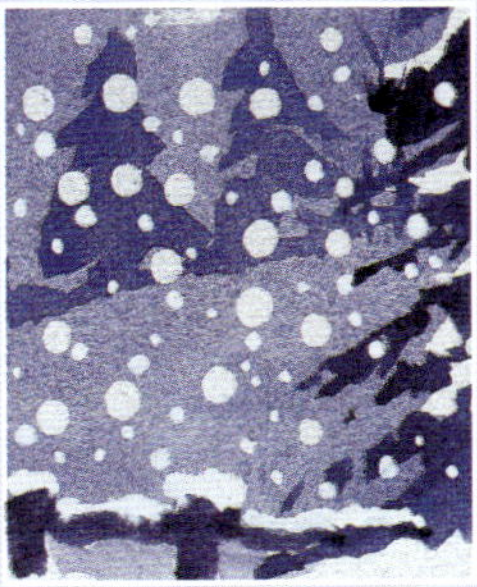

This produces much finer lines than can be made with a brush.

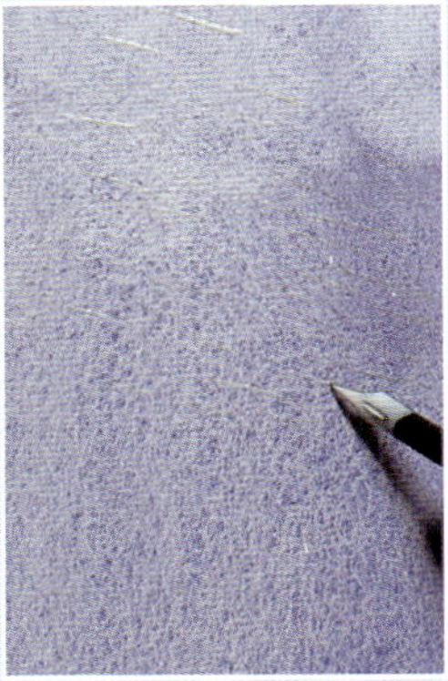

Washes applied over masking fluid applied with a pen.

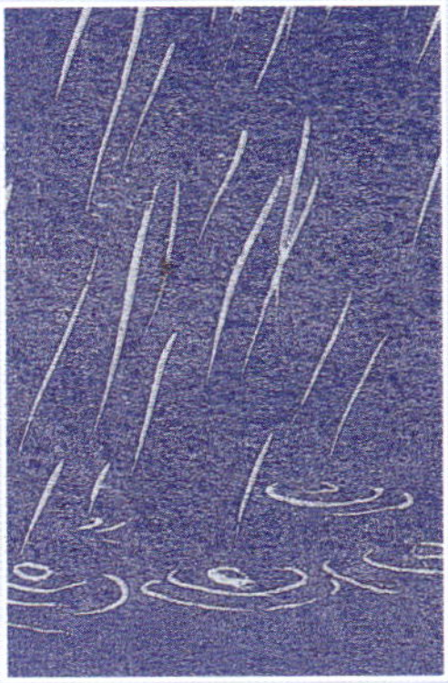

This has produced very even, regular white shapes.

82

CANDLE WAX

Wax from an ordinary household candle can be used instead of masking fluid to "block" the paint. It is, however, more difficult to remove than masking fluid and is thus usually left on the paper to provide an interesting texture.

Hot candle wax has been dripped onto the paper before the paint is applied.

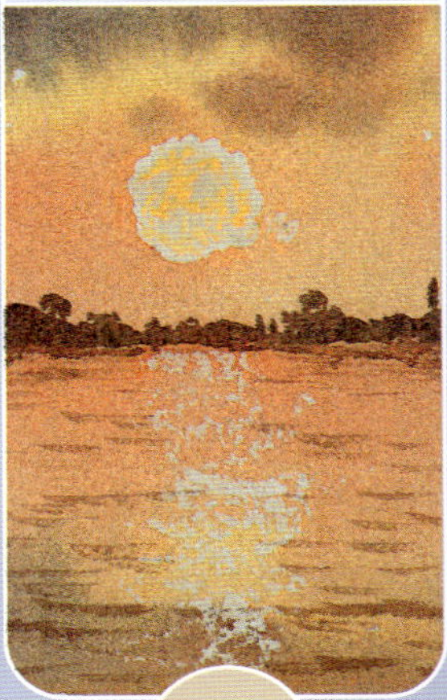

83

ALTERING AND ERASING

Watercolor painting can be a nerve-racking business, as things often go wrong. But you seldom need to throw the paper away and start again if a wash dries blotchy, or if you find you have slopped paint over an edge that was meant to be white. There are many ways of making corrections, and if you are dissatisfied with a finished picture, why not draw on top of the paint with colored pencil or pastel?

BRUSHING OUT

84

If the edge of a brushstroke is too hard or soft, and you want to get smooth edges, "tickle" them out with the tip of a damp brush.

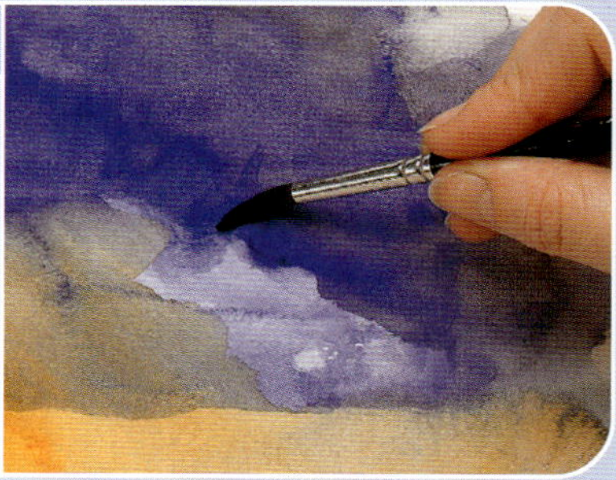

REMOVING PAINT

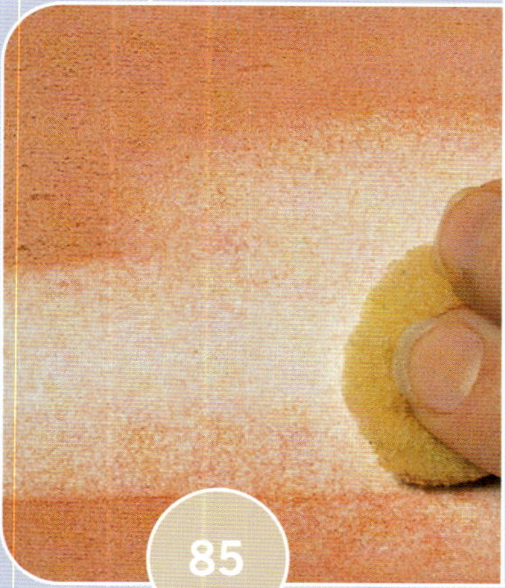

85

Trying to move watercolor once it has dried can be difficult, but it is possible. Once your watercolor has dried, it can still be re-wet, moved around, or partially removed from the paper. A sponge may work better than a brush for this purpose. Bear in mind, however, that most colors can never be completely removed because the pigment in the paint will have stained fibers in the paper. Let the paper dry thoroughly before repainting.

DISGUISING STAINS

After washing out a wrong tone or color, you may have been left with a slight stain. You can paint a thin film of white or suitably tinted acrylic over this, smoothing the edges with a cotton swab. When the acrylic has dried, transparent watercolor can be washed over it.

86

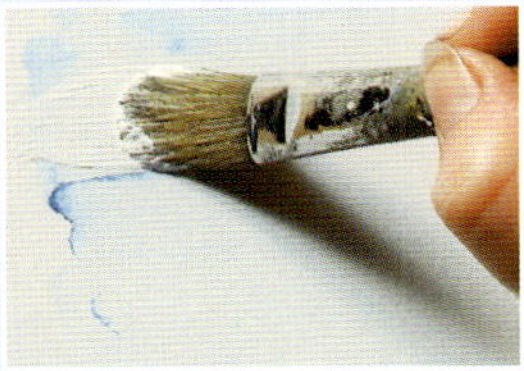

White acrylic masks mistake.

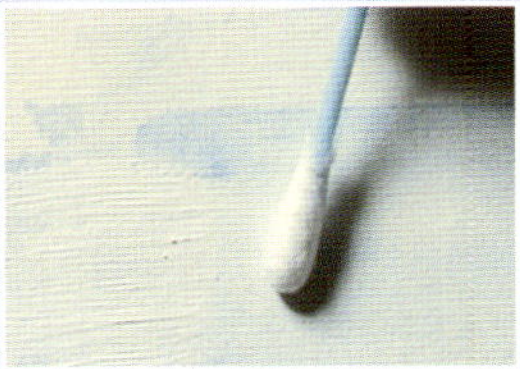

Cotton swab blends white.

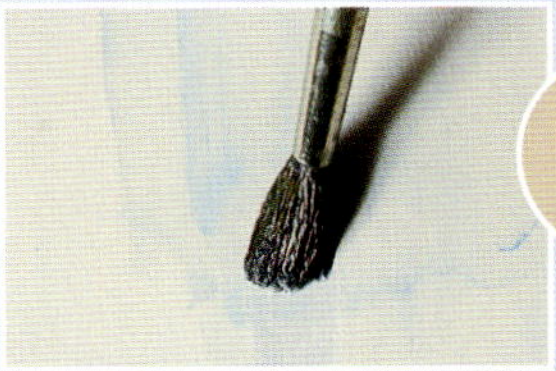

Watercolor is reapplied.

ACRYLIC SEALER

If your watercolor paper is too absorbent, or has become roughened by too much rubbing, a thin wash of white or tinted acrylic will seal the surface. When using acrylic for underpainting or corrections, it should be used thinly, or superimposed layers of watercolor may not adhere.

87

CRAYON REMEDY

Colored pencil or pastel on top of an abandoned or aborted watercolor can pull it all together and create attractive effects at the same time.

In Hazel Soan's "Fish River Canyon," colored pencil gives texture.

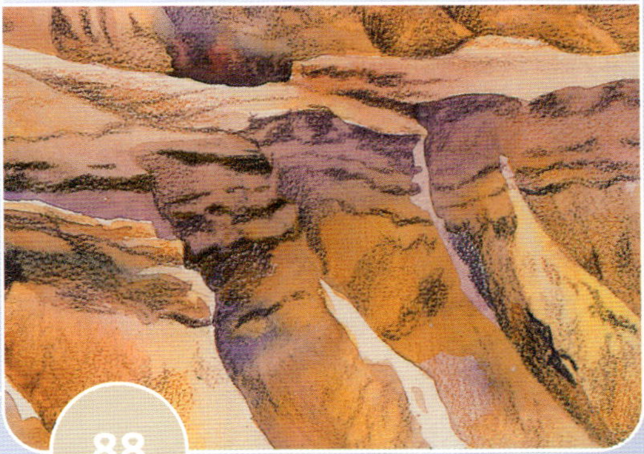

88

OPACITY

Watercolor is usually thought of as a transparent medium, but it need not be. Some of the great watercolor painters of the past mixed their colors with opaque white paint, and many contemporary artists follow the same practice. If you want to give the paint more body, there are substances you can add to it, such as soap or starchy water—and you won't even need to visit the art store for these.

TINTED GROUNDS

89

Try tinting watercolor paper with diluted coffee. This was a common practice among early watercolorists and is still a very good way of producing a pale, warm ground. In China, artists use tea leaves to produce similar grounds. You could even tint paper with a used teabag.

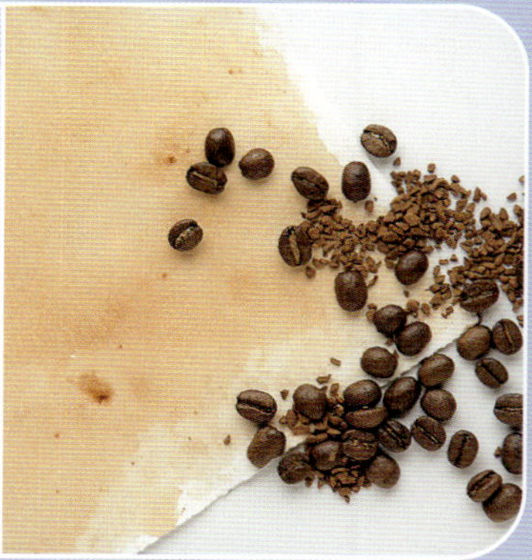

ORDER OF WORKING

90

You do not have to follow the convention of painting from light to dark with watercolor—Turner certainly did not always adhere to this practice. Working on blue-tinted paper, he would first apply "body color" (opaque watercolor), building from dark to light as in oil painting, the reverse of the traditional watercolor process.

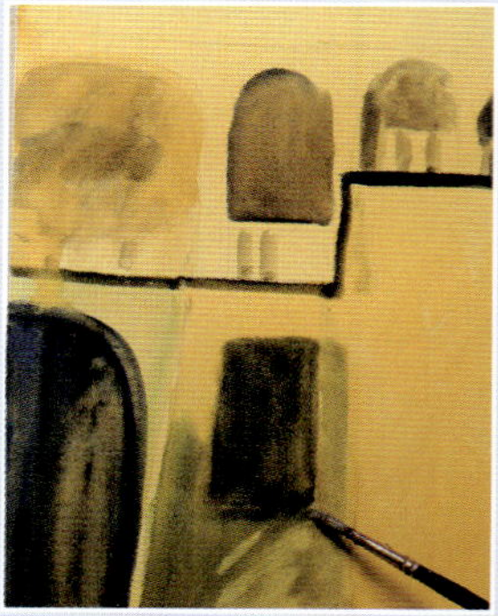

Diluted white paint modifies the darker colors.

OPAQUE MEDIUM

91

To make your brushstrokes more opaque, follow Turner's example and mix your paint with rice water. You can also try soap, which thickens the paint nicely and leaves small bubbles if applied with a stiff brush.

OPAQUE PAINT

92

Mixing gouache with Chinese White or White Gouache will produce more opaque pale colors. You could also try undiluted watercolor, for example, Yellow Ocher, on colored Ingres or Canson papers.

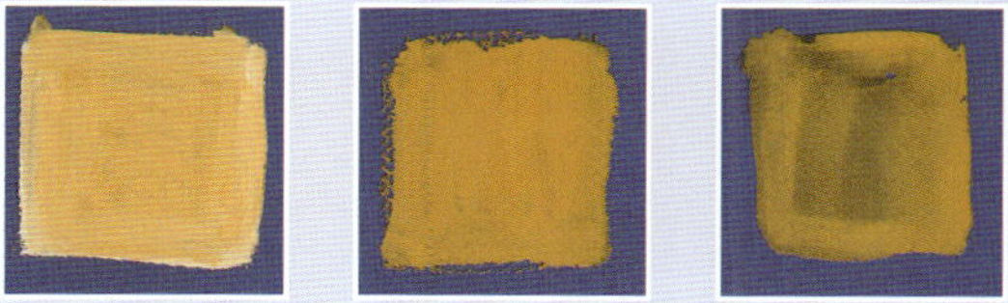

With gouache. *Undiluted.* *With water.*

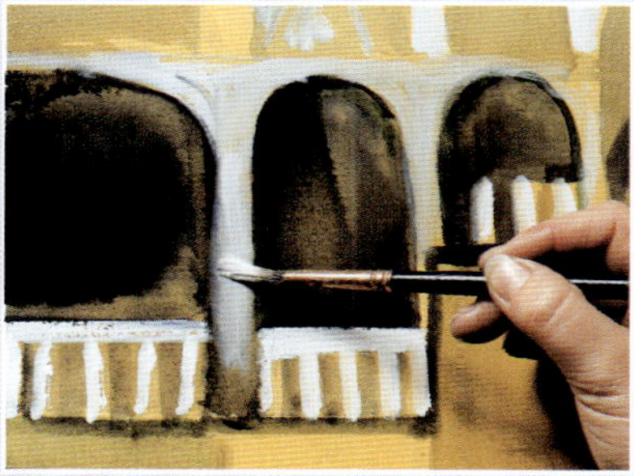

Thicker white paint is now used.

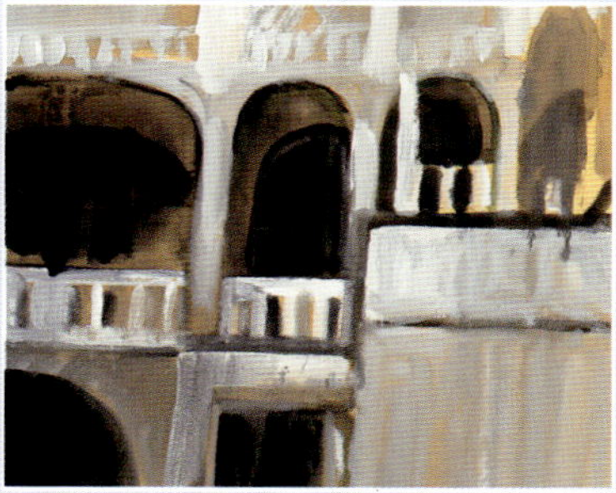

White mixes with colors to create a milky effect.

TRAVELING LIGHT

It's always a problem going to paint in an unfamiliar place because you may encounter quite unexpected different colors. But resist the temptation to buy a whole new set of paints—take as few as possible and welcome the opportunity to practice your color-mixing skills. Some of the greatest watercolors of all time were painted with no more than five or six colors.

ADVANCE PREPARATION

93

If you like to work on tinted paper, prepare it in advance, so that when you arrive at your chosen location you will be ready to start painting. You could even prepare several sheets, mixing up a large quantity of the desired color.

RESTRICTED PALETTE

If you use tube paints and are uncertain which you will need, take only two versions of each primary color—red, yellow, and blue. This will give you valuable practice in color mixing and will also help to unify your paintings. Experiment at home before you go.

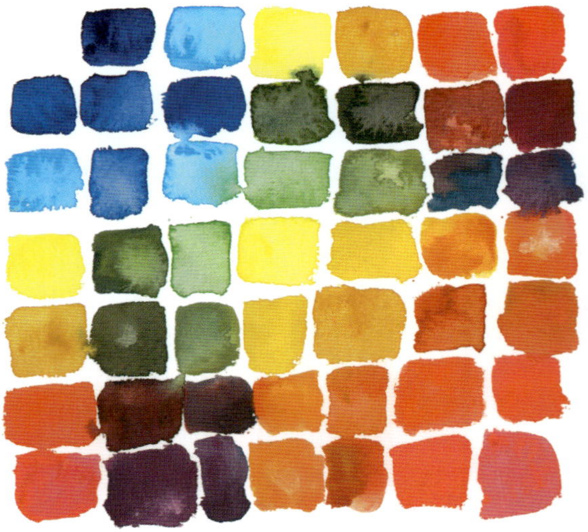

94

RANGE OF TONES

When painting outdoors, you may not be able to take a wide palette. If you experiment, you will find that with one color you can create infinite tonal variations—for instance, Raw Umber can appear as everything from a dark brown to a brick brown to a Yellow Ocher to a cream, simply by the addition of more water.

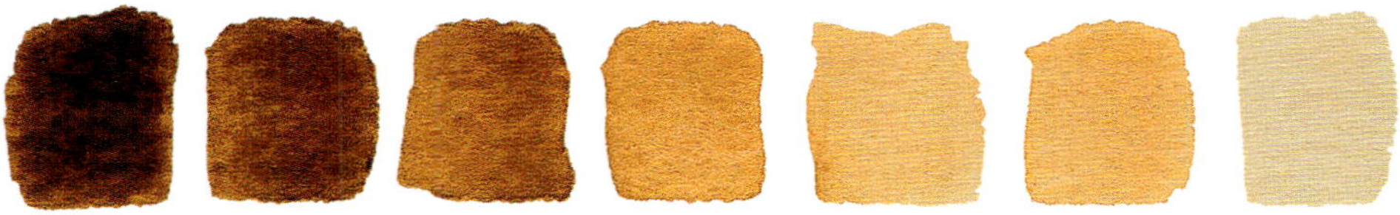

95

COLOR PATCHES

Choose the colors you will need from a set of watercolor pencils and rub a 2 inch (5cm) square of dry pigment from each onto the last page of your sketchbook. Take this, a brush, and some water and, when you are ready to paint, just wet the brush and touch it to the squares of color. You can then blend them and paint on the front pages.

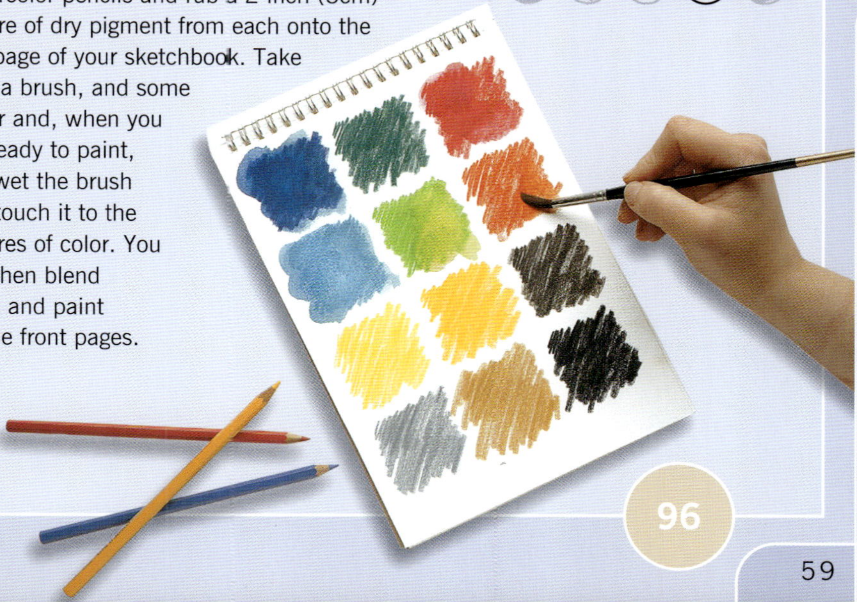

96

WATER SUBSTITUTE

97

If you run out of water or need to mix color on a palette without much water, a touch of saliva makes an adequate alternative to water.

FINGERNAIL TRICK

98

When painting on location without your usual “tool kit,” use your fingernails when you need to scratch out dry paint for highlights.

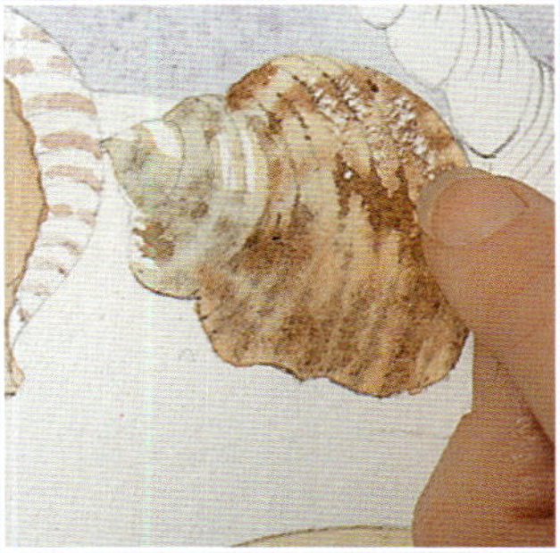

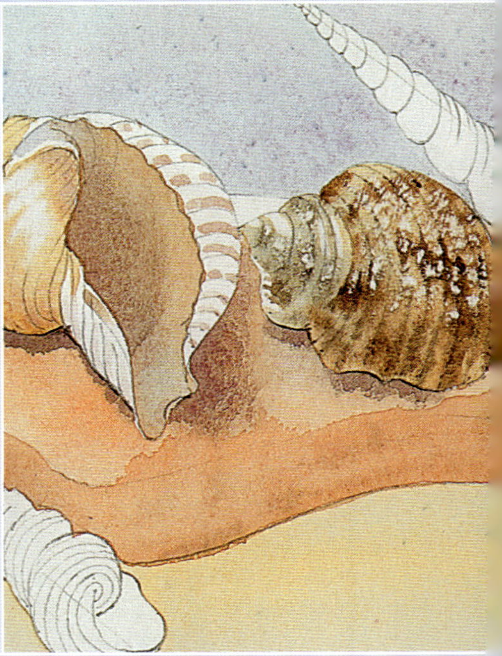

ALTERNATIVE ERASER

If you find you have left your eraser behind, dry French bread left over from your picnic can make an excellent alternative.

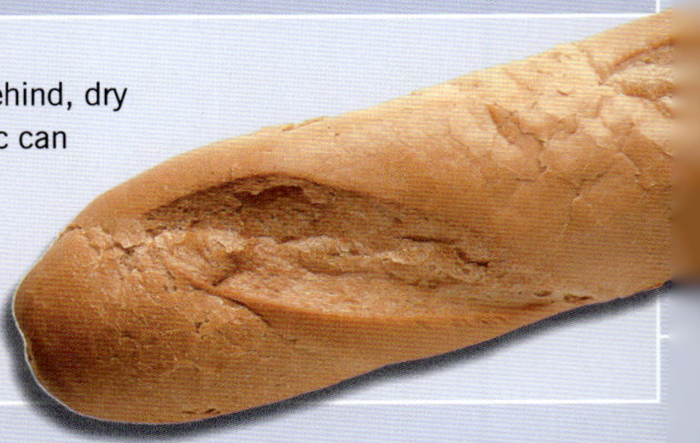

99

LANDSCAPES

When painting a landscape, don't make the common mistake of becoming bogged down in detail—think about the painting as a personal interpretation of nature, not as a copy of it.

KEY ELEMENTS

100

When working on a landscape, it is all too easy to concentrate too much on detail rather than seeing the work as a whole, so that your picture becomes too busy and your final image does not hold together. To create a convincing landscape, concentrate on a few interesting features and use creative license. To practice this, half-close your eyes to blur the image in front of you and reduce it in your mind's eye to basic areas of tone and form. By freeing yourself of detail, you will find it much easier to concentrate on those elements that will make your landscape more successful.

UNIFIED COLOR

101

Paint the sky first and then allow the tonal values across the land to complement the air mass above. To unite the colors in your landscape, repeat sky colors in the landscape below, using blues among the greens, for example. To create a sense of depth, use cooler colors toward the mid-distance and warmer ones in the foreground.

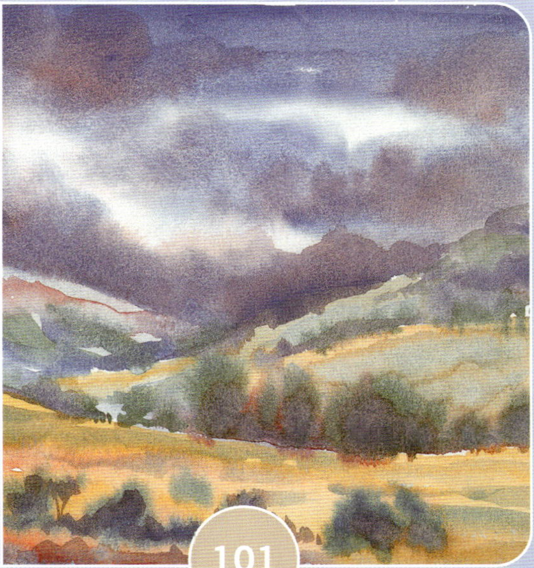

CLOUDS

102

To gauge the true color of white clouds, hold a piece of white paper against the sky and note what tonal variations there are. You may be surprised to realize that few are really white. When the light of the sun is shining directly through a cloud from behind, the outline of the cloud will be clearly defined. If there is no direct sunlight through a cloud formation, the outline will be much more hazy.

CONVINCING REFLECTIONS

To test the effectiveness of your reflections, turn your painting upside down and see how convincing the image seems the "right way" up.

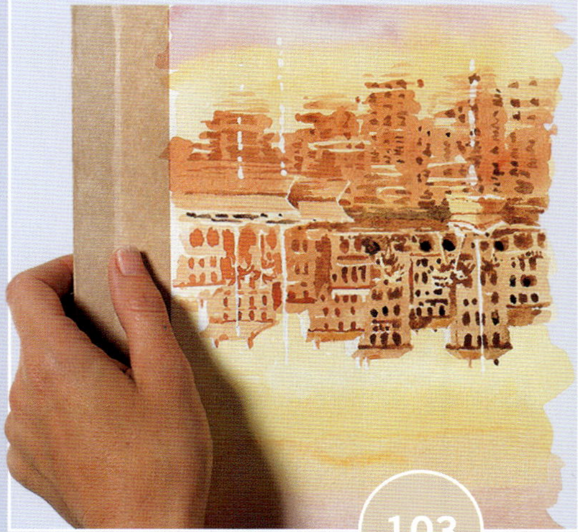

103

UNDERWATER SUBJECTS

When painting subjects submerged under water try to make the surface waterline as clear as possible to make sure that the water retains a sense of depth. To create a fine edge, sharpen a suitably colored watercolor pencil to a point and lightly mark the line with it.

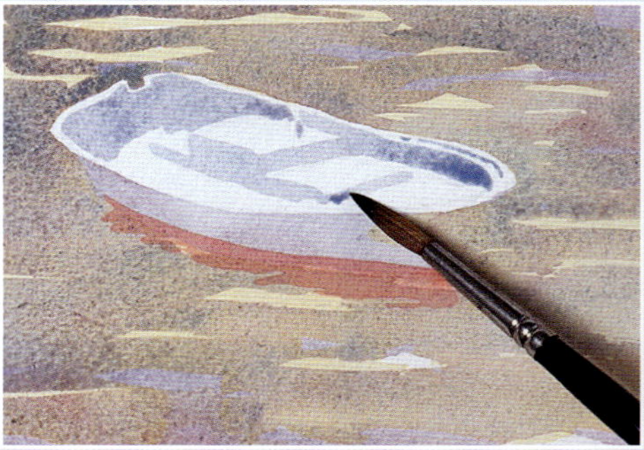

Subject is painted.

104

REFLECTED COLOR

105

The colors of reflections in water should both mirror the colors of the reflected object while incorporating the main color affecting the surface of the water—usually that of the sky. To achieve this balance, try painting a light wash over the reflection using the same color you have used for the sky.

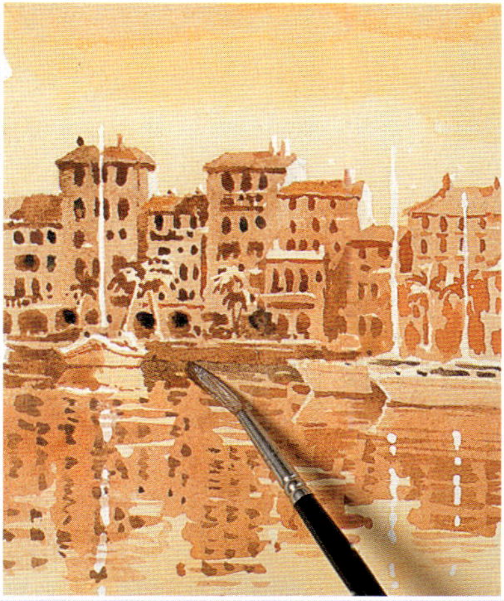

A light wash of sky color is brushed over the reflections.

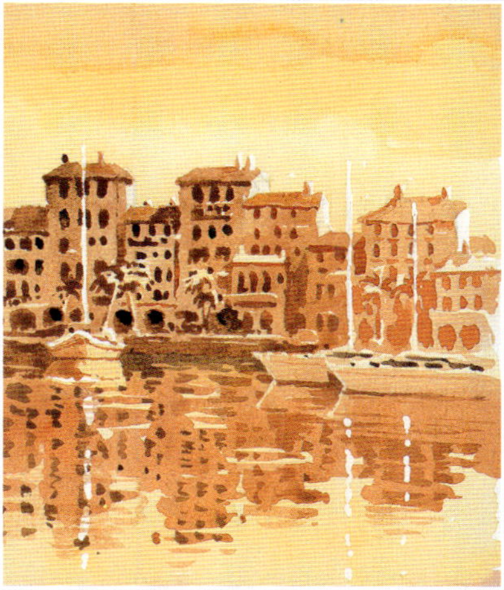

The colors of the reflections are slightly richer than those of the buildings.

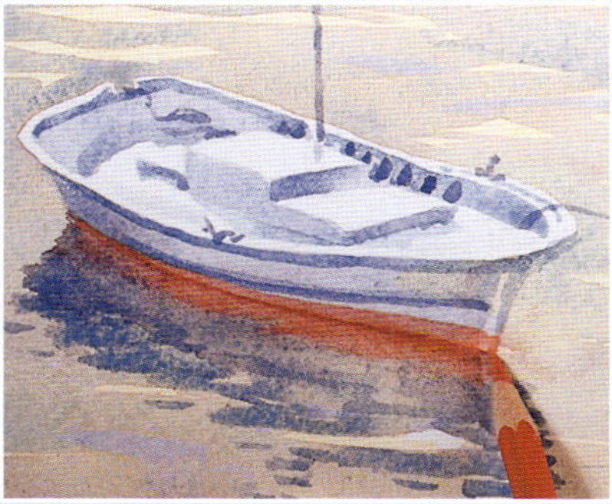

The waterline is marked in.

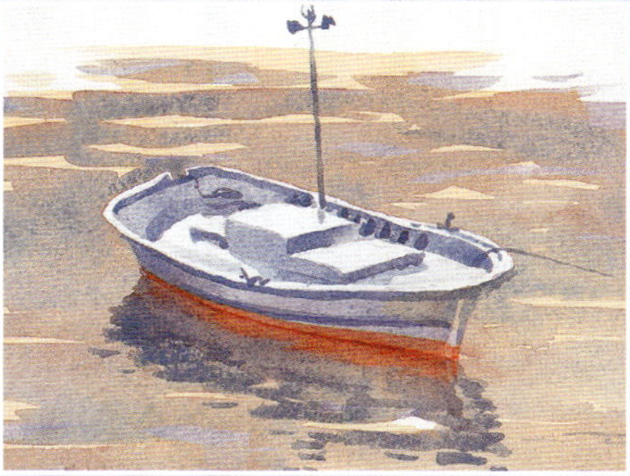

The line has helped to create a sense of depth.

TREES AND FOLIAGE

The main cause of failure when painting trees is poor observation; look for the real colors of foliage, trunks, and branches instead of painting everything in shades of green and brown. Always remember that texture is important, too.

FOLIAGE

106

The texture of foliage can be hard to recreate in watercolor. A good way to achieve convincing texture is by using wax crayon or oil pastel over flat, dry watercolor.

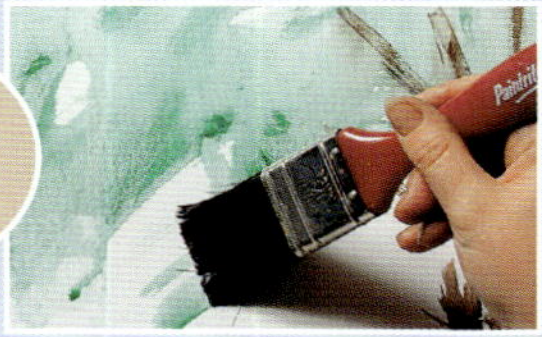

An ordinary household paintbrush is ideal for large blocks of color.

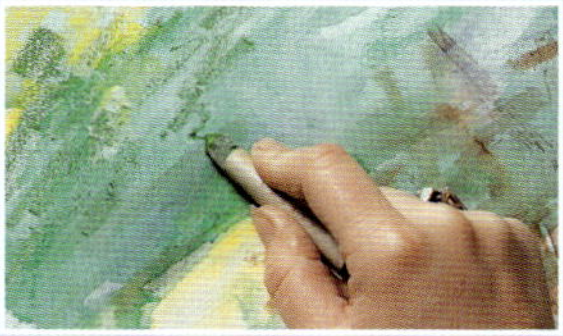

Wax crayon or oil pastel can be added once color is dry.

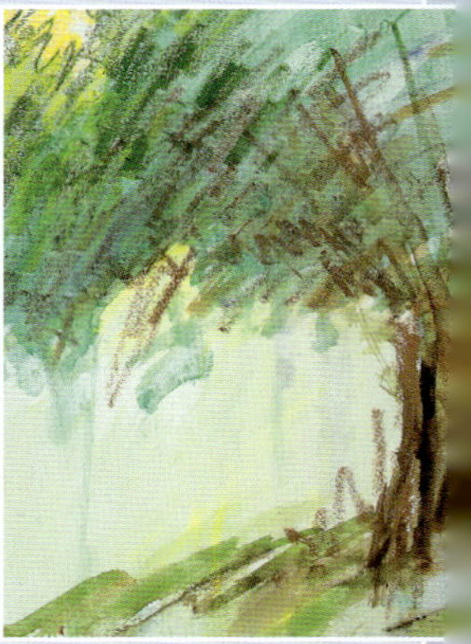

The mixture of media creates interesting textured effects.

FRESH FLOWERS

107

To convey the organic nature of flowers, paint the overall shapes in lightly, then drop in the centers, wet into wet. Allow the paper to dry and then fill in the fine details, either with a brush or watercolor pencil. In this way, your flowers will appear as a vivid combination of spontaneity and intricate design.

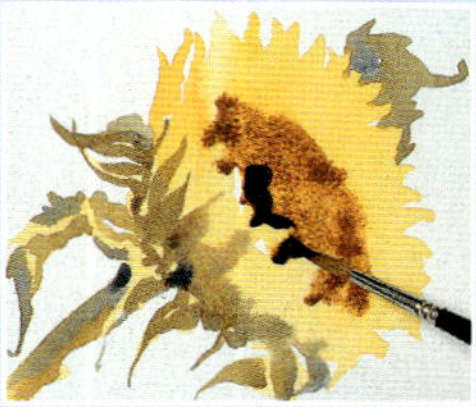

Overall shapes blocked in lightly.

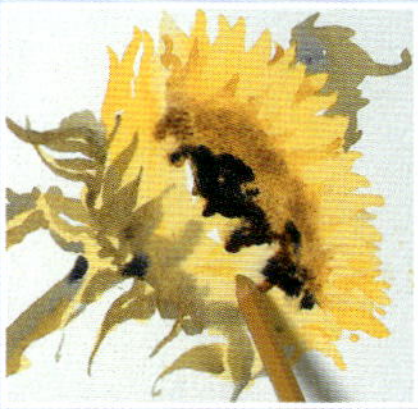

Centers painted wet into wet with watercolor pencil details.

LEAF PATTERNS

108

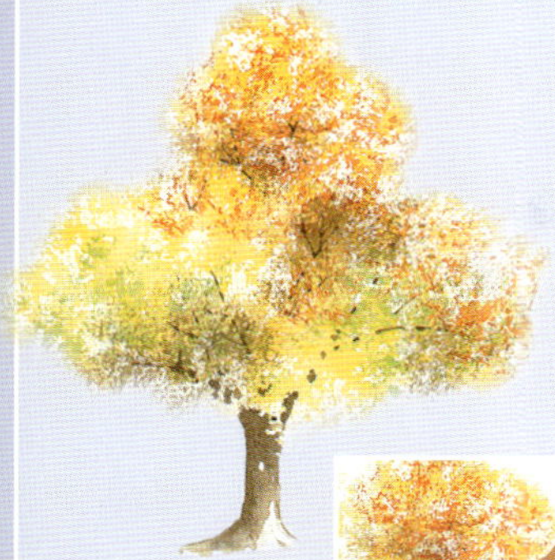

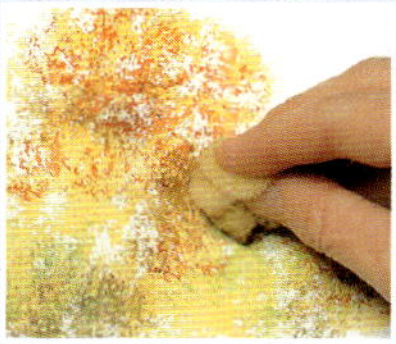

Sponging dark colors over light gives depth.

To create a pattern of leaves or foliage, try applying paint with a sponge, dabbing first a lighter tone, such as a yellow, then laying a darker tone of green or orange over the top to create the shadowy areas.

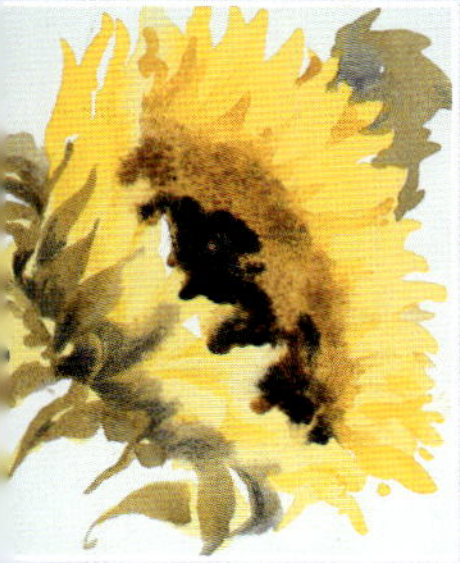

Soft effects contrast with touches of crisper, clearer detail.

LEAF VEINS

109

Once you have applied the initial wash of color to the petals and leaves of flowers, mask out the veins while you build up tonal variations. When you have finished, remove the masking fluid; the delicate veining will give the leaves and petals greater authenticity.

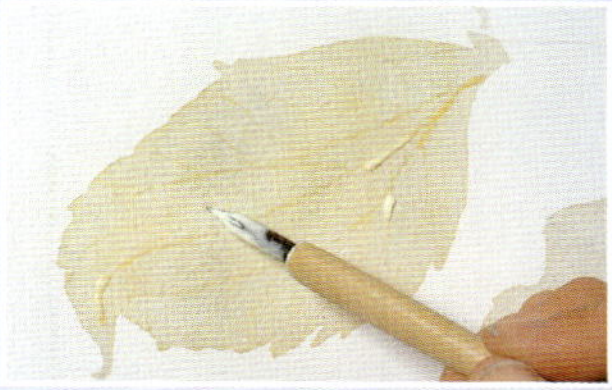

Masking fluid is applied over the dry wash.

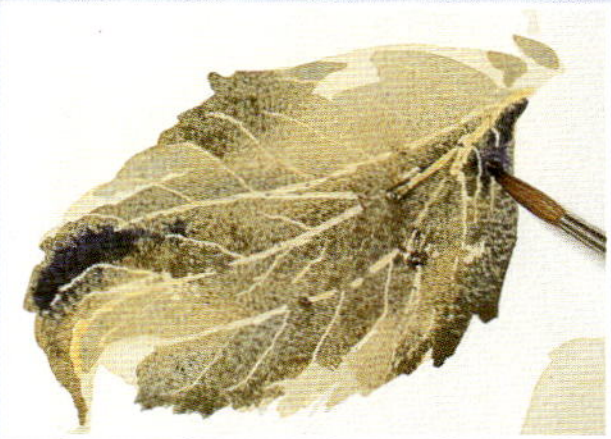

The tones and colors are built up with further washes, and the fluid is removed.

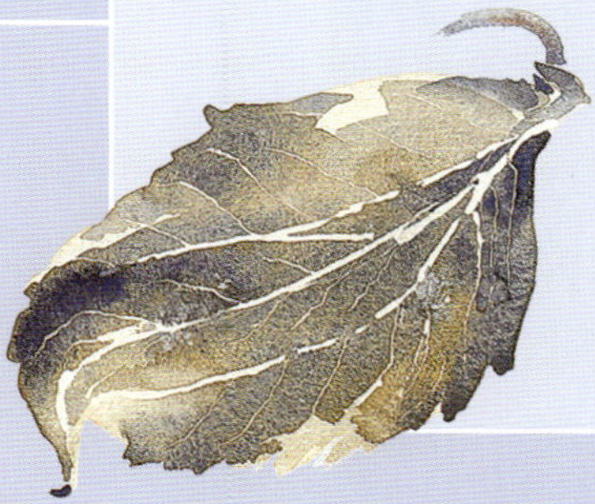

BUILDINGS

Watercolor is well suited to painting buildings, as the combination of broad washes and fine, delicate brushwork can describe architectural features with accuracy and sensitivity.

BRICKWORK

110

When painting a brick wall, remember that from a distance not every brick will be clearly defined—rather the viewer will see the overall fabric of the wall, so describing a few bricks here and there will suffice. Begin by laying in a pale wash of Raw Sienna to provide the background tone. When dry, use a No. 6 chisel brush to paint the bricks and leave spaces between them to indicate mortar. Bricks are not uniform in color, so mix three or four tones before you begin and alternate between them. When the first washes are dry, paint a weak solution of Payne's Gray over the top of the brickwork to unify it. Finally, spatter a mixture of Payne's Gray and Raw Umber over the surface to create more pronounced textural effects.

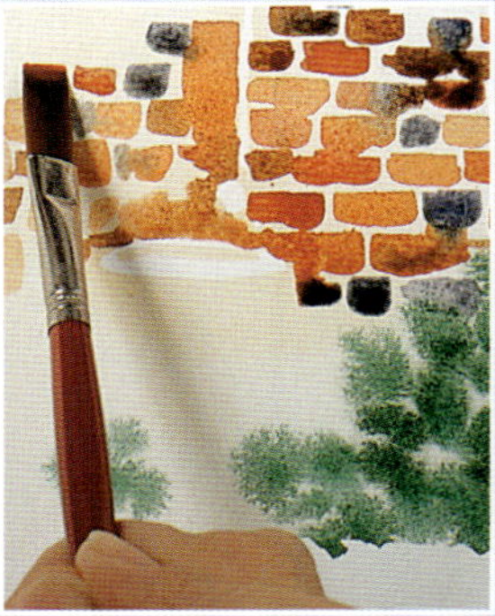

The bricks are painted with a chisel brush, leaving white spaces for the mortar.

SHADING STEPS

111

To paint steps, apply a thin line of paint under the ridges of the steps, and, using a wet brush, pull the paint downward to form the shadow, blotting out rogue runs that you do not want shaded. Alternatively, try wetting under the ridge of the step with plain water first, and then, while it is still wet, draw a line of color under the ridge, allowing it to run into the clean water. Make sure that the band of clear water covers the whole of the vertical plane of the step, but is not so wet that the color runs right down it.

WARM TONES

112

Burnt Sienna, with its rich, luminous red tone, makes a good color for adding warmth to natural brickwork.

STRAIGHT STROKES

113

To avoid crooked window frames, use the brushing technique: hold a ruler at the correct angle to the paper and then carefully glide the brush along it with the ferrule held tightly against the edge of the ruler.

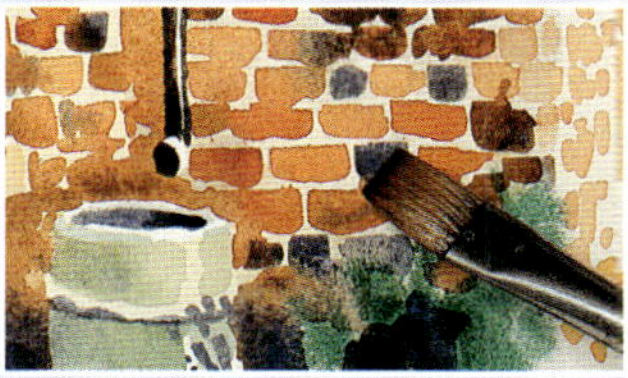

Three or four tones are used to enhance the texture.

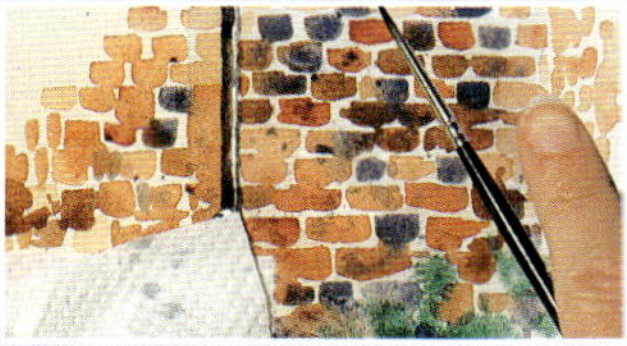

A light spatter of Payne's Gray builds up the texture.

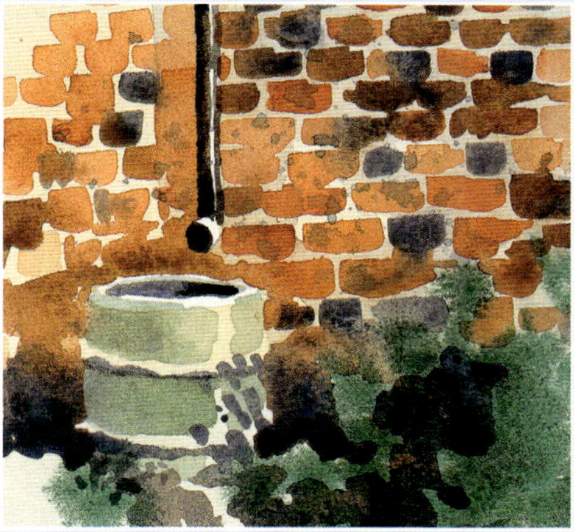

The loose series of brushmarks creates a convincing impression.

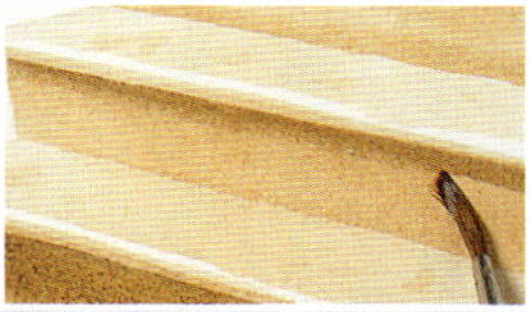

A thin line of paint is applied under the ridges of the steps.

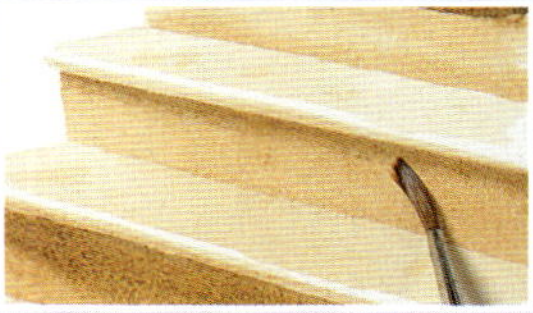

A wet brush is used to soften the edge.

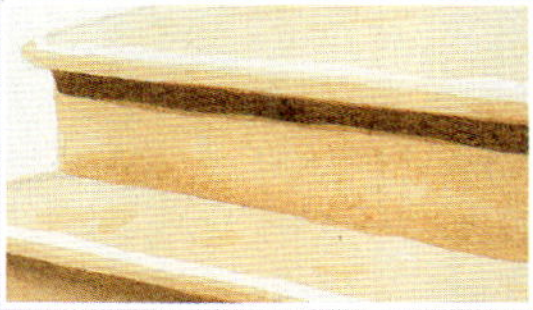

Alternatively, draw a line of color under the ridge.

PAINTING PEOPLE

Although portrait painting is best avoided until you are sure of your skills, painting people in a landscape is no harder than painting trees or rocks, and will often give the painting the extra touch it needs.

SKIN TONES

114

If you find it difficult to achieve lively skin tones, try using smooth (hot-pressed) paper instead of standard cold-pressed. Because it has a much harder, flatter surface, it will not soak up watercolor so quickly, making it easier to move the colors around and create soft effects. If you decide to experiment with this surface, you will have to control more backruns and pools of paint. Although the paper is more unpredictable, you will be able to achieve spontaneous and sparkling results.

PEOPLE IN A LANDSCAPE

115

It is best to paint people in a landscape with two simple strokes, one lighter to indicate flesh tones, and the other over the top when dry to indicate hair or head covering and garments. The overall shape of the stroke is important: it must be simple and direct.

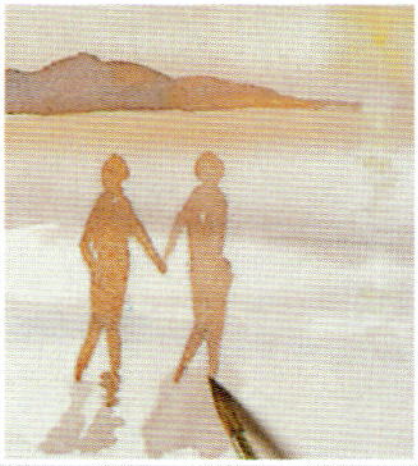

Light brushstrokes over dried washes suggest the figures.

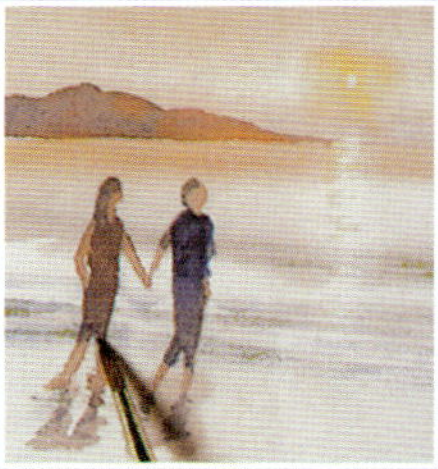

Darker colors are now added for hair and clothing.

The figures are well integrated into their surroundings.

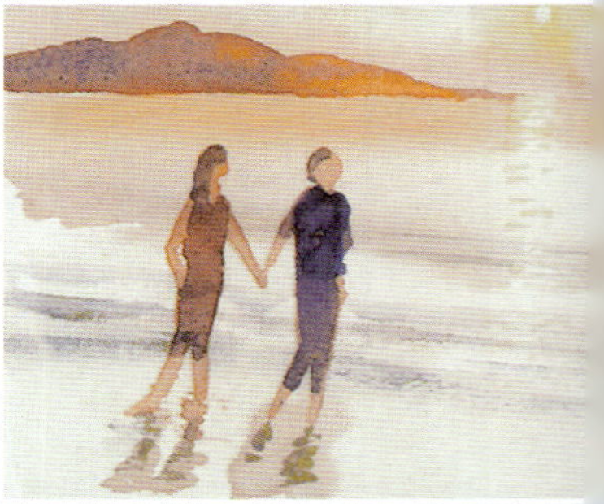

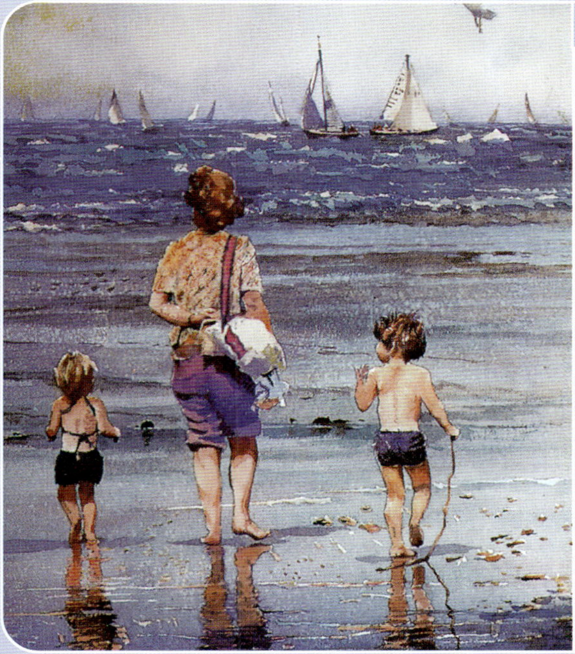

LAYERED TONES

Build up skin tones gradually, with very thin, light washes of paint, allowing the painting to dry in between applications to achieve subtle tonal variations. The less you drag the paint around, the more lively the portrait will be.

La Vere Hutchings' "A Day at the Beach" (detail) is a perfect example of layered tones.

116

FLESH HIGHLIGHTS

When painting pale skin, allow untouched white paper to depict the lightest flesh tones.

In Paul Bartlett's "Face Looking Through" (detail), the colors have been worked rapidly wet into wet.

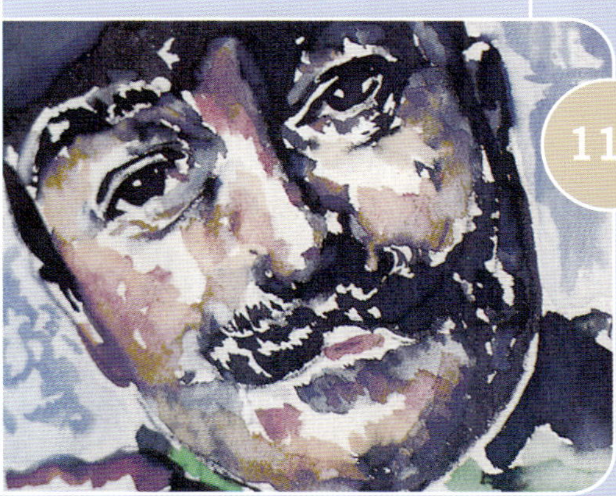

117

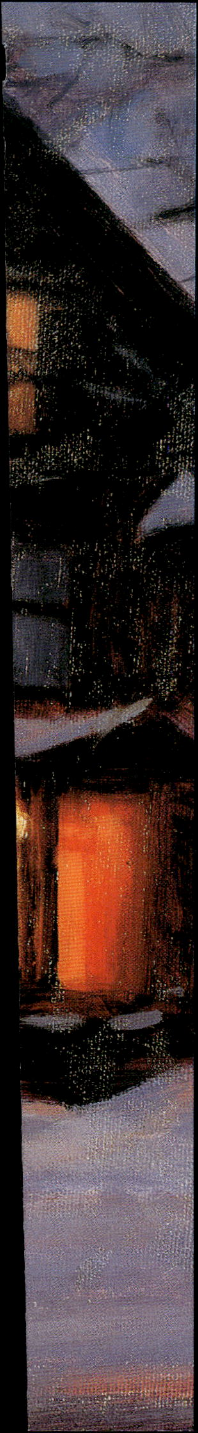

2

OIL PAINTING

There are almost as many approaches to oil painting as there are artists, and the fact that there are so few rules can make the whole process more rather than less confusing. The tips that follow—spanning paints, materials and equipment, brushes and brushmarks, color theory and ways of mixing color, methods of applying paint, making modifications and changes, special effects, working on location, and coping with difficult subjects—will help you avoid the pitfalls and get maximum enjoyment out of working in oils.

Doug Dawson, "Denver Snow" (detail).

INTRODUCTION TO OILS

THERE ARE almost as many approaches and techniques for oil painting as there are artists, and the fact that there are so few rules can make the whole process more, rather than less, confusing. This section is designed to answer the queries that are often raised about the materials and techniques of painting with oils, to dispel confusion about what is or is not possible, and to suggest new techniques to try. Many beginners assume that oils are more difficult to use than other types of paint, such as watercolor or acrylics, but armed with a little knowledge you may well find it easier than you imagined to get good results. Tips are included on paints and equipment, covering selection, re-use and recycling, and alternatives to purchased materials. There are different ways of mixing colors and getting color effects with oil paints, and there are also many ways to begin and build up a painting.

Oil paint can be applied into wet paint or over dry paint, it can be built up in thin, transparent layers or thick, opaque ones. It can be applied with a brush or a knife, and it can be scraped or drawn into or wiped off. With oil paint it is also possible to return to a painting to do further work after a gap of some weeks, or even months.

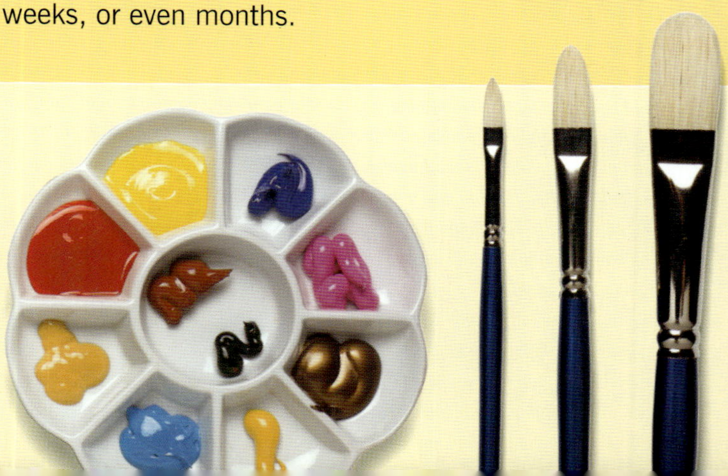

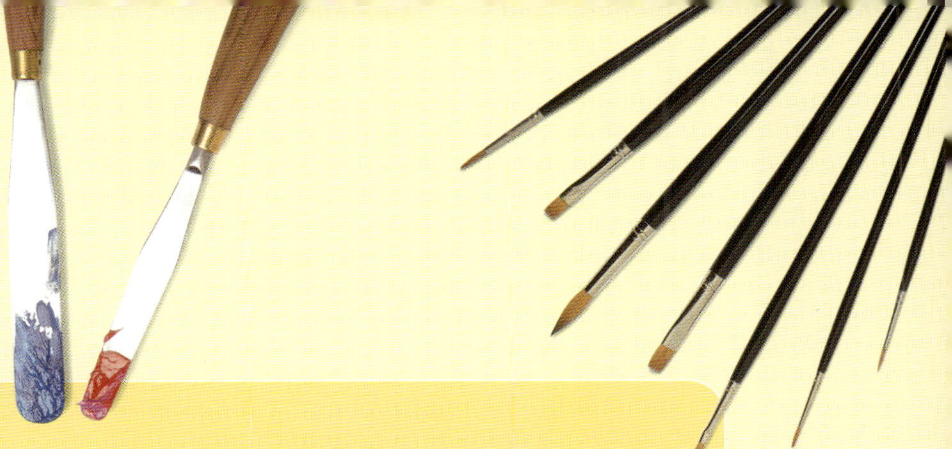

One of the great advantages of oil paint is that you can keep on removing paint and reworking or painting over areas you are not happy with until they look right. And there are different ways of taking the paint off, depending on how much you want to leave behind to build on again. Oil paints can be cumbersome to take on location, but with careful selection of equipment and materials it is possible to lighten the load. There are also various strategies to help with the other problems—such as constantly changing conditions and limited time—associated with working out of doors. And then there is the problem of transporting wet paintings home again.

Dramatic special effects can be created with oils by adding in materials to give the paint additional substance and texture, or by combining it with other media. Oils can also be used to produce monoprints—the only additional equipment needed is a sheet of glass. In short, oil paint is one of the most versatile of all the painting mediums, and these tips will help you avoid the pitfalls and get maximum enjoyment out of using it.

MATERIALS

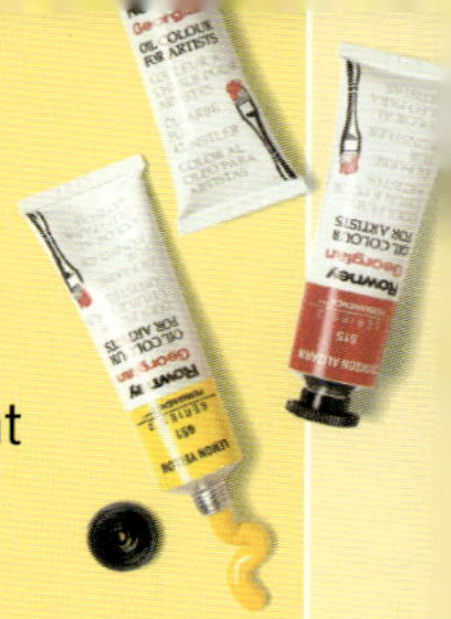

When you are starting out with a new medium, you may be confused by the choice of materials available to you. This section combines practical advice on paint types and mixing mediums with helpful hints. For example, did you know that you can recycle mineral spirits and save paint, or that you can make your own palette from a sheet of glass?

PAINT QUALITY

118

Oil paints are available from most manufacturers in two qualities, artists' and students'. The more expensive of the two, artists' quality paints contain a higher proportion of pigment to oil, whereas students' paints are bulked out with fillers. Because they contain more pigment, artists' quality paints have more tinting power in mixtures, so you end up using less of them.

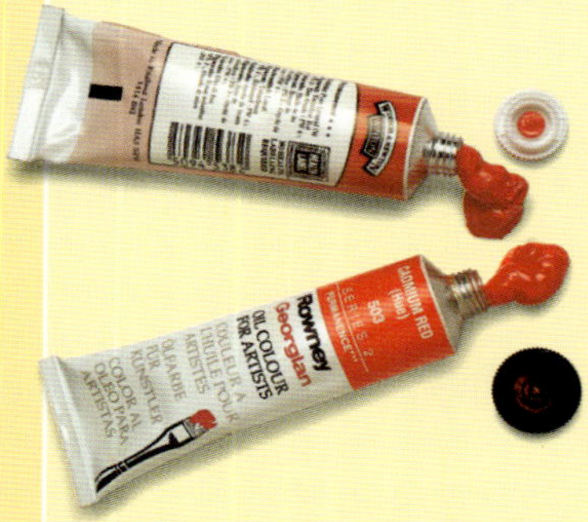

TUBES AND JARS

119

If you get through paint quickly, or are planning to work on a very large canvas, it may be more convenient, and is probably cheaper, to buy it in large tubes or pint jars instead of standard tubes. It is particularly worth buying white in a large quantity.

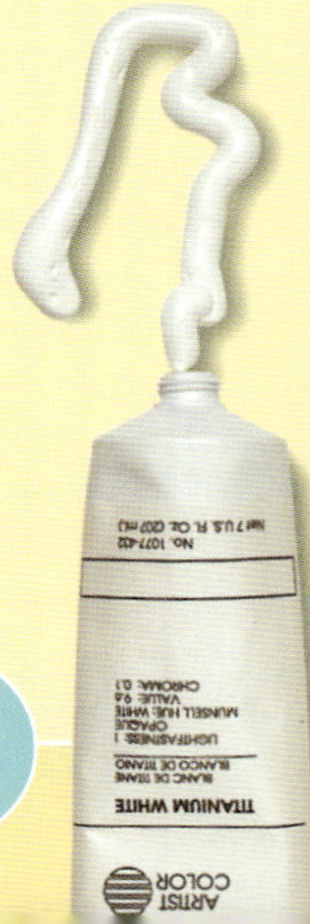

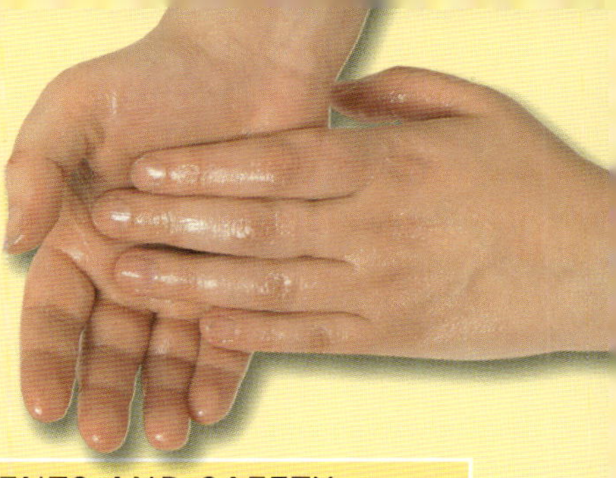

LIGHTFASTNESS

Pigments vary in their lightfastness—or resistance to fading in sunlight. Paint manufacturers provide information on the lightfastness of their colors. The number of categories varies, but they usually range from excellent to poor. Colors with an excellent rating will retain their intensity over a long period of time, whereas those with a poor rating will gradually fade and should be avoided.

120

PIGMENTS AND SAFETY

121

Some pigments used in paints are poisonous if ingested over a period of time, and it is advisable to take measures to prevent paint from getting all over your hands, as it can work into the skin. Thin surgical gloves are one answer. Barrier cream is another possibility. Barrier cream prevents paint from seeping into the skin, and hands can be cleaned just by washing in soap and hot water. Avoid eating, drinking, or smoking until you have cleaned all paint smudges off your hands.

USING PAINT CHARTS

Colors vary in transparency and lightfastness, and this information is available on manufacturers' paint charts. The chart lists the pigment(s) used in each color, using the Color Index Generic Name for each pigment (an international index of pigments used in artists' paints), and information about the transparency and lightfastness of each tube color.

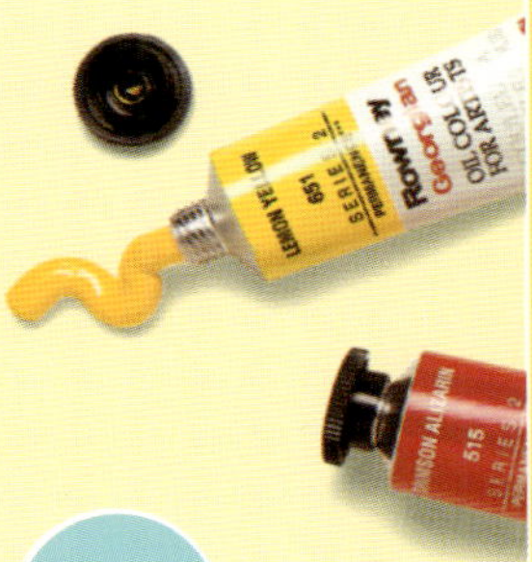

122

PALETTE KNIVES

123

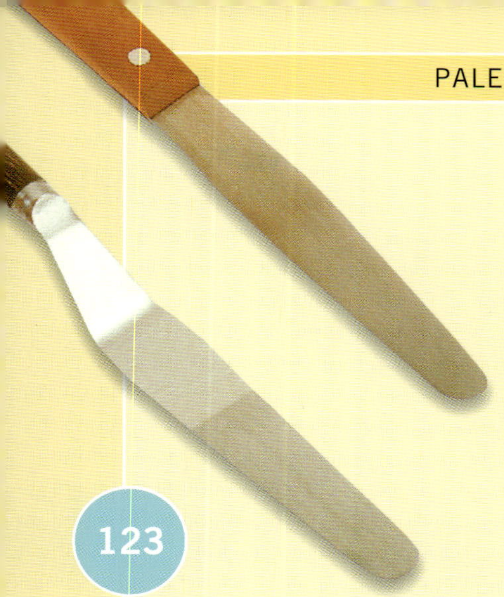

If you use a palette knife for applying or taking off paint as well as for mixing, you will probably find the cantilevered type much easier to work with than a straight one, because it keeps your hand away from the wet paint on the canvas or board.

Uncantilevered palette knife for scraping off paint.

Cantilevered palette knife for mixing paint.

MIXING MEDIUMS

Paint mediums (used to improve the flow of the paint) can be mixed easily and quickly. Recipes usually quote quantities in parts, and the easiest way to mix them is to take a jar or bottle with a tight-fitting lid and pour in the correct quantity of each ingredient in turn, marking the level on the outside of the bottle after each addition. Subsequently, as long as you add the ingredients in the same order each time, you've got a quick guide to mixing the correct quantities.

Mix ingredients in a jar with a tight-fitting lid.

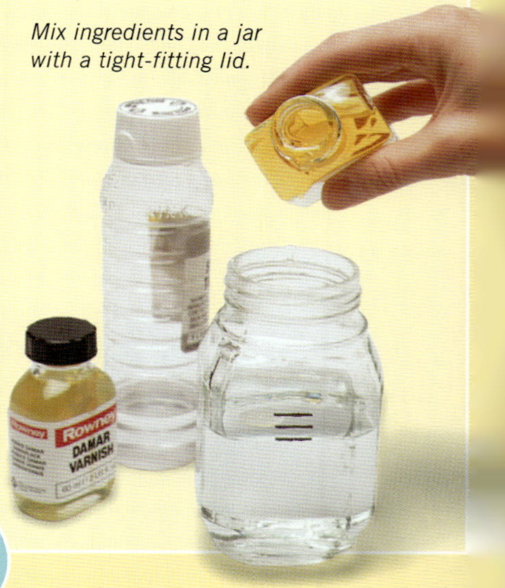

124

PALETTE ALTERNATIVE

There are several alternatives to wooden artists' palettes that are both cheaper and available in larger sizes. A sheet of glass laid over a sheet of white, neutral, or medium-toned paper is one possibility. Apply masking tape along each side of the glass so you cannot cut yourself on it. Other possibilities are formica-covered board, available from hardware stores or lumber yards.

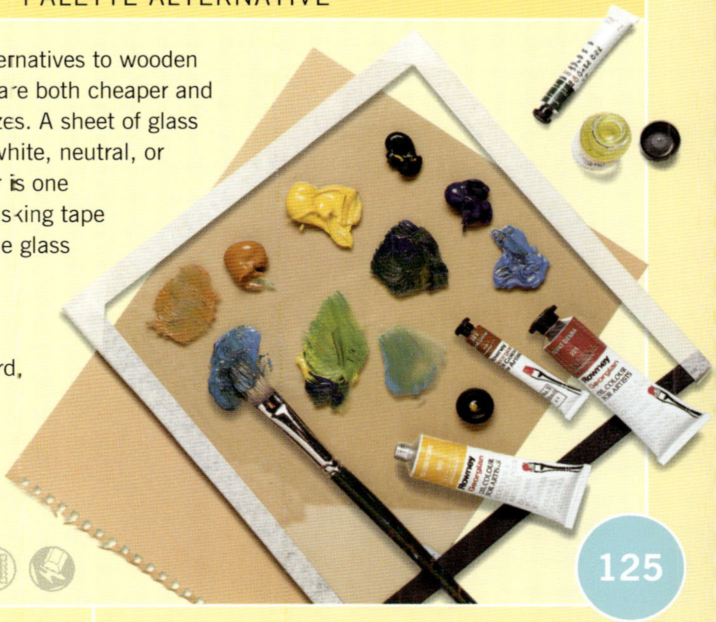

125

MINERAL SPIRITS

126

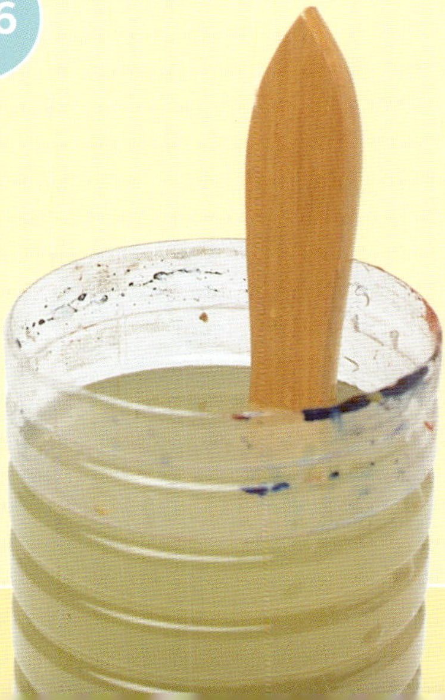

Mineral spirit that has been used for cleaning brushes needn't be poured away. Cut the top from a large plastic bottle or use a large glass jar and leave dirty spirits to stand in it until clear, although it will still be discolored. This mixture can then be poured into a clean container and stored for re-use.

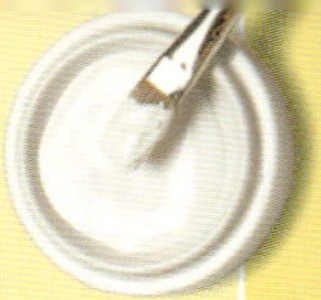

SUPPORTS

You can use oil paint on a variety of supports: on stretchers, canvas (such as cotton or linen), plywood, strong cardboard, or you can try more unusual textures such as a board covered with cheesecloth and white glue. Try out different supports until you find one that suits you.

ECONOMICAL BOARD

127

If you like painting on board, an economical way of buying it is in big sheets from a hardware store that has a cutting service. Large 9 x 12 foot (2.75 x 3.65m) sheets of masonite, for example, are available at an economical price, and you can have them cut up into different sizes.

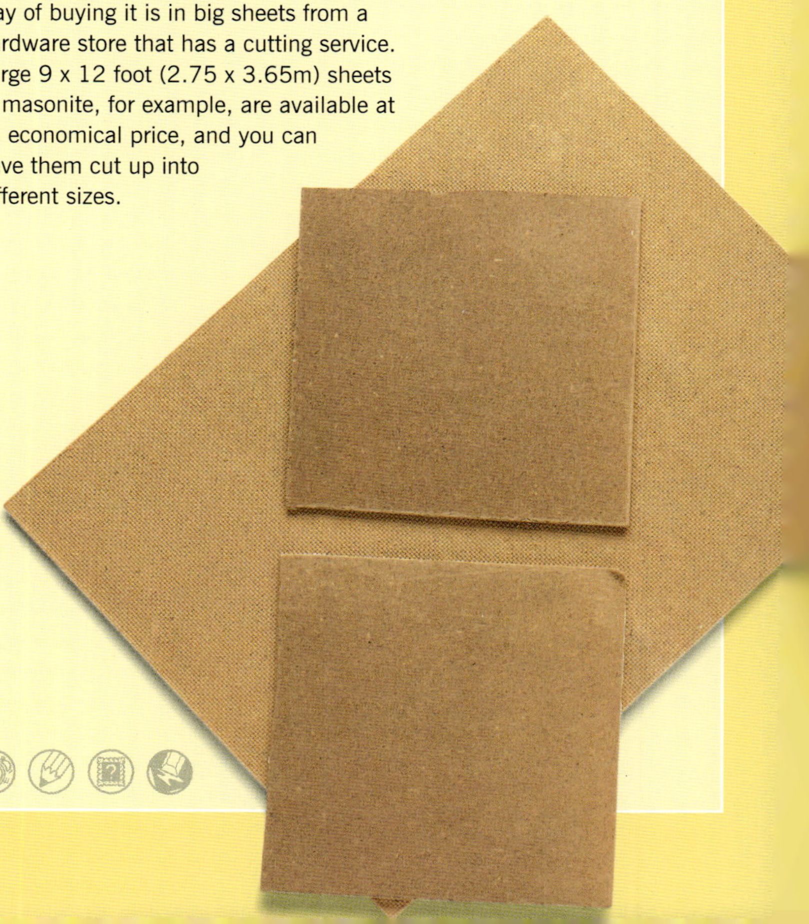

PREPARING BOARDS

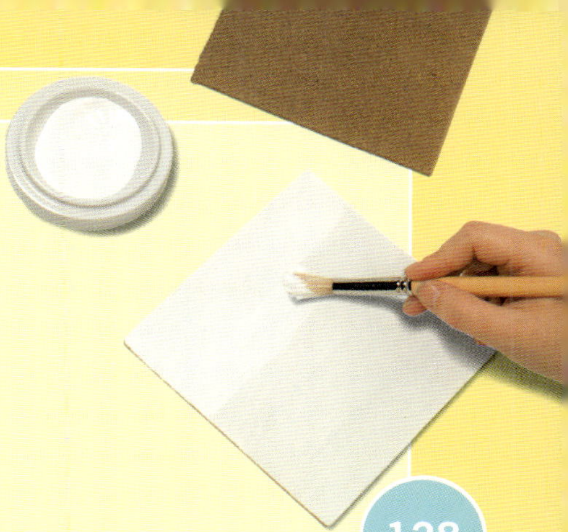

Before priming a piece of masonite, wipe over the surface with denatured alcohol to degrease it, so that it takes the paint well. When it is dry, prime with two or three coats of acrylic primer. To add texture to the surface, you can mix some acrylic texture paste into the final coat. If you want to use an oil primer, the board will need to be sized (given a coat of diluted rabbit-skin glue) first.

128

VARIED TEXTURES

An interesting surface can be created by covering a board with cheesecloth and white craft glue. Cover the surface of the board with the glue, applied roughly with a knife or scraper; don't worry about getting it smooth. Take a piece of cheesecloth 2 inches (5cm) larger than the board all around, press it down over the glue, fold the edges over to the back, and stick them down. Then apply glue unevenly over the cheesecloth, covering it in places and leaving it bare in others. When dry, the board should be primed, and a colored ground can be rubbed on lightly with a cloth. This creates a varied surface, smooth in some places, and with the weave of the cloth evident in others.

White glue is applied thinly in some areas and more thickly in others before cheesecloth is applied, which will give a varied final surface.

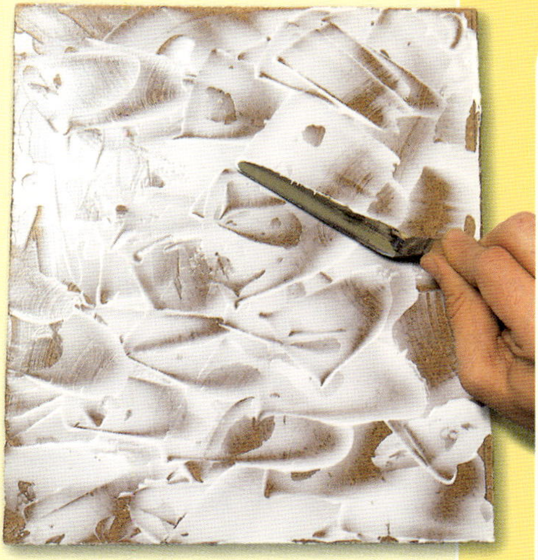

129

CANVAS

130 If you like to work on canvas but want to experiment with different textures, you should consider stretching and preparing your own canvases. The standard materials are cotton duck, available in a selection of weights, and artists' linen, which gives a lively and interesting surface but is more expensive. There is also braided cotton, a heavy, textured cotton with a loose weave, and fabrics such as flax and burlap, which have quite coarse surfaces, making them very interesting to experiment with.

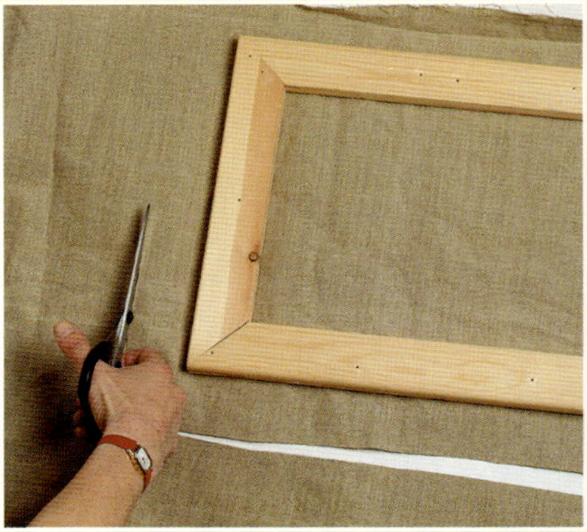

Assemble the stretchers and cut the canvas to size. Staple or tack the center of each side.

PRIMING

131 Either acrylic or oil primers can be used under oil paints. The canvas should not be sized if acrylic primer is going to be used, but should be sized (given a coat of a weak solution of rabbit-skin glue) if an oil-based primer is going to be used. Acrylic primers dry much more quickly than oil-based ones. However, sizing has the advantage that it tightens up the canvas as it dries, helping to produce a good, drum-tight surface to paint on.

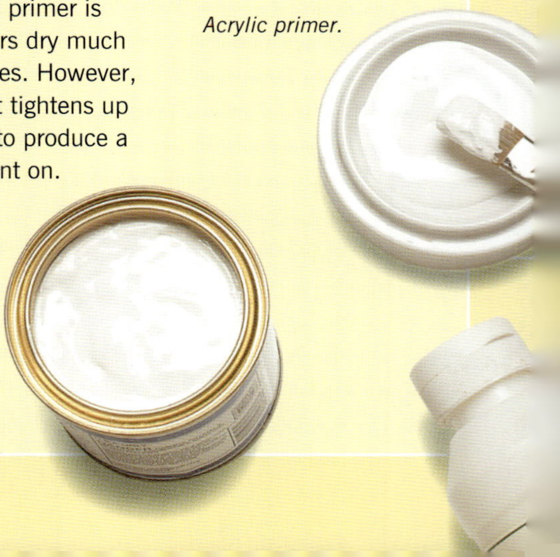

Acrylic primer.

Oil-based primer; size canvas before application.

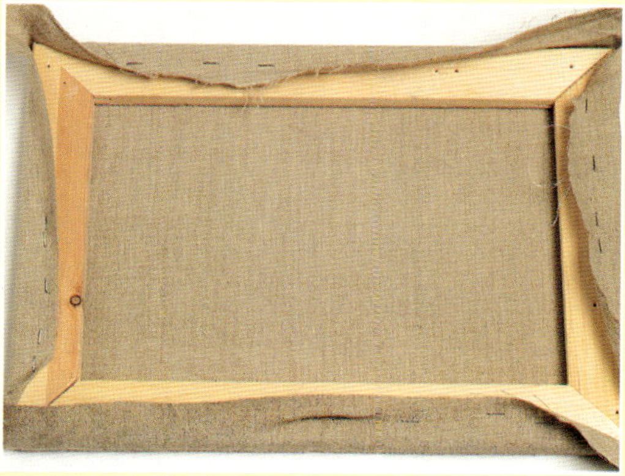

Working on alternate sides, staple or tack from the center out to the corners

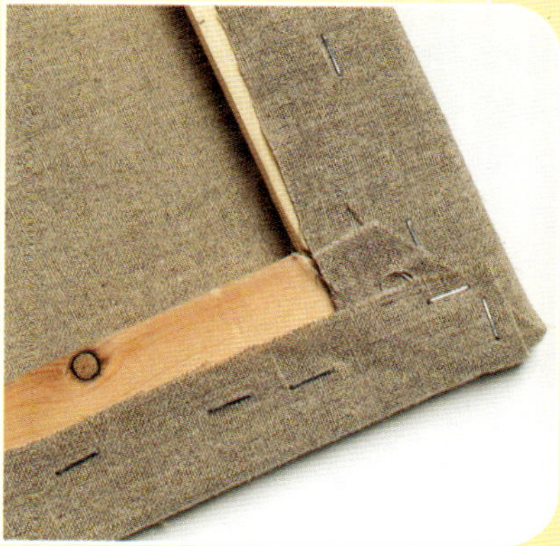

Staple each side before folding the corners over.

OILS ON PAPER

Oil paint can be used on paper, but the paper should be primed first. Paper absorbs oil in the paint, which makes the paint difficult to work with, and will eventually rot the paper. The answer is to prime paper with acrylic primer first. For smaller sheets of paper or cardboard for oil sketches, you could prime with acrylic paint from a tube, thinned with water, which will dry very quickly so you can start painting almost immediately.

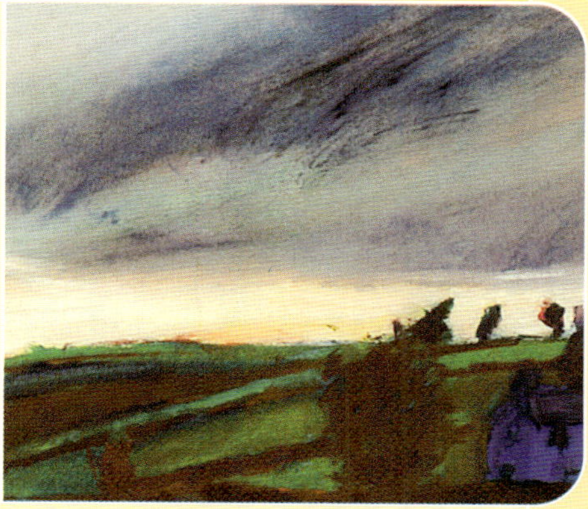

Jane Strother's "One Welsh Hillside" (detail) is painted on paper. The paint has been used thinly, and the smooth white surface of the paper gives the colors great luminosity.

132

WEDGES

To avoid damaging a prepared canvas surface when hammering wedges into the corners, slip a piece of cardboard into each corner between the stretcher (the wooden frame supporting the canvas) and the canvas itself. This will protect the canvas if the hammer knocks against it as you hammer the wedges in, which can cause the size layer and priming to crack. Work around each corner one way, and then the other, to increase pressure on the canvas evenly.

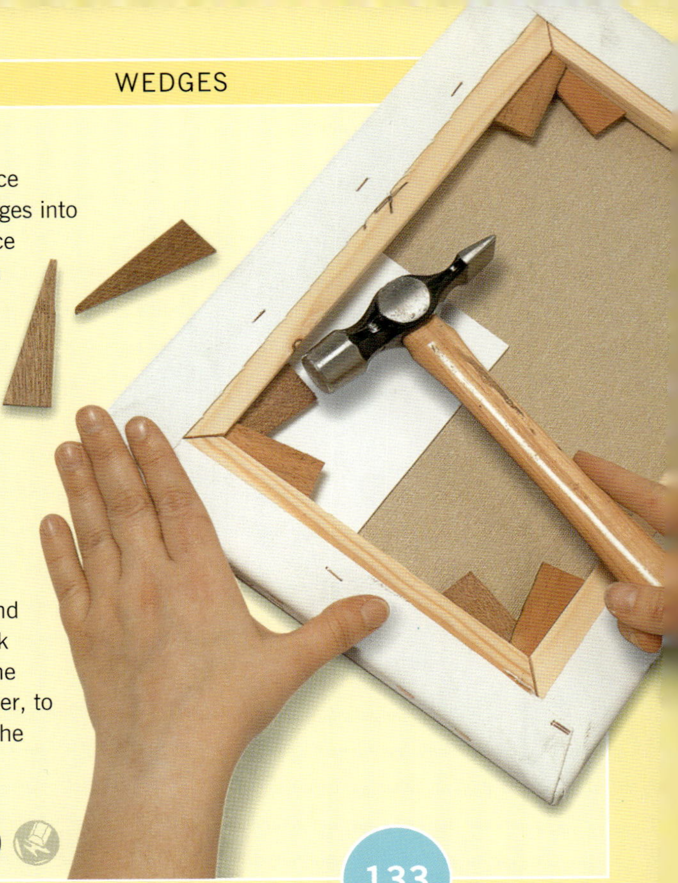

133

STRETCHER MARKS

Irritating lines can appear near the sides of a canvas, caused by pressure against the stretcher bars behind. This can often happen when you do lots of rubbing and scraping off. The lines can be prevented by inserting strips of thin foam or bubble-wrap between the stretcher bars and the canvas to cushion the canvas, if it is likely to be pressed against the edge of the bars while you work.

134

DENTS IN A CANVAS

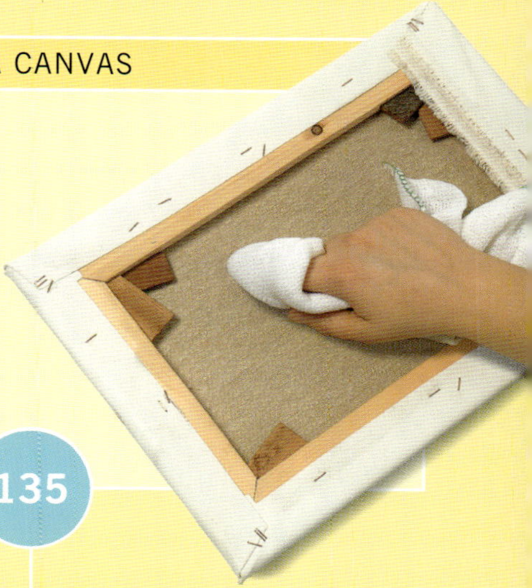

To get rid of any dents that have appeared in a canvas, take a damp, well squeezed-out rag or sponge and rub it lightly over the dent on the back of the canvas a few times. As the canvas dries, it will tighten up and the dent will disappear.

135

RE-USING SUPPORTS

It is better not to re-use canvas or boards unless the paint already applied is not entirely dry and can be scraped off. The new paint may not adhere properly to the surface, and the texture of the original painting may interfere with the new one. If you are re-using a support, scrape it down and wash off as much paint as possible with turpentine. When dry, re-prime with an oil-based primer.

136

ROLLING A CANVAS

137

Canvases shouldn't be rolled unless it is unavoidable, because it can cause cracks in the sizing and paint layers. If a canvas does have to be taken off the stretchers and rolled, for storage or carrying for example, roll it around a cylinder with as wide a diameter as possible, and roll it with the paint surface facing out. This way, when the canvas is unrolled, any cracks will close up again.

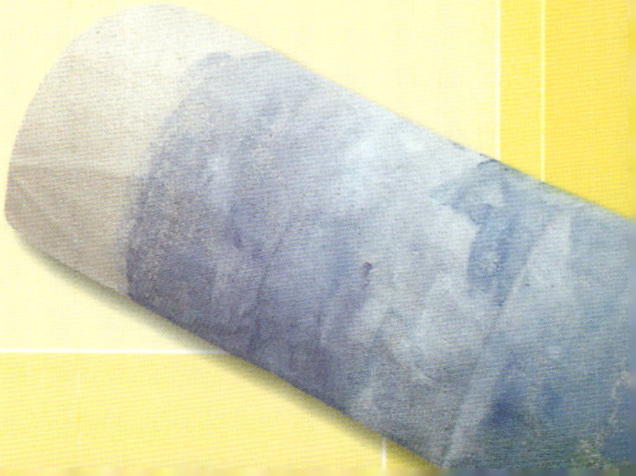

BRUSHES AND BRUSHMARKS

To get the best results from your painting, you need to know the different brush shapes and the marks they make. This section covers choice and care of brushes, plus hints on achieving smooth surfaces and gradations, as well as experimenting with ways of handling your own brushes to create different effects.

BRUSH SHAPES

138

You need to select the shape of brush according to the way in which you want to apply the paint. Flat-ended brushes, known as brights, are best used for covering large areas of paint, while short flats are good for dragging paint across the surface. Round-ended brushes—filberts—make tapering marks, while round brushes are good for detail.

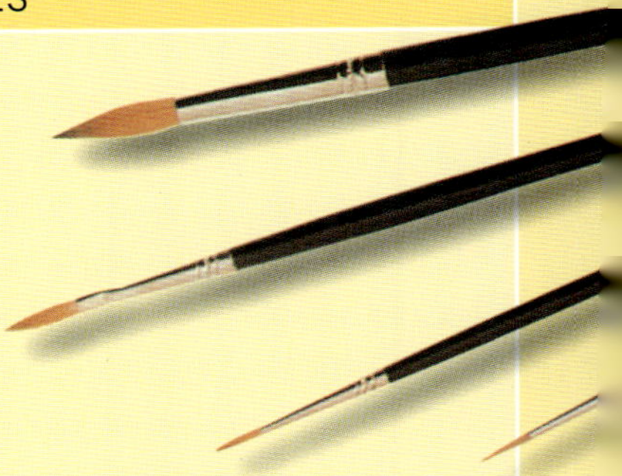

Round brushes: use these for small areas and details.

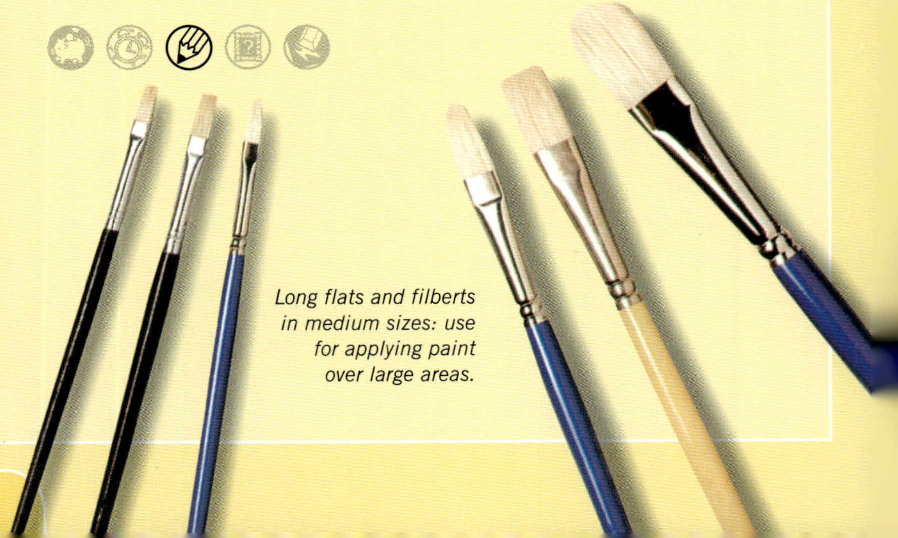

Long flats and filberts in medium sizes: use for applying paint over large areas.

HARD OR SOFT BRUSHES

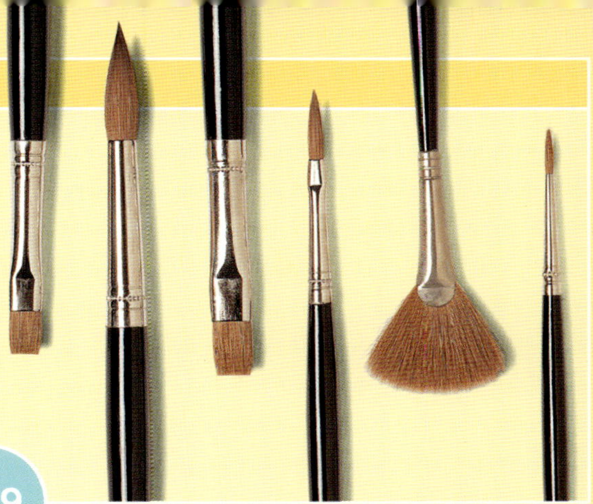

139

To apply paint to large areas, or to apply very thick paint, bristle brushes are best. For a smooth surface, fine detail, or applying thin paint such as glazes, soft brushes such as sable should be used.

SABLE OR SYNTHETIC

140

Sable brushes are the best quality soft brushes. However, cheaper alternatives are available in the form of sable/synthetic mixtures and synthetic brushes. Although these are satisfactory, they lack the springiness in the bristles that sable brushes have and do not retain their shape over time, so they may turn out to be a false economy in the long run.

CLEANING BRUSHES

141

To get all the paint out of a brush, first rinse it in mineral spirits to get as much paint out as possible. Then draw the brush across the top of a bar of soap, with the bristles horizontal to the surface of the soap, under running water a few times. Work the soap through the bristles, drawing paint out of the ferrule, and rinse. Repeat this process until no more paint comes out.

NEW BRUSHES

142

The bristles of new brushes are dipped in sizing to protect them, which is why they are stiff. If you try to soften them, being stiff, the bristles may crack and break off. Before using a brush for the first time, you should soak it in water for a while, and then rinse it with warm water and soap to get all the sizing out of the bristles.

VISIBLE BRUSHMARKS

143

To make brushmarks that hold their shape, use a reasonably stiff bristle brush. Linseed oil mixed into the paint will also help to hold the brushmarks in shape. It is also important to have a firm support—for example, a canvas should be tightly stretched, with some resistance in it, so that it does not give under pressure from the brush.

VARIETY OF MARKS

144

To create a varied surface, experiment with different ways of handling your brushes. You can stab the painting with the tip of the brush for very textural marks. You can hold the brush horizontal to the paint surface and drag it across the surface for broken application of paint, or apply thin paint with a scrubbing motion for a scumbled effect.

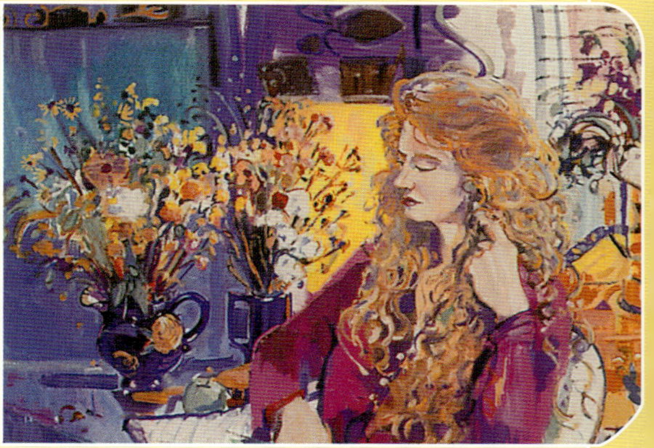

In "Anne Amongst Flowers" (detail) by Peter Graham, paint has been put on in a range of ways. Energetic vertical brushstrokes in the figure and furniture, offset with long flowing brushstrokes in the hair and distinct marks in the flowers, produce a lively image.

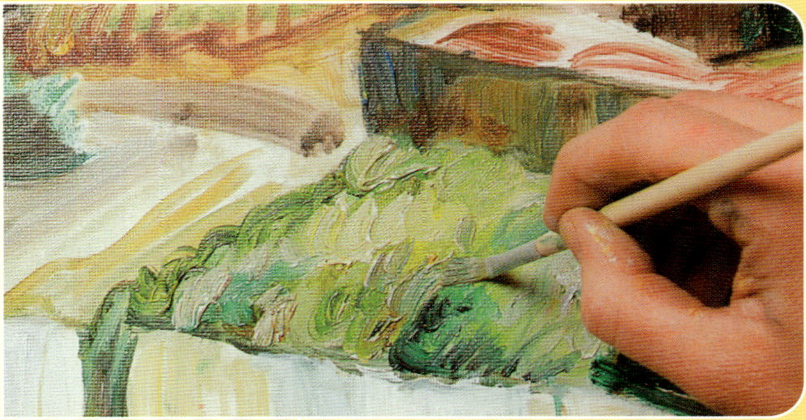

Slightly thinned paint is applied with a bristle brush and holds the brushmarks well.

A SMOOTH SURFACE

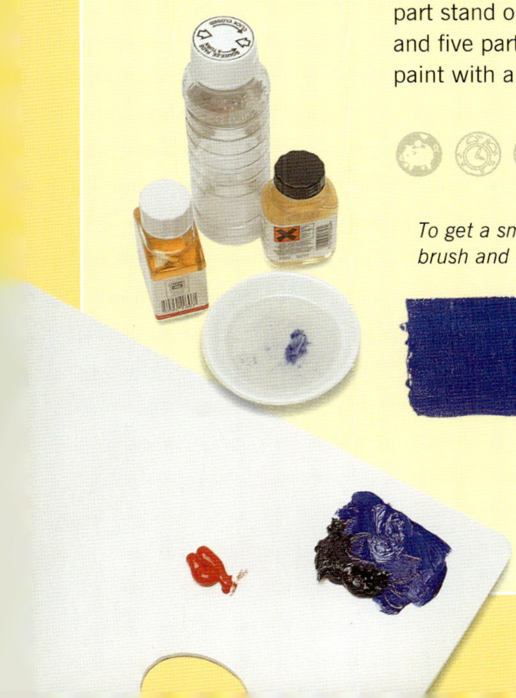

For a smooth surface with no brushmarks, mix a medium into the paint, either a commercial one, or one mixed from one part stand oil, one part damar varnish, and five parts turpentine. Also apply the paint with a soft brush such as sable.

To get a smooth surface use a soft brush and long strokes.

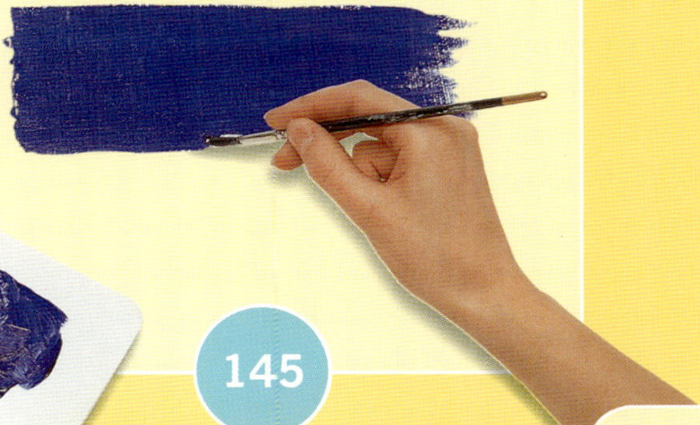

145

A SMOOTH GRADATION

146

To get an absolutely smooth, barely perceptible gradation from one tone or color to another, prepare a color mixture for each. Apply the colors separately, the darkest one first and the lighter one next to it, with a clean brush. Blend the two, initially with a bristle brush, and then switch to a fan brush, using short strokes and working across the edge between the two areas of paint.

Two colors are laid down and then pulled into each other.

The colors have been blended together until a smooth gradation is achieved.

ROUGH BLENDING

147

Apply two tones or colors next to each other, and knit them together with short zigzag strokes to create a broken edge.

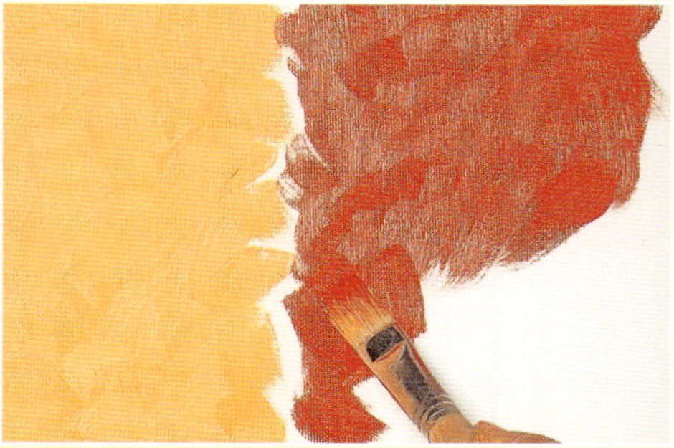

Two areas of color are laid next to each other.

LOOSENING UP

If your work has become very tight, of if you tend to be distracted by detail, try using very large brushes and other implements that force you to apply the paint in large, simplified blocks of color. Household painting brushes, signwriters' brushes and paint scrapers are all good implements to try. Also, try using the paint very thinly in the early stages as this will make it that much easier to apply quickly.

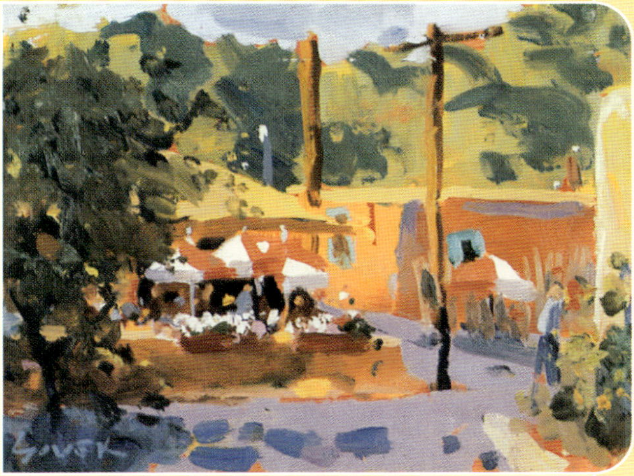

In Charles Sovek's "Canyon Road Café" very loose, broad marks are used to suggest different elements in the subject.

148

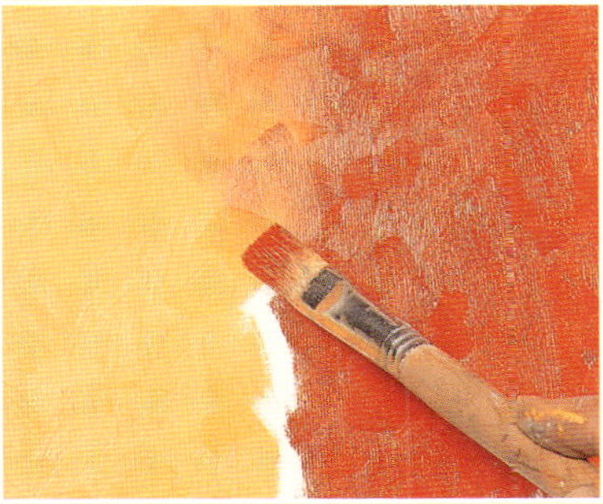

The two colors are pulled into each other with short, zigzag strokes.

The transition from one color to another is gradual but broken.

COLORS

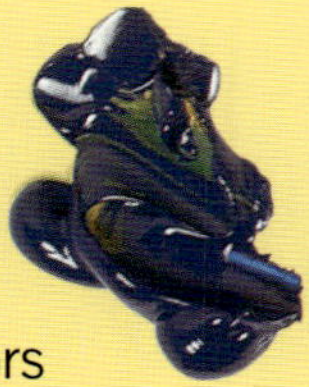

For fresh, lively colors, it is easier to begin with a small selection of individual tubes, rather than painting sets. In this way, you learn to identify the colors you see and to mix them accurately. This section explains which colors you need, and gives tips on mixing colors and on methods of harmonizing colors.

CHOICE OF COLORS

149

It is best to avoid sets of paints and to buy individual tubes. Warm and cool versions of each of the three primaries—Cadmium Yellow and Lemon Yellow, Cadmium Red and Alizarin Crimson, Ultramarine Blue and Cerulean Blue—a green, such as Viridian, and one or two earth colors, such as Yellow Ocher or Raw Sienna, and Burnt Sienna, plus Titanium White, will allow you to mix a wide range of colors.

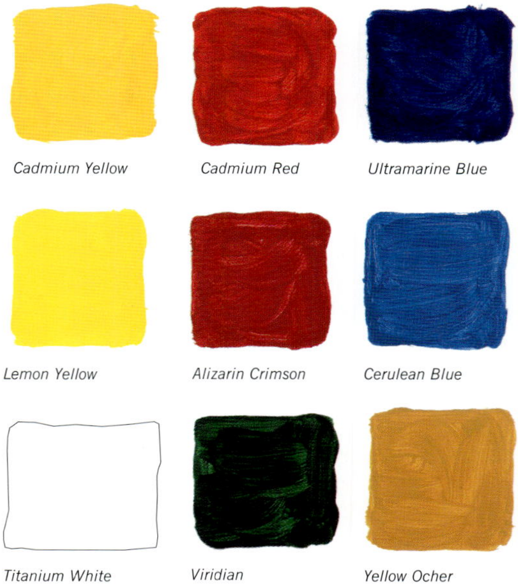

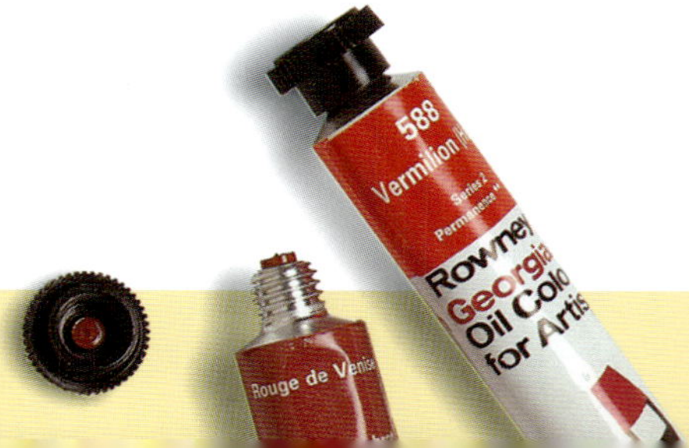

LAYING OUT COLORS

150

Colors can be laid out on a palette in various ways—light to dark, warm to cool, or in the order of the spectrum. The order in which you lay them out is less important than always laying them out in the same order, because then you'll know approximately where each color is without having to look for it. This is a particular advantage when you're on location and mixing colors quickly. It also reduces the chances of picking up the wrong colors on the brush by mistake.

CLEANER COLORS

151

If your colors look muddy on the canvas, it could be that you've mixed too many colors together. For fresh, lively colors, mix the minimum number—preferably two or three. Unwanted colors can creep into a mix from a dirty brush, so keep cleaning your brushes after each application, and have separate jars of mineral spirits for cleaning brushes used for different colors.

Muddy

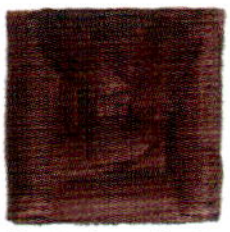

Cadmium Red
Cobalt Blue
Payne's Gray
Yellow Ocher

Chrome Yellow
Yellow Ocher
Cerulean Blue
Cobalt Blue

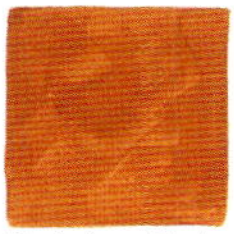

Cadmium Red
Alizarin Crimson
Chrome Orange
Cobalt Blue

Bright

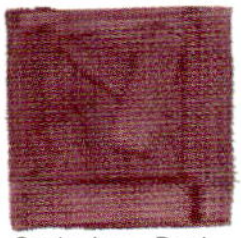

Cadmium Red
Cobalt Blue

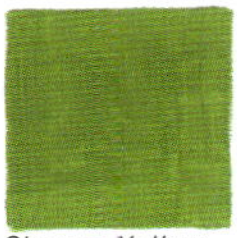

Chrome Yellow
Cerulean Blue

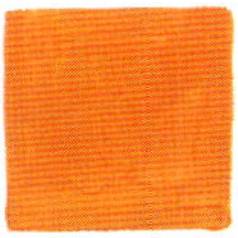

Cadmium Red
Chrome Orange

MIXING COLORS

152

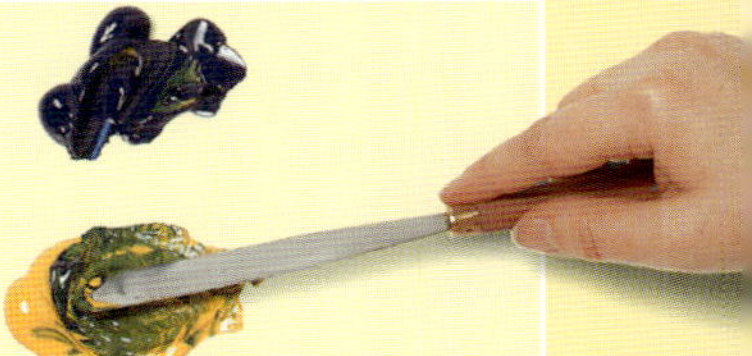

To save wear on your brushes, mix paint on the palette with a palette knife, or reserve some old brushes just for this purpose. A knife is also quicker than a brush for mixing large quantities. Mix the darker color into the lighter one, a small amount at a time, until you have the shade and color that you want. Mix up more of a color than you think you'll need so that you don't have to try to match the mix again later.

BROKEN COLOR

153

Very vibrant color effects can be achieved through broken color—applying a layer of color so that the color underneath shows through in places, with the two mixing in the viewer's eye to create a third color—through techniques such as scumbling and pointillism. Complementary colors used in this way will create an effect of shimmering light.

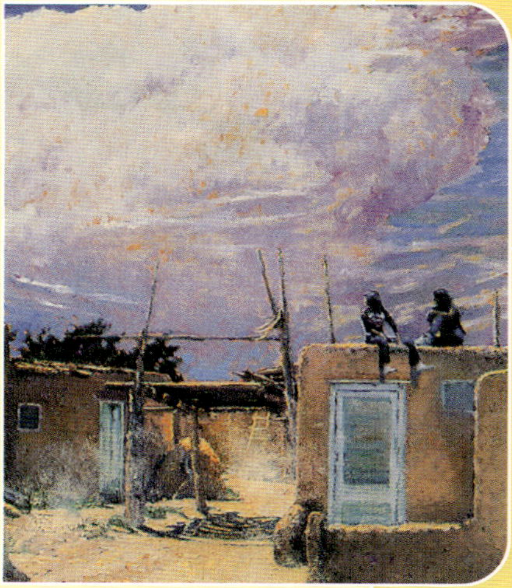

In "Before the Storm" by Nelda Pieper, the light in the sky is created by dragging bluish sky and cloud colors over a burnt sienna background.

DARKS WITHOUT BLACK

154

Mix darks rather than using black: Ultramarine and Burnt Sienna, or Alizarin and Viridian make good vibrant darks, and Ultramarine and Cadmium Red Dark produces a color that is almost black but is capable of subtle modulations of warmth and coolness.

SUBTLE COLOR MIXES

155

To get more subtle color mixes than those produced by mixing colors on the palette, you could try glazing transparent layers or scumbling broken layers of color one over another. The colors will be the same, but they will be very subtle and luminous.

In "Anna's Daughters" (detail) by Nelda Pieper, color is caught by scumbling and dragging one color over another.

DARKENING TONES

Black added to colors to darken them can produce dull, dirty-looking results. Instead, try mixing in a darker version of the same or a similar color, or mix in a little of the color's complementary color for a darker, but slightly grayed version. The complementary pairs of colors are red and green, blue and orange, and violet and yellow.

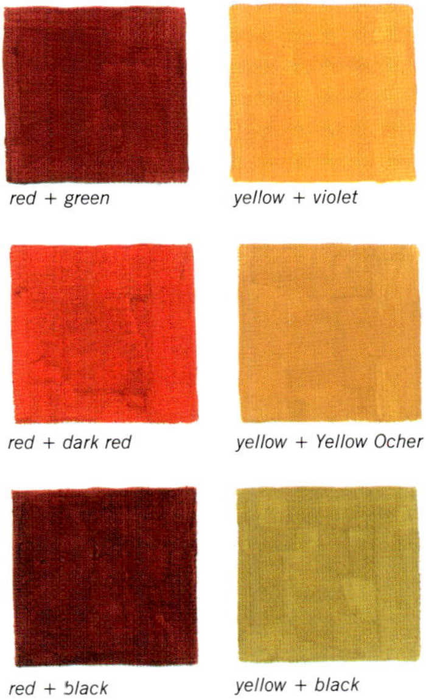

156

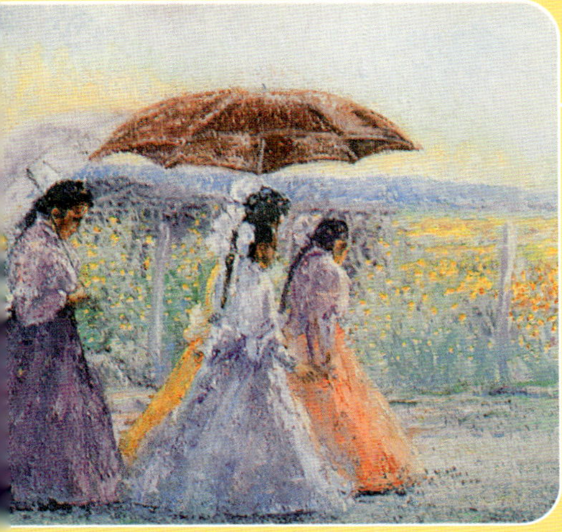

A UNIFIED EFFECT

In order to harmonize the colors used across a painting, apply a layer of color to the white ground—known as a toned ground—before starting the painting. If glazing and scumbling techniques are used to allow the ground color to show through in places, then this will have a unifying effect on the painting.

157

APPLYING PAINT

A pure white canvas can be inhibiting, whereas if you stain or color the surface, this gives you a good basis to work on. Build up your confidence by experimenting with ways of creating light with glazes, achieving lost-and-found edges, or adding in highlights, following the useful advice in this section.

TO PREVENT CRACKING

158

Cracking occurs when a top layer of paint dries more quickly than those underneath. To prevent this from happening, you need to follow the principle of "fat over lean." This means that each successive layer of paint should have more oil mixed into it than the previous layer. Other ways to prevent cracking are to let one layer dry before applying another, and to avoid the slower-drying colors, such as Alizarin Crimson, in the early stages of a painting.

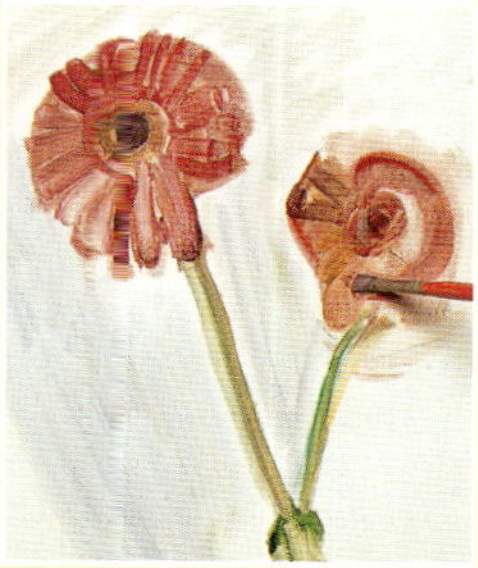

Broad areas of color are blocked in using paint thinned down with turpentine.

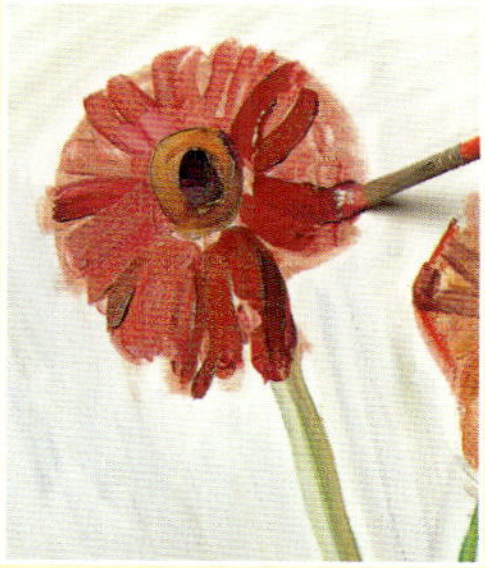

Next, a layer of thicker paint, mixed with a little linseed oil, is applied over the top.

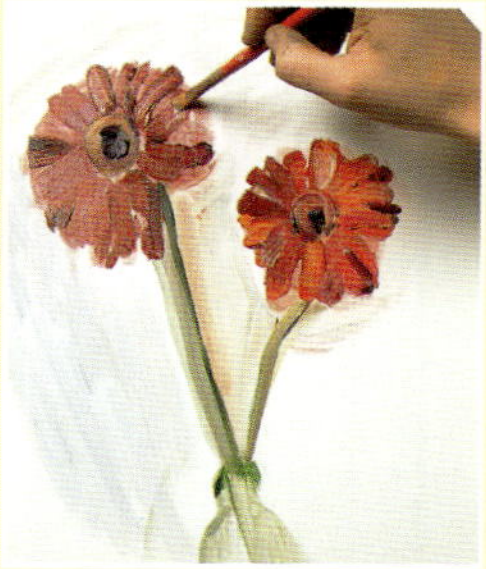

Layers of paint continue to be built up to give texture and definition.

STAINING A GROUND

To stain a white ground with transparent color, choose or mix a color that is darker than the final result you want to achieve, and thin it with turpentine until it is quite runny. Apply this all over the surface with a wide brush, and then rub back with a cloth until you have the tone and degree of transparency that you want. Alternatively, you can rub the paint on with a rag.

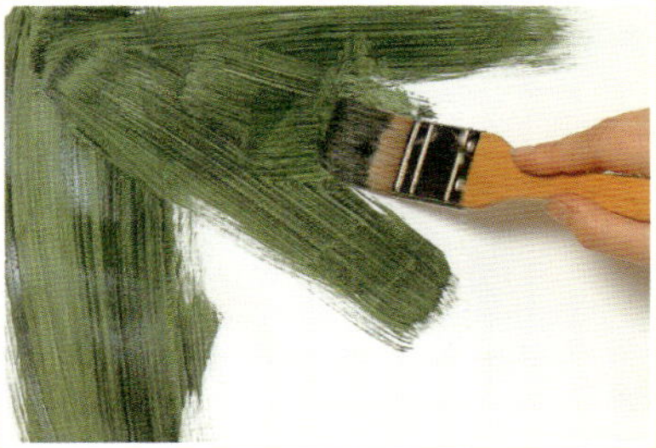

Paint thinned with turpentine is applied with loose brushmarks.

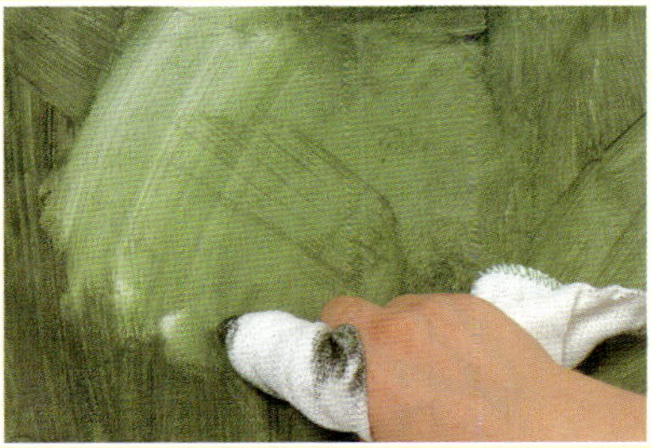

A cloth is used to take off some of the paint to give a very light, transparent layer of color to work on.

159

EASY START

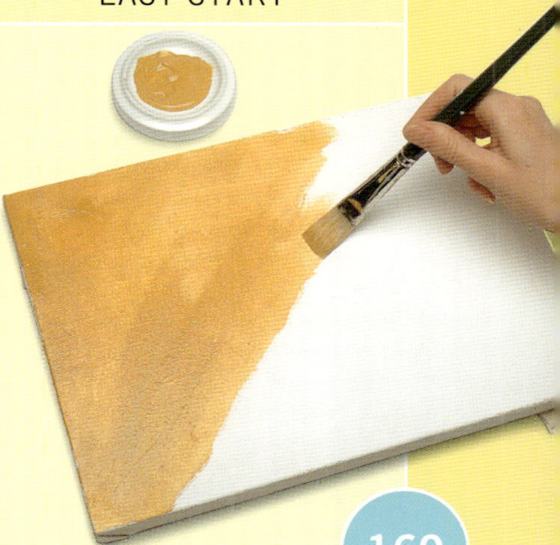

160

If you find a pure white canvas inhibiting to work on, try applying a colored ground—a layer of color put on over the primer. Transparent colors such as Yellow Ocher, Raw Sienna, Burnt Sienna or a neutral gray are good choices. Then begin the painting either by wiping out the light areas with a rag, or by putting in the dark areas, either of which will give you a good basis to build on.

161

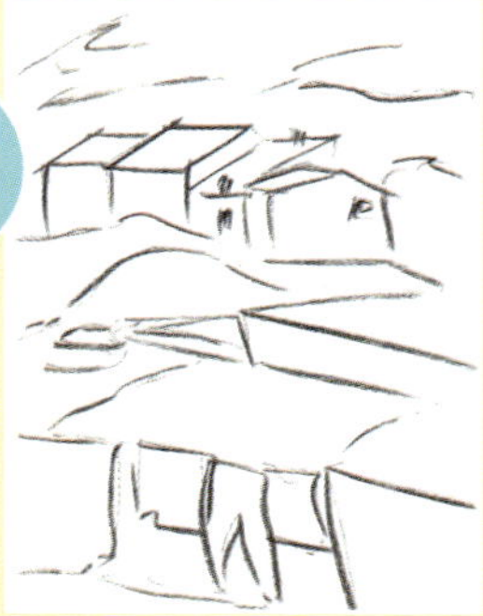

Preliminary charcoal sketch.

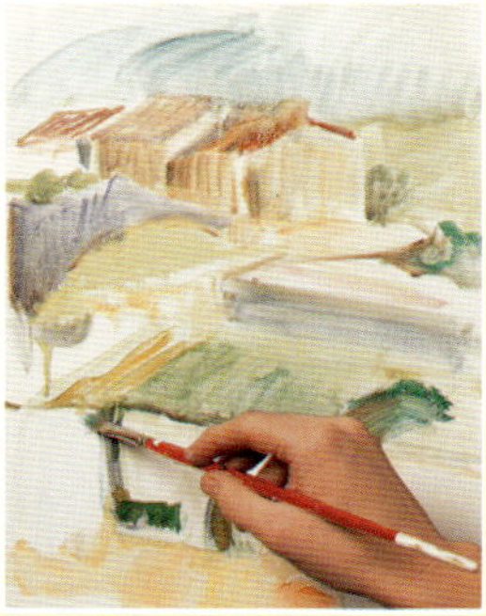

Main shapes filled in.

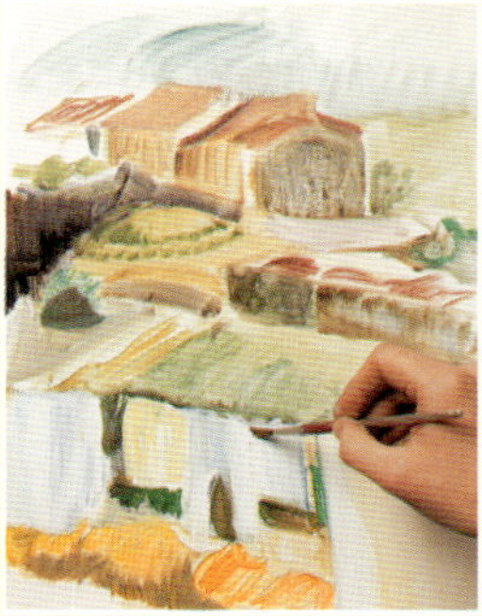

Details added.

The main shapes of the composition can be drawn in with pencil, charcoal, or paint. If charcoal is used, either brush away the excess or spray it with fixative if you don't want it to be picked up and blended into the first layer of color.

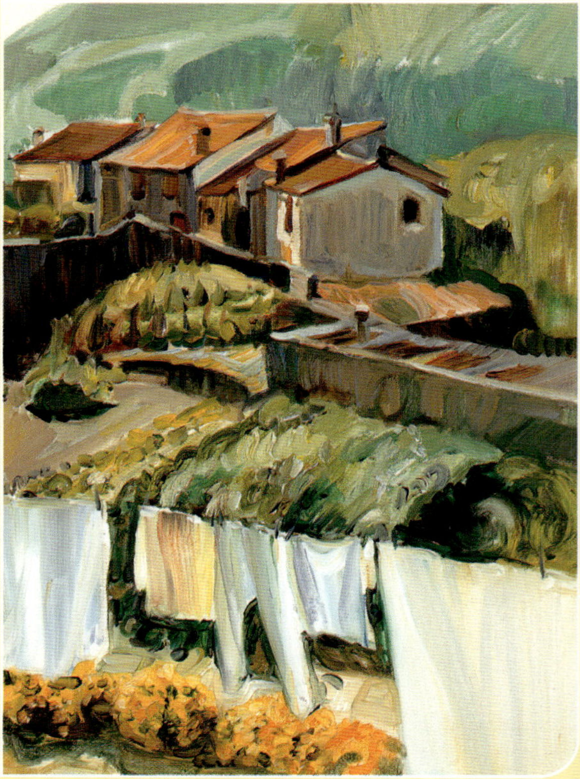

UNDERPAINTING

If you have trouble making tonal sense of colors, a monochrome underpainting provides a good guide for a painting. Working in one color, or a gray mixed from two colors, make a tonal painting of the subject in thin paint. The lighter tones can be created either by thinning the paint right down or by mixing in a little white. Let the underpainting dry and then apply colors over the top.

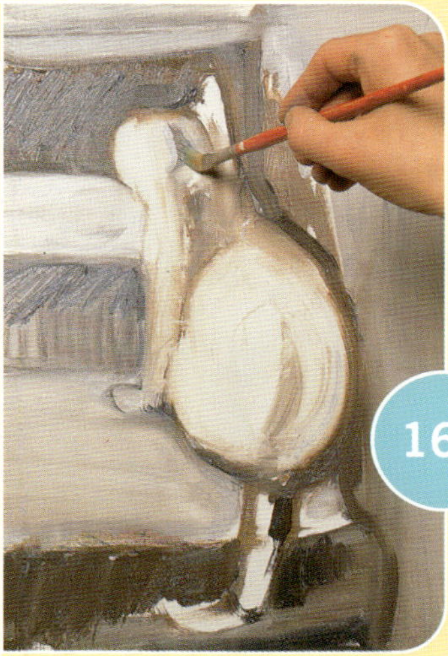

162

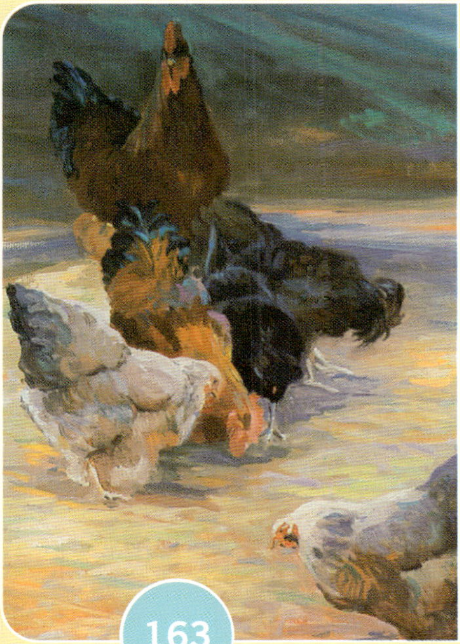

163

WET INTO WET

To keep the colors clean and vibrant when working into wet paint, work with a limited palette and have a plentiful supply of brushes. Load the brush with plenty of paint, and make a quick stroke holding the brush as nearly horizontal to the painting surface as you can.

In "Pecking Order" by Denise Burns, individual brushstrokes of strong color are worked into wet paint with decisive marks to create an image that has clean and vibrant color.

164

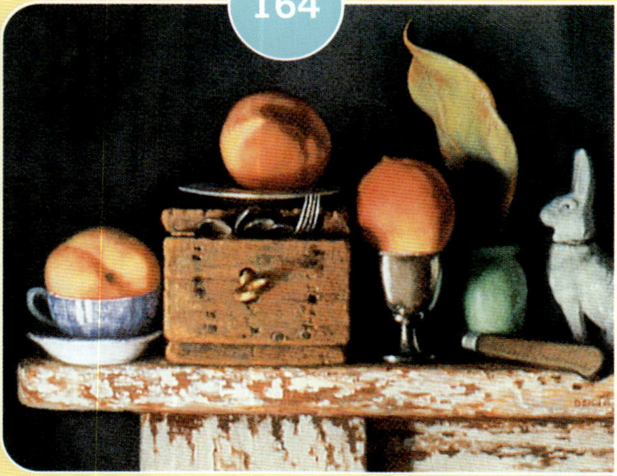

GLAZING

To get a smooth, transparent layer of color, for surfaces such as water or glass, or to create interesting darks, mix the paint with a glaze medium, either one you have mixed yourself or a commercial one—not with turpentine, which will take off the previous layer of paint—and apply it with a soft brush.

In "March Peaches and Hare" by Deborah Deichler, the layers of thin paint give depth to the shadow areas.

LIGHT WITH GLAZES

165

To retain a sense of light, apply glazes over light or neutral colors because they reflect light best and because the color will darken with each layer of color added.

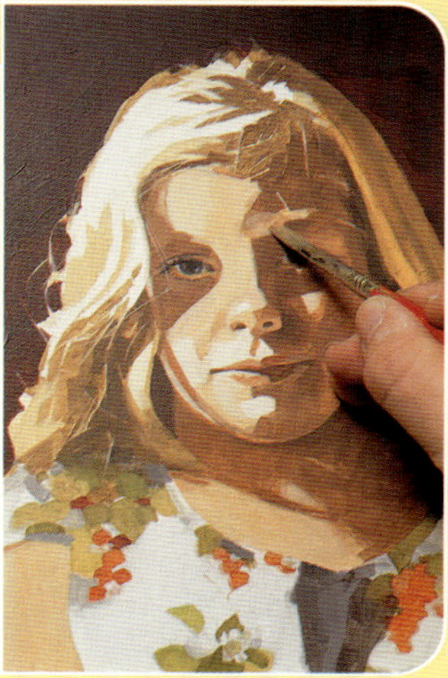

Depth of tone is achieved by applying layers of thin paint to model the face.

QUICK GLAZING

Some commercial glazing mediums increase the flow and transparency of the paint, although some also make the paint very shiny, so you will need to experiment with them to find out what you like. They may also speed up the drying time, which makes it possible to continue to the next stage on the following day.

166

SPEEDING UP DRYING

You can slightly speed up the time each layer of paint takes to dry by mixing in either a small amount of one of the commercial oil-painting mediums that has this effect, or by mixing a little damar varnish into linseed oil and mixing this into the paint. It isn't a good idea to speed up the drying time too much, as the painting will probably either crack or develop an unpleasant skin.

167

HIGHLIGHTS

To look convincing, highlights shouldn't be painted with pure white. Even the brightest highlights contain a hint of color, so mix in a touch of warmth or coolness, or a more distinct color if that is appropriate. Apply highlights at the very end of the painting.

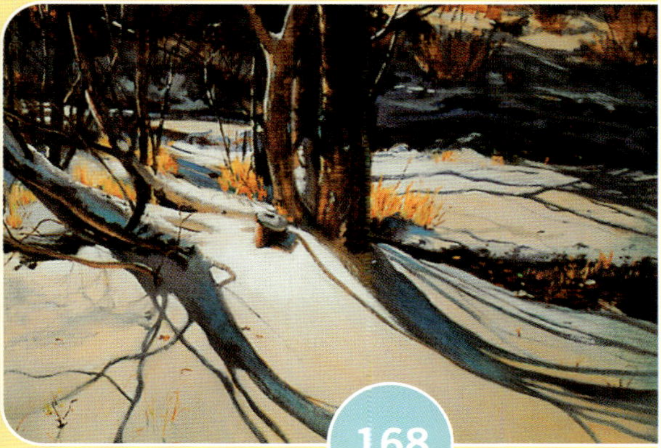

168

Even the lightest areas in a scene contain a hint of warm or cool color, as shown in Martha Saudek's "Sierra November."

SHARP EDGES

169

When you want to achieve sharp edges, you have two options. One is to work wet over dry. If you are working wet into wet, lay one color down with a stroke that runs in the same direction as the edge, and then lay the second color beside it, manipulating the brush so that the two colors butt up against each other.

Lay the second color so that it just butts up against the first color.

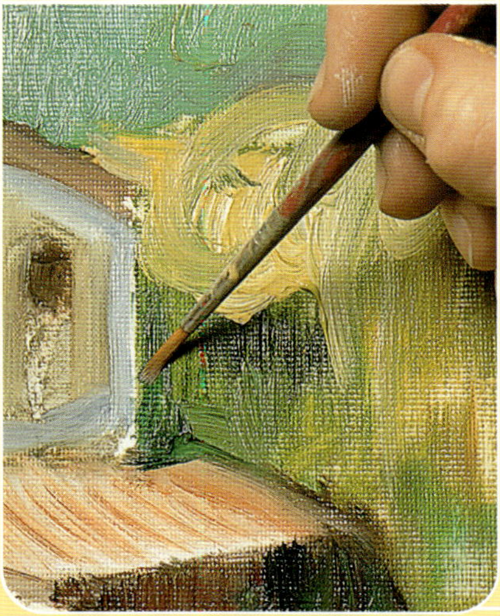

BROKEN EDGES

170

For edges where you want a broken, lost-and-found effect, such as for clouds' shadows, work wet into wet and slightly mix the two tones or colors by pulling one into the other here and there on the canvas. Or scumble paint along the edge.

Areas of color are laid down next to each other.

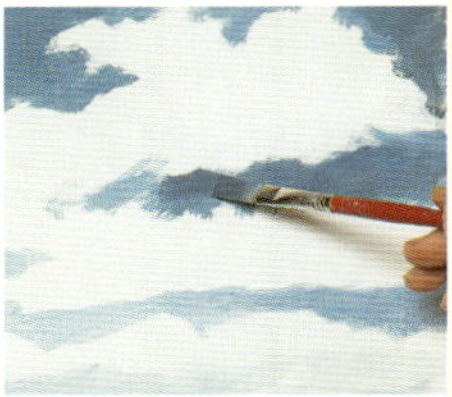

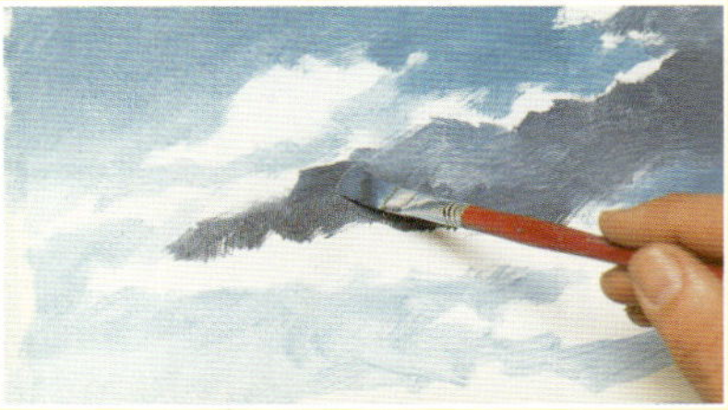

Colors are pulled into each other around the edges.

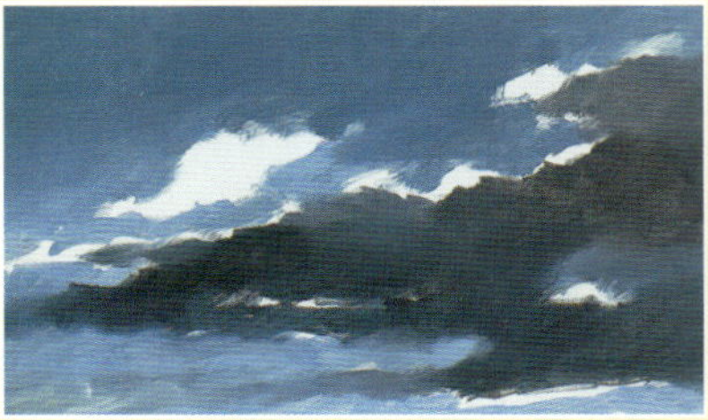

A mixture of hard, soft and broken edges create depth.

ADDITIONAL TECHNIQUES

As your painting progresses, you may want to try some of the interesting ideas and more advanced methods featured in this section. Knife painting, drawing with paint, and the techniques of impasto and pointillism are some of the ways of adding character to your paintings.

DRAWING WITH PAINT

171

Details such as foreground grasses in a landscape, hair, or fur textures can be drawn in. Thin the paint with a glazing medium, not turpentine, and using a very fine, soft brush, such as a sable watercolor brush, put them in with distinct, separate strokes, reloading the brush each time. This technique can also be used to put in larger details and can be used in a looser, freer way.

The ripples in the water are drawn in using thin paint and a small brush.

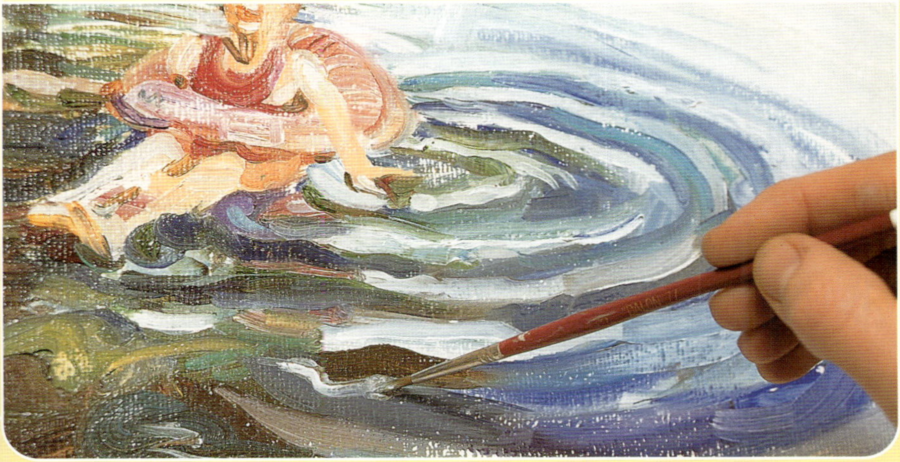

172

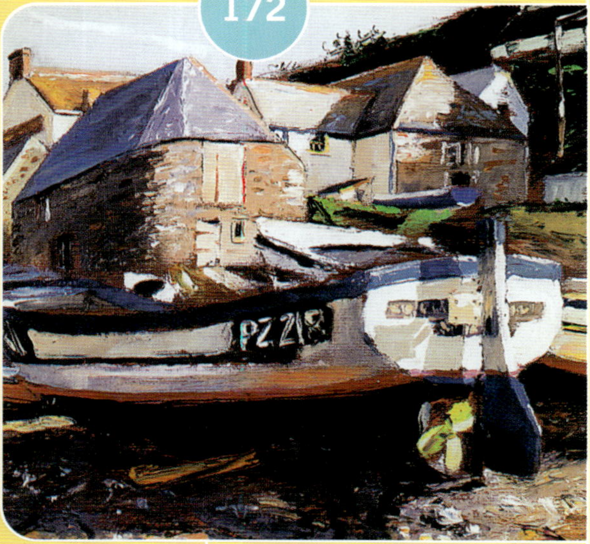

KNIFE PAINTING

For a highly reflective paint surface and bright colors using opaque paint, the paint can be applied with a knife. To get the smooth surface needed to reflect the maximum amount of light, apply the paint boldly and lift the knife off cleanly at the end of the stroke. Resist the temptation to go over the stroke once it is made, as this will disturb the paint surface and kill the effect.

In "Early Morning in Cadgewith" (detail), Jeremy Sanders has applied the paint over a colored ground with a palette knife and a credit card cut in half, using them flat and on their edges to create a variety of different types of marks and textural effects.

SCUMBLING

Scumbling involves applying paint over a previous layer in a way that allows the color underneath to show through. To get a broken application of paint, use an almost dry brush and thick paint. Keeping the brush horizontal to the surface, pull it across quickly and lightly, and don't go over the application again. It works best on a textured surface, as only the raised points in the weave pick up paint from the brush.

173

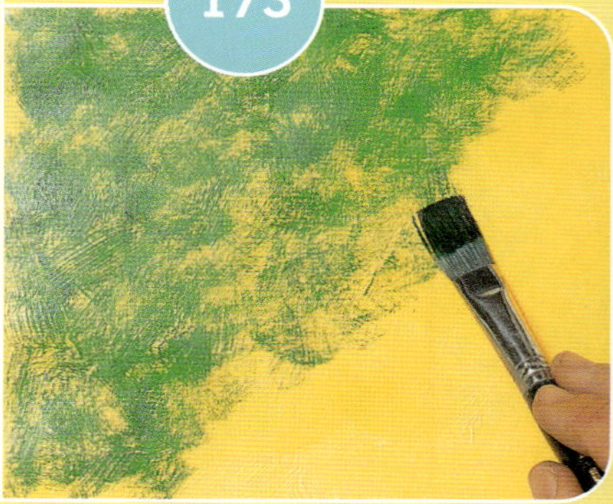

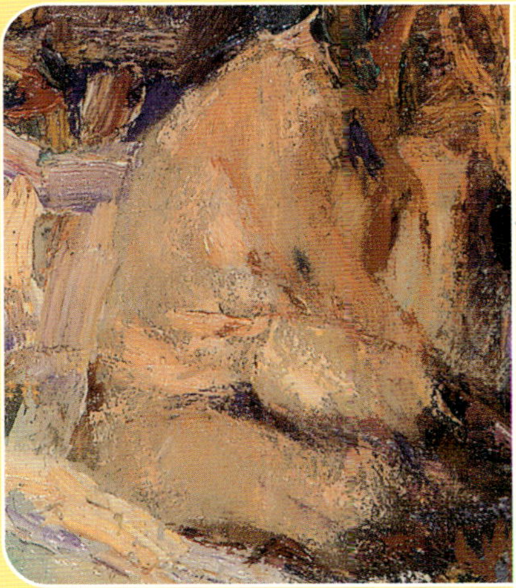

IMPASTO

174

If you want an application of thick paint, it is best to build up the paint in layers, letting each layer dry before applying the next, in order to avoid cracking. Apply the paint with short strokes, using a brush or a knife.

In "Bedroom Study" by Arthur Maderson, the image has been built up with thick, rich applications of paint, giving the paint itself a three-dimensional quality.

SGRAFFITO

An alternative way to indicate intricate details, such as details on windows, rain, or fabric such as lace, rather than painting them in, is to use the technique called sgraffito—scraping through the paint to reveal the color underneath. With wet paint, just draw into the paint with a knife or the end of a paintbrush. With dry paint, more vigorous drawing and scraping is required.

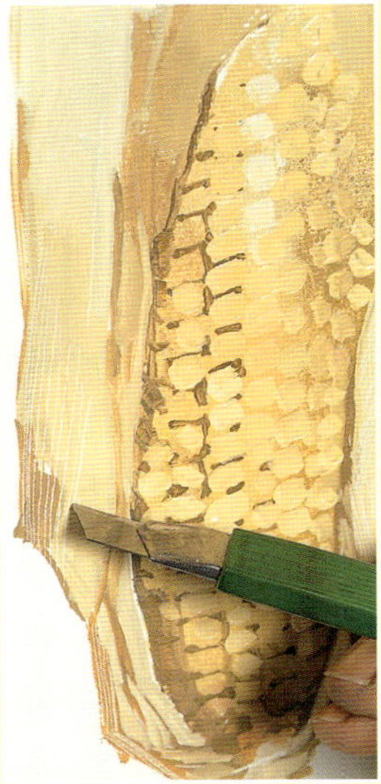

The veins of the leaf are drawn into the paint.

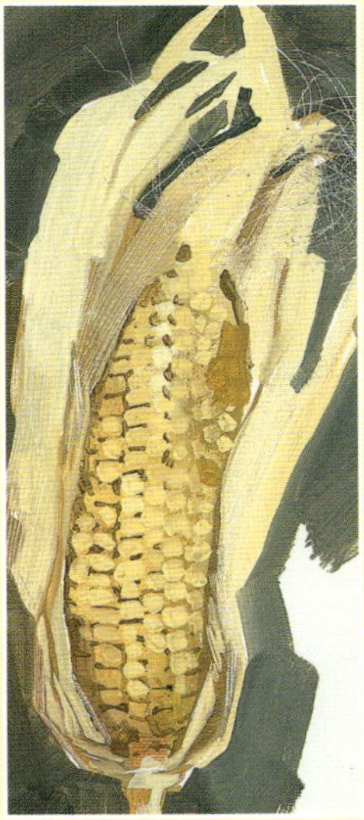

Very fine details can be added with this technique.

175

176 POINTILLISM

If you have tried the pointillist technique and the colors don't seem to be mixing, it could be because the colors you are using vary too much in shade. To work effectively, the colors used should be the same shade. Use dryish paint, and apply it in short strokes, making sure that the brushstrokes don't blend together.

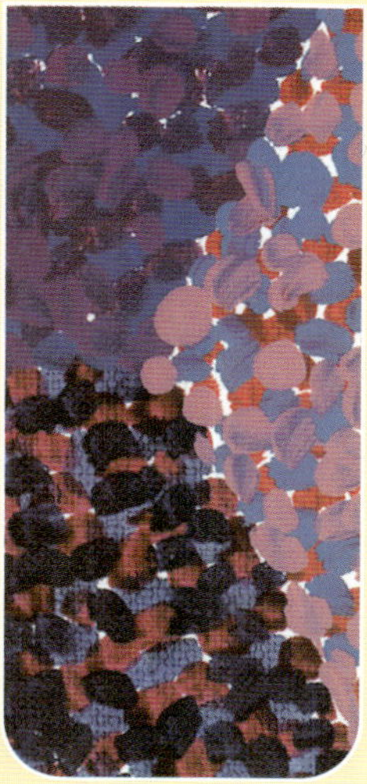

177 CREATING TEXTURE

One way to suggest texture is to press crumpled or textured paper to the paint surface and lift it off again, leaving an imprint of the texture in the paint—a technique known as frottage. Experiment with different textures to see what effect they create.

178 STRONG CONTRAST

Subjects with a strong contrast between light and dark can be captured by applying a dark-colored ground over the primed canvas and using light-toned or brightly colored opaque paint over the top.

179 VARNISHING

In order to get a smooth finish when varnishing, and to minimize reflections on a varnished painting, place the painting flat on a firm, level surface and apply the varnish in brushstrokes that run vertical to the image. Use a varnishing brush, which will pick up plenty of varnish, as each stroke needs to be made in one continuous sweep from the top to the bottom edge of the painting.

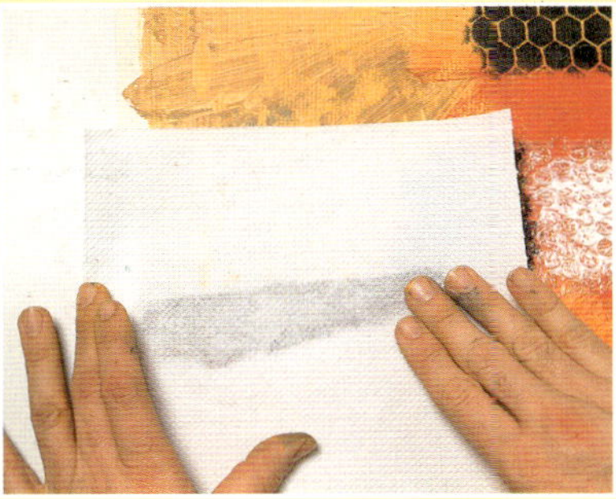

Paper towels are pressed into the paint.

The texture is transferred to the paint surface.

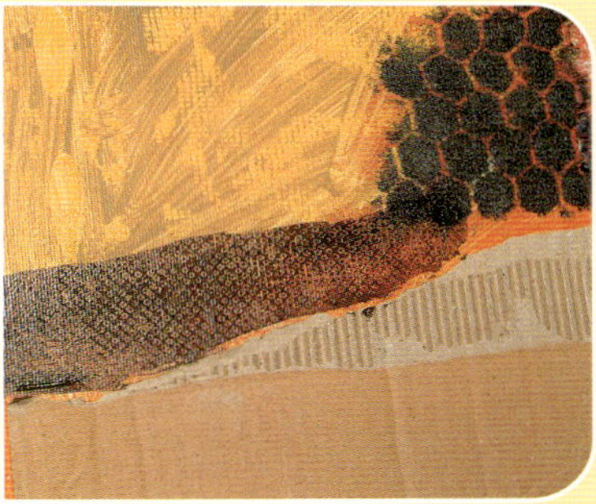

VARIETY OF MARKS

180

To create a varied surface, experiment with different ways of handling your brushes. You can stab the painting with the tip of the brush for very textural marks. You can hold the brush horizontal to the paint surface and drag it across the surface for broken application of paint, and you can apply thin paint with a scrubbing motion for a scumbled effect.

Fresh paint added to a painting that has been allowed to dry looks much brighter than the previous application.

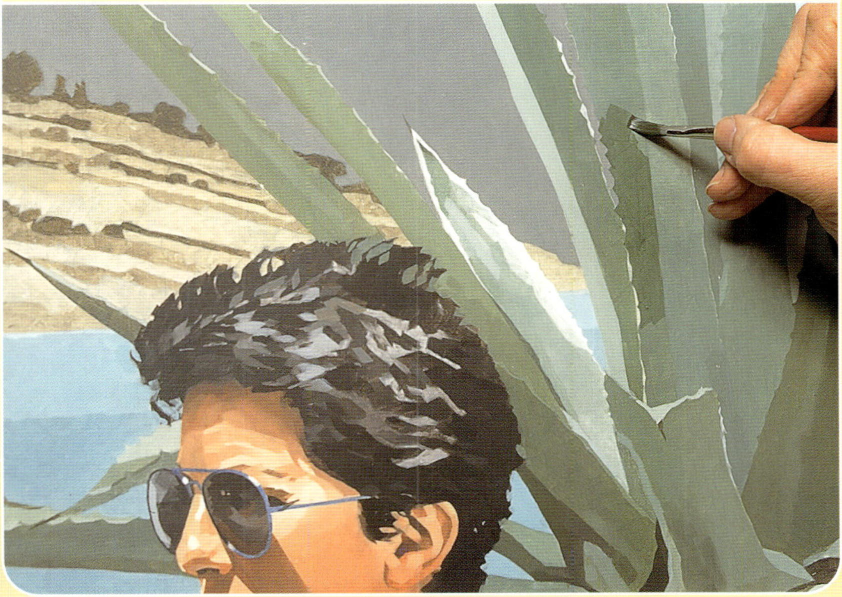

MODIFICATIONS

There are a number of ways to correct your paintings, even when you think it is too late to do anything. For example, dull, flat sections can be enlivened with scumbling, or knocking back over-bright color can be done with your fingers. These are just two of the helpful hints described in this section.

LIGHTENING A COLOR

181

To lighten a color on the canvas, you don't need to work white into it, or to apply a lighter shade over the top. As long as the paint isn't dry, try rubbing or scraping off some of the paint so that more light is reflected by the white ground. Another possibility may be to darken other colors nearby—as long as this won't upset the overall tonal balance. The original color will appear lighter against the darkened ones.

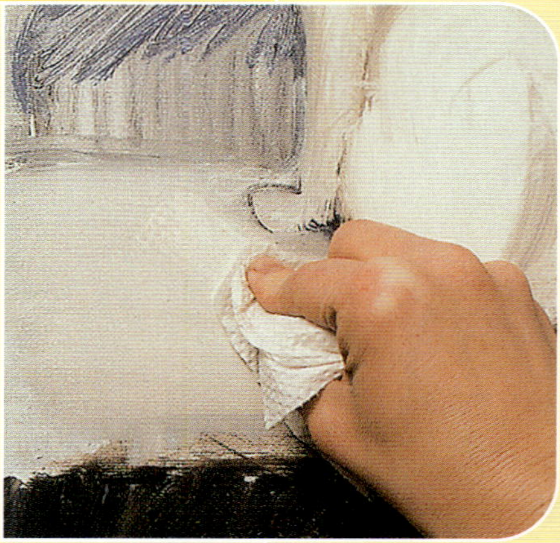

Rubbing back lightens the color.

DARKENING A COLOR

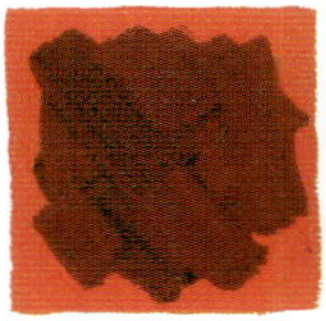

Cadmium Red + Phthalo Green

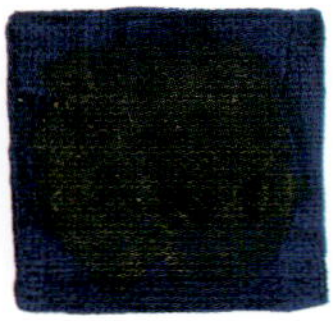

Dioxazine Purple + Lemon Yellow

To darken a color that has already been applied to the canvas, let it dry, then glaze its complementary color over the top.

182

MAKING CHANGES

183

When working wet into wet you may find that a build-up of paint becomes difficult to work with, especially if you want to make changes; and if you apply fresh paint to make a change or correction over wet paint, the colors will probably become overmixed. It is best to scrape off excess paint with a knife or remove it with a rag.

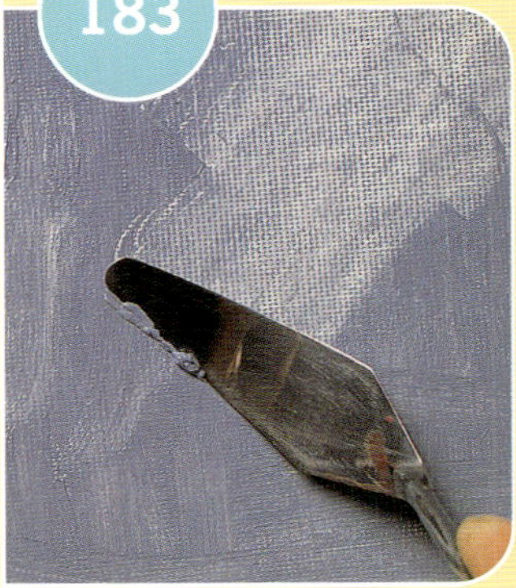

Scrape off as much paint as possible before making changes to the painting.

OVERWORKED AREAS

184

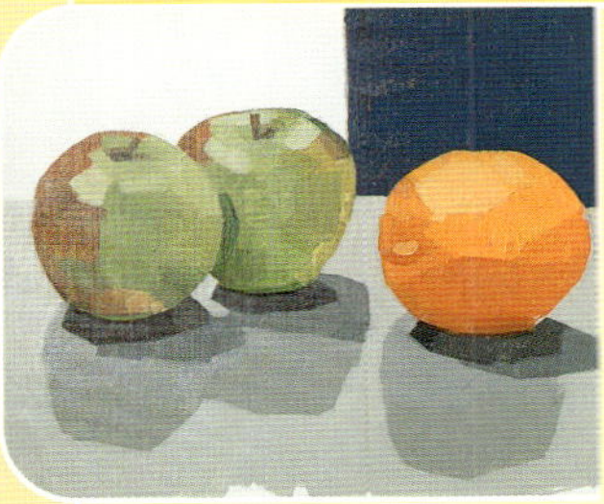

This background is too heavy.

To unclog an overworked area without removing all the paint, leaving a basic layer of color to build on again and the texture of the support still in evidence, you can use the technique known as tonking. Press a smooth, absorbent paper, such as newsprint, against the paint surface and remove it. Repeat with a fresh piece of paper until you have removed as much paint as you wish.

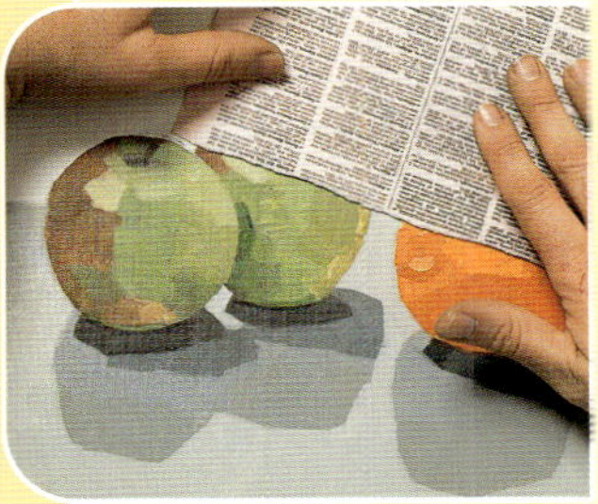

Newspaper is applied to the overworked area.

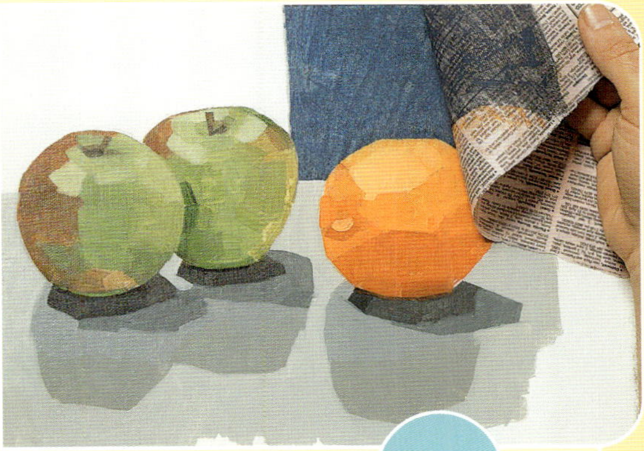

ENLIVENING DULLNESS

185

If there are dull, flat areas in a painting, try scumbling another color, such as the complementary color, over the top. Adjusting other colors nearby or introducing tiny touches of a bright color may also do the trick.

Bright yellow scumbled over the foreground field and added into the trees brightens up these areas and introduces a feeling of light into the scene.

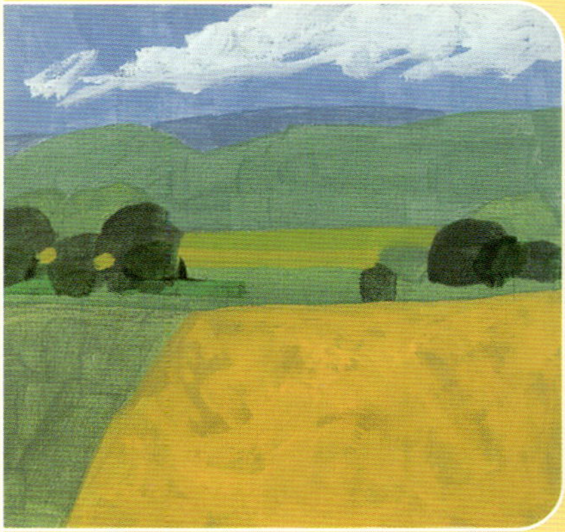

SINKING COLORS

Sometimes areas of color appear to "sink." This can be cured either by "oiling out"—rubbing a little linseed oil sparingly over the area in question with a soft cloth and leaving it for 24 hours—or by giving it a thin coat of retouching varnish using a soft brush and leaving it to dry, which takes up to about 15 minutes.

187

OVER-BRIGHT AREAS

An area of color that is too strong can be knocked back by blending the edges with the colors next to it, or by knocking it back with a finger. Or, the color can be modified by scumbling or glazing another color over it.

The yellow is toned down by blending it around the edges with the color next to it.

186

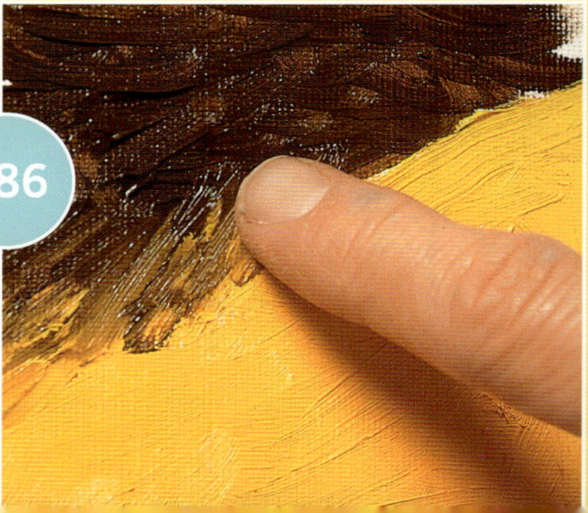

SPECIAL EFFECTS

Oil paints can be used to achieve a number of exciting and unpredictable results, for example, by mixing media, such as using oil or soft pastels over dry oil paint, or experimenting with fabric or paper collage. Monoprinting, also featured in this section, is another interesting method to add to your range of painting skills.

ADDING TEXTURE

188

It is not a good idea to apply paint too thickly because you run the risk of cracking. If you want a very heavy impasto effect, it is better to add something to the paint to thicken it. It can then be applied to the support with a palette knife. A grainy effect can be achieved by mixing in sand, while a slightly granular effect is provided by sawdust.

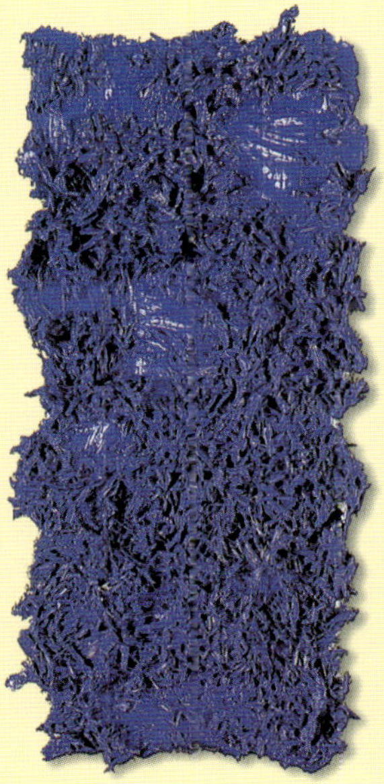

Sawdust produces a very rough textured surface.

Sand mixed into the paint makes it thick and textured.

COLLAGE

189

To collage fabric, paper, or objects to an oil painting, it is best to attach them directly to the support with glue before applying any paint. A board will support the weight of collaged materials much better than canvas. In this instance you should prime the support with acrylic primer and use white glue to attach the materials, which can then be painted over with oil paint.

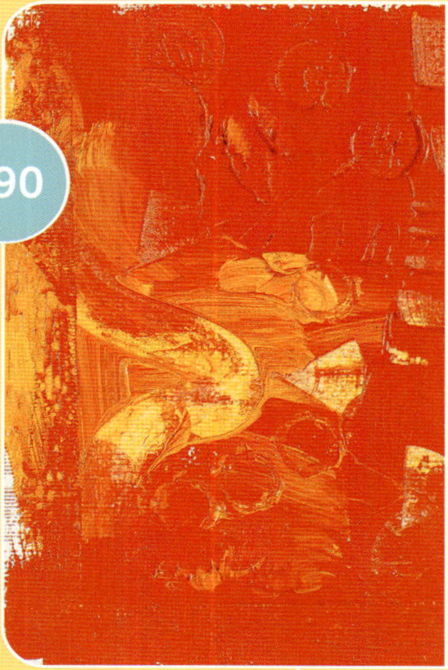

190

IMPRINTING

If you can't get the texture you want in a thick paint surface with knives or brushes, try making marks and patterns with other implements, such as a fork, a slotted spoon, or the end of a canister, drawing them across the surface or pressing them into the paint, depending on the type of pattern you need. Experiment with this technique before trying it in a painting.

Patterns have been pushed into thick paint: the round marks were made with a film canister, the triangular ones by twisting the end of a ruler, and the rough areas by dabbing with a crumpled facial tissue.

MIXED MEDIA

Interesting textural effects can be created by using oil or soft pastels over dry oil paint. They can also be used to add in or redefine small details and to emphasize the separation between one area and another.

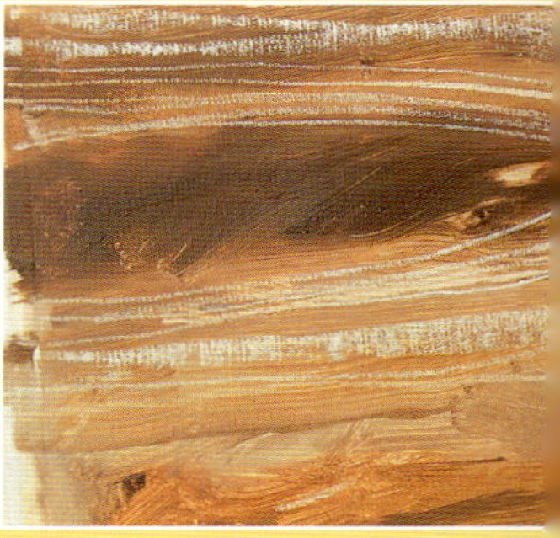

191

To produce exciting and unpredictable results with oil paints, try making monoprints. These are created by using a sheet of glass and thinly applied paint. Either paint the image directly onto the glass, or spread the glass evenly with paint and create the image by removing paint—wiping it off with a rag and drawing into it with different instruments. Then place a sheet of drawing paper over the top, press gently, and peel the paper off again. The print can be worked into further with more paint or with oil pastels.

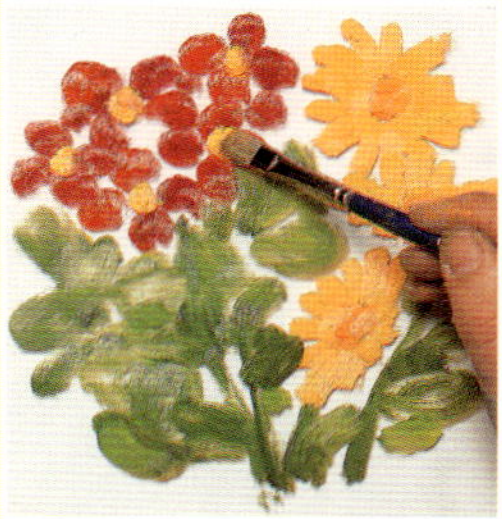

Oil paint is applied to a sheet of glass.

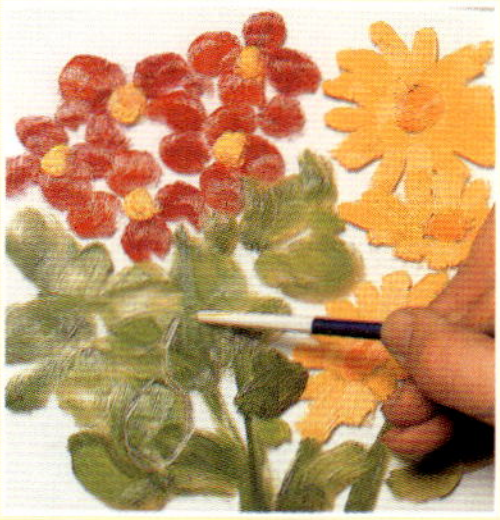

Texture is added by drawing into the paint.

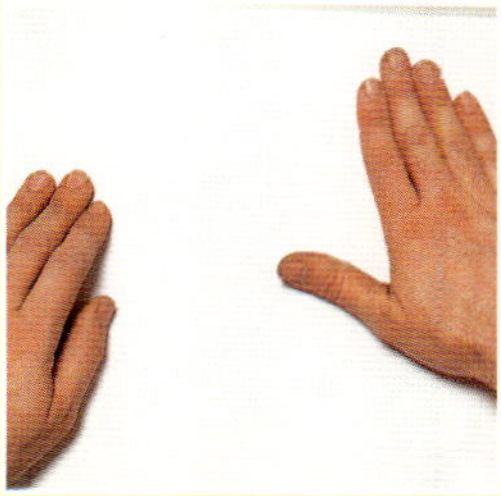

Paper is laid over the top.

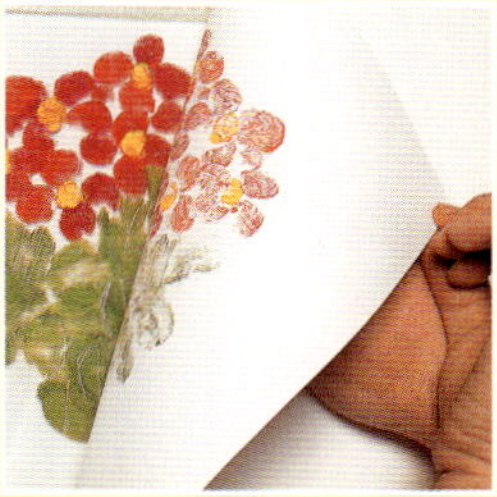

The paper is peeled away.

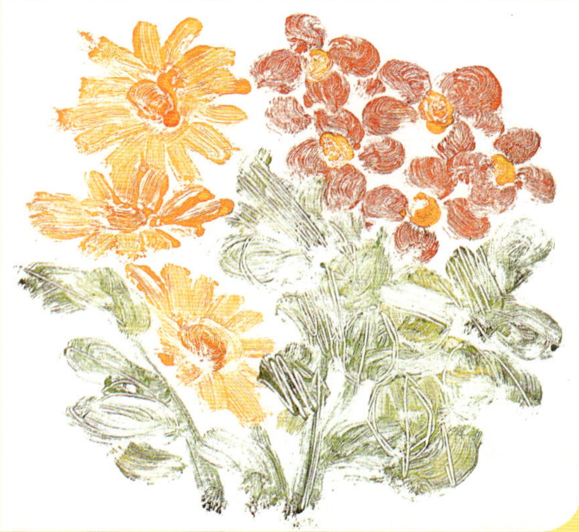

A very delicate and textural print is produced from the original. Only one print can be made from each painting on glass.

192

ON LOCATION

It is not easy to decide what to take when you are setting off to paint in a new place. To make the most of working outdoors, you should reduce your equipment to a minimum and organize it so that it is as light and easy to carry as possible.

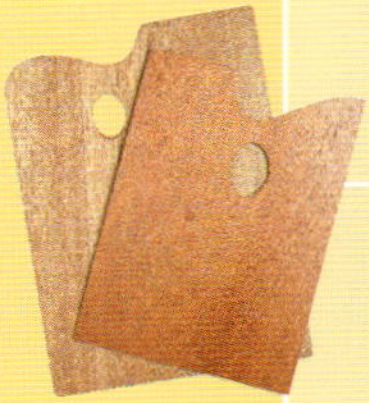

PAINT BOXES

193

A convenient type of paint box for working on location is a ready-made box which combines palette and paint box in one and holds boards in the lid. These boxes are available in a choice of sizes. The smaller sizes can be held in one hand, while leaving the other free to paint, or they can be rested on a wall or on the knees if you are sitting.

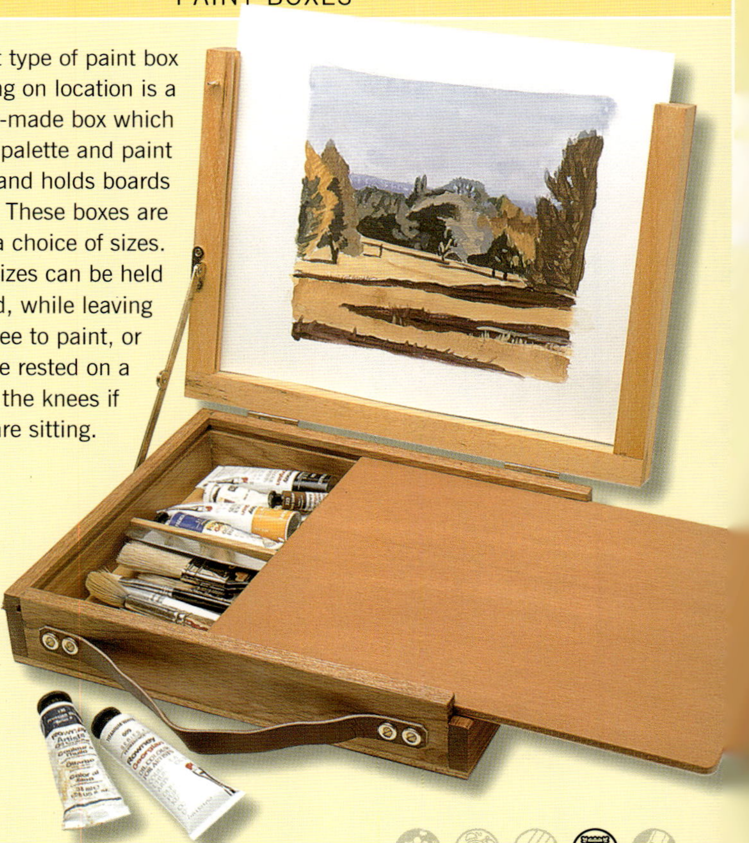

LIMITED PALETTE

194

When you are working fast or in difficult conditions, it helps to limit the number of colors that you use. You will need one each of the primary colors in some form: a yellow, a red or reddish orange, and a blue, plus white. Lemon Yellow, Burnt Sienna, and Cobalt Blue give a selection of fresh colors; Yellow Ocher, Cadmium Red, and Cerulean Blue give a choice of bright or subtle colors.

Very limited palettes can provide a good choice of colors to work with. They can be mixed to produce a range of interesting grays and browns, darkened through the mixing of complementaries, and made lighter and more opaque with the addition of white.

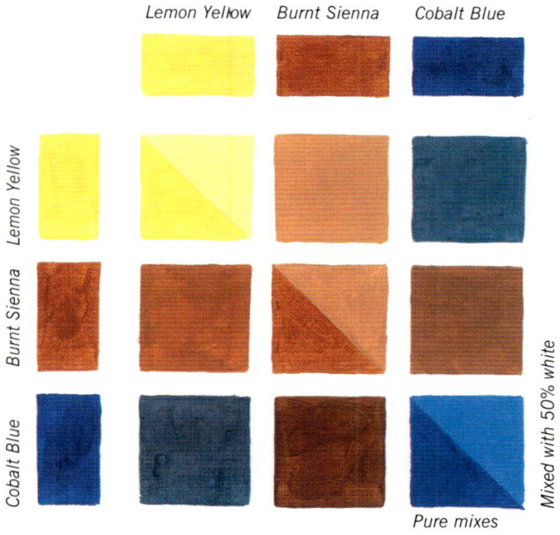

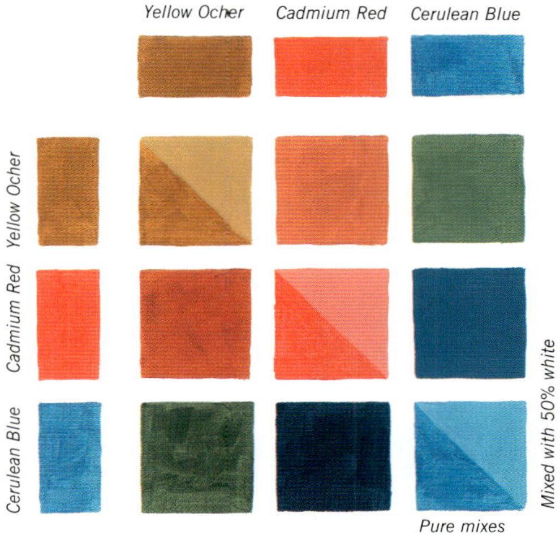

A STEADY EASEL

195

Even quite a mild breeze can catch a large board or canvas on a sketching easel and blow it over. To prevent this from happening, suspend a bag—a plastic shopping bag will do well—filled with something heavy, such as stones that you can collect on the spot, from the center of the easel to weight it down.

SMALL PALETTES

196

Two small palettes are easier to manage than one large one on outdoor painting trips, if you need plenty of space for mixing colors. A small palette is easier to hold in difficult weather conditions, and smaller sizes are easier to pack away for carrying.

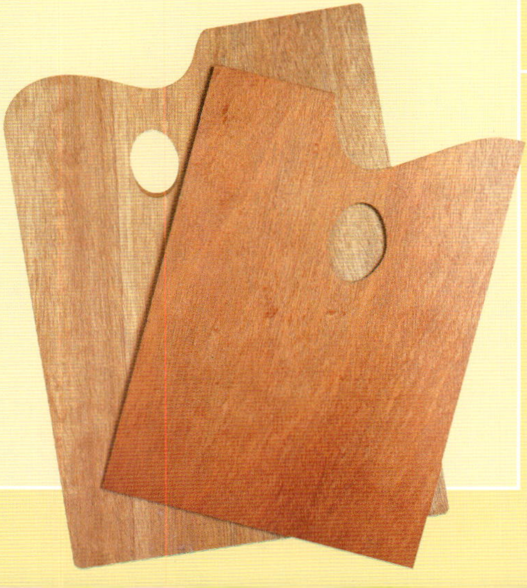

LIMITED TIME

197

When you have a limited time in which to complete a painting, the best approach is to break down the subject into simple overall shapes and block these in with thinned-down paint. At this stage don't mix more than two colors together and don't add white. Control the tones through the thinness of the paint, and wipe back any areas that are too dark. This will give you a clear foundation on which to build the painting.

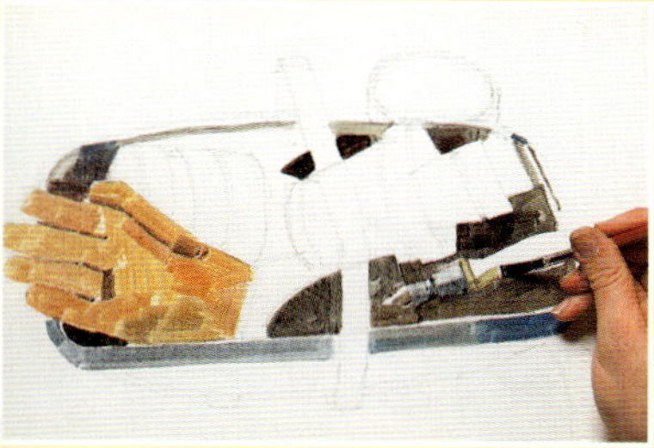

The subject is reduced to a series of simple shapes.

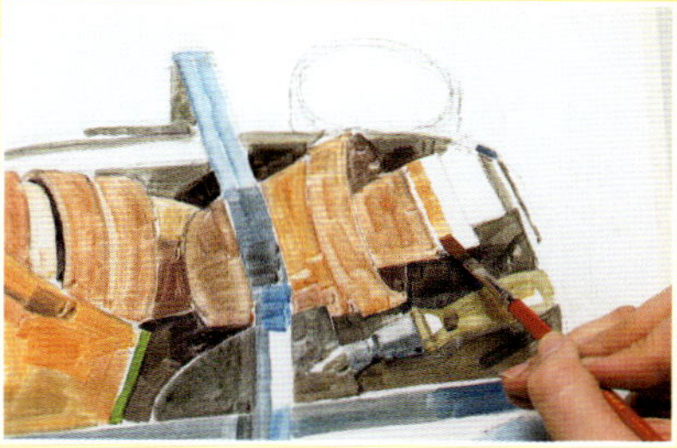

The composition is blocked in simple, flat areas of color using thinned-down paint.

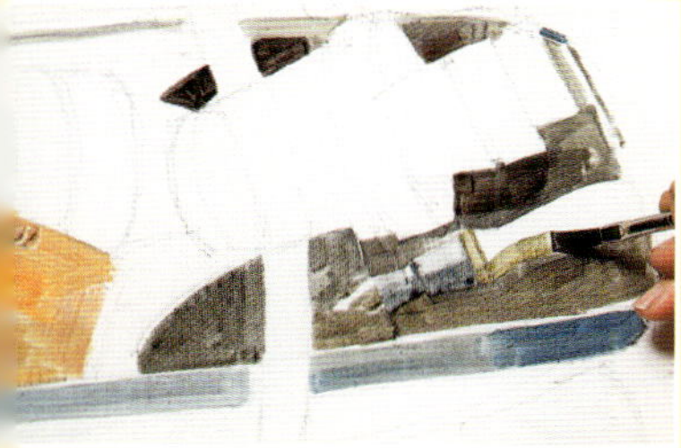

The paint is used very thin for the lightest tones of the painting.

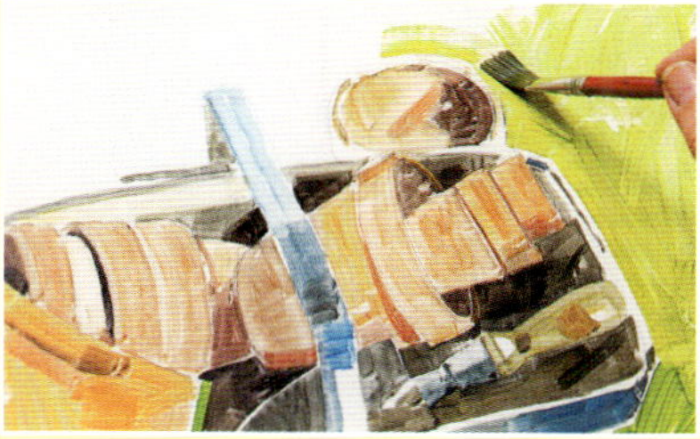

The background is put in with a suggestion of light and shadow.

The painting has been kept simple and controlled to provide a good guide for building up subsequent layers of thicker paint and more varied tones and colors.

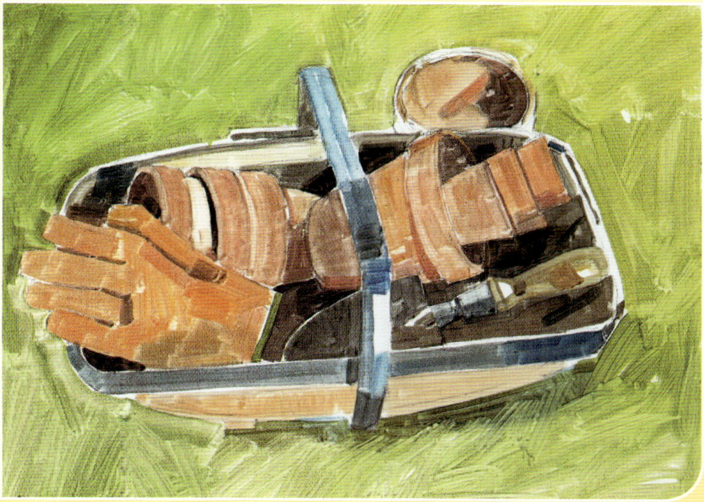

SHORT-TERM SUBJECTS

Some subjects, such as market scenes, are only there for a short time. To retain the immediacy of working directly from life, make a pencil drawing of the scene on the spot on stretched watercolor paper, recording all the information you want to include in the painting. Additional color notes will be useful. When you get home, give the paper a coat of shellac varnish, which will seal the surface without concealing the drawing. When the shellac is dry, apply paint, working fast over the drawing to complete it in one session.

Use a varnishing brush to give the drawing a coat of shellac varnish to seal the surface.

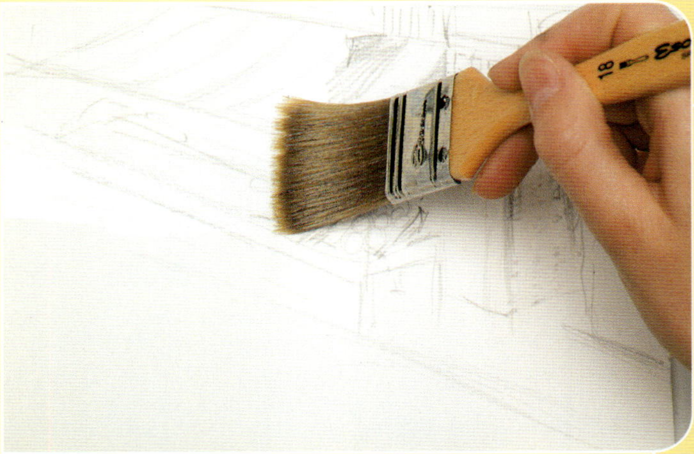

198

QUICK DRYING TIME

199

Quick-drying alkyd gel medium will speed up the drying time of the paint. It is available in tubes and can be squeezed out on the palette. Add a little to the paint that you mix for blocking in the composition to prevent subsequent layers picking up color from the first layer.

TRANSPORTING WET PAINTINGS

To carry a wet canvas or board, you will need a second canvas or board of roughly the same size, plus four small pieces of cork about 1 inch (2.5cm) thick, and some masking tape. Lay the painting flat and place a piece of cork in each corner. Place the second board or canvas on top, and tape the corners together. The painted surfaces are held apart, but face in and so protect each other. If the corks leave a mark, the corners can be touched up again at home.

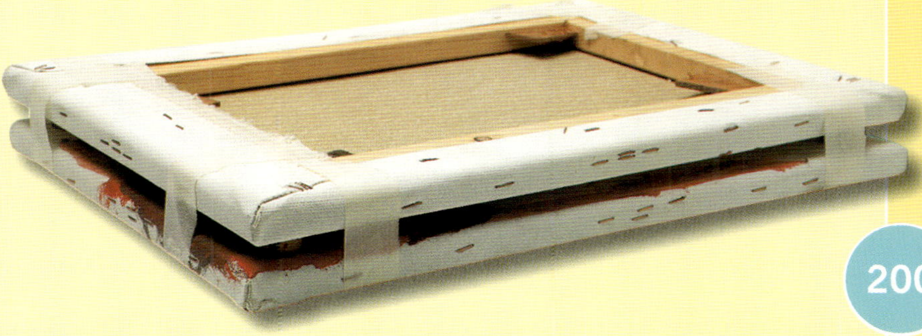

200

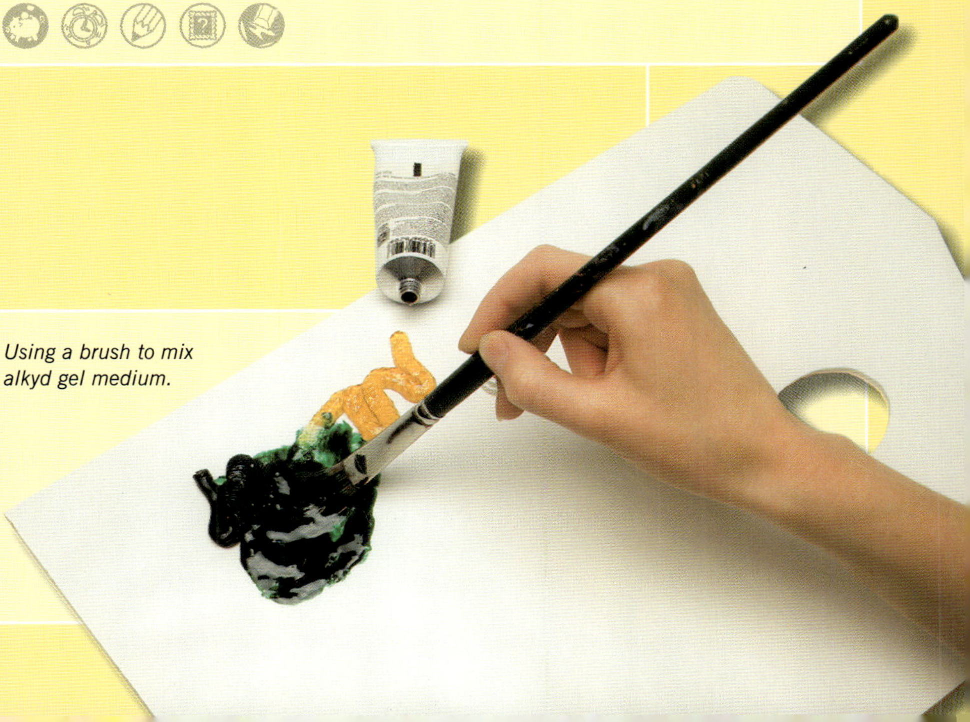

Using a brush to mix alkyd gel medium.

SUBJECTS

As experience will show you, there is no correct way to paint a particular subject—a still life and a portrait painted by the same artist will not vary much in style or technique. However, there are still a few subject-related problems, and this section contains some useful ideas for solving them. With all subjects, it is best to concentrate on portraying them in terms of light and dark, rather than including too much detail.

SKY HOLES

201

To depict "sky holes" seen through foliage, paint in the foliage first, then add in the patches of sky over the top, roughly blending them into the foliage around the edges so that they are not too stark.

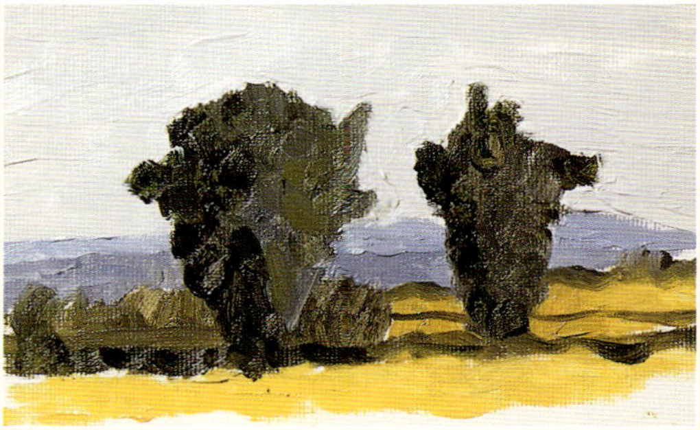

Trees are put in as solid areas of foliage and modeled with light and dark tones.

Sky holes are added into the trees to create a natural effect.

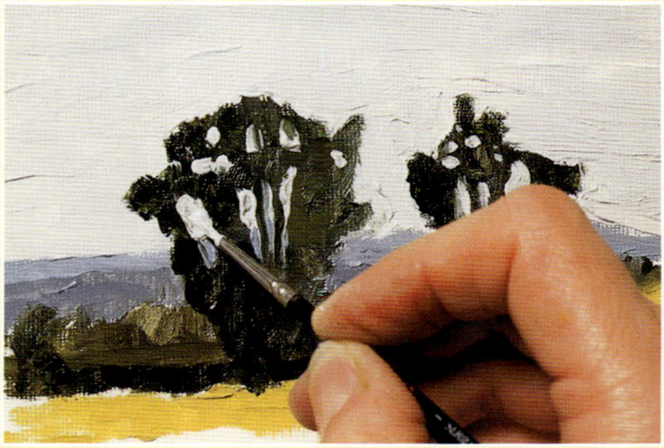

KEEP IT SIMPLE

Avoid including too much detail, and observe correct color relationships. The temptation is to look at colors individually, which can lead to their being too bright. Put down as many of the main colors as possible quickly, at the blocking-in stage, so that you can assess all the colors in the painting in relation to each other.

202

In "Footprints" (detail) by Denise Burns, the quality of light is created through the contrast between yellow highlights and violet shadows. Where there are extreme color or tonal contrasts, establish them early and then work between them.

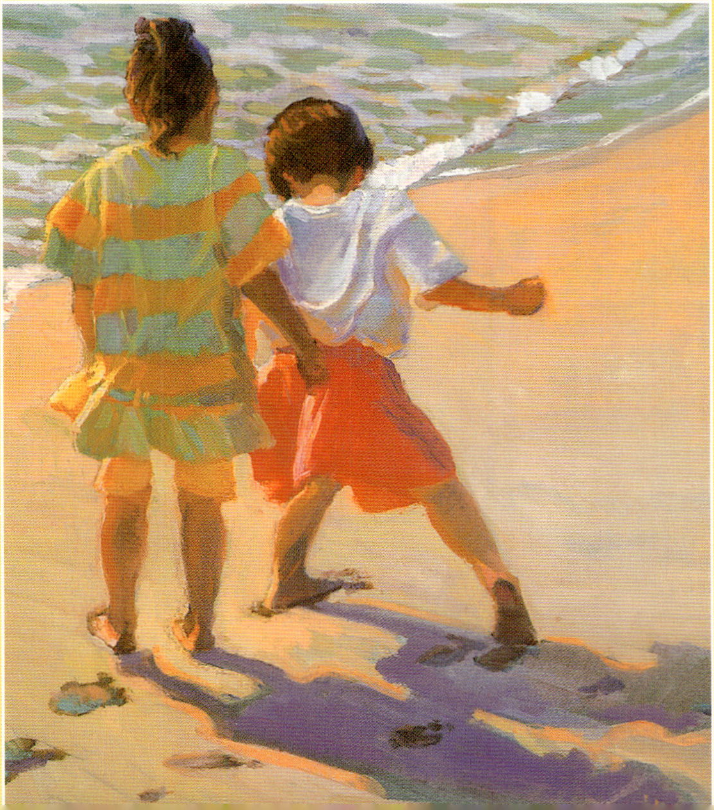

FLAT FIELDS

In order to make a field extend forward from a hedge, work a line of darker tone along the bottom of the hedge. Then put in a light line along the edge of the field where it meets the hedge and blend it back, if necessary, so that it isn't obvious.

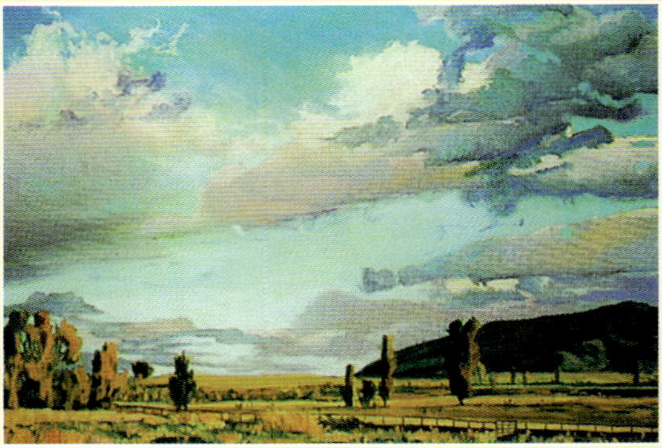

In "Evening Skies" by Martha Saudek, the light across the distant fields makes the land recede back toward the horizon.

203

SKY AND LAND

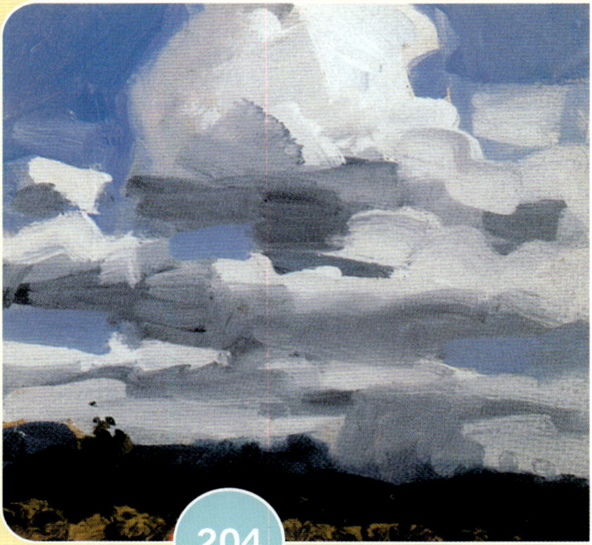

204

The sky shouldn't be painted with smooth, thin paint just because that seems to express insubstantial air. It should be painted in the same style as the land or sea in order to unify the two areas. Keep the brushstrokes in scale with the scene as a whole.

In Charles Sovek's "Clouds over Sante Fe" land and sky are unified.

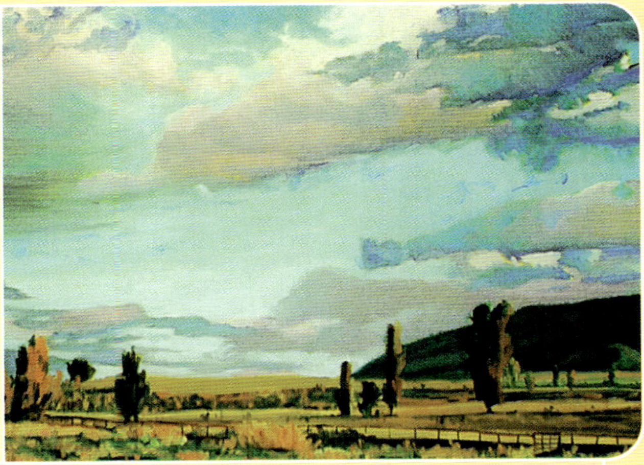

The detail shows the point is kept smooth for the land itself, and the plants in the foreground emphasize the feeling of depth in the scene.

SUBSTANTIAL CLOUDS

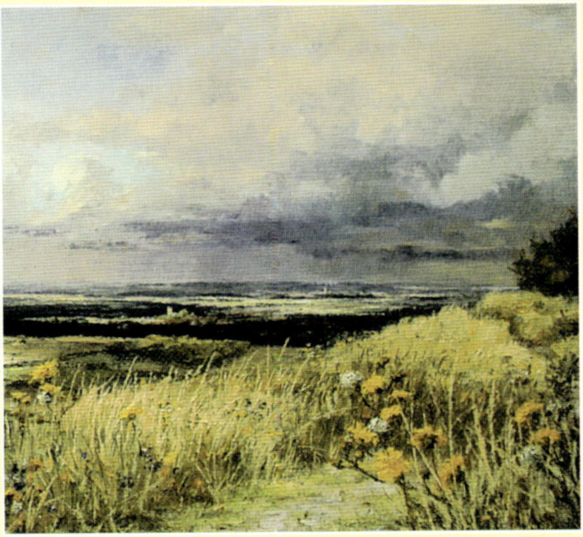

In this detail from "From the Ridgeway" by Brian Bennet, thick paint gives the clouds substance.

To create clouds with form and volume, remember that the lightest area is not at the edges unless the clouds are backlit. The upper surfaces will reflect sky color while the underside will reflect earth tones. The lightest area will be within the body of the cloud, and it should be painted quite thickly.

205

206

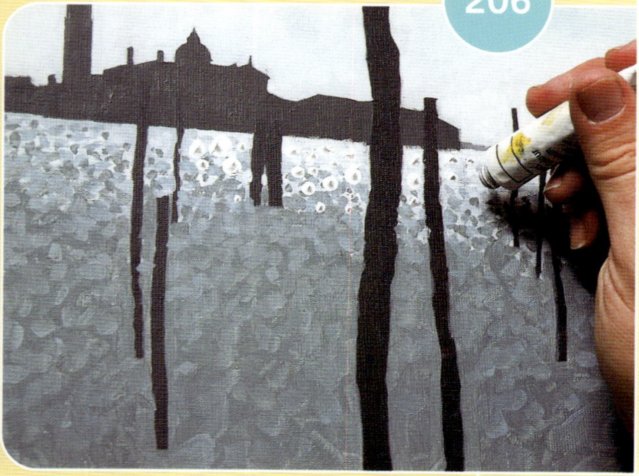

LIGHT ON WATER

To capture light on water, either put in the darker shades first and add highlights over the top; or apply patches of a light color first, and when it's dry, drag darker colors over the top, letting the light color show through.

Highlights are being added with paint straight from the tube.

FOCUS ON FOLIAGE

207

If you are including a clump of branches or foliage in the foreground, concentrate on portraying it in terms of areas of light and dark, instead of trying to paint individual branches or leaves.

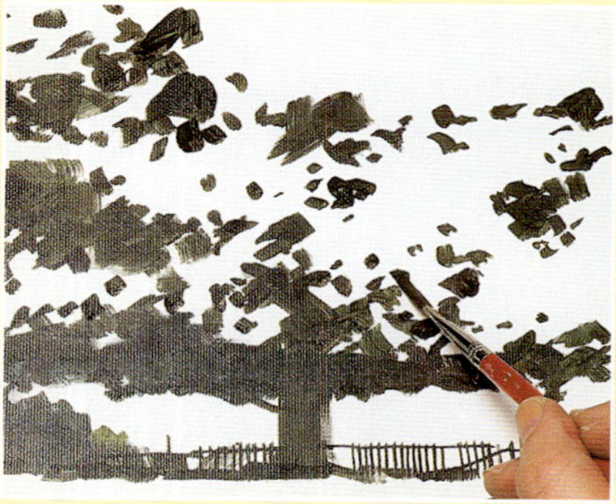

The shadow areas are blocked in with a dark shade of green.

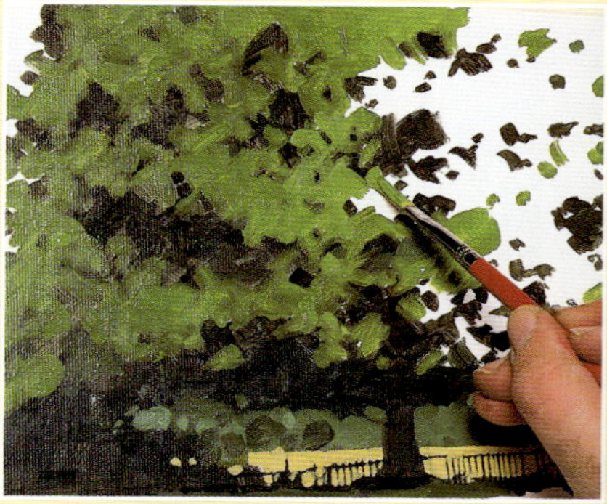

A medium green is worked over the rest of the foliage area.

PORTRAITS

Keep the paint thin, and remember that removing paint is as important as putting it on. Paint can be removed with a rag, a clean brush, or a knife. Remove it gradually until you have worked back to an effect you like.

Features are easier to model if you keep the paint thin, as shown in "Self Portrait" by Ashley Hold.

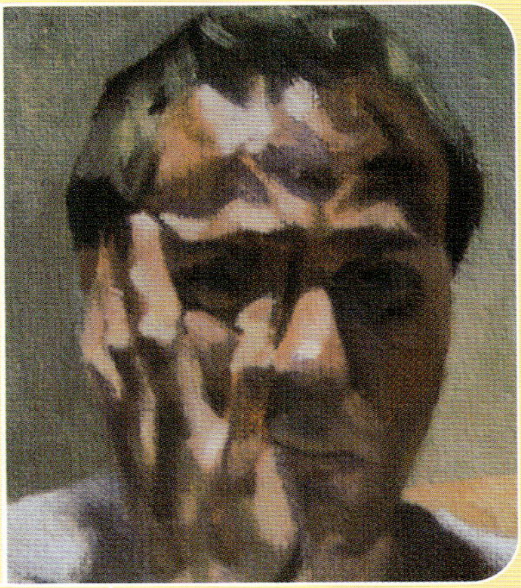

208

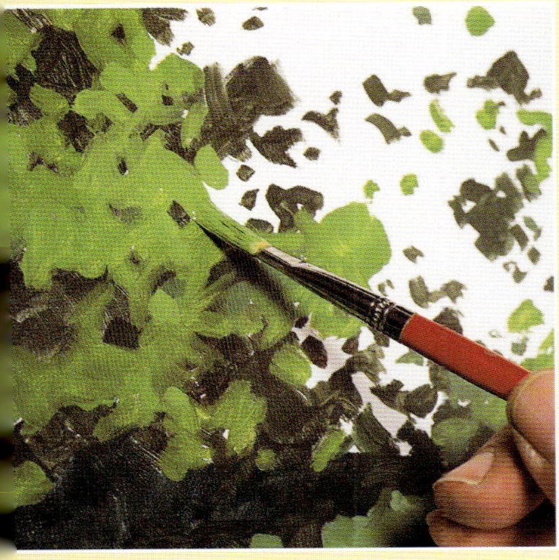

Multidirectional brushstrokes suggest foliage, but no attempt is made to paint leaves.

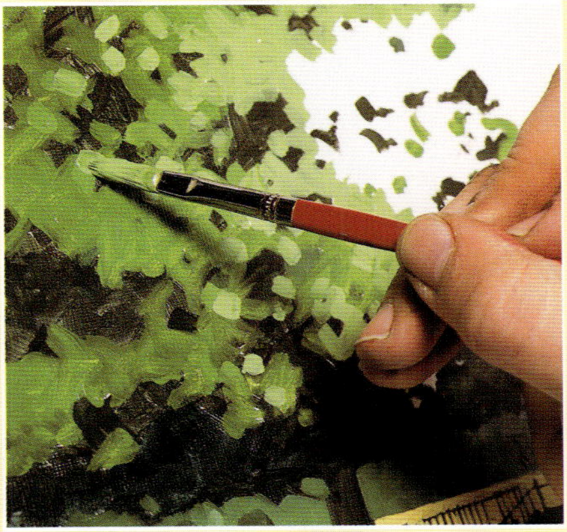

A light green is added. The combination of shades creates a feeling of depth.

SKIN COLORS

209

Mix the colors you need, rather than buying flesh colors, which will be flat and uninteresting. Take three or four colors—such as Alizarin Crimson, Yellow Ocher, and white, or Burnt Umber, Alizarin, Cobalt Blue, and white—and use them to mix a base color that you can warm and cool, lighten and darken as needed.

In "Dianna" by Tom Coates, the skin and background colors are mixed from the same palette of earth yellows and reds, blue, and white.

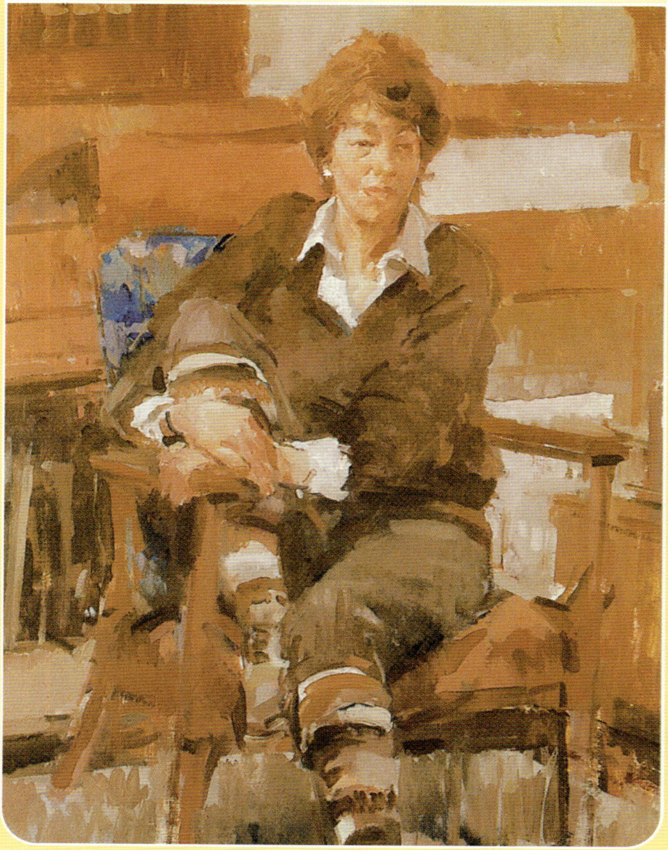

MOVING FIGURES

210

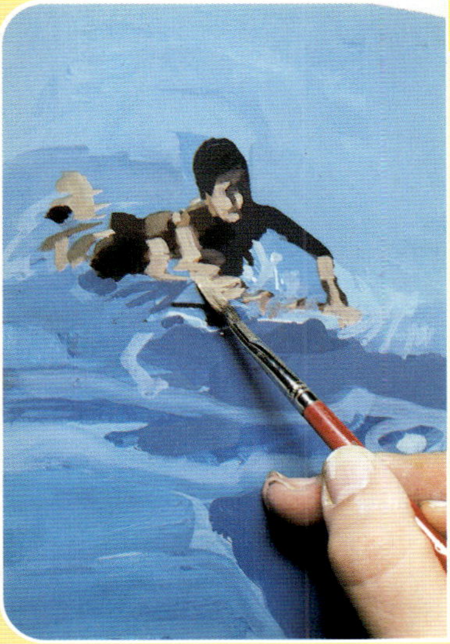

Wet into wet is the best technique for portraying figures in action because it is easy to blur areas of the body—especially legs and feet—to suggest motion, and no part will end up too sharply defined.

The head and shoulders are in sharp focus, but the arms and legs are painted as a blur of activity and movement.

GROUPS

211

Groups of figures, including just two together, should be blocked in initially as one overall shape. Then indicate where the light is falling on each figure to distinguish it from the others and from the surroundings.

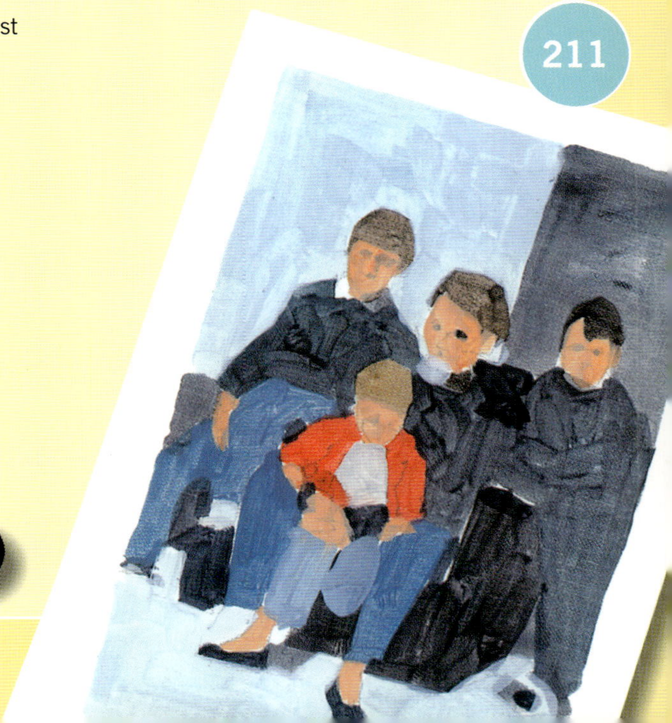

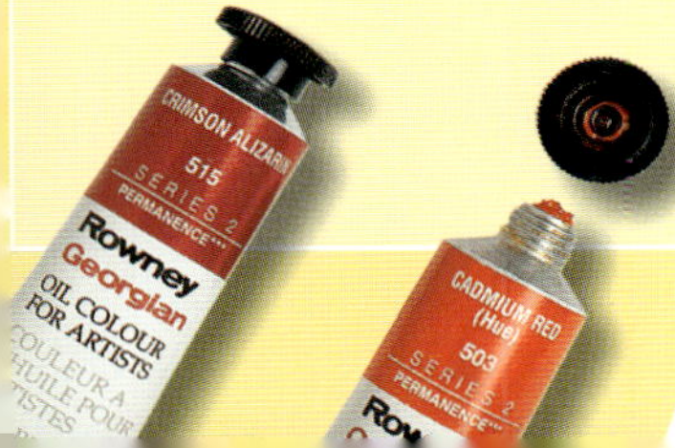

CHILDREN

212

Young subjects will find it difficult to keep still for any length of time while you paint them. One way to speed up the process is to make a monochromatic underpainting in acrylics, which will dry quickly, and you can add color over the top with oil paint.

CONVINCING FOLDS

To paint folds in cloth, work in about five shades, exaggerating the warm and cool darker tones so that the highlights stand out. Also, work dark to light, keeping the paint thin to start with, and applying the highlights last in thicker paint.

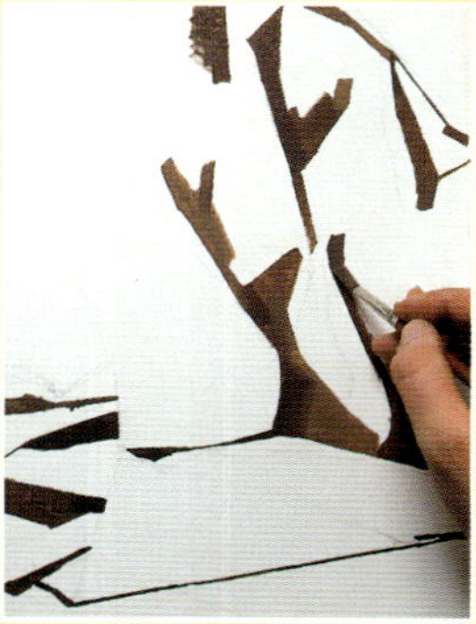

The recessed parts of the folds, that is, the dark shadow areas, are put in first in a dark tone of the fabric color.

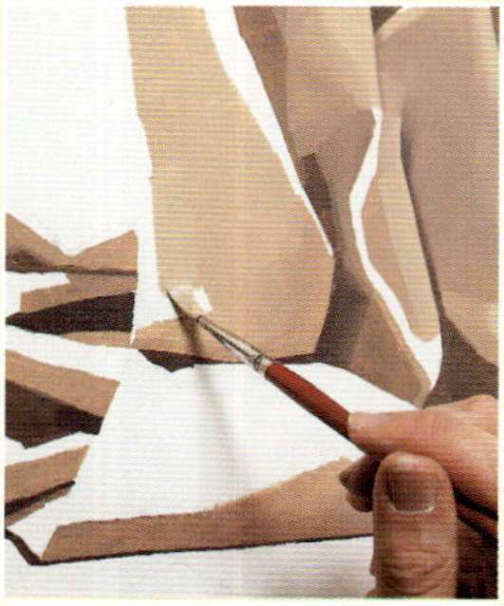

The middle tones are added next. They are carefully blended with the darks to suggest a continuous surface.

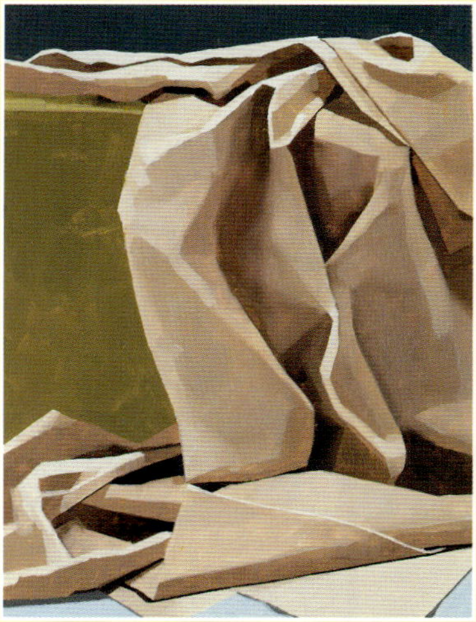

The lightest tones are added. A light tone against a dark gives a sharp change in plane, whereas a gradual transition describes a curving surface.

213

214

The background is as important as the subject and should be seen and painted as an integral part of the composition. Build it up using the same kind of marks and techniques as for the main subject, and keep moving to and fro between the subject and the background so that you can keep judging the colors and tones of one against the other.

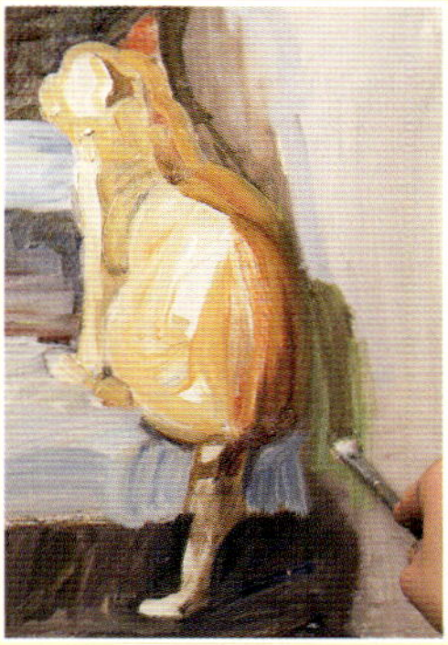

The background is blocked in, establishing the space and tonal range.

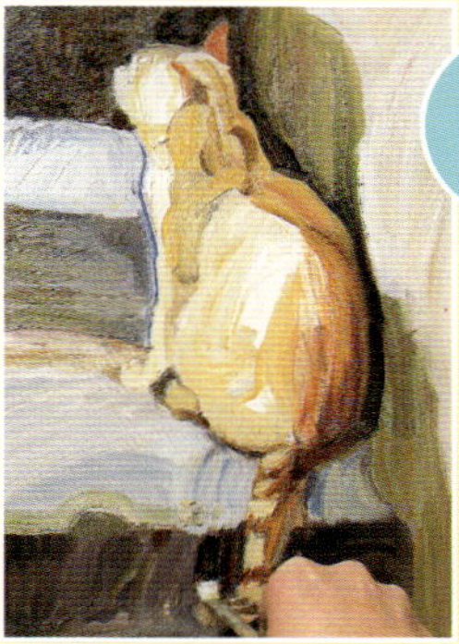

Background tones are darkened in places, giving definition to the cat. The paper is peeled away.

Subject and background are painted in the same style, giving the painting a unified feel.

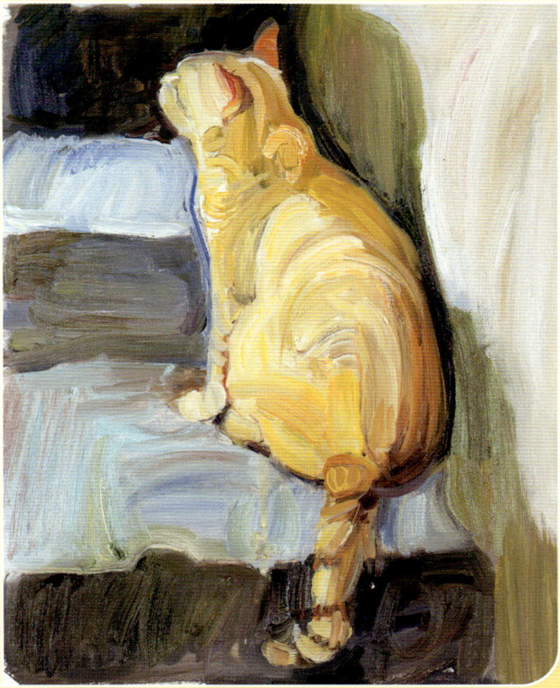

PAINTING GLASS

215

To capture glass, first paint the background and anything inside the glass, such as flowers and stems, observing the distortions caused by glass or water. Then indicate the edges of the object in terms of the light and dark tones that you see, and put in simplified reflections and highlights.

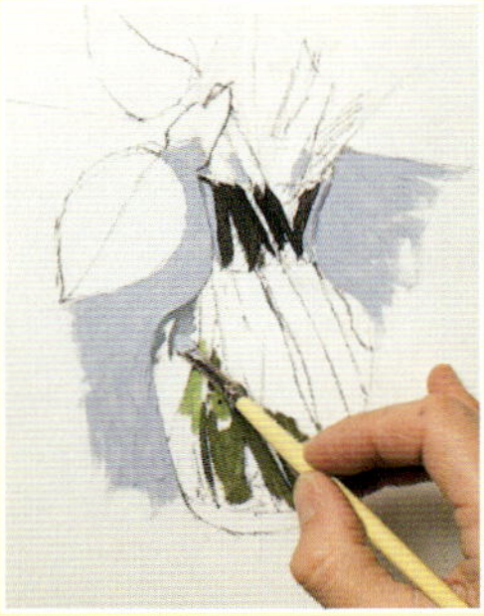

Anything that can be seen through the glass, such as flower stems and glimpses of the background, is painted in.

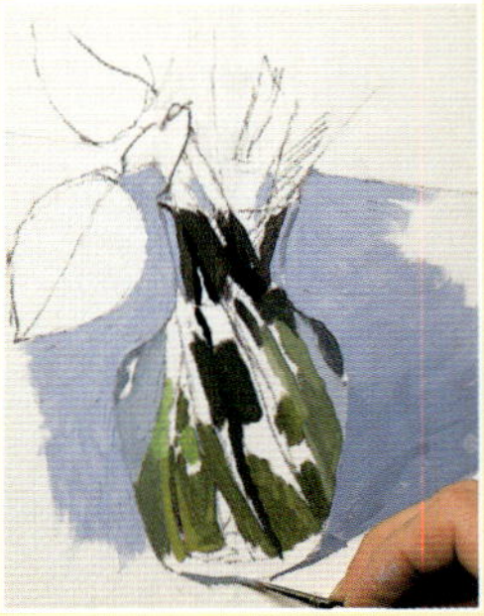

The edges of the vase are indicated through changes of tone between the glass and the background.

FLOWERS

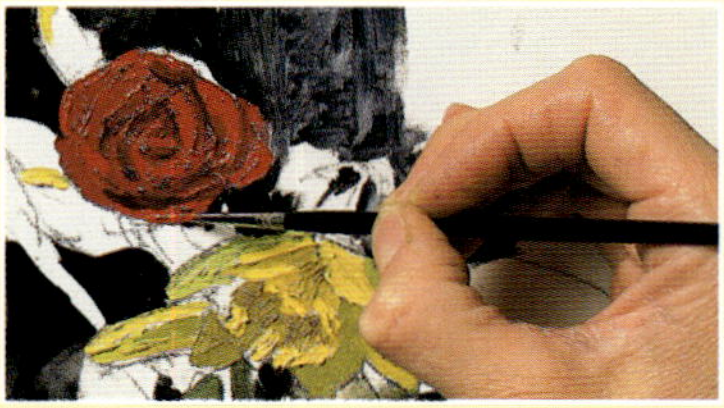

The rose is painted by following the circular arrangement of the leaves, leaving the paint thin in the lit areas.

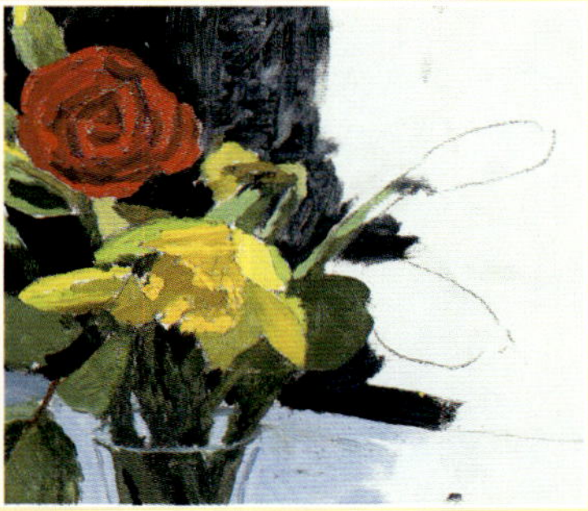

The daffodil buds are put in with short, directional marks that establish their roundness and solidity.

To prevent a painting of flowers from becoming fussy and overworked, plan the composition carefully to begin with, and then try to work using bold brushstrokes to describe the shape and direction of the petals and leaves, and leave them alone once made. If you are not happy with any area, scrape off the paint and try again.

216

PAINTING METAL

217

Metallic surfaces reflect their surroundings, but the colors will be duller than the things they are reflecting, except in highlights. You can use the reflections to describe the shape of the object itself.

The shape and reflective quality of metallic objects are described through the way they reflect light and colors from the surrounding objects, as demonstrated in this work, "Tomato with Salt and Pepper," by Deborah Deichler.

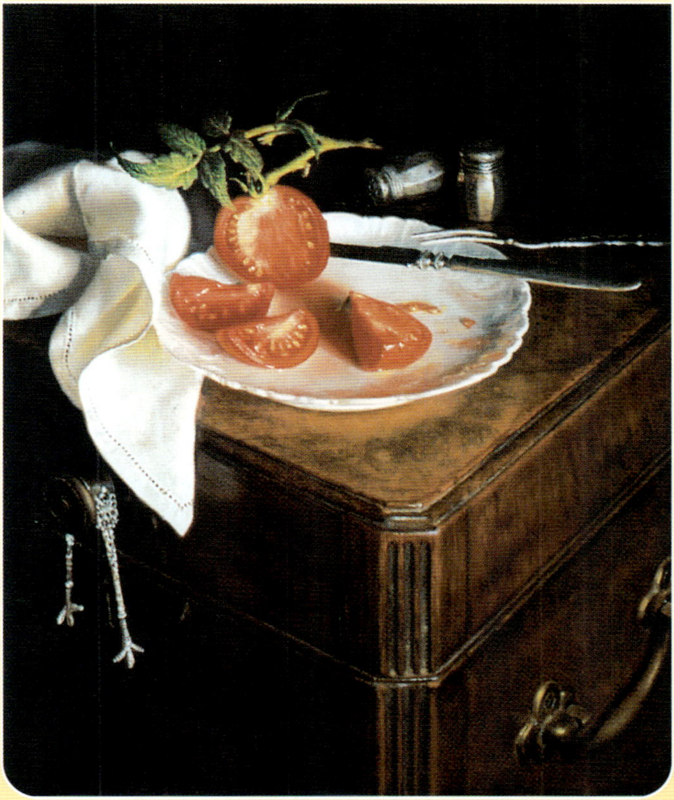

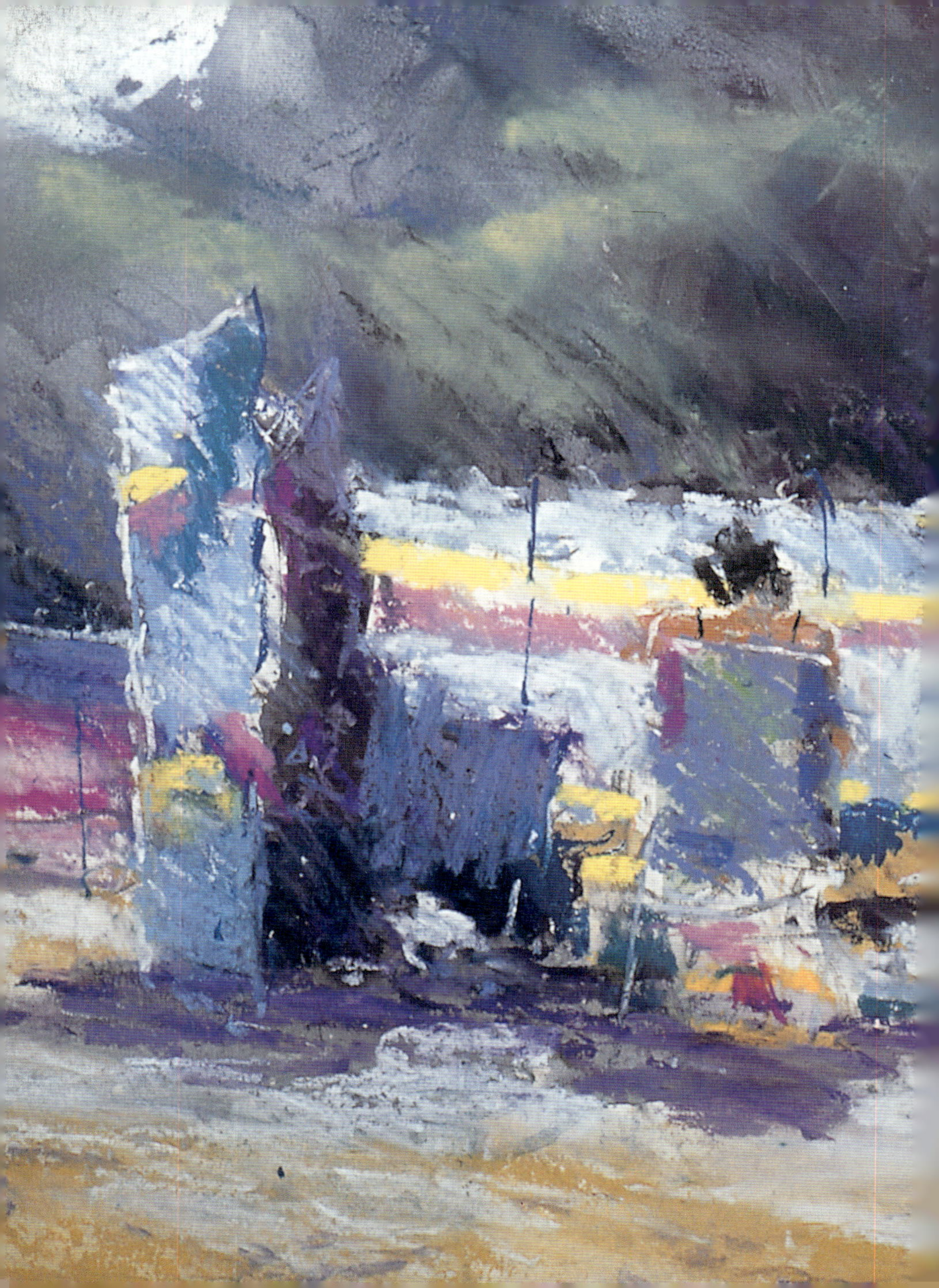

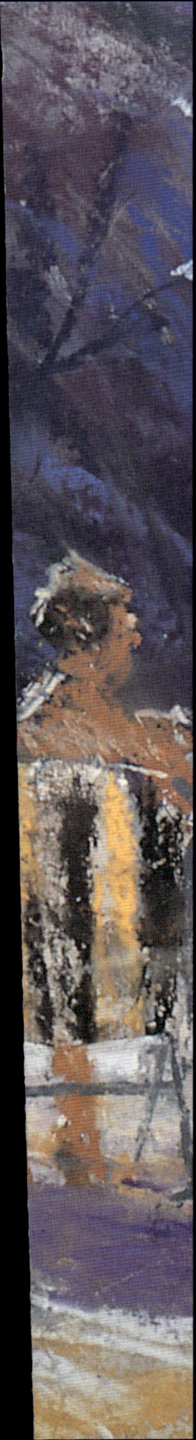

3

PASTEL

The range of colors and ease of application of pastel make it an exciting medium to use, but problems can occur. The tips that follow cover not only the essentials, such as color selection, making a start, papers and grounds, preparatory drawings, special effects, creating highlights, fixing, and making alterations, but also include advice on ways to retain the appealing surface effects and vibrant color of pastels in well-worked, finished paintings. Practical advice is also included on traveling light, storage of work, framing, and safety when using pastels.

Alan Oliver, "The Blue Windbreak" (detail).

INTRODUCTION TO PASTELS

HAVE YOU ever looked at a pastel painting in a gallery and wondered how a particular effect was achieved? Or watched an artist demonstrating a technique that suddenly opened up new possibilities? Have you despaired of a pastel because the colors look too bright or too dull, and you don't know how to save the situation? Or, on a more mundane level, have you perhaps gone out sketching and found that you have the wrong color of paper?

Pastel is a wonderfully direct and expressive medium, combining the virtues of paint—pure, glowing color—with the handling properties of the drawing media. With a stick of hard or soft pastel, or of oil pastel, for example, you can draw as you would with a stick of charcoal, but you can also spread, blend, and overlay colors to build up a thick, painterly effect. There are so many different ways of working with pastels that it is impossible to lay down a set of rules, but, once you know what can be done, you will be halfway to finding your own style.

This section starts with general advice on colors and papers and moves on to help with specific techniques and effects, including ways of "saving" a picture that has not

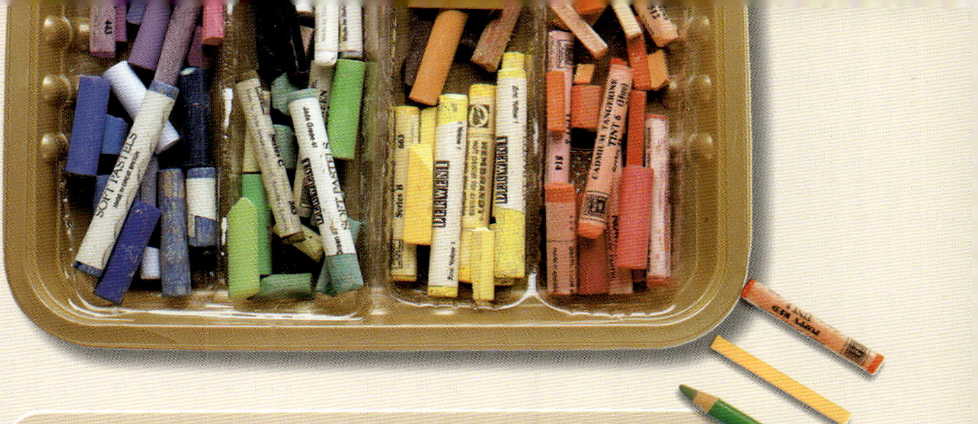

quite worked. You will learn how to tint your own paper (did you know that you can do this with a used teabag?), how to create textured effects by working over an acrylic ground, how to turn oil pastel into paint by spreading it with mineral spirits, how to combine pastel with other media such as paint and charcoal, and many other invaluable techniques. There is a short section on erasing (always a problem in pastel work), some hints for the traveling artist, and a section on caring for your work, because pastel is a fragile medium and your pictures won't last if you don't look after them. You can also use this section retrospectively—look back at some of your finished pastel paintings and see whether a different method might have improved them. If you find any of the tips here particularly inspiring, try them out—you will learn a lot simply by experimenting with the medium, and you will enjoy yourself in the process.

MAKING A START

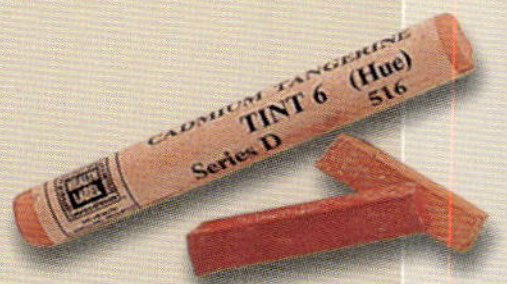

This section combines practical advice on pastel types and colors with some more unusual hints. Did you know, for example, that you can clean your pastels with ground rice? Had you thought of using supermarket vegetable trays as "palettes" to hold the selection of pastels you will need for each picture? These are just two of the many helpful tips that you will find on the following pages.

A BASIC PALETTE

To build up a selective yet versatile palette, buy one cool and one warm version of the most important colors in the spectrum. Basic cool colors include Poppy Red, Lemon Yellow, Olive Green, Cobalt Blue, and Burnt Sienna. Useful warm colors include Crimson Lake, Cadmium Yellow, Viridian, French Ultramarine, and Burnt Umber. To broaden your palette, supplement these colors with black, white, and a few earth tones such as Madder Brown and Raw Sienna.

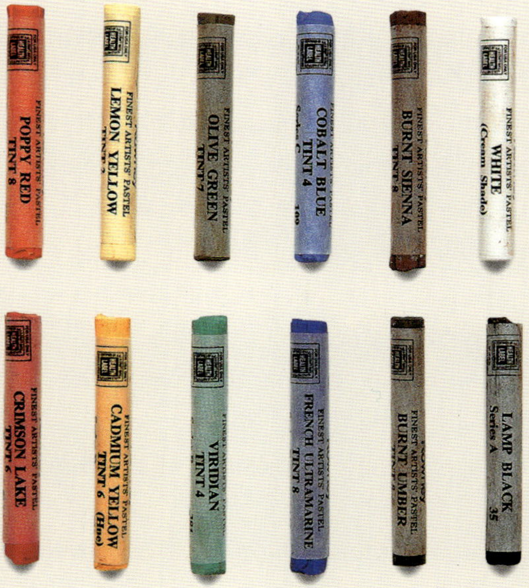

WORKING IN PASTELS

218

A LIMITED PALETTE

219

To try out pastels using just a few colors, select an initial palette to suit your favorite subject. If you paint landscapes, choose a wide selection of greens, but if you paint portraits you will need a range of flesh tones plus a few extra colors for the sitters' clothing. Add to these a selection of neutral colors for creating highlights and shadow areas.

USING PRIMARY COLORS

220

All colors can theoretically be mixed from the three primaries, red, blue, and yellow. Experiments will improve your mixing skills and your perception of color.

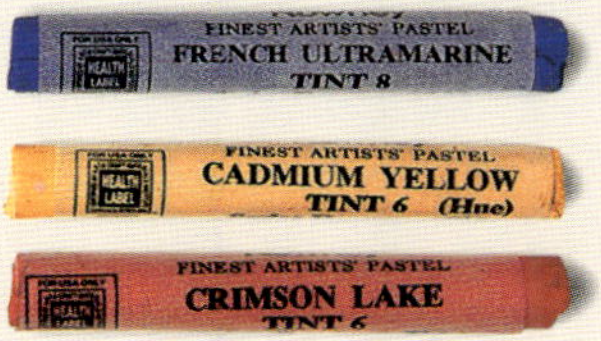

CHOOSING COLORS

Avoid ending up with superfluous colors by buying pastels selectively. Although you can choose a boxed set of colors that is specially put together for a specific subject—portrait, landscape, or still life—there is a real danger that some of the colors supplied in it will be superfluous to your needs. If you select individual colors you will have a more versatile range.

221

SELECTING PASTELS

222

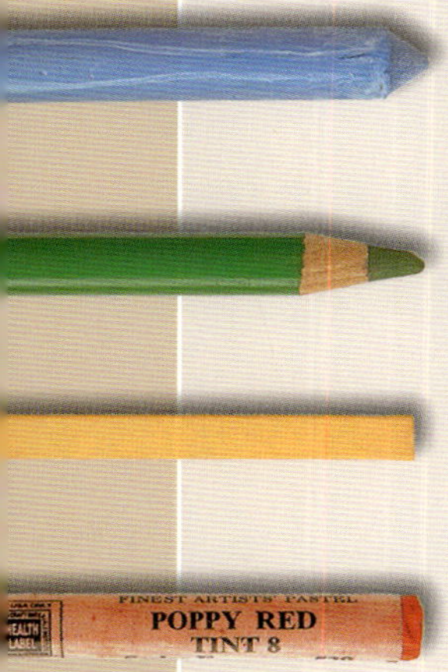

There are four types of pastels—bear in mind the following characteristics when making your choice. Soft: crumbly, vibrant; use to blend, smudge, and cover large areas. Hard: less crumbly, easily erased; use for preliminary drawing and detail. Pencil: clean, does not crumble or smudge easily; use for intricate work and crosshatching. Oil: does not crumble, makes buttery marks; does not mix with other pastels.

BUY THE BEST

If you want to make sure that your paintings retain their brightness and freshness of color over the years, always use the best-quality pastels in your work. Even though cheap pastels are available, the greater amount of chalk, and therefore clay content (used to extend the pastel mixture), reduces the lightfastness of the pigments so the colors fade over time.

223

AN IMPROVISED STORAGE BOX

If you do not have a ready-made pastel box to keep your pastels in, try using corrugated cardboard to line boxes or drawers to keep pastels apart from each other and therefore clean. Plastic containers with separate compartments also make good "paint boxes."

224

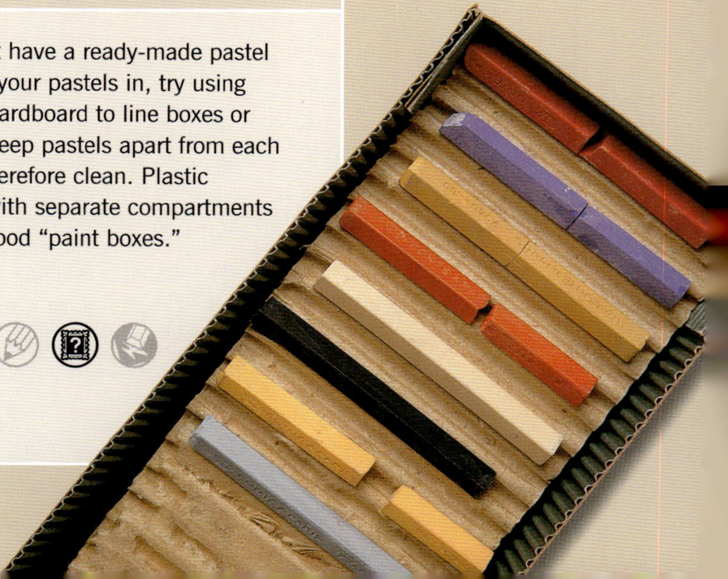

FINDING THE RIGHT COLOR

225

If you have a wide selection of pastels it is essential to store them in separate containers according to color: greens in one, reds in another, and so on. When working, you will easily be able to see your tint options across a color and select those that are most appropriate.

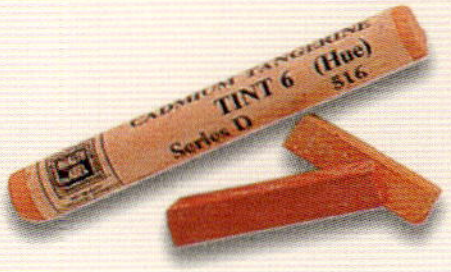

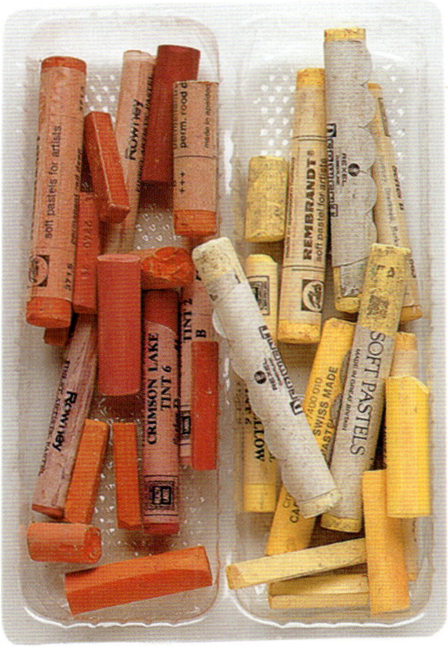

KEEPING PASTELS CLEAN

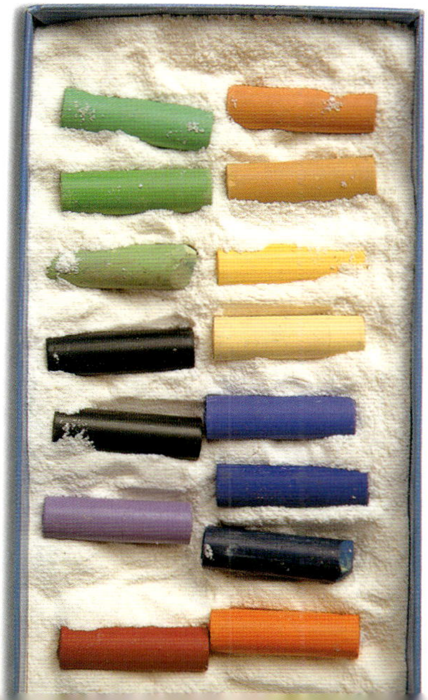

226

If you store all your soft pastels in one box, line it with ground rice, because this will help to keep the pastel sticks apart. The slightly rough-textured rice will also rub against the pastels, removing dust that they have picked up from other sticks and keeping them clean. Remove any particles of rice before use.

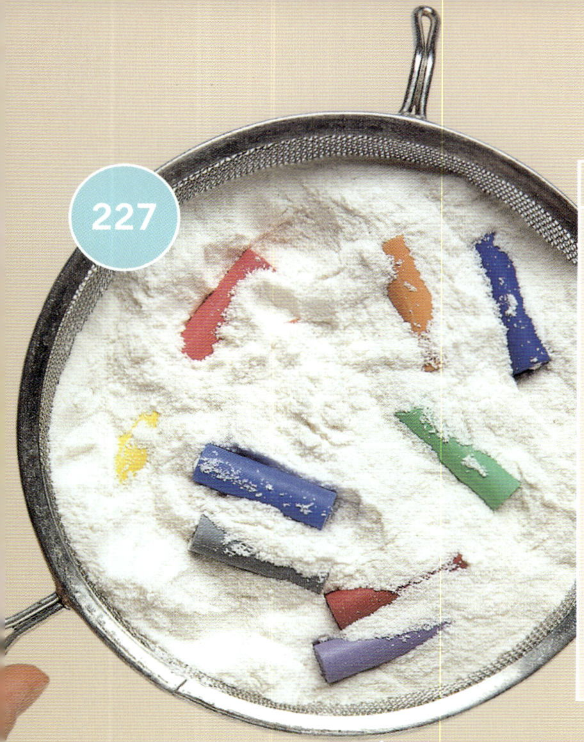

227

CLEANING DIRTY PASTELS

If your soft pastels have acquired a film of gray dust, as they quickly do, you can clean them by placing them in a large plastic bag together with enough ground rice to coat the pastels. Shake the bag well, and then pour the contents into a sifter. The dirty ground rice will fall through leaving sparkling-clean pastels.

228

SETTING UP A WORKSTATION

If you have trouble keeping your pastels orderly while working, establish a special place for them. An old television table, serving trolley, or occasional table all make excellent pastel worktables. You should be able to pick up one of the above cheaply from a junk shop. The important thing to look for is a raised rim around the edge of the trolley or tabletop, which will prevent the pastels from rolling off. The shelf below will hold corrugated boxes, fixatives, sprays, rags, paper, towels, torchons, and so on.

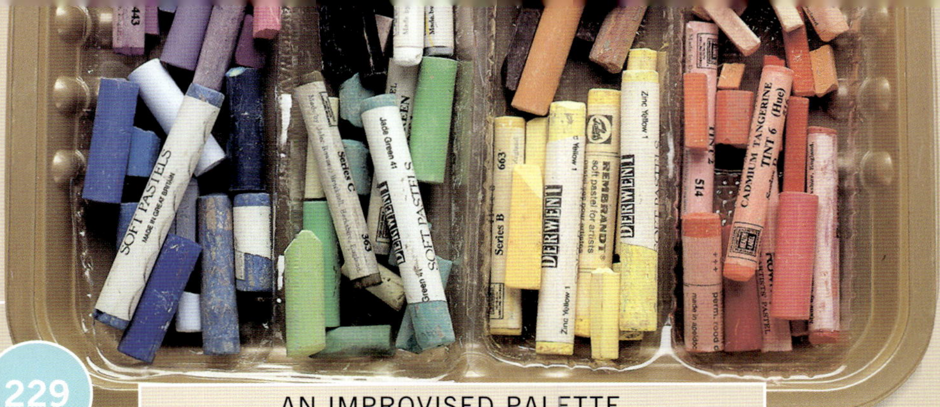

229

AN IMPROVISED PALETTE

Most supermarkets and delis now sell vegetables in small plastic trays. Do not throw away the trays, as they make ideal, lightweight, easy-to-hold palettes in which to keep the particular pastels that you are using for a painting.

KEEPING YOUR WORK CLEAN

To stop crumbles of soft-pastel residue from collecting over your painting surface when working, work on a slight tilt or with the board held vertically on an easel. Loose powder will then fall away from the paper onto the table or floor, and can be removed with a vacuum cleaner.

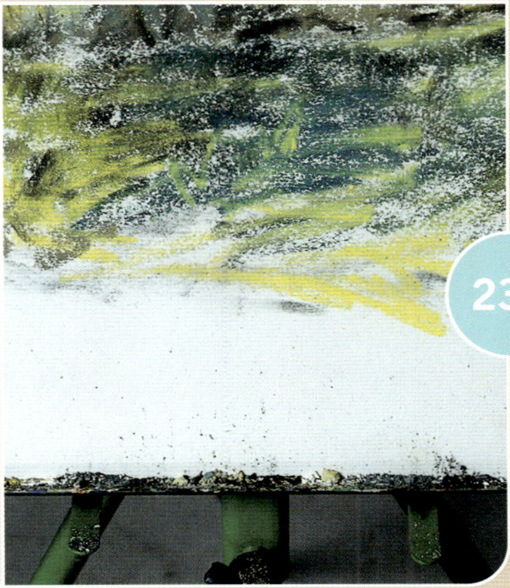

230

ADVICE ON BOARDS

231 Make sure that your drawing board is wider on all sides than your paper, as this will improve the way that you work. If the board is the same size as your paper, it will cramp the composition, and you will tighten your style to counteract the effect. The board can also act as a "frame" for the picture, enabling you to judge the proportion and scale correctly.

A HOMEMADE COLOR CHART

232 If you think you will want to remove the wrappers from pastels while you are working, thus losing the color and tint information that is given on them, make a chart of the colors you are using before you start, Lay down a patch of each color along the edge of a piece of paper and write the color name and tint beside it. You can then identify a color you have used in a painting by overlapping the edge of your chart with the relevant color in the work. You can also use the chart to identify pastels that have lost their wrappers along the way.

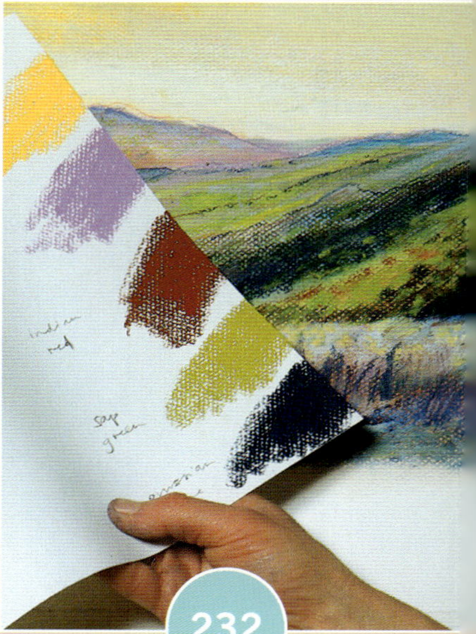

A PERFECT SURFACE

233

If imperfections appear on the surface of your work, they could well be caused by the texture of the ground under your paper. Any pit, bump, or cut-line on the board under the paper will be picked up by the pastels in a "brass-rubbing" effect. To avoid this problem, cushion your pastel paper with layers of acid-free paper attached between it and the board. This will give you a smooth, soft surface to work on.

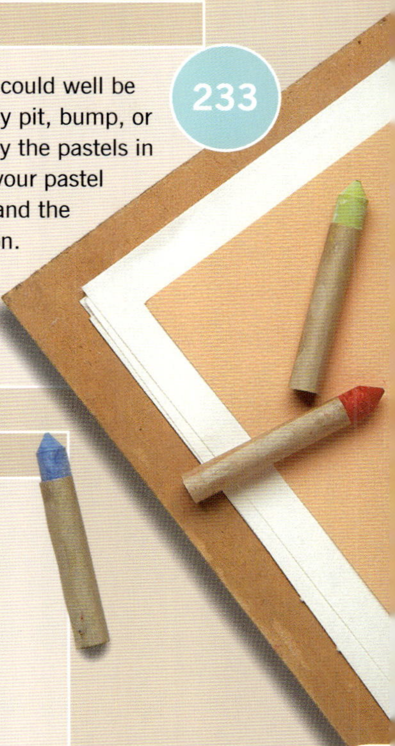

WORK HARD TO SOFT

234

When using both hard and soft pastels, start working with the harder pastels. Resist the temptation to start with ultrasoft pastels, as they will clog the paper and make later adjustments difficult.

SMUDGE-FREE PAINTINGS

235

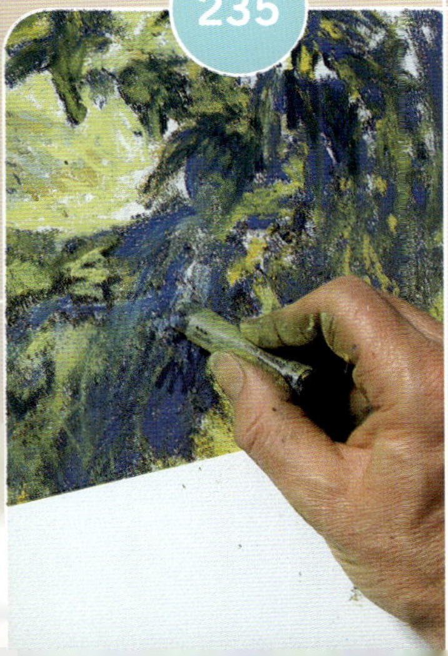

To avoid smudging your pastel painting with your hand as you work, become accustomed to working from left to right if you are right-handed and from right to left if you are left-handed, and from the top of the paper down. In this way, you will always be resting your hand on clean paper and will not accidentally disturb the work already done. If it is not practical to work methodically across the paper, you can cover completed areas with a sheet of paper and rest your hand on that while working on the next area.

PAPERS AND GROUNDS

The "standard" papers sold for pastel work, which come in a wide choice of colors, are adequate for most needs, but there are many other kinds of paper with which to experiment. Sandpaper, for example, is a favorite with many artists, as is watercolor paper, which you can tint with water-based paints in any color you choose. If you like a good texture to work on, you can also lay a special ground with acrylic paint or gesso.

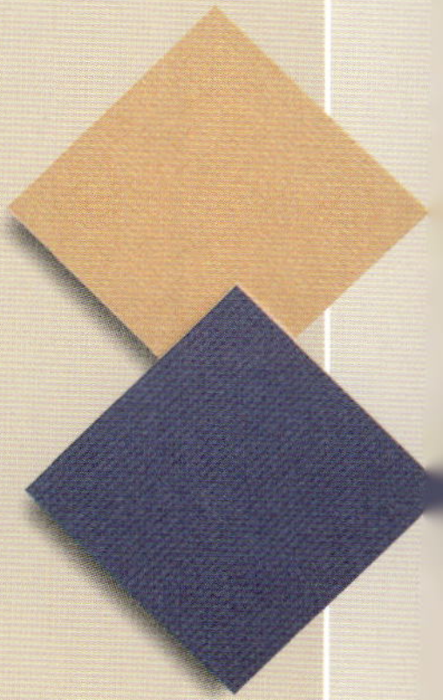

PAPERS FOR SOFT PASTEL

If you have trouble with soft pastel not adhering, you may be using the wrong surface. Soft pastels adhere best to paper with some "tooth," as the particles are held in the texture.

1 Mi-Teintes paper has a textured surface resembling fine chicken wire. The "wrong" side has a different texture and can also be used. Mi-Teintes is tough and therefore ideal for heavily worked pastel.

2 The "laid" surface of Ingres paper consists of close parallel lines. It comes in a choice of colors, from pale neutrals to stronger and darker tones, or with a fleck, which gives a mottled effect to the surface color.

3 Not watercolor paper is a popular choice. It is only produced in white, but can easily be tinted with watercolor, acrylic, or a dry wash of pastel.

4 Velour paper has a coating of powdered cotton. It holds pigment particles well and is a good choice for heavily worked paintings.

5 Flour paper is ideal for pastel work, but is only sold in small sheets.

6 There are two types of sandpaper suitable for soft pastel. Artists' quality sandpaper is a neutral color and comes in large sheets. Wet-and-dry sandpaper can take a wash, but is only available in small sizes and is black in color. Use the finest grit (400) for pastel work.

7 Pastel cloth is a synthetic fabric backed with fiberglass for strength. It absorbs underpainting much like paper, but does not buckle when wet.

236

SURFACES FOR OIL PASTEL

237

Oil pastel does not fall off the paper as soft pastel does, but if you want to build up colors thickly, a textured paper will give the best results.

1 Mi-Teintes paper is well suited to oil-pastel work. Either the "right" (textured) side or the "wrong" (smoother) side can be used. This paper is fairly tough and will allow you to spread the oil pastel with mineral spirits and manipulate the color without harming the paper.

2 Ingres paper can also be used. Although it is thinner than Mi-Teintes, the surface is not easily damaged and will allow manipulation of the color with mineral spirits.

8 Watercolor paper, either smooth (hot-pressed) or medium (Not) is a good choice for oil pastel. You can also tint it with a wash of oil paint thinned with mineral spirits, or with acrylic diluted with water.

9 Oil-sketching paper, which has a texture resembling canvas, is ideal for "painterly" approaches in oil pastel. It is very strong, allowing you to combine brush and line techniques. Mistakes can be corrected by wiping off the color with mineral spirits.

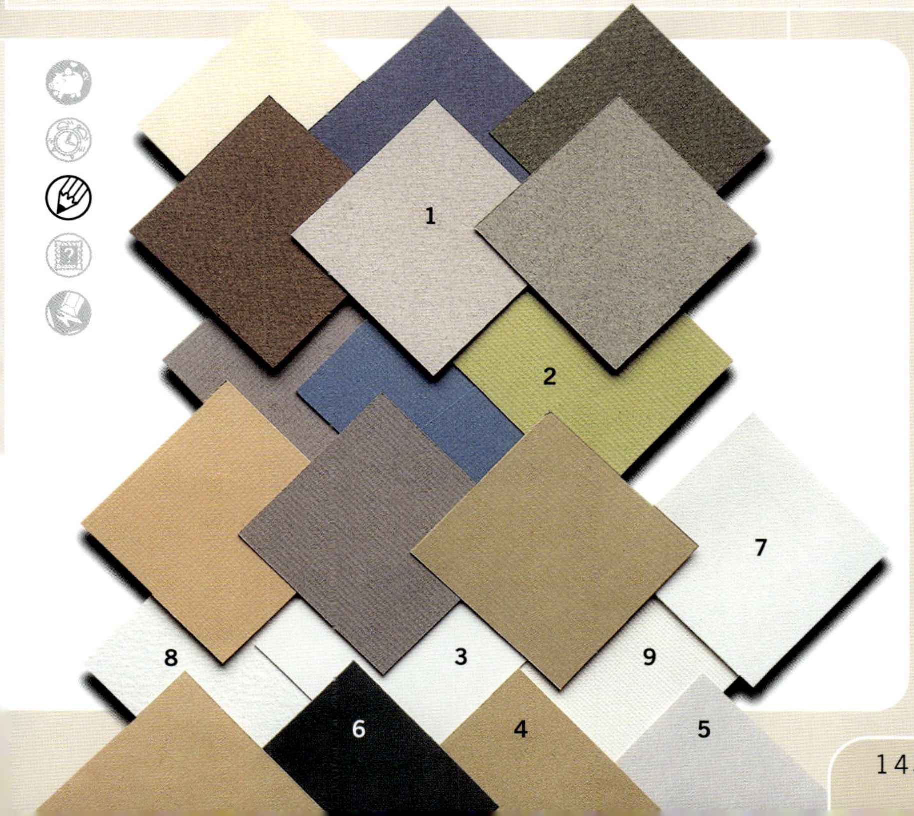

AVOIDING DISCOLORATION

238

If you want your work to last, use an acid-free paper, as this will not disintegrate or discolor with age, or cause the colors of the pastels to change over time.

A CHOICE OF SURFACES

239

Experimenting with different paper textures will help you to achieve varied effects in your work. Ingres paper, shown below, has one slightly textured and one smooth surface. Mi-Teintes paper also has two surface options.

PAPER ALTERNATIVES

If you cannot obtain standard pastel papers, construction paper or recycled paper make good alternatives, although the colors may fade in time if the paper is not acid-free.

240

A SMOOTH FINISH

241

If you want to create a smooth finish, the papers produced for etching or printmaking are a better choice than hot-pressed watercolor paper, because they are slightly absorbent and hold the pastel better.

NO FIXING NEEDED

242

If you want to avoid fixing your work, use a paper with a good tooth. The better the paper grips the pastel, the less it will need fixing.

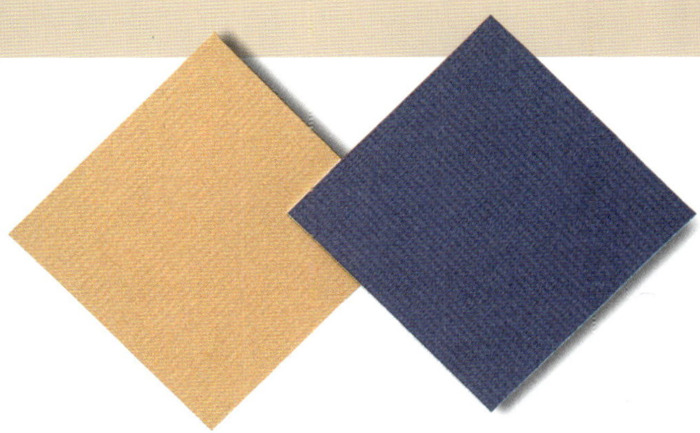

PAPER FOR HEAVY WORKING

243

For vigorous working it is possible to buy pastel papers attached to mat board. You then have all the advantages of a paper surface ready-stretched on a rigid ground.

A LAST RESORT

244

If you have nothing else, you can use brown wrapping paper as a cheap alternative to pastel paper. See the pastels of Venice by James McNeil Whistler (1834–1903) for proof of this! Be careful, though, as the paper is unlikely to be acid-free and is best reserved for pastel sketches and rough work.

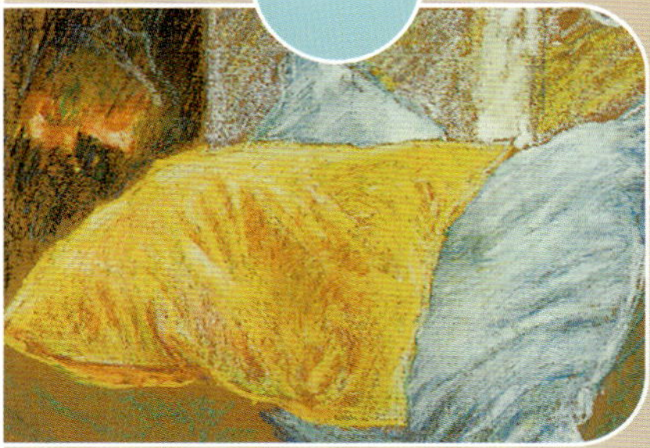

In "Yellow and Blue Cushions" (detail) by Olivia Thomas, the paper color contrasts with the pastels.

SETTING UP A CONTRAST

245

Most pastel painters like to use a paper which tones with the overall color scheme of the subject, but an alternative approach that can be exciting to try is to use an "opposite" color for the paper. For example, if you paint a snow scene or a predominantly blue-gray landscape on warm yellow or brown paper, it will provide a color contrast from the start. If small patches of the paper color are allowed to show through in the finished painting, they will enhance the blues and grays.

Olivia Thomas has used black paper for "White Chrysanthemums" (detail) to create contrast.

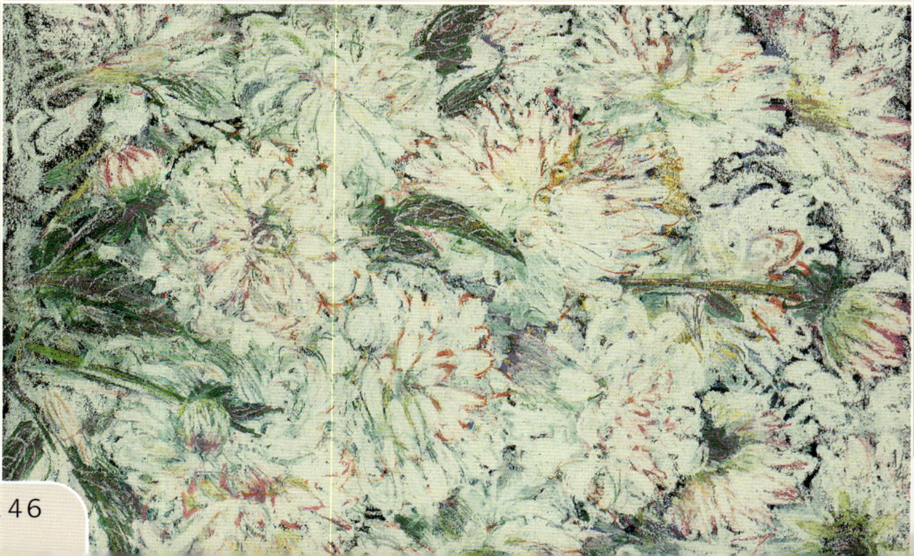

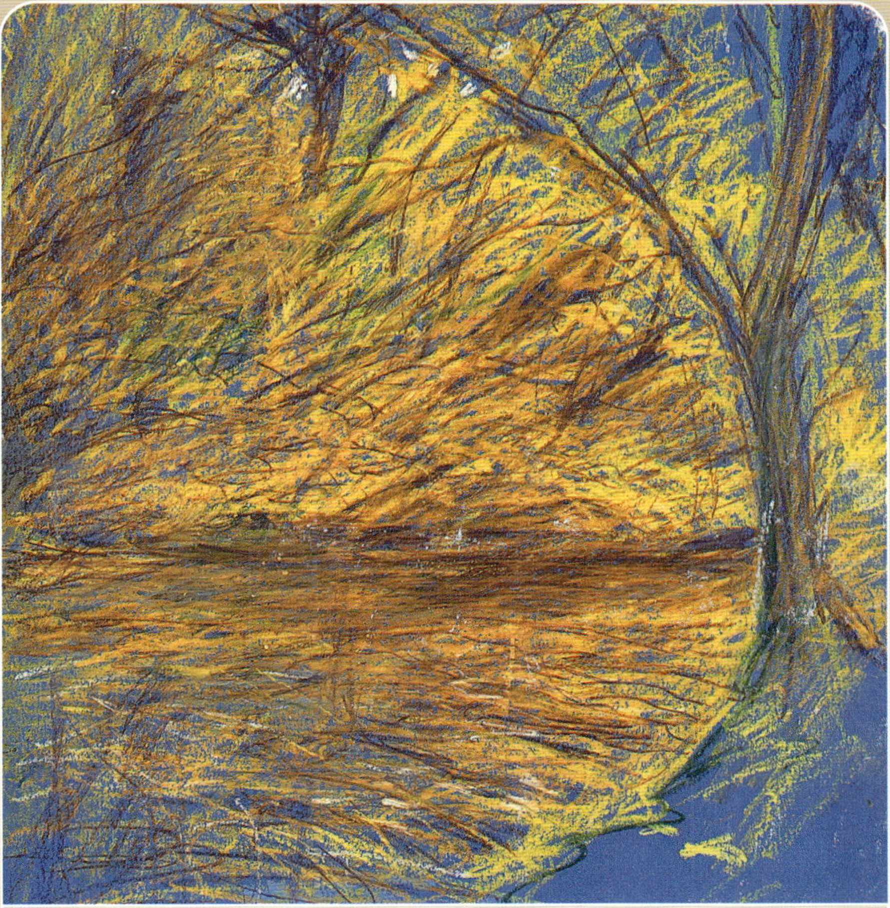

COLORED PAPER

If your pictures appear dull in color, or convey the wrong mood, try working on different-colored papers. Colored paper can be left uncovered in places, which means that you do not have to put on so much pastel. A gray sky, for example, might consist almost entirely of the paper color.

In "Autumn Colors at Chiswick House" by Olivia Thomas, blue paper gives additional brilliance to the yellows and oranges.

246

CHANGING THE GROUND COLOR

247

If the paper color that you have is not what you want, and provided that the paper is thick enough, you can alter it with a wash of watercolor or acrylic paint. Remember to stretch the paper first to prevent it from buckling.

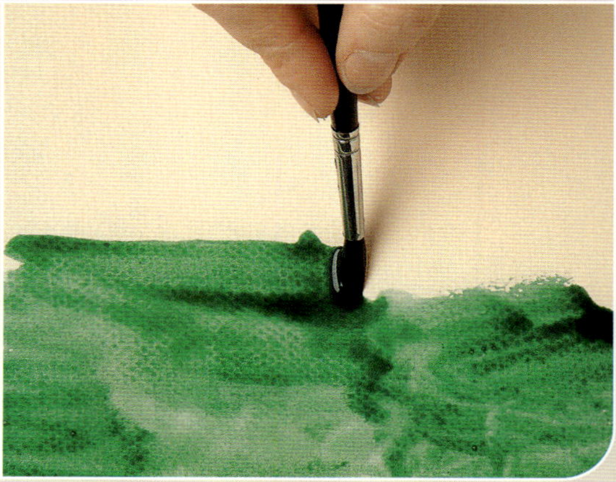

LAYING A PASTEL GROUND

248

You can change the color of the paper, or lay a tint of your choosing on watercolor paper, by putting down what is known as a dry wash. This is very simple; all you do is scrape a soft-pastel stick with a sharp blade until you have a good quantity of colored dust and spread this over the paper with a rag or piece of absorbent cotton. Fix the wash before working over it. If required, you can make the color darker in some places than others, or even use different colors. In a landscape, for example, you might lay a blue or gray dry wash for the sky area and a yellow or brown one for the land.

Three colors of pastel have been used here, providing base tints for both sky and land.

249

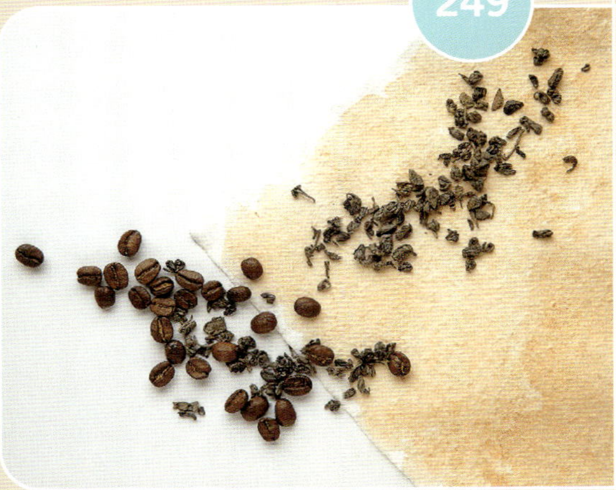

UNUSUAL TINTS

An unusual way to tint watercolor paper is to follow the Chinese example and rub damp tea leaves across the paper surface—or you could gain the same effect by dabbing with a used teabag. Coffee also makes a good stainer.

RETAINING THE TOOTH

If you tint the paper with acrylic, be careful not to apply it too thickly and smoothly, as it will impair the surface tooth, making it more difficult for the pastel to adhere.

250

A CHARCOAL GROUND

Scene painters' charcoal on watercolor paper makes an interesting colored and textured background and mixes well with soft pastels. Blend it into the paper, and then brush off excess dust before applying pastels.

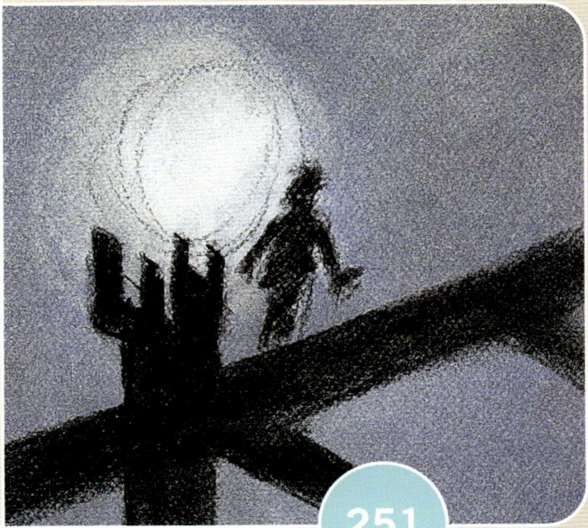

251

252

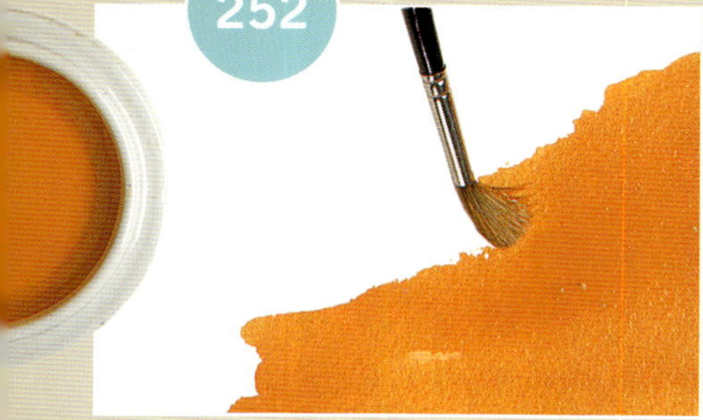

EXTRA TEXTURE

For a rough-textured look, try using rough watercolor paper. If you don't like working on white paper, you can tint it first with acrylic or watercolor.

A TEXTURED GROUND

253

Try laying a ground of acrylic gesso or acrylic modeling paste on smooth, heavy watercolor paper to achieve a rough-textured look. Apply it in roughly diagonal or multidirectional strokes with a large bristle brush. The texture of the brushmarks will be visible through the overlaid pastel, giving an extra quality of movement to the finished painting.

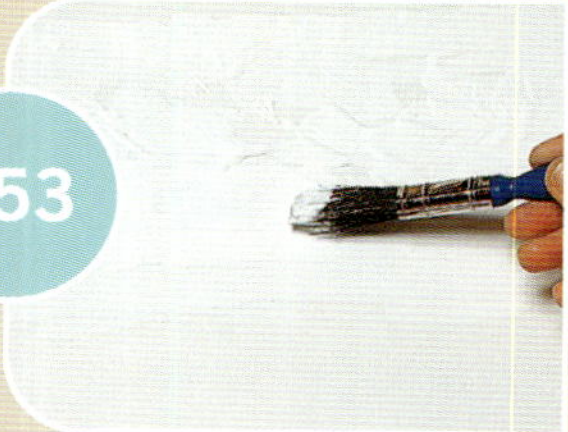

Acrylic modeling paste is laid with a household paintbrush.

The pastel color catches on the ridges.

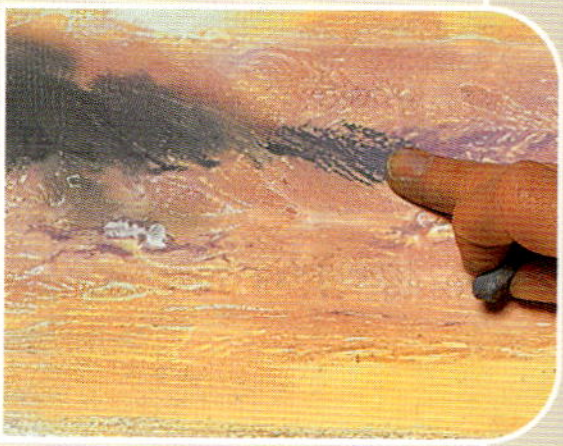

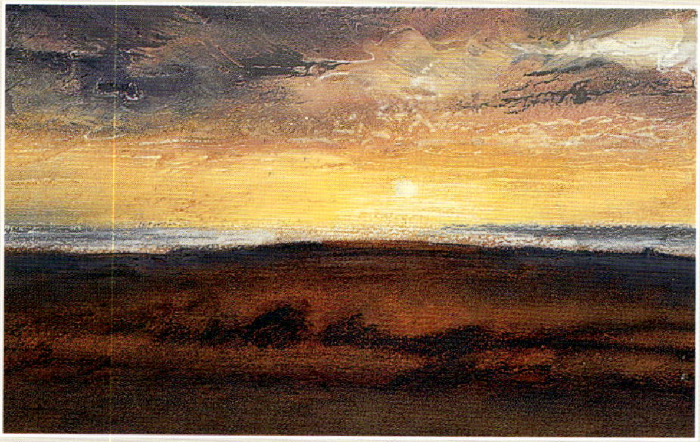

The textured ground has only been used for the sky area.

DARK DARKS

254

If you find it difficult to establish dark values because the dark colors you want to use are not available or seem to dull your work, try washing in the darks with a different medium, such as diluted ink or very thin acrylic, when you begin the painting.

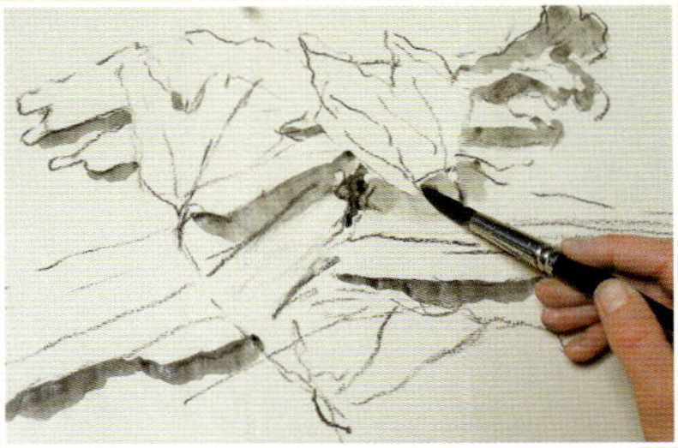

Diluted black ink is applied with a brush.

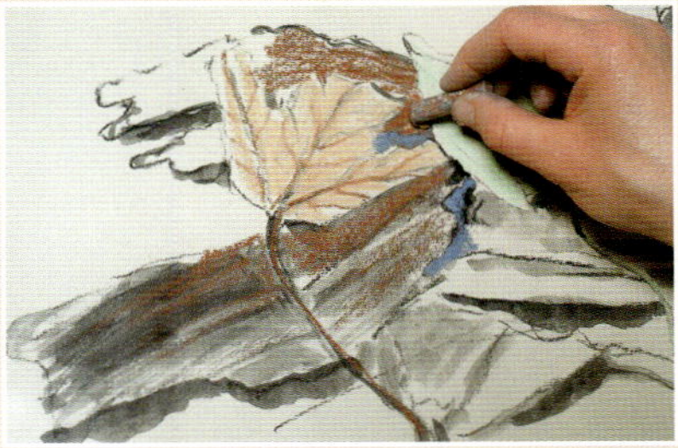

It is allowed to dry before pastel is used.

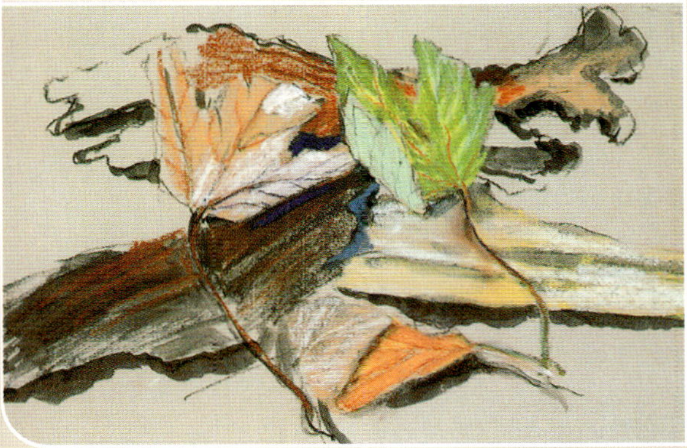

The red-brown pastel over the ink creates a rich brown.

ELIMINATING SPOTS

The slightly rough texture of heavy watercolor paper breaks up the pastel strokes, and you may find that small, unwanted white spots remain across the surface when the painting is complete. If you give the paper an initial watercolor or thin acrylic wash in a color that is harmonious with the subject before you start, any spots not covered by pastel will be unnoticeable.

255

PREPARATORY DRAWINGS

One of the problems with pastel work is that you cannot erase easily, so you need to begin with a good drawing. But how do you make this drawing? Ordinary pencil is not suitable for use under pastel, but you can use charcoal or pastel pencil, and there are several other useful methods, too, such as pouncing and tracing, which are ideal for intricate and complex designs.

UNDERDRAWING

256

Don't make preliminary drawings for soft-pastel paintings with graphite pencil, as it is slightly greasy and repels the pastel pigment. Instead, use hard pastel, a pastel pencil, or charcoal.

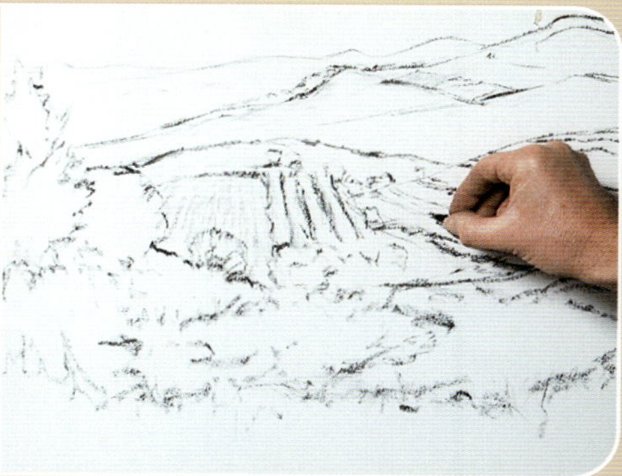

TRACING THE IMAGE

257

If you feel that you need to work from a detailed sketch in pencil, but are worried about the graphite repelling the pastel color, try tracing the original sketch on pastel paper. To do this, first draw the detailed sketch on a piece of typing paper, and then trace it using a 2B pencil. Go over the sketch on the reverse of the tracing paper with a 2B pencil. Then place the tracing paper with the right side up over the pastel paper and transfer the sketch. This takes a little extra time, but it will keep your paper in pristine condition and will give you a pale yet detailed sketch to work over that will not affect the pastel's adhesion to the board.

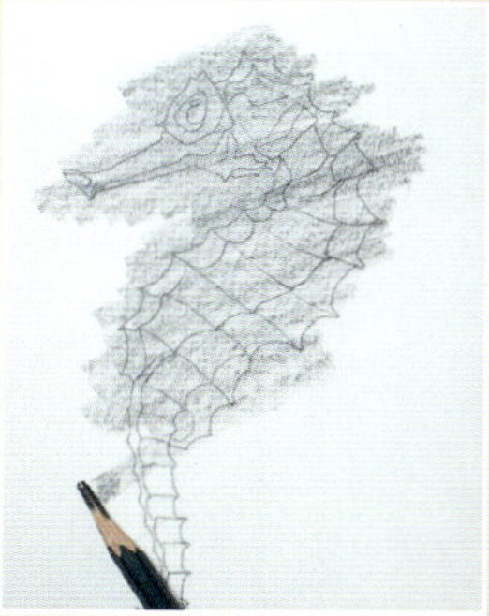

Scribble over the back of the tracing.

POUNCING

258

Another way of transferring an image is pouncing, which is most suitable for small-scale work involving a complex design. Prick holes all along the lines of your original drawing with a long needle, an awl, or similar implement, then lay the drawing on the pastel paper and push powdered pastel through the holes by rubbing it over the surface with a soft rag or piece of absorbent cotton. This produces faint dotted lines, which you can strengthen if needed by drawing over them with a pastel pencil of the appropriate color.

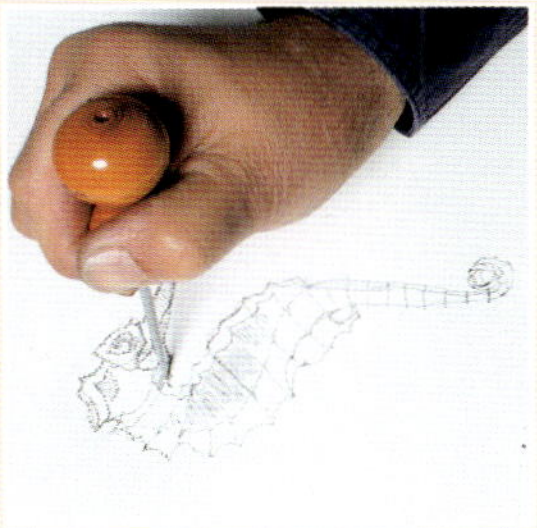

First the tracing is pricked with an awl.

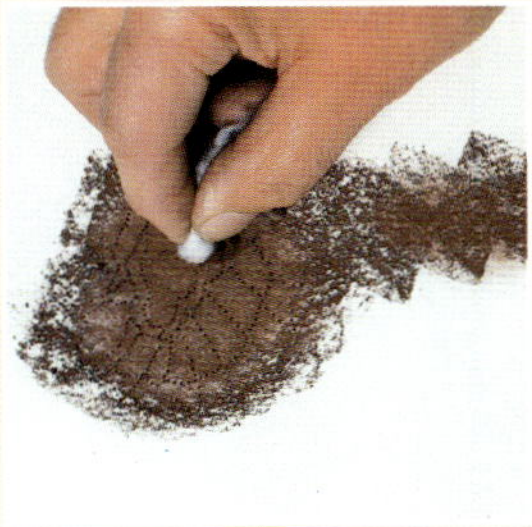

Soft pastel is rubbed through the holes.

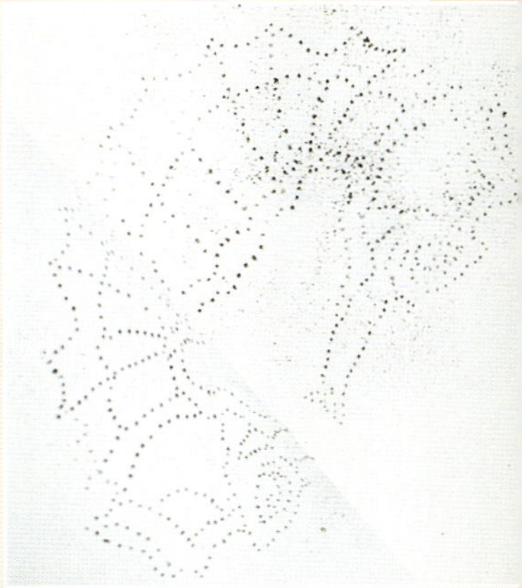

The dots are easy to follow.

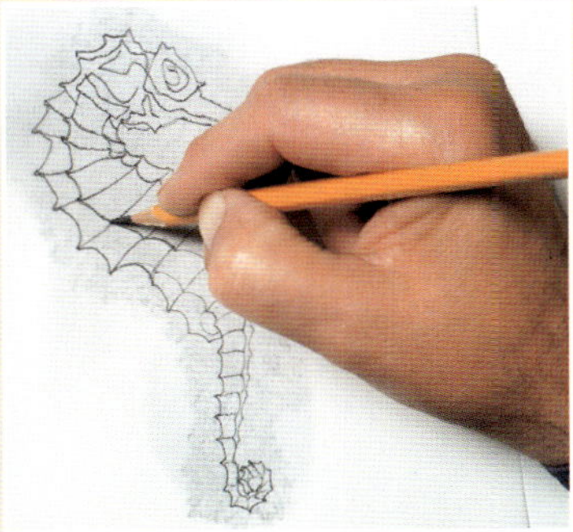

Use a hard pencil to transfer the lines.

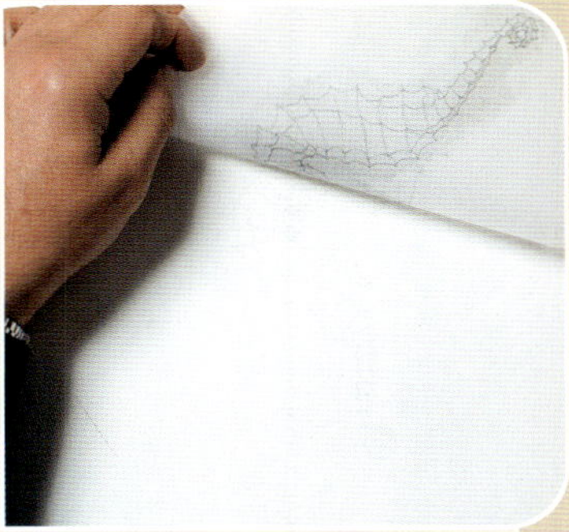

The lines will be faint but clear.

WHITE-LINE DRAWING

259

Interesting effects can be achieved by indenting the surface of the paper and then laying pastel on top, so that the indentations show as a series of white lines. Watercolor paper is best for this, as it needs to be fairly tough. Either draw "blind" onto the paper with an implement such as a knitting needle, or draw the design on tracing paper first, place it on the paper, and go over the lines with a hard pencil or ballpoint pen.

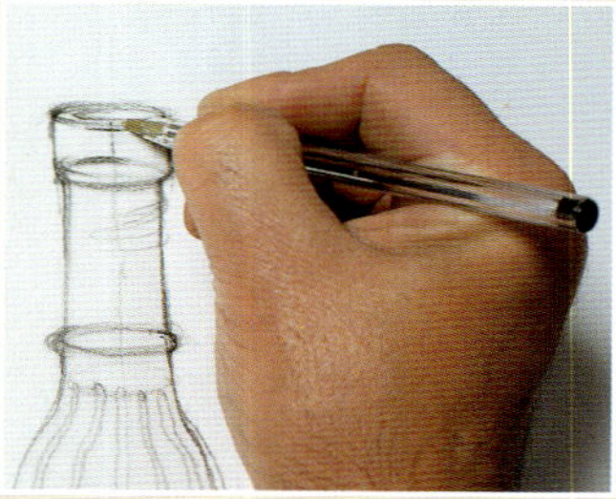

A ballpoint pen makes clear indentations.

The indented lines show up white.

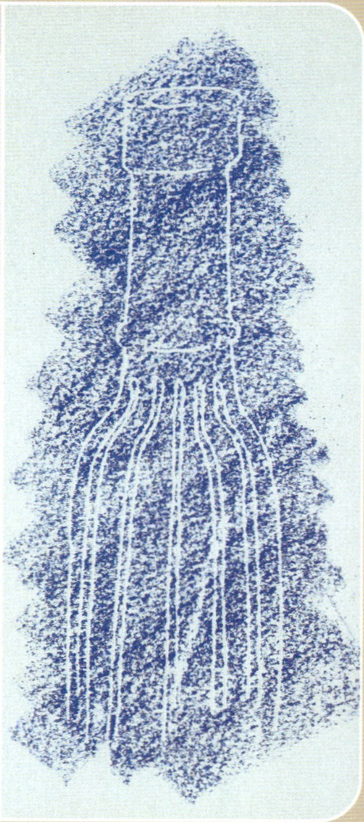

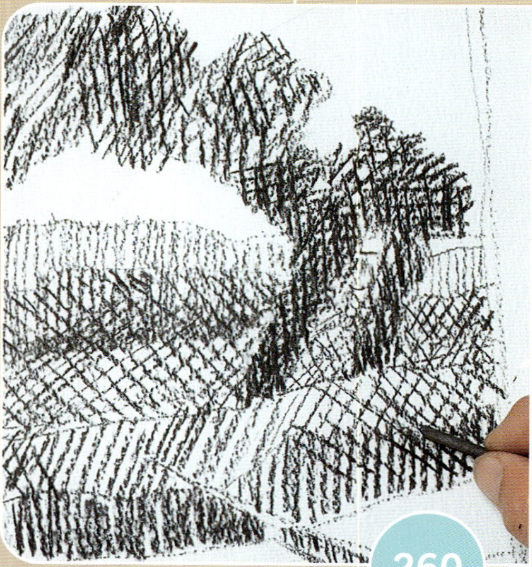

SHADOW AREAS

260

If you are creating a preliminary sketch with charcoal, light crosshatching in the shadow areas makes a useful reference for later stages of the work. Remember to brush off any excess charcoal dust or to spray on fixative before starting to apply pastels, to avoid contamination.

CHARCOAL DRAWING

261

Charcoal is a good medium with which to create your initial drawing, as its texture complements the pastel medium. Once you are ready to apply pastels, flick the drawing with a rag and most of the charcoal will fall away, leaving you with a light "ghost image" from which to work.

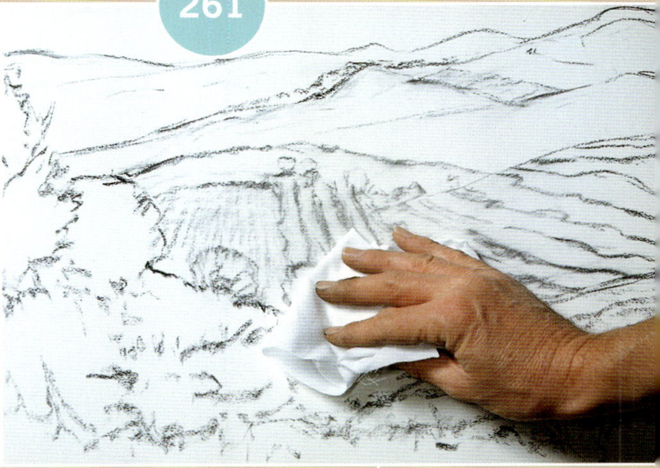

ENHANCING SHADOWS

262

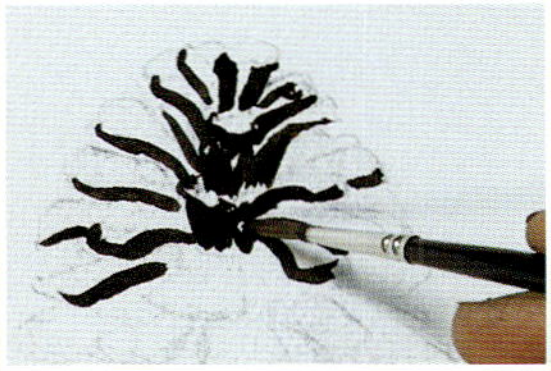

The ink is used undiluted to give a strong black.

Dark colors can be difficult to achieve in soft pastel, so, to enhance the shadow areas in the composition, try making your initial sketch in black ink. Before it is completely dry, smudge it slightly and then begin applying pastel, allowing the ink to smudge further with it.

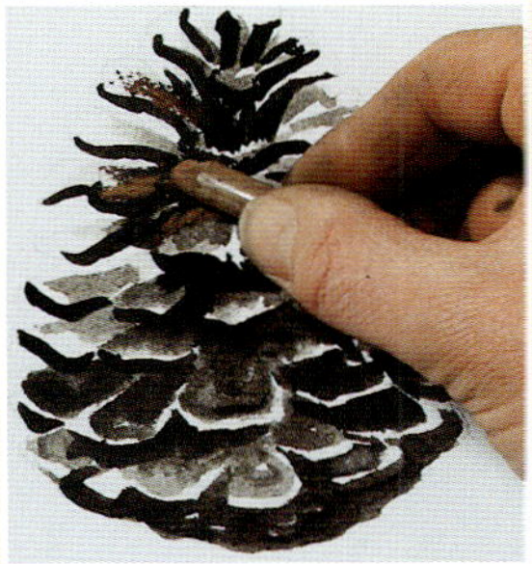

Water makes a middle tone, and then pastel is applied.

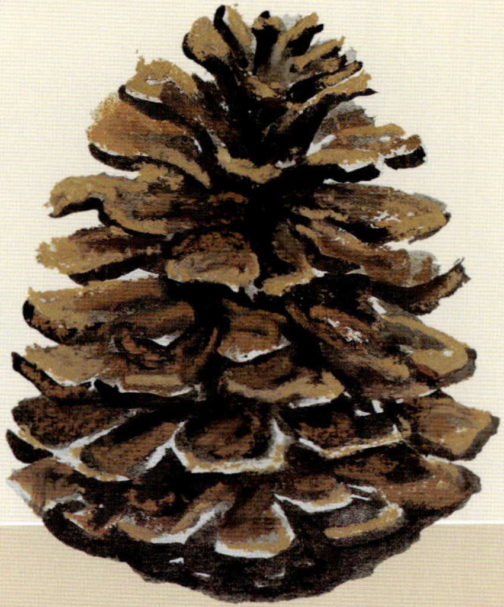

SPECIAL EFFECTS

The tips here will help you to develop your own pastel style by experimenting with different techniques. Not only will you discover how to create subtle shades by blending or dragging colors, but you can also try out some more unusual ways of working, such as wet brushing and sgraffito with oil pastel. There are also hints on how to rescue areas that may have become tired or overworked.

FEATHERING

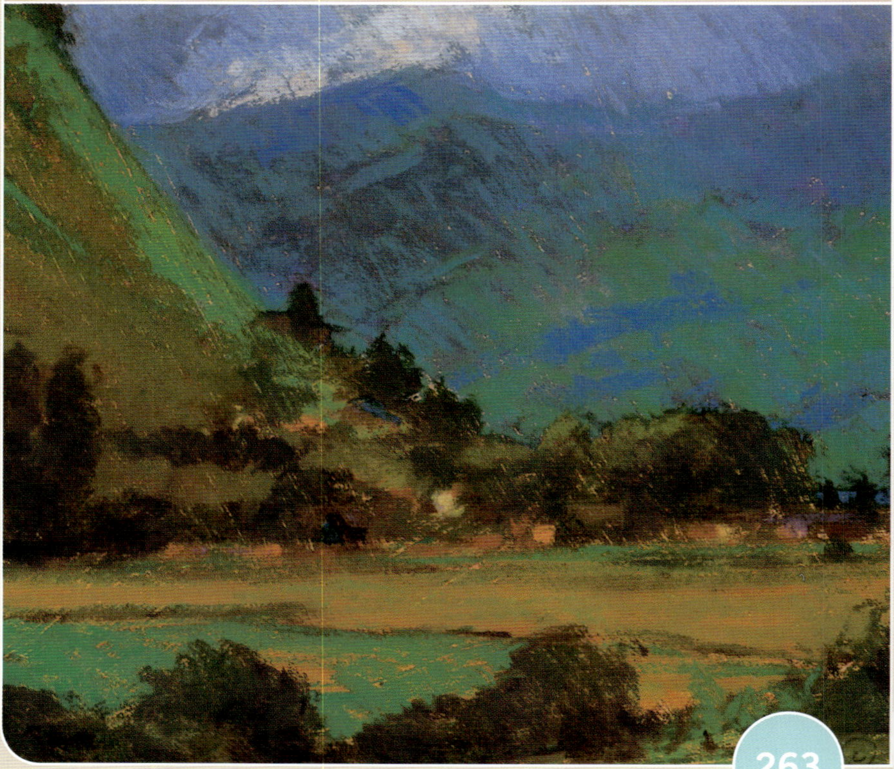

263

264

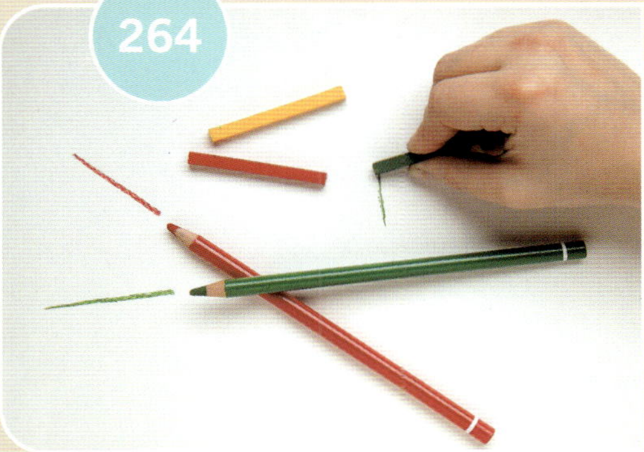

HARD PASTEL OVER SOFT

When you plan to use hard pastel or pastel pencils in the later stages of a soft-pastel painting, avoid a heavy buildup of soft pastel in the initial stages, as the hard pastel will not adhere over it and will also remove earlier working.

TONING DOWN COLORS

265

Feathering can be used to "knock back" a color that is too bright. For example, if a red looks too fiery, you can modify it by feathering over it with its complementary, green. This technique works best with a hard pastel or pastel pencil, but with a thick buildup of pigment, you may have to use soft pastel.

If you have overblended a color when working in soft pastel or oil pastel, and it has lost its vibrancy, feathering can rescue the situation. Make quick linear strokes across the overblended areas in either a lighter or darker color.

In "Outside Jackson Hole," Doug Dawson has used a version of feathering for the sky and mountains.

SOLID FORMS

266

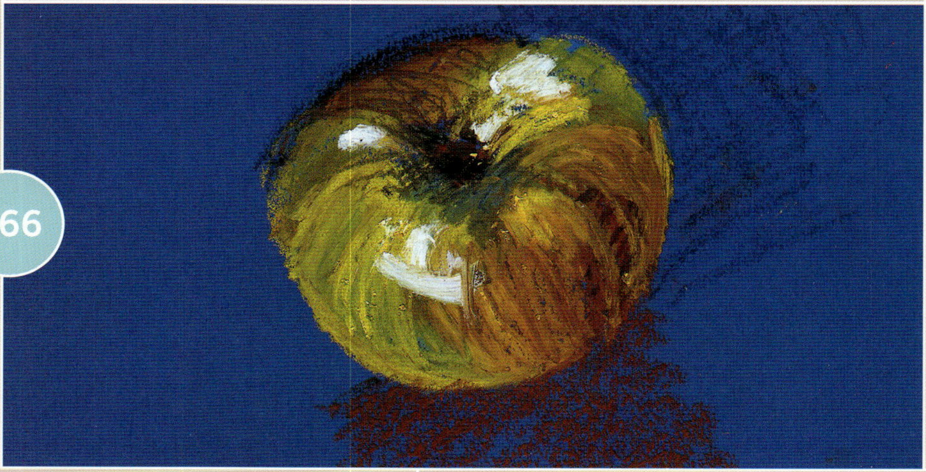

SPACE AND DEPTH

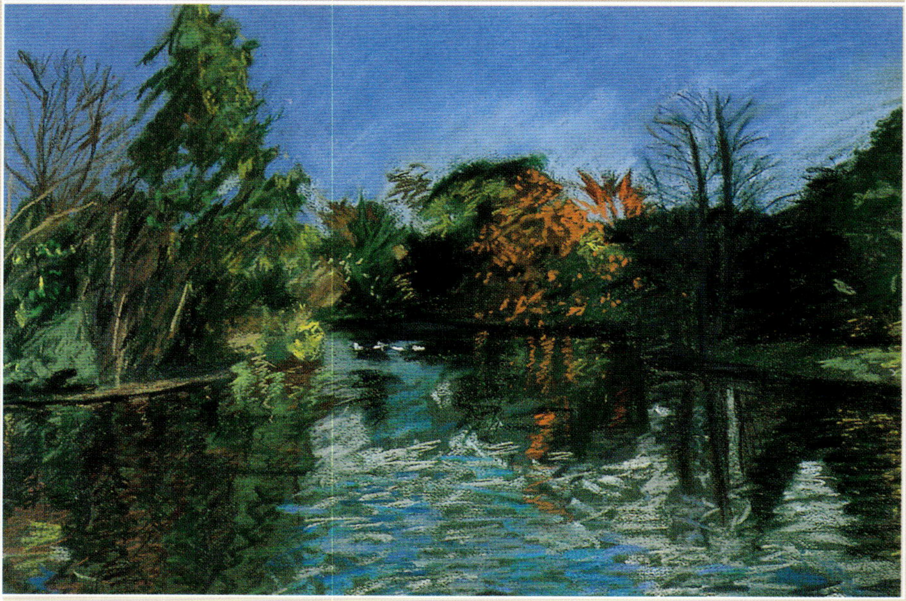

Suzie Balazs has reserved the strongest strokes for the foreground in "End of Autumn, Dulwich Park."

Do you have the problem of three-dimensional forms looking flat? If so, your strokes are probably too straight. Curved strokes that follow the form (known as bracelet shading) will reinforce the illusion of solidity.

If your paintings appear too flat, you may be using uniform marks across the entire painting surface. If this is the case, try using vivid, more definite strokes in the foreground and softer, smaller, less well-defined marks in the distance. This will greatly enhance the illusion of depth.

267

EXTREMES OF LIGHT

268

If you want to create areas of bright light or deep shadow in a painting, make sure that your marks are softened and blended.

"Celebration" (detail), by Urania Christy Tarbet.

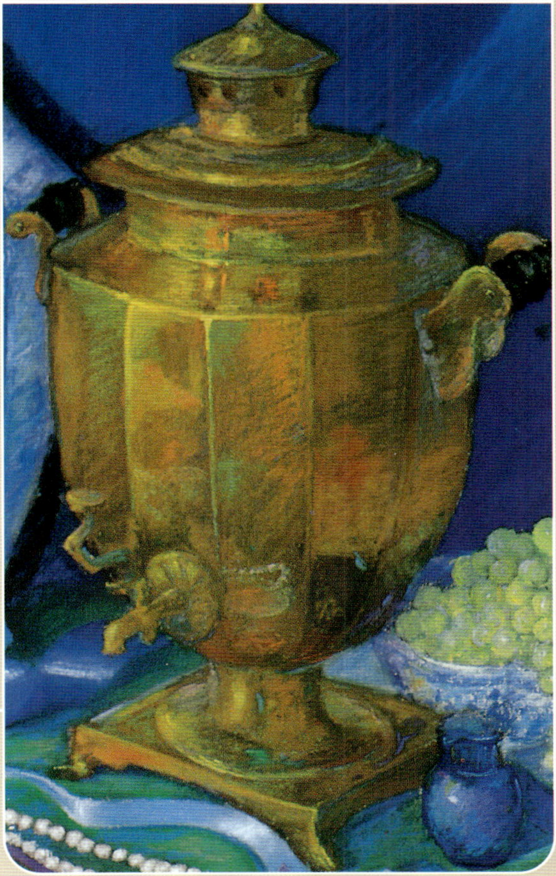

A LIVELY SURFACE

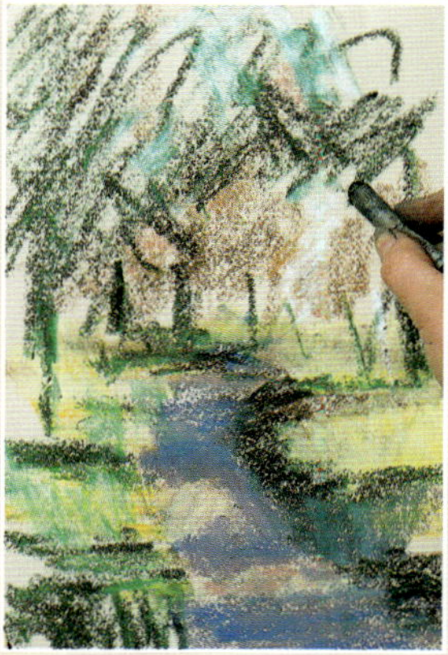

Lightly scribbled strokes, laid over side strokes.

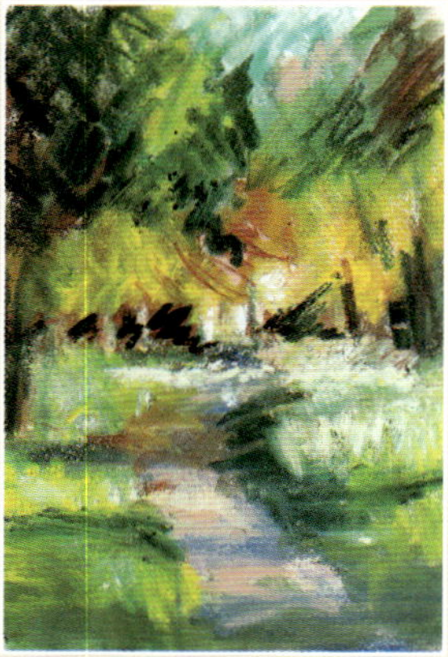

Diagonal strokes give movement to the trees.

If your work seems dull and lacking in expression, you may be applying your pastel strokes too consistently, in similar lengths and directions. Vary the direction of your strokes to counteract this.

269

EMPHASIZING A FOCAL POINT

To make a focal point—the center of interest—more powerful, render it in strong, definite strokes and surround it with softer strokes.

In Gary Michael's "Scholar" the lively use of marks not only describes texture but also means that the face is the center of interest.

270

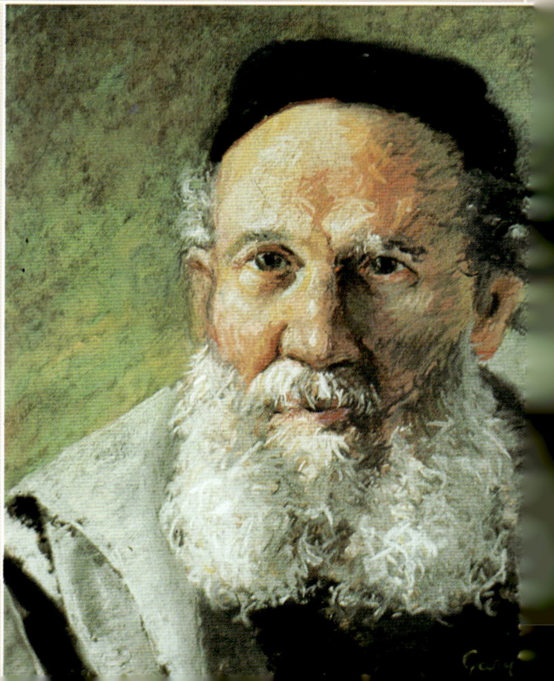

CREATING UNITY

If your work appears somewhat choppy, it could be because all your strokes vary in length and direction. For the most interesting effects, vary your strokes, but repeat each type enough to give a sense of overall consistency.

In "Afternoon, Ville Fagnan" by Debra Manifold, the marks are all of the same kind, although there is variety within the overall unity.

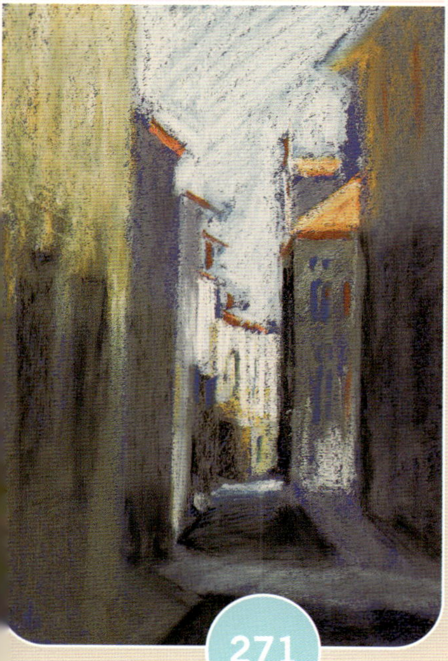

271

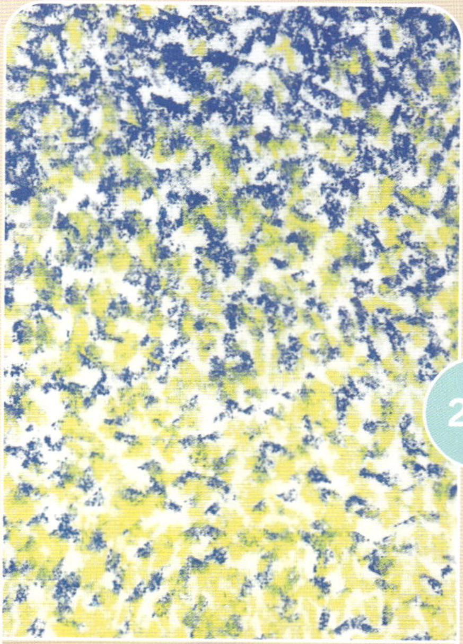

272

POINTILLIST COLOR

If you have trouble creating a sense of depth or good tonal variation when blending pastels on the paper, look at the works of Jean Edouard Vuillard, Odilon Redon, Pierre Bonnard, and Henri Matisse for examples of the pointillist technique of color mixing. The color is not always blended in their work. Instead, it is applied as individual colors in dots and dashes over the paper, and the colors mix in the eye of the viewer to create interesting surface textures and color vibrations.

QUIET COLORS

As the range of neutral mid-toned colors is limited, it can be difficult to achieve successful subtle colors and "low-key" effects in soft pastel. Try using charcoal hand-in-hand with pastel wherever you want to "knock back" the colors. In a landscape, for example, the gray-greens and blue-greens seen in the middle distance can often be achieved by laying a light veil of charcoal over pastel color. Alternatively, block in the area with charcoal first, but don't fix it; this way, you will be deliberately "polluting" the pastel color laid on top.

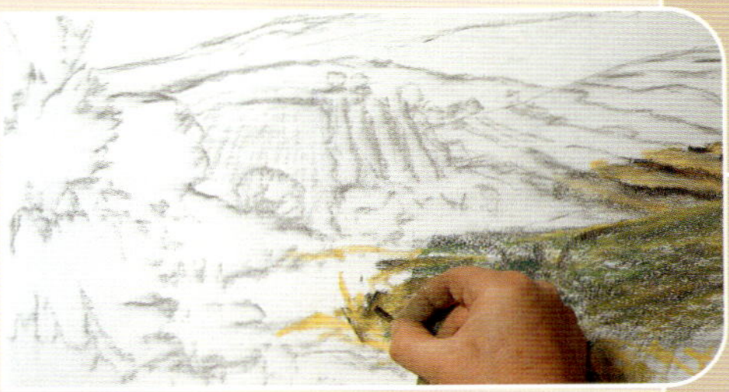

The two media blend together very well.

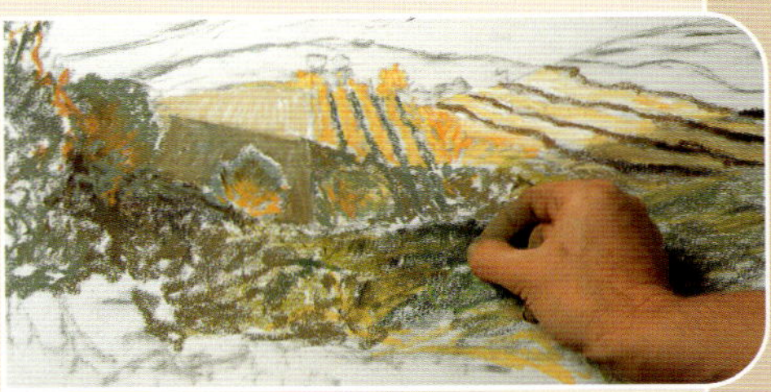

Charcoal can be used under or over soft pastel.

273

CROSSHATCHED COLOR

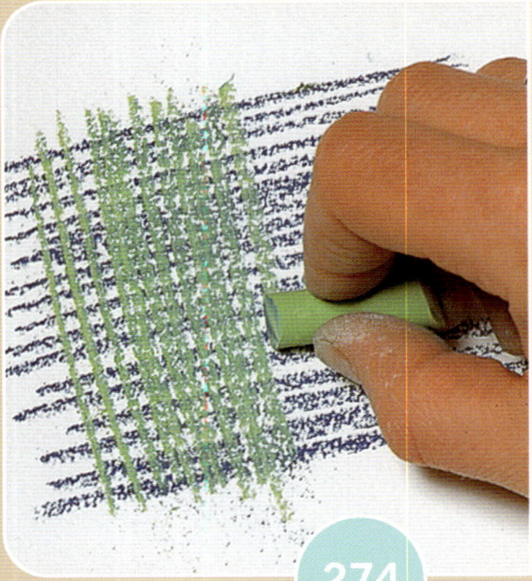

274

To create crosshatched effects, hold the first pastel color as if it were a pencil and make quick strokes in one direction. Then use the second color to make marks over and roughly at right angles to the first. Always apply the stronger color first, otherwise the overlapping color will obliterate the color underneath. For instance, if you apply pale green with strong blue over it, the green will disappear.

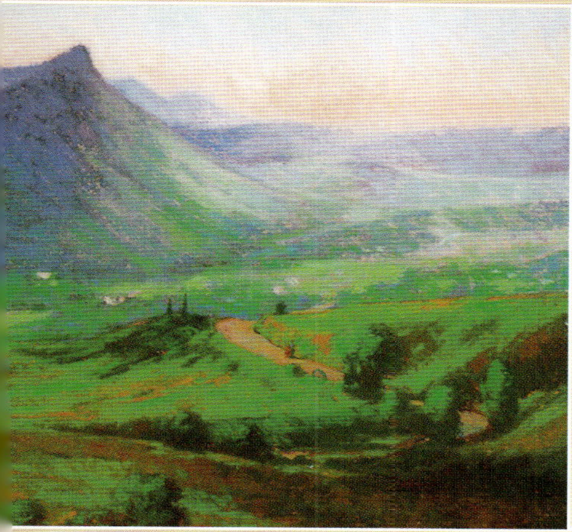

DRAGGED COLOR

When dragging one color over another, put down the first color with firm pressure, and then drag the second color across it very lightly, using the side of the stick. This creates a light veil of color, which modifies the original one while leaving it partially visible.

In "View Over Morrison" Doug Dawson makes extensive use of dragged color, particularly in the distant mountains.

275

WET-BRUSHED COLOR

276

Soft pastel consists almost entirely of pure pigment, so it can be spread with water in a very similar way to powder paints. A technique that is often used either to soften pastel strokes or to cover large areas of the paper quickly is wet brushing, in which a soft brush is dipped into clean water and then washed over the pastel. This can create attractive effects in a painting, as it releases some of the color to form a watercolor like wash, while leaving the pastel strokes intact.

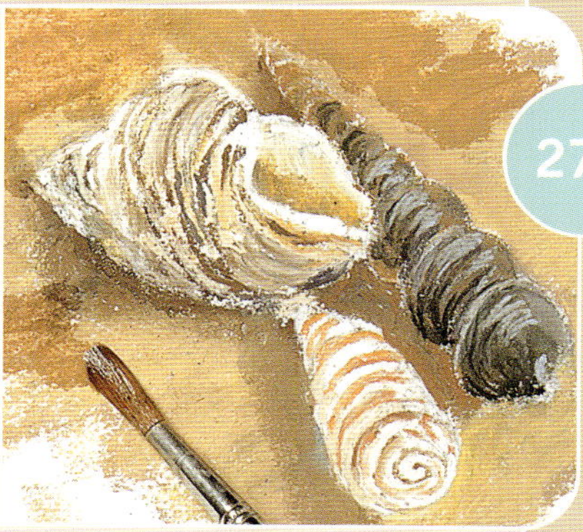

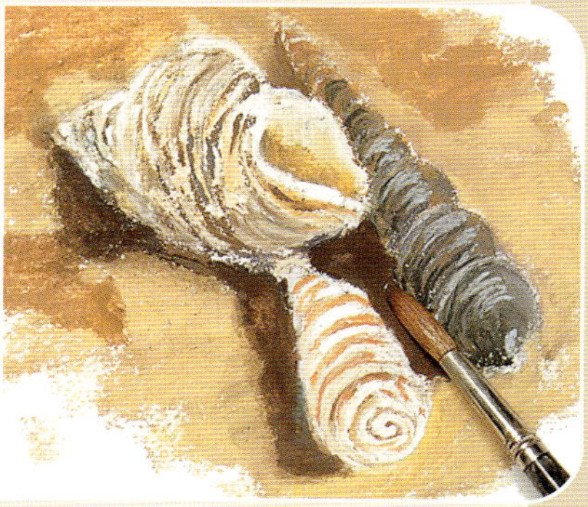

Soft pastel is almost pure pigment, which is released and spread by adding water.

BLENDING SOFT PASTEL

277

If you want to achieve a smooth effect in a painting, or subtle gradations of tone and color, blending is the answer. For large areas, lay the pastel down lightly and then rub over it with a rag or your hand. Several colors can be laid one on top of another and blended to produce a mixture on the paper surface. For smaller areas, the traditional blending implement is a torchon—a tight roll of paper made for the purpose—but you can also use cotton swabs. Remember that you will not be able to blend to any great extent on sandpaper or velour paper.

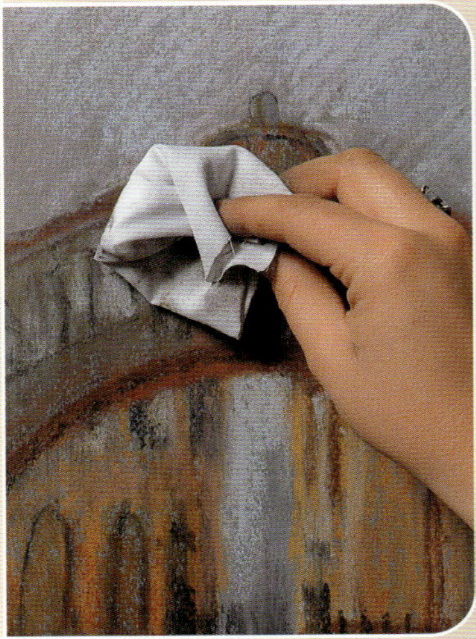

BLENDING OIL PASTEL

Oil pastels cannot be rubbed into each other as easily as soft pastels, but you can blend just as successfully if you "melt" the color with mineral spirits. For large areas, lay down the colors and go over them with a brush or rag dipped in mineral spirits. For smaller areas, use a spirit-moistened small brush, a cotton swab, a torchon, or your finger.

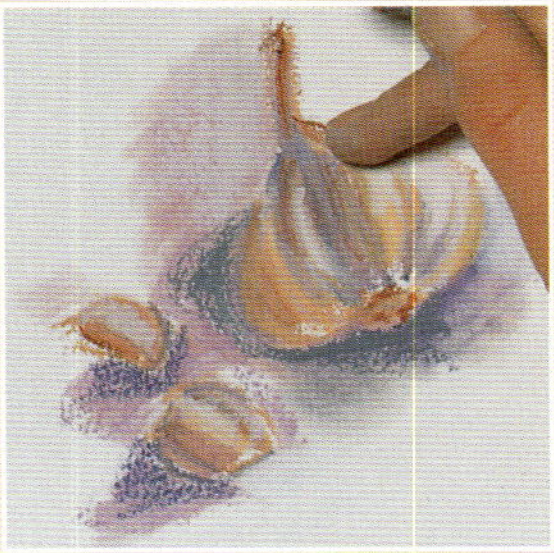

Colors are blended with mineral spirits.

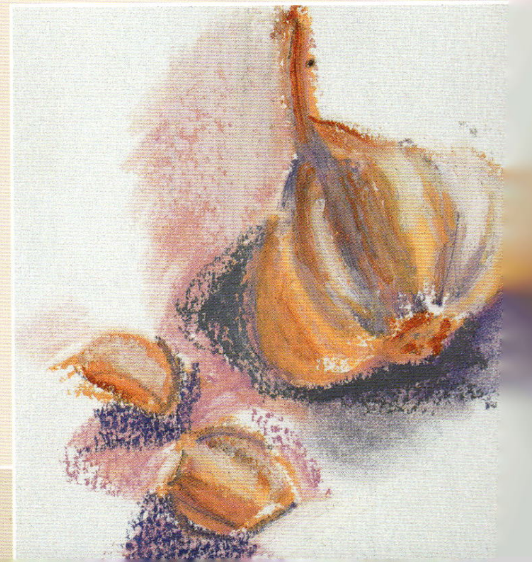

Soft gradations of tone can be achieved.

278

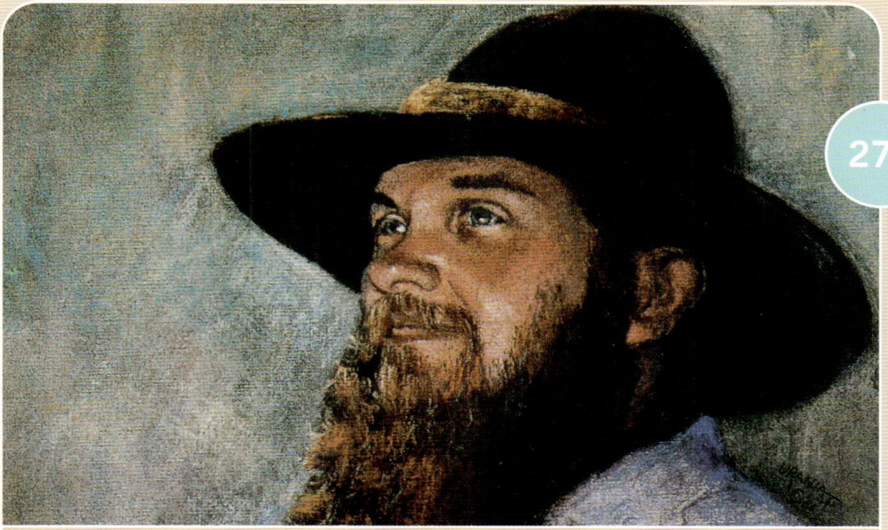

279

SHARP EDGES

It can be difficult to create sharp edges with pastel, as it smudges so easily. A good technique for dealing with this is to work on the color areas on each side of the edge simultaneously, pushing the colors up against each other.

For "The Sod Buster" (detail), Urania Christy Tarbet has worked on canvas to reduce smudging.

CLEAR OUTLINES

You can use the edge of a sheet of paper as a mask while you work. Lift the paper up carefully to avoid disrupting the outline once you have applied the necessary pastel.

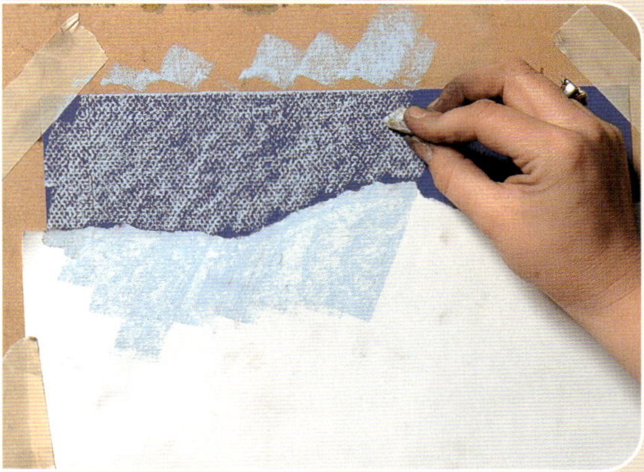

280

PENCILS AND STICKS

281

Pastel pencils cut to very sharp points, used in conjunction with pastel sticks, are very good for emphasizing sharp edges and adding definition to outlines.

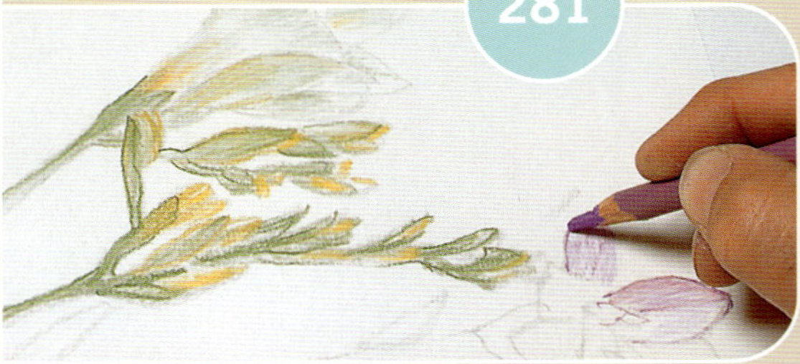

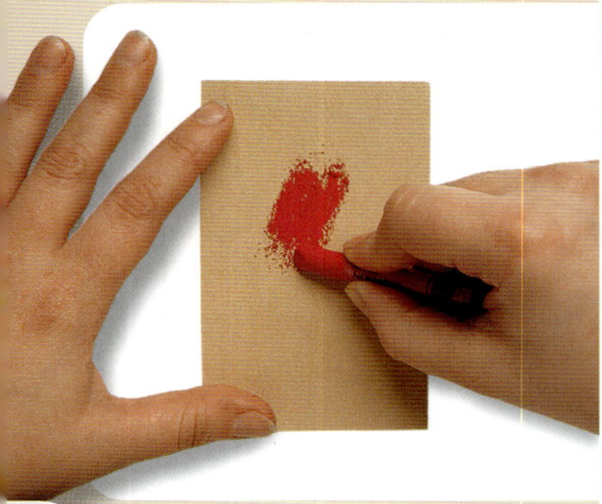

SHARPENING SOFT PASTELS

282

To make fine lines with soft pastels you can either break a stick in half and use the side of the broken edge, or sharpen the tip itself by rubbing it gently on a piece of sandpaper. Leave this kind of fine-line detail to the last stages of a painting, since there is a risk of smudging.

PENCIL TECHNIQUES

283

If you have trouble creating, crosshatching, or feathering with sticks of soft pastel, try using pastel pencils or hard pastels in these areas. Because of their length and resistance to snapping, they give you greater control, and your hands stay clean!

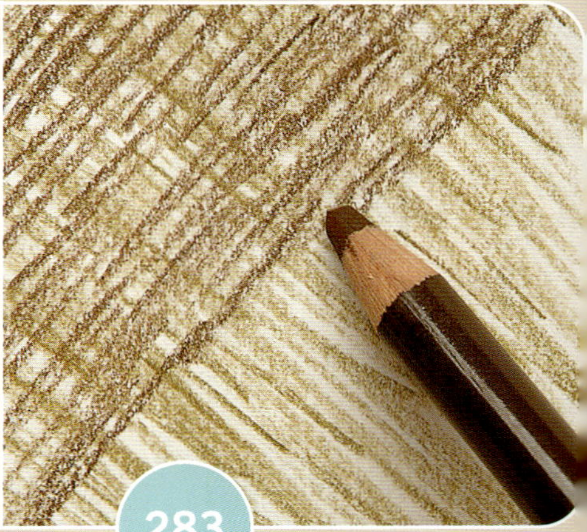

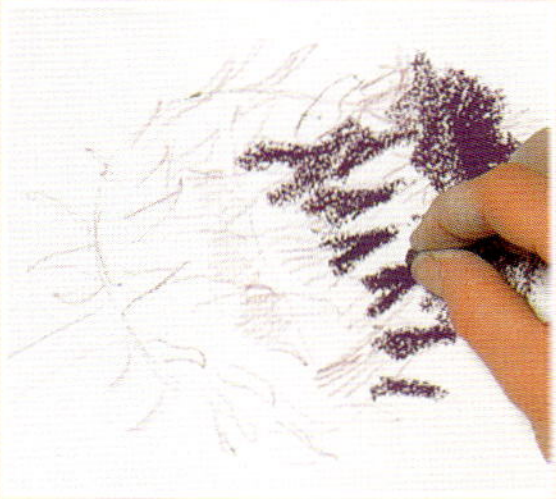
The layers of oil pastel are applied.

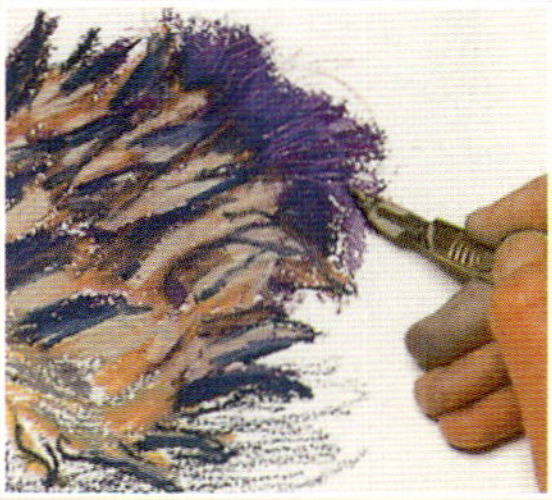
The point of a mat knife makes very fine lines.

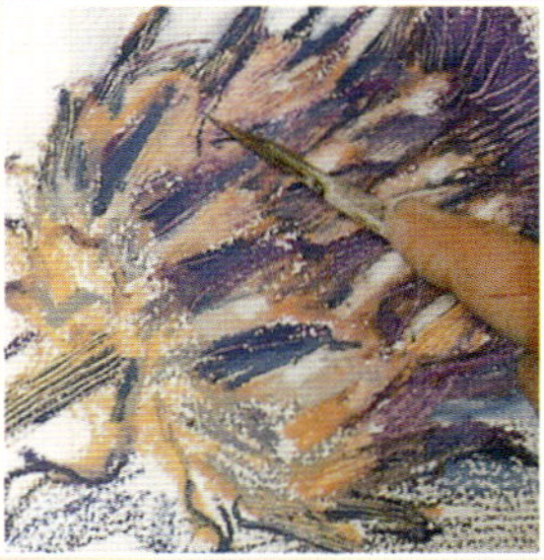
The effect varies with the pressure applied.

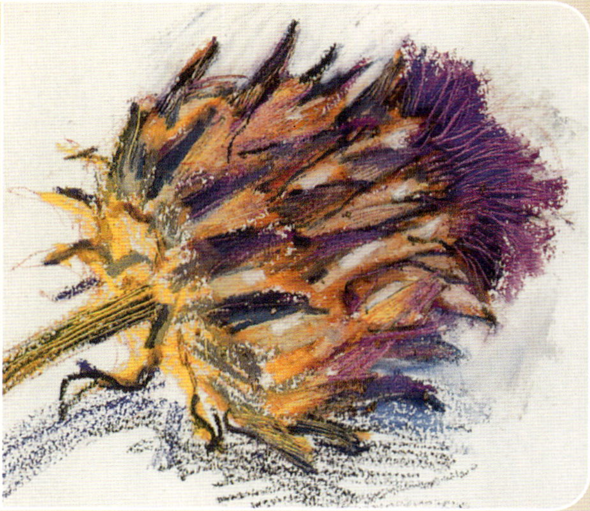
Sgraffito is ideal for a delicate subject that needs fine lines.

284

In oil pastel, highlights and various color effects are often achieved by scratching into one color to reveal another one below. The method involves covering the paper, or a selected area, with a solid layer of color, well rubbed into the paper grain, before laying another on top. This also needs to be quite heavy, but should not be rubbed in. Any sharp implement can then be used to draw or scrape into the top layer of color. A fine point, such as the tip of a mat knife, will obviously give fine lines, but you can also achieve interesting broken-color effects by scraping gently with the side of a knife, which removes the color from the top of the grain only. The method can also be used in soft pastel, but you must work on a solid surface, such as pastel board. Make sure that you fix the first layer of color before putting on the second.

HOMEMADE TORCHONS

285

Try making your own torchons for blending detailed areas. Take a toothpick and a small piece of paper towel. Soak the towel in water and then roll it around the stick, without letting the paper protrude too far beyond the points of the stick. The paper will shrink as it dries to form a tight covering, without the need for any further adhesion. When the torchon becomes dirty in use, simply pull off the paper and re-use the stick. Homemade torchons can be used dry with soft pastels, or dipped in mineral spirits or turpentine to blend details in oil-pastel painting.

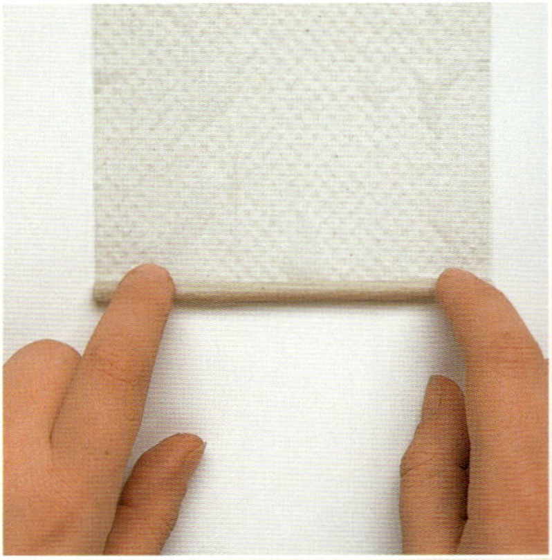

Damp paper towel is wound onto a toothpick

SOFT-FOCUS EFFECTS

To create very soft, out-of-focus paintings, you can blur the outlines of images using your finger, a tissue, or a rag. Edouard Manet did this to give the impression of out-of-focus photographs, which were in vogue at that time.

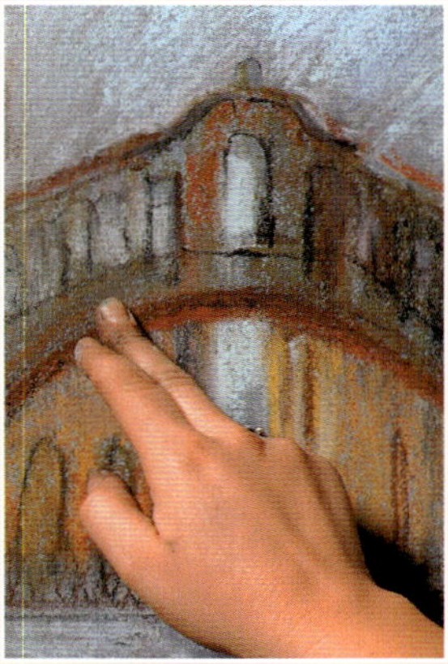

Unwanted edges can be softened with a finger.

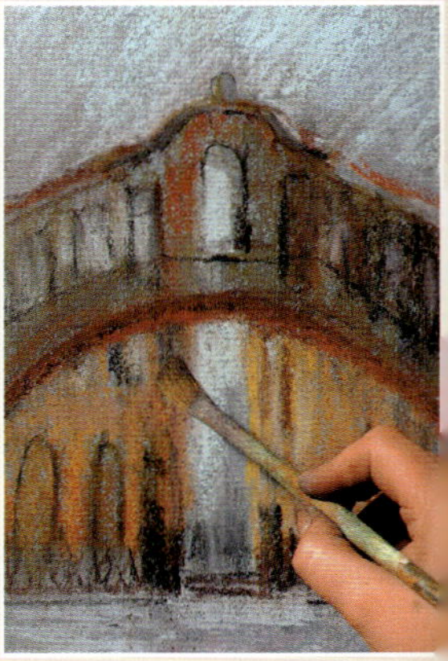

For larger areas, a bristle brush or rag can be used.

286

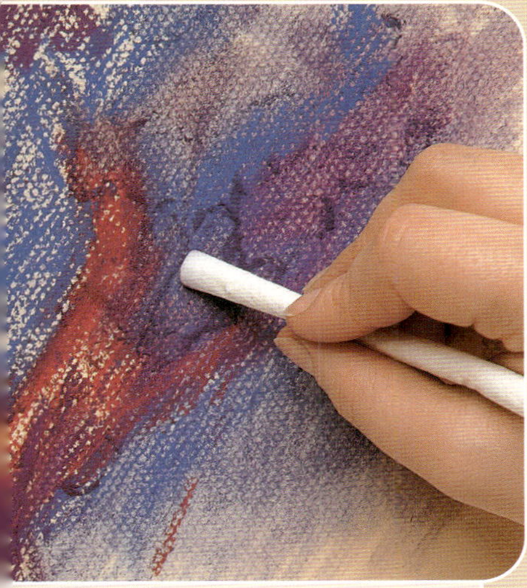

The homemade torchon is used for blending.

CREATING TEXTURE

287

To achieve a textured effect, perhaps for distant clumps of trees, dab into soft pastels with a fingertip or small cotton ball. For a more pronounced effect, dip your finger or the cotton ball into water first. The same method can be employed with oil pastels, but using mineral spirits instead of water.

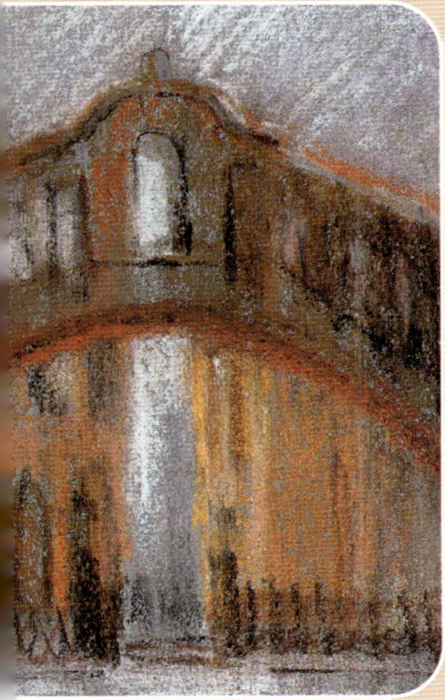

The overall effect is gentle and atmospheric.

APPLYING DETAILS

When applying details over pastel work that has used up the grain of the paper, the additional pastel will not adhere. To overcome this, try dipping your pastels in water and working over the top quite heavily.

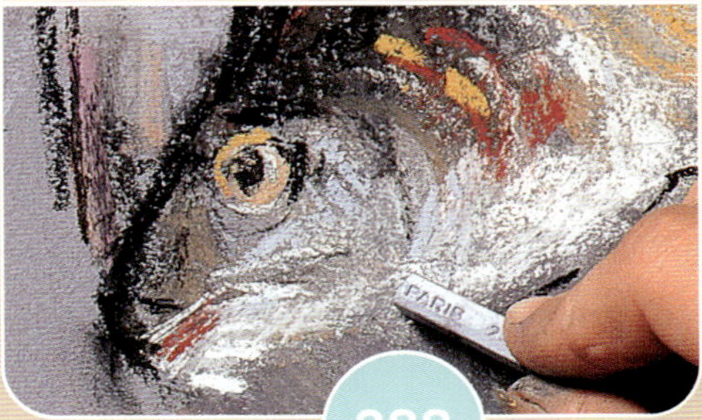

288

289 FIXATIVE AS MEDIUM

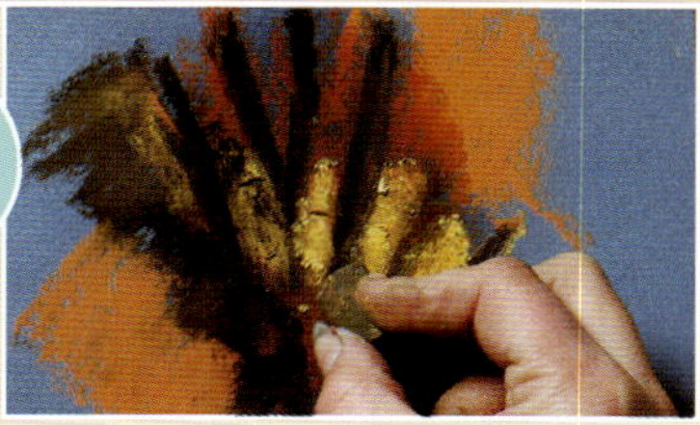

Having sprayed the first pastel application with fixative, further pastel is worked on top.

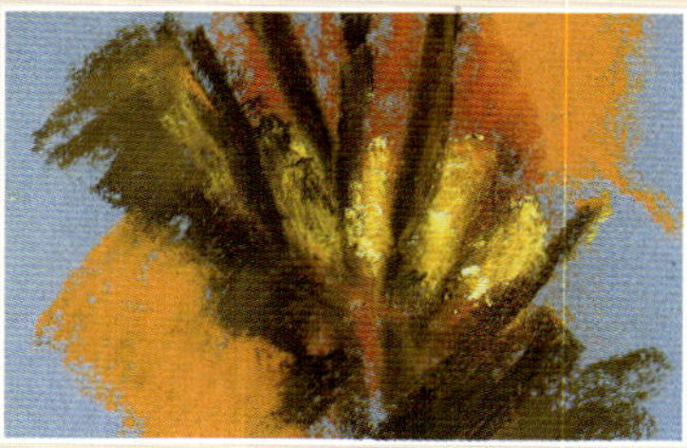

Pastel and fixative resembles oil pastel.

To create unusual surface textures, try using fixative in a positive way and mixing it with soft pastel. You can do this either by spraying the paper and then working into it with pastel while the fixative is still wet, or by spraying existing color quite heavily and then working into it with brushes or more pastel.
A more extreme approach is to dip a brush into fixative and work over pastel. Edgar Degas used to make a kind of paste with his pastels in a similar way, although no one is sure of his precise methods.

290 STEAMING THE SURFACE

Edgar Degas invented a technique of steaming soft pastel in certain areas of a work. This created a paste that could then be worked over with a brush, extending the repertoire of possible surface textures. If you want to experiment with this, work on stretched paper so that it does not buckle when it becomes damp from the steam.

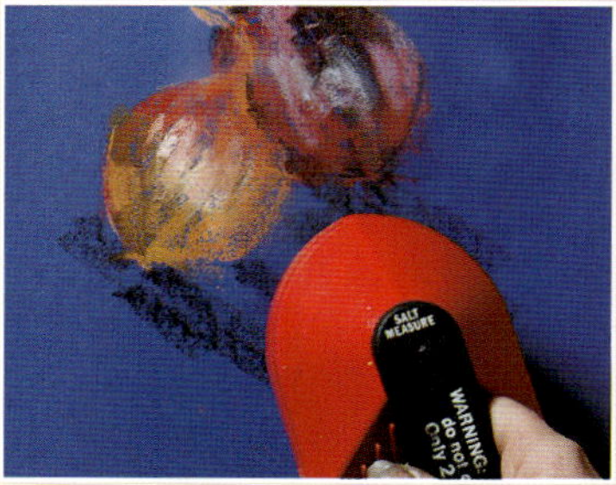

A tailor's steamer wets the pastel and paper. (Below) The damp pastel is then spread with a brush.

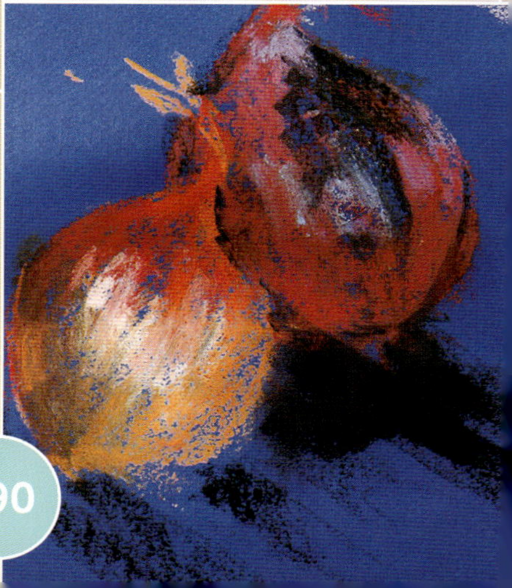

HIGHLIGHTS

Creating highlights is an important part of successful pastel painting. As pastel is an opaque medium, light colors can be laid over dark ones, so it is sometimes possible to leave the highlights until last and to concentrate on the darks first. Take care with last-minute highlights, however, particularly if you have used the pastel thickly, or the highlights may become muddied through mixing with the layers of color beneath.

291

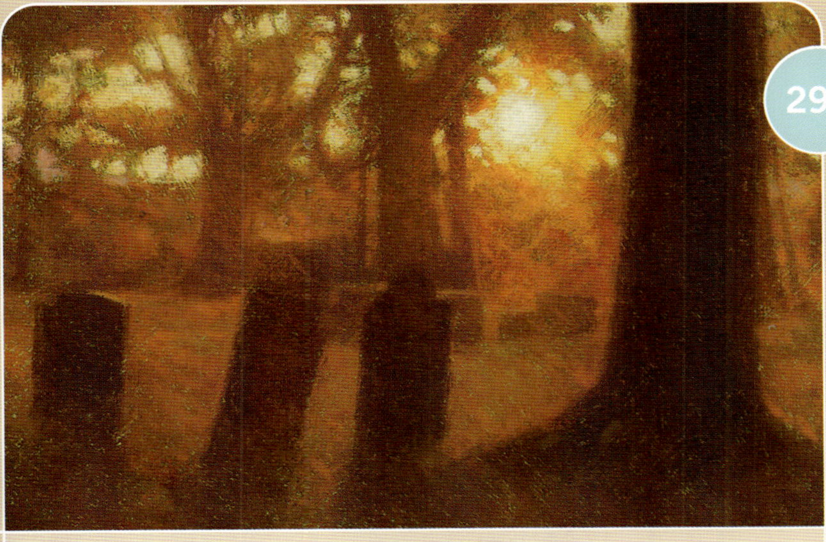

DARKS FIRST

Don't add light colors during the early stages of a painting. If you use the lights too freely or too soon, you will find it difficult to get the darks dark enough, and the painting will become pale and washed-out. Spend time getting shadows and mid-tones right first.

In "The Graveyard," Doug Dawson has painted patches of light sky over and around the middle tones.

HIGHLIGHTS GUIDE

292

If your subject has large, definite highlight areas, such as white buildings in a landscape, map them out in white pastel pencil so that you can develop them later in the work.

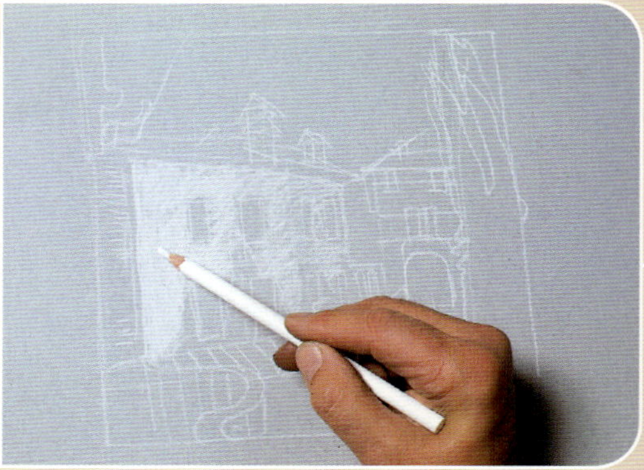

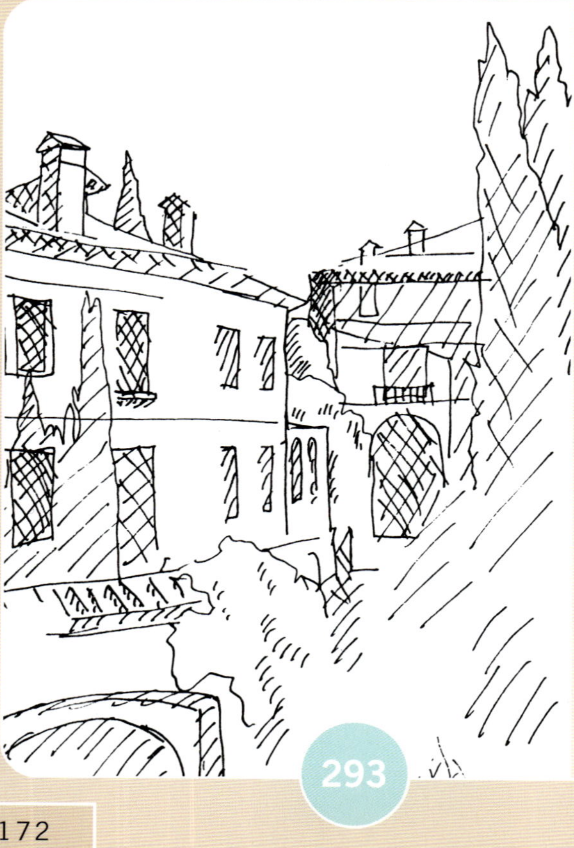

CHANGING LIGHT

When working outdoors, remember that, as time moves on, the direction of the light changes, altering the highlights. Make a note of the direction of the light falling on your view before you begin, and stick to that throughout the painting. This will prevent you from producing conflicting highlights and shadows. If you have time, work on a painting at the same time over several days in order to record the effect of the light more accurately.

293

FIXING

There is constant argument about the use of fixative in pastel-painting circles. Some artists avoid it altogether, claiming that it spoils the freshness of the colors; some fix at regular intervals as they work, but leave the completed picture unfixed; and others fix only at the final stage. If you do like to use fixative, but find it difficult, the following tips explain how to achieve the best results.

DIFFUSERS

294

If you use a mouth diffuser to apply fixative to a soft-pastel painting, you probably find that it clogs easily. If you pass a thin piece of wire through the diffuser after each use, this will clean the passage for the next time.

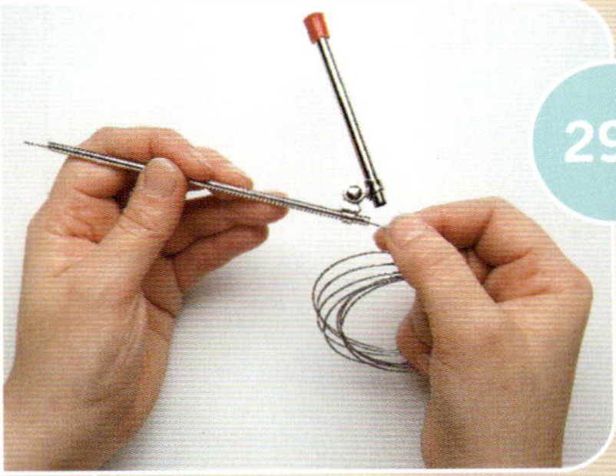

NON-SPRAY FIXING

295

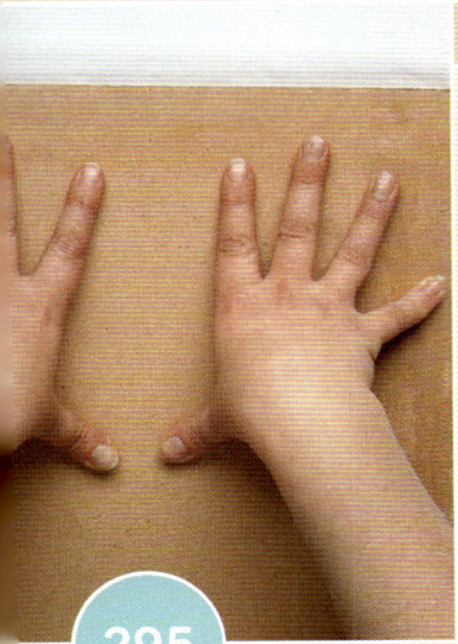

Many artists find that fixative alters the color and texture of a soft-pastel painting. An effective alternative to the use of fixative is to lay a sheet of tissue paper or cellophane over the painting, cover it with a board, and apply pressure. The pressure will push the pastel particles more firmly into the grain of the paper without affecting the surface. Be careful that you do not apply too much pressure, however, as this will alter the surface textures of the painting.

KEEPING COLORS BRIGHT

If you like to fix your work, but are disappointed by the dulling effect created by fixative, spray it on during the painting process but before you add the final layer of color or highlights. In this way, the finished work will retain its freshness.

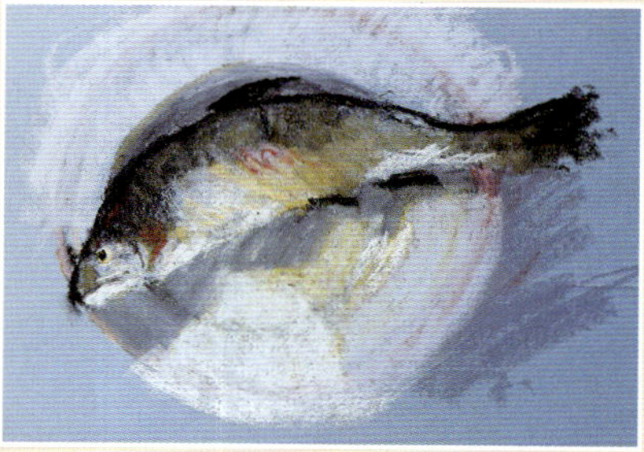

This picture is at the halfway stage, with colors laid over one another quite thickly.

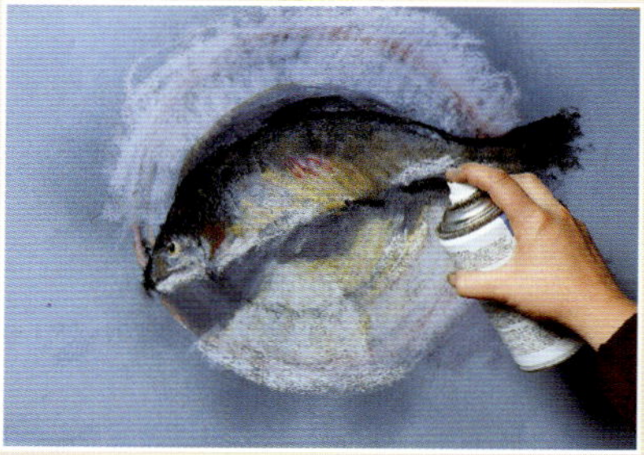

Fixative is applied in order to prevent the new colors from mixing with earlier ones.

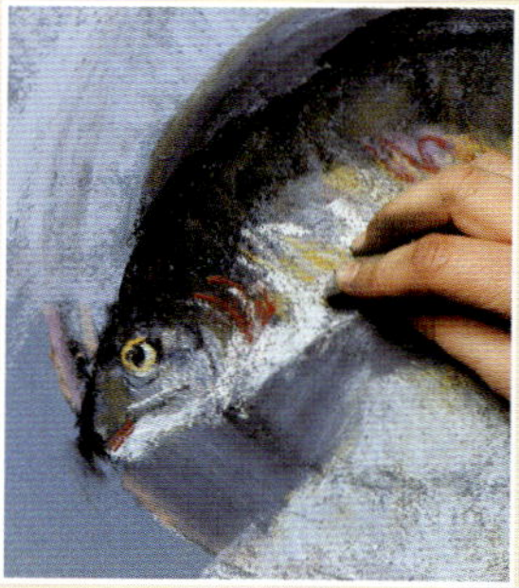

The white can now safely be applied over the other colors.

The final colors are left unfixed to retain their freshness.

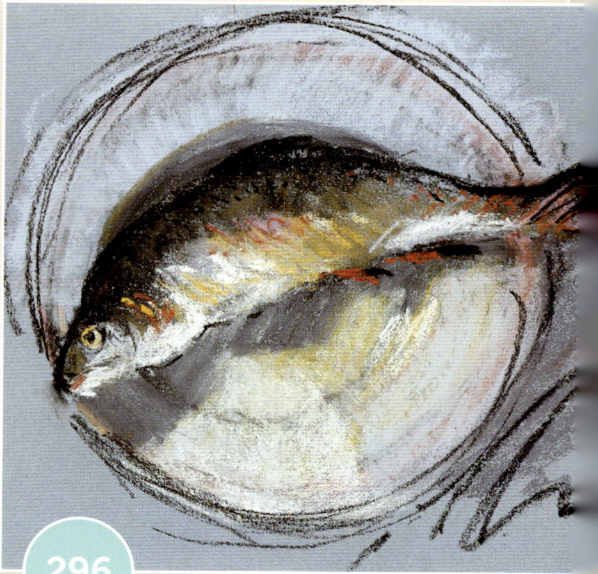

296

FIXING FROM THE BACK

297

To avoid overspraying a painting with fixative, try spraying the back of the paper. The fixative will soak through and dampen the pastel to hold it in place, but will not disturb the surface of the work. If you are using absorbent paper, this is a better way of fixing than spraying a skin of fixative over unstable pigment.

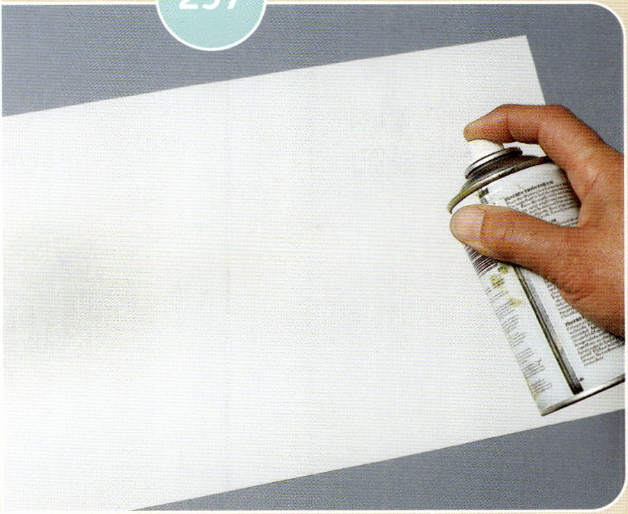

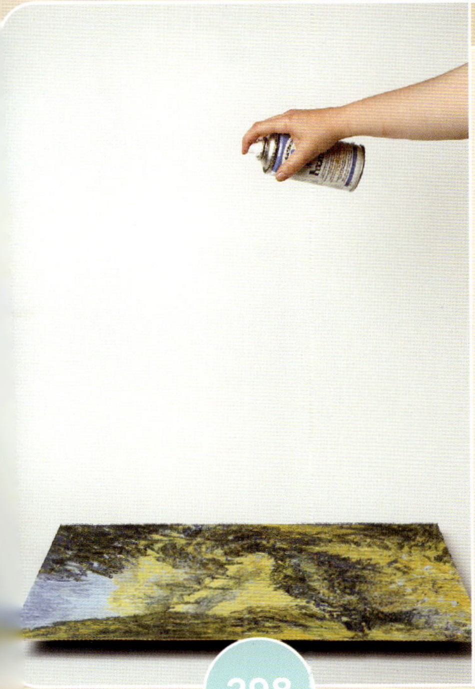

298

PERFECT FIXING

If you consistently overspray your paintings, perhaps you are standing too close to the work. Stand at least 2 feet (60cm) away from your picture and begin spraying from outside the picture plane. Work back and forth across the painting with a slow, controlled motion, always going beyond the edge of the painting before stopping. You should apply a fine, even spray, and keep your arm moving all the time so that the spray does not build up in one spot. Too much fixative in one spot will create dark patches or drip down the work.

ALTERING AND ERASING

Beginners can sometimes find early attempts at pastel rather nerve-racking because they have been told that it is not possible to erase. Although it is true that you cannot rub out the marks as you would a pencil drawing, there are ways to erase, as you will see from the tips that follow. And there really is no need to worry, because you can easily work over wrong lines and colors if you brush off the loose pigment first.

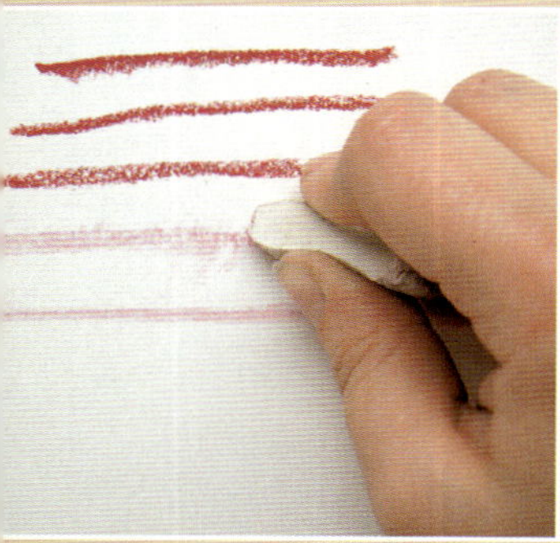

USING A PLASTIC ERASER

Pastel cannot be erased completely, and if you try to rub out unwanted marks with a standard eraser you will damage the paper and lose the surface texture. However, if you use a kneaded plastic eraser in a gentle dabbing motion, you will be able to remove most of the pigment, leaving a faint "ghost" line that you can then work over.

299

ERASING WITH BREAD

A small piece of kneaded fresh white bread makes a very effective alternative to a plastic eraser.

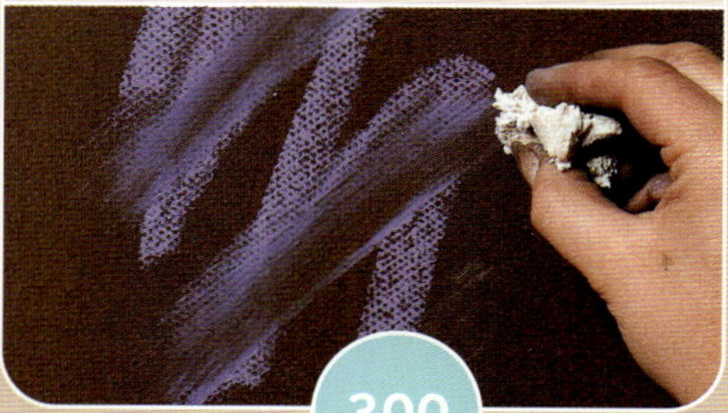

300

UNWANTED MARKS

Try using a stiff hoghair brush to remove unwanted pastel marks. This makes a very good substitute if you do not have an eraser on hand.

301

RE-USING PAPER

If you give up on a picture, don't waste the paper. Apply a wash of acrylic paint over the painting and allow it to dry, and you will find that new pastel will work well over it. This is only possible on papers that do not buckle, such as heavy-grade watercolor papers. The acrylic paint will mix with the pastel as you apply it, creating a tint upon which to work.

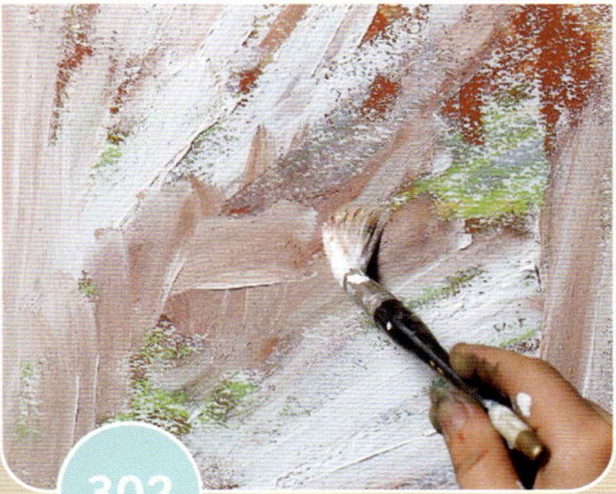

302

MINOR ALTERATIONS

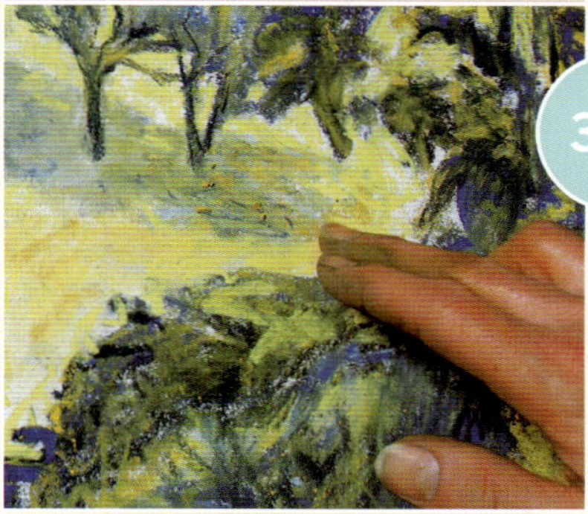

303

To make very small alterations to a soft pastel painting without damaging the surface of your work, try making short, dabbing strokes with your finger. This does not have the same effect as rubbing the area. Alternate the direction of these strokes to mirror the direction used to apply the pastel in the first place.

ERASING OIL PASTEL

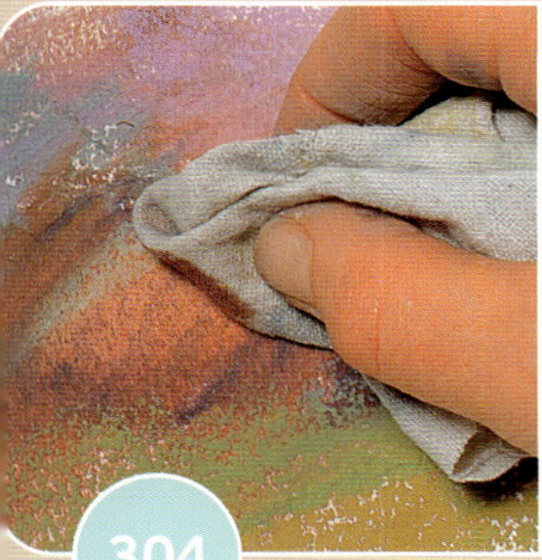

304

One of the joys of oil pastel is that mistakes can be rectified very easily. Instead of an eraser, simply moisten a cotton ball with mineral spirits and wipe off the color. You can remove it quite cleanly, and the spirits will not harm the picture surface because it evaporates almost immediately.

TRANSFERRING THE IMAGE

If you are happy with the structure of a soft-pastel image that you have drawn, but have overworked it and cannot rectify the errors, try a technique often used by Degas. Soak a new piece of paper in water and let it drain. Then place it firmly over your existing picture; make sure that it does not move at all once placed down. Rub the back of the paper firmly with your hand or a damp sponge. Then lift it gently off the picture, and you will have lightly transferred the image onto the new piece of paper, albeit in reverse. Tape it to a board and allow it to dry, so that the paper does not buckle. You can then start work on the image again.

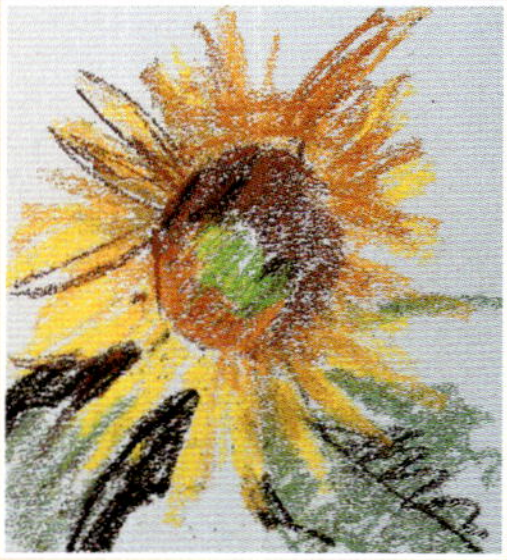
The image to be transferred is on watercolor paper.

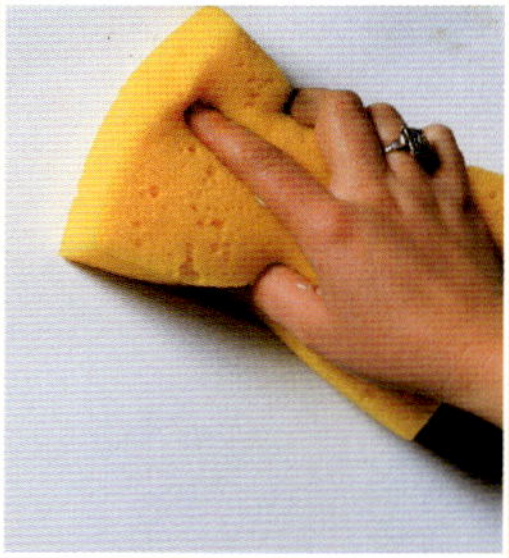
A sheet of the same paper is placed on top and dampened.

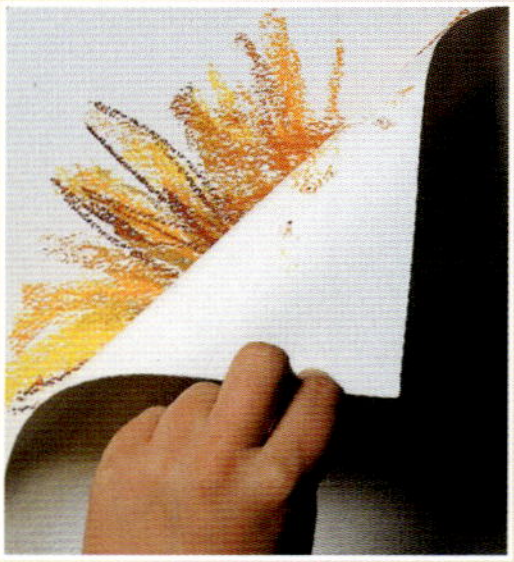
The top sheet is lifted away from the painting.

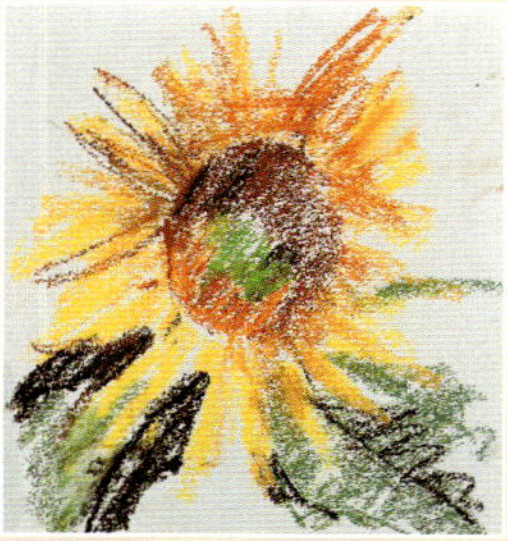
The original image is unchanged.

And a reversed version of it appears.

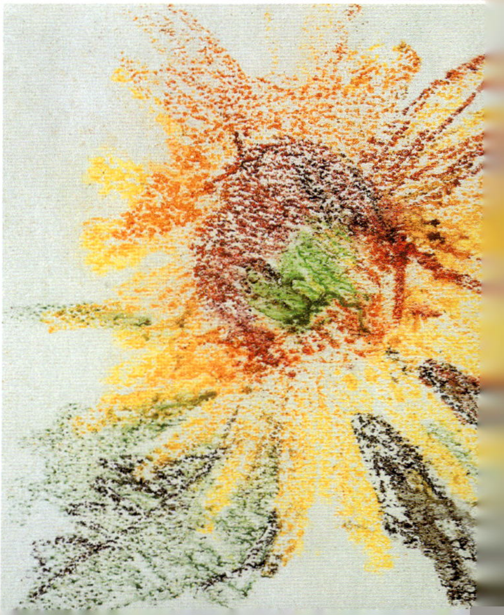

305

TRAVEL

It can be hard to decide what you will need when you are setting off to paint in a new place. The colors of the scenery may be quite different from those to which you are accustomed, so which pastels do you take, and what color paper? It is best to take the minimum—don't forget that colors can be mixed, and paper tinted. Make sure, too, that you have a supply of tissue paper to protect your work.

STAYING CLEAN

306

Carry some wet wipes with you when pastel painting on location so that you can clean your hands whenever necessary. If you are working with oil pastels, take rags and a bottle of mineral spirits.

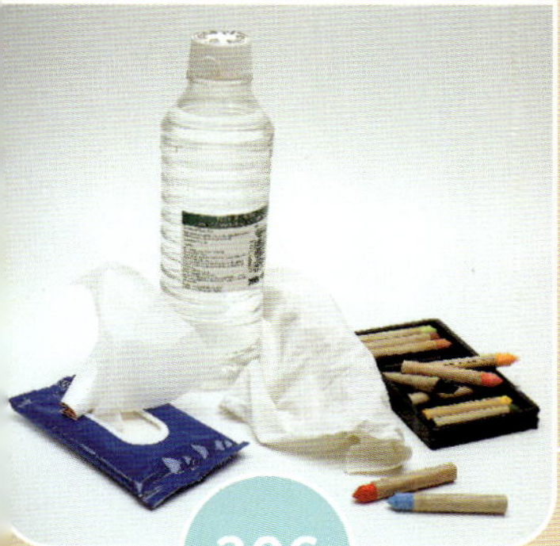

PROTECTING YOUR WORK

307

When working away from home, take some acid-free tissue paper to place between your paintings to prevent them smudging while in transit.

NON-AEROSOL FIXATIVES

308

When traveling, you may not be allowed to take aerosol fixative on an airplane for safety reasons. Hairspray, which is now available in non-aerosol containers, makes a cheap and satisfactory alternative, or you could take a bottle of fixative and a diffuser instead.

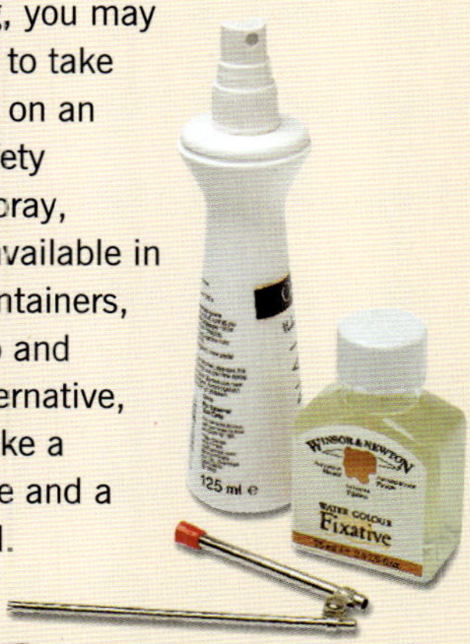

309

TRAVEL KIT

Always keep a travel set of materials ready for expeditions. This should include everything you need for working outdoors when the wind blows, including clips and masking tape. Take only the very basic range of colors. This is a good discipline and means that you don't carry unnecessary colors with you. While the exact color may not be in your box, you can always make a note to the effect that the real tone is sharper or softer, or closer to another color, for later work back in the studio.

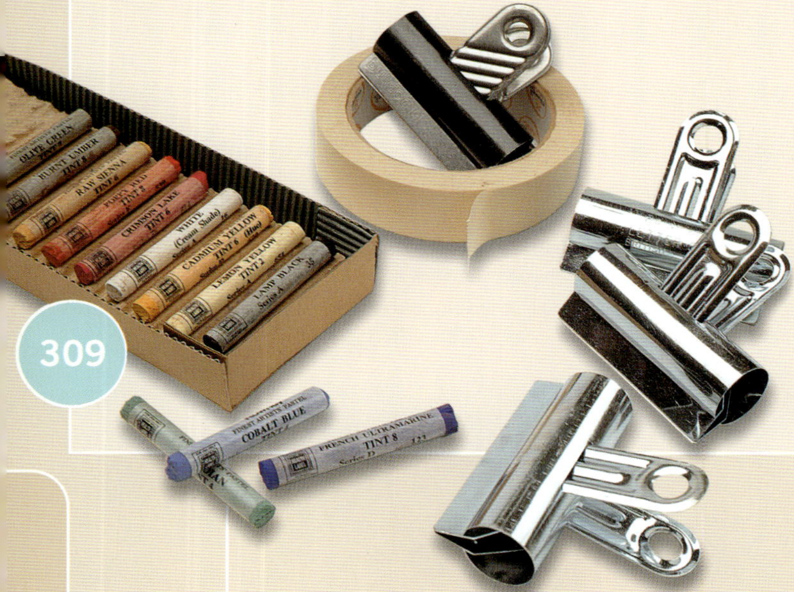

310

ALL-PURPOSE PAPERS

Rather than taking a large selection of papers with you when working outside, stick to one or two mid-toned neutrals that will be suitable for most subjects. If you find you need a darker or more positive color, you can alter it quickly with the dry-wash technique.

STORAGE AND SAFETY

Pastel paintings are fragile and can easily become smudged and dirty. If you do not intend to frame your picture immediately, make sure that it is protected—the following tips will show you how to do this, as well as providing advice on mounting and framing. There are also some valuable hints on safety measures. Remember that some pigments can be harmful, and that pastel makes a good deal of dust that should not be inhaled.

CARE OF PAINTINGS

311

To protect finished pastel paintings while they are stored, cover each with a sheet of acid-free tissue paper or tracing paper. Don't use newspaper, as the acids and residue of the printing ink could damage your work.

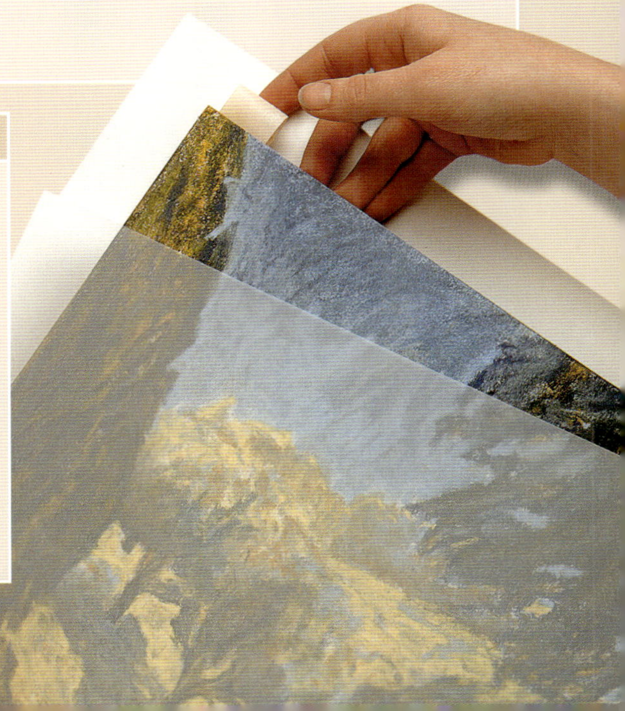

LONG-TERM PROTECTION

If you are intending to store a picture for a long period of time, attach it to an acid-free board with masking tape, then place a larger piece of tissue or tracing paper over it, taping that down onto the board around the pastel painting.

312

FRAMING FACTS

When framing your work, it is essential to keep the pastel away from the glass with a thick mat around the picture (if the two come into contact, the moisture in the atmosphere will increase condensation on the glass, causing spots on the work). Pastel does not have to be fixed if it is to be kept under glass and will remain undisturbed for many years.

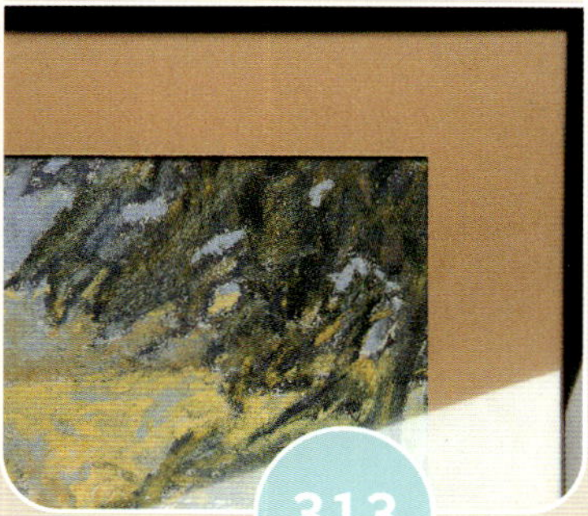

313

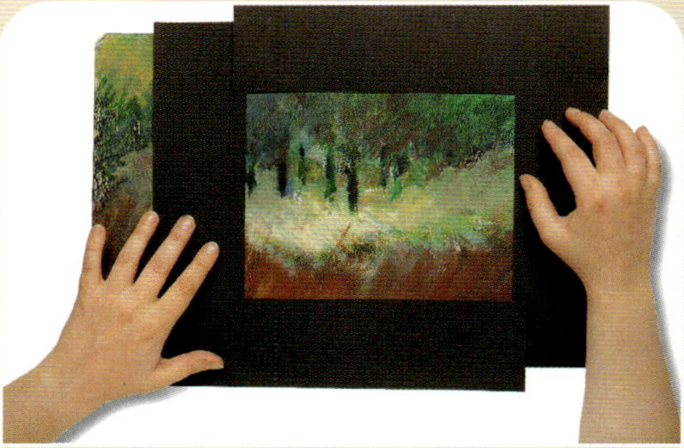

SECOND THOUGHTS

Mounting your work gives you a chance to reassess it and consider where there are any minor changes to be made. Often you can improve the composition simply by cropping: that is, taking an inch or two off the foreground or one side. This can be a simple way to "recompose" a picture that is over-symmetrical or unbalanced. Before you measure and cut the mat, make two corners of mat board or thick paper and move them around on the painting to see whether cropping will help the composition.

314

FIXATIVE SAFETY

315

To avoid inhaling fixative fumes, which can be harmful, either make sure that the room in which you are spraying is well-ventilated, or, better still, spray your paintings outdoors.

A DUST-FREE ENVIRONMENT

316

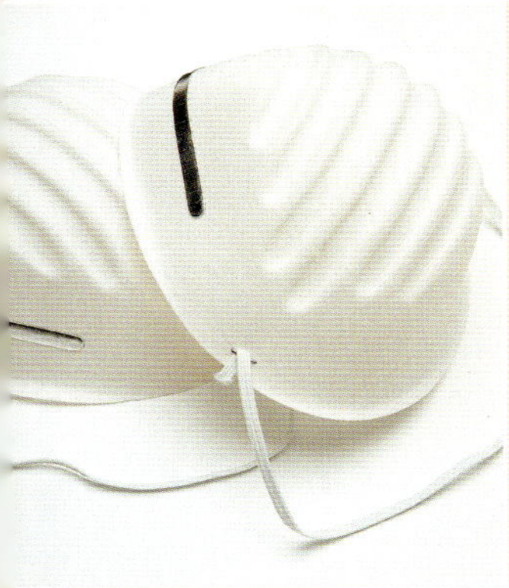

If your nose becomes congested when using soft pastel, you need to improve the air ventilation in your studio. An air-filter machine is a sensible option. Pastel makes a lot of dust, and the disposable filter can become clogged very quickly. If you are seriously allergic, try wearing a protective ventilation mask over your mouth and nose, such as those worn by cyclists. This will enable you to breathe freely while it filters pastel dust from the air.

SAFE PRACTICE

317

Manufacturers are careful to avoid the inclusion of the most toxic pigments in pastel colors, because of the risk of absorption through the skin. Nevertheless, it is wise to reduce the chance of transferring pastel colors from your hands to your mouth by making sure that you keep your hands as clean as possible when working. Always clean them thoroughly whenever you take a break.

FIXATIVE RECIPE

318

Fixatives can be toxic or inflammable. To avoid these health-and-safety dangers, try making your own, ozone-friendly solution. For a clear, nonstaining, permanent fixative, dissolve half a teaspoon of gelatin powder in two pints of hot water. Leave this until it is lukewarm, then apply it immediately to a painting with a brush or spray. If the mixture is allowed to cool, it will begin to set.

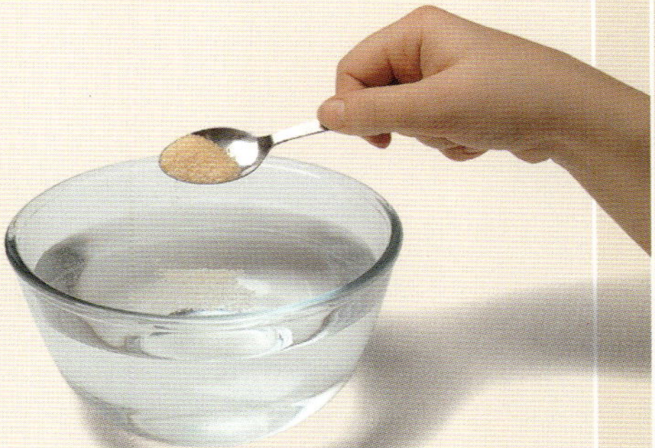

LANDSCAPES

Nature presents such wide variations of color—particularly greens—that you will need to exercise your color-mixing skills when painting the landscape. Make the paper color work for you too, or create exciting effects by starting with an underpainting.

LANDSCAPE COLORS

319

It can be difficult selecting from the wide choice of greens available, especially if you work in landscapes. You can, however, produce many variations on green without ever using green pastels, by mixing on the picture surface. Try a limited palette of Lemon Yellow, Deep Yellow, and Yellow Ocher mixed with Prussian Blue, Cobalt Blue, and French Ultramarine. These color combinations will offer you at least nine shades of green.

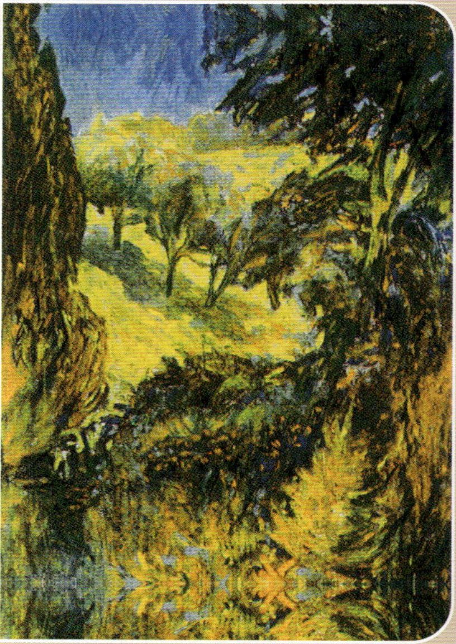

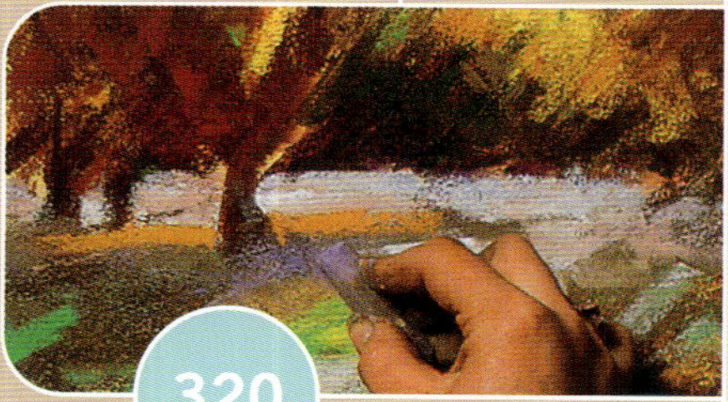

320

SHADOW COLORS

The colors that you use for shadows will depend on the subject of your painting. However, if you want to achieve a sense of coolness in a landscape scene, you could try a technique used by the Impressionists, and choose blues or mauves for shadow areas.

UNDERPAINTING FOR INTENSITY

Do you feel that your pastel landscapes look lightweight, and not rooted in the nature that they are attempting to convey? If so, try starting with an underpainting in either acrylic or watercolor. For example, when painting a traditional landscape scene, begin by painting a loose wash of blue watercolor where the sky will be, a darker tone of brown where the trees on the horizon will be situated, and a loose wash of green for the landscape. When this is dry and you come to apply your pastel, the colors will appear far more intense than before.

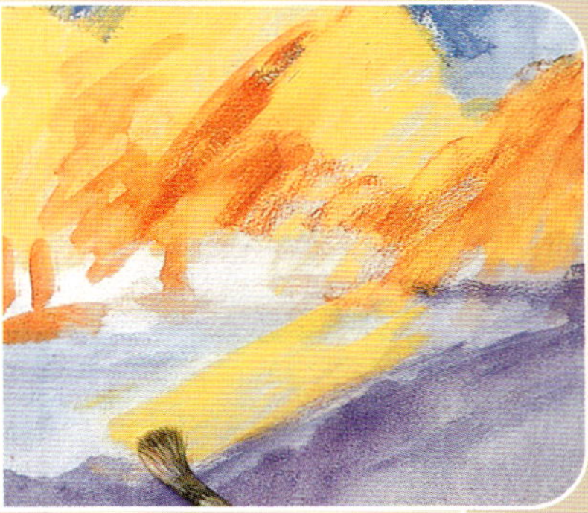

Acrylic is used to make a vivid underpainting that will set the key for the picture.

321

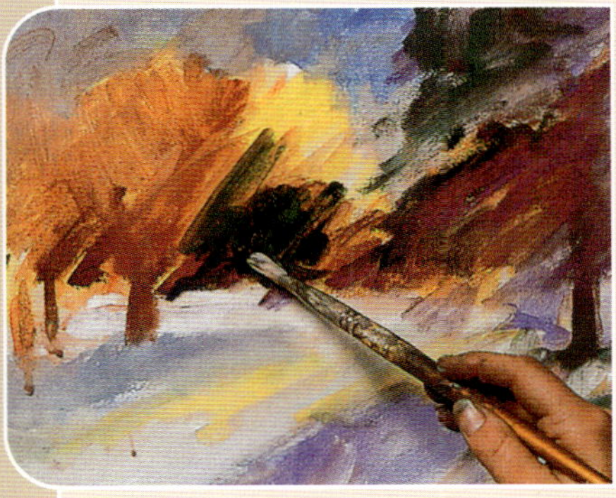

Applying the acrylic provides texture.

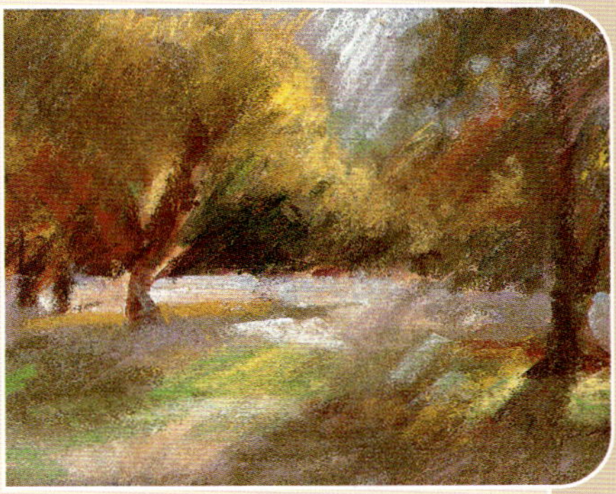

Colors must be chosen with the finished effect in mind.

UNDERPAINTING FOR OIL PASTEL

When using oil pastel you don't have to use a different medium for the underpainting. Spread the oil-pastel color with mineral spirits and a brush or rag to produce a series of washes. You can then work over these with linear strokes of "dry" pastels.

322

WORKING FROM A PHOTOGRAPH

If you are working on a landscape painting indoors, try using a black-and-white photograph as your reference. Whereas a color photograph will tempt you to imitate or copy the colors, a black-and-white one will offer tonal suggestions while leaving room for your own color interpretation.

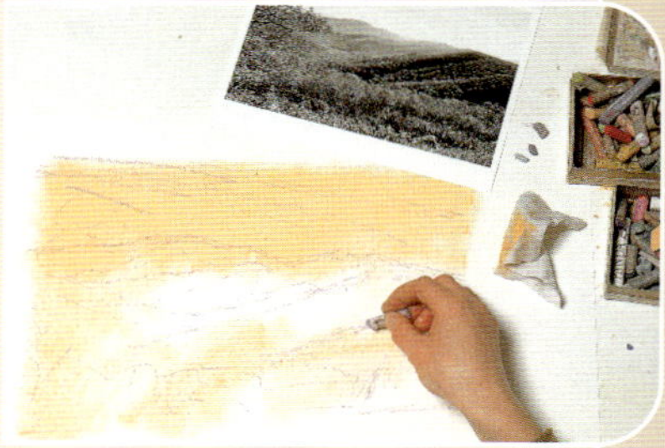

A dry wash has been laid over the sky area, and the composition is mapped out in line.

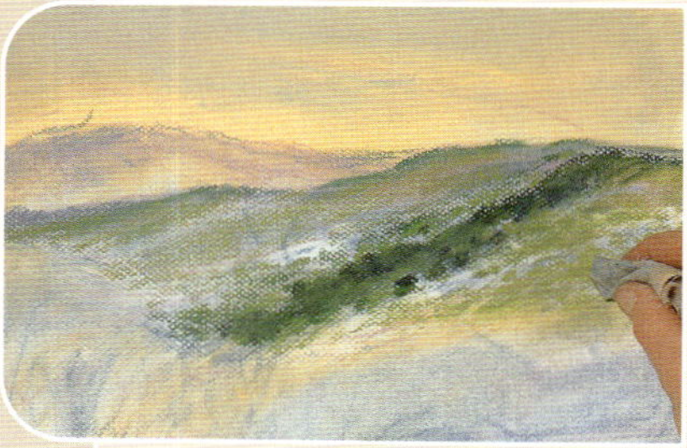

Colors are lightly blended with a rag.

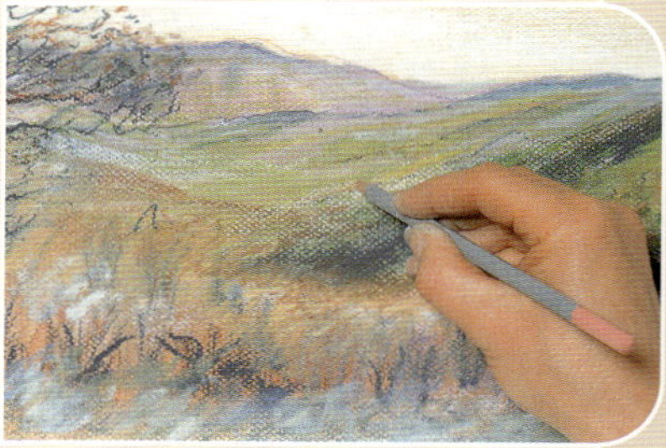

A pastel pencil is used for delicate lines.

323

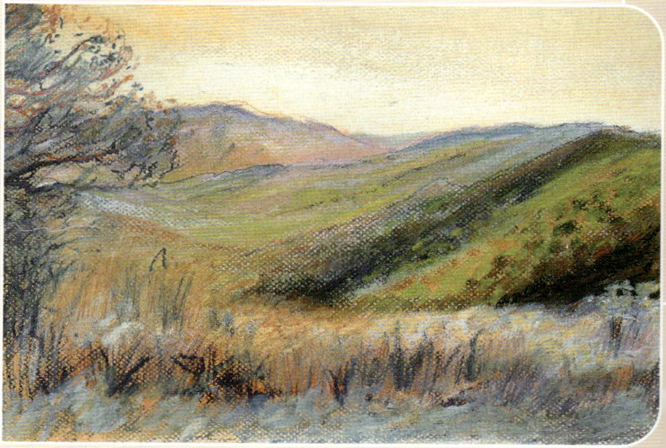

The photograph has provided the basic composition, but the colors spring from memory and imagination.

PORTRAITS

Although a variety of colors can be discerned in skin, they are all very closely related. Start with a good drawing in pastel pencil or charcoal, keep to a limited range of colors, and choose a paper color that will stand in for the middle tones or shadows.

SKIN TONES

Skin tones are difficult to master, and if you start off with too wide a palette, you will quickly run into difficulties. Much more can be done with a few colors than you might realize. The first step is to identify the main color of the person's skin. If you block this in lightly, you can then bring in lighter and darker colors for shadows and highlights.

In Doug Dawson's "Lois," thickly applied colors have been laid over and pushed into one another.

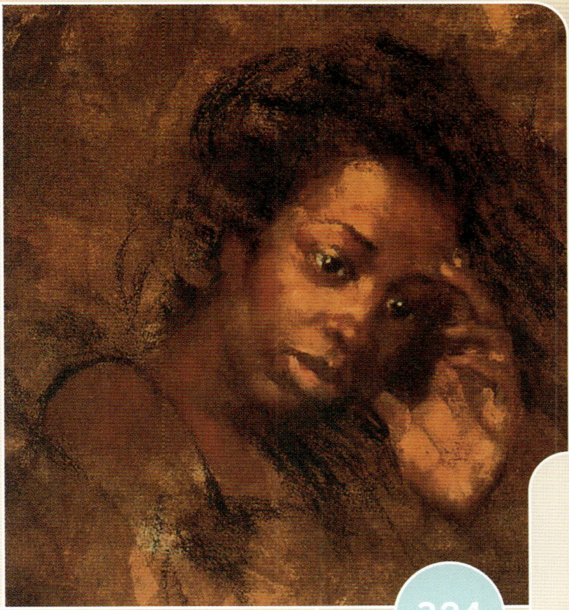

324

325

SMUDGING FOR EFFECT

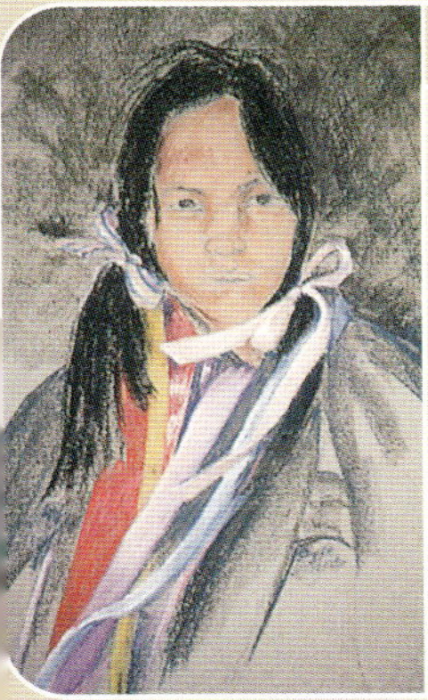

The surface of pastel paper tends to fill up very quickly, and it can be tricky to build up layers of color and a sense of depth because the later layers of pastel will smear and smudge. However, for soft skin tones, these effects can enhance your work.

In "Spring Blossom" by Urania Christy Tarbet, the skin tones have been softly smudged and blended.

FLOWERS

Flowers are well-suited to the brilliance of pastel. Unless you intend to simplify and treat a floral subject as broad mass of color, however, it is easy to go wrong with the complex structures. Keep your pastel marks light initially and build up the colors gradually.

CONVEYING FRAGILITY

326

To create a sense of fragility when painting flowers, try working directly on white paper. This will soften all your colors and make the flowers appear less solid.

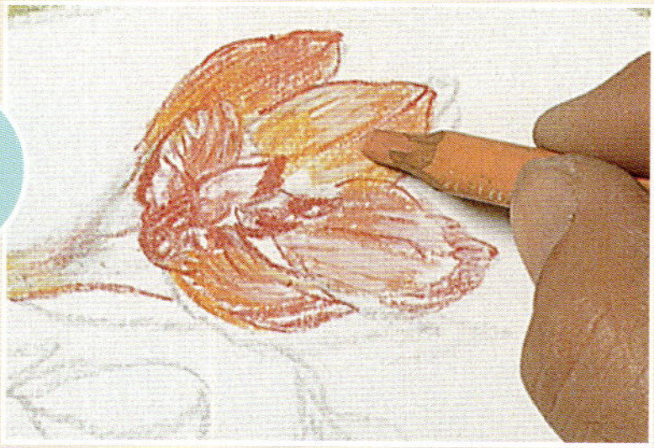

Light marks are made with a pastel pencil.

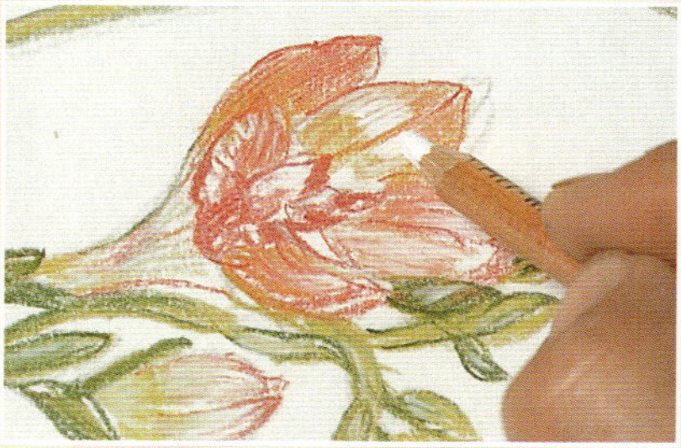

Highlights are built up, again with a pastel pencil.

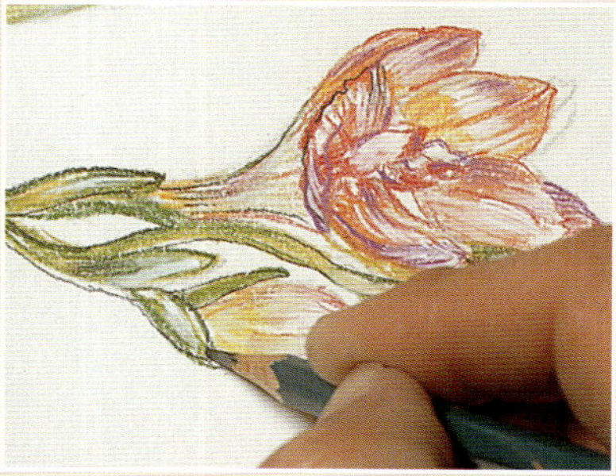

The drawing is sharpened up with a 6B pencil.

(Below) The smooth watercolor paper helps to keep the lines light and delicate.

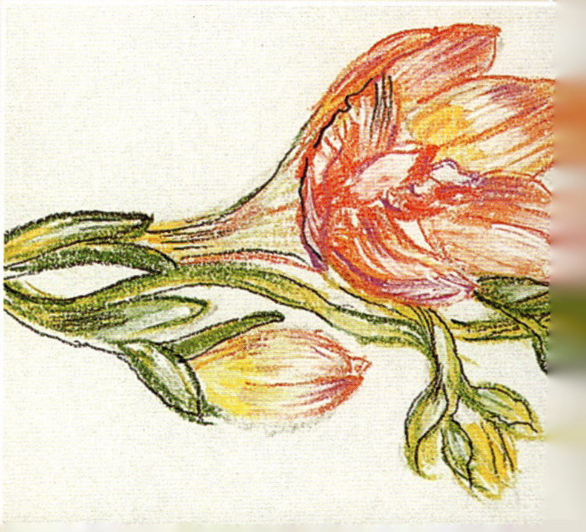

UNDERSTANDING THE STRUCTURE

Flowers are extremely hard to paint because their structures are so complex. When you begin, try drawing the flowers on tinted paper with pastel pencil. Follow the line of the plant up the stem in the direction of growth to the tips, following the natural line of the plant. Then fill in the petals with softer pastels to create intensity of color and lightness of form.

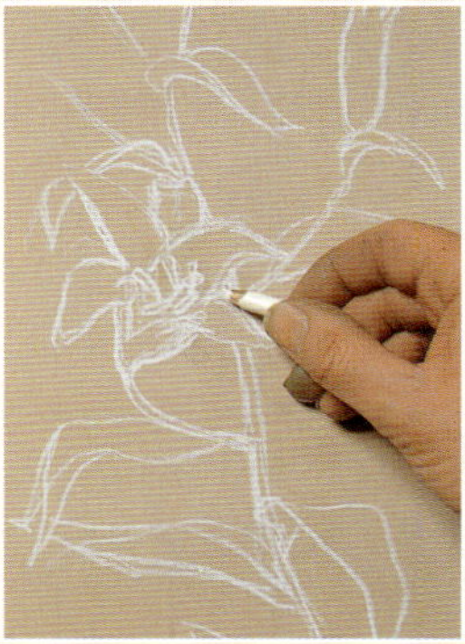

White pastel pencil is taken around the main shapes.

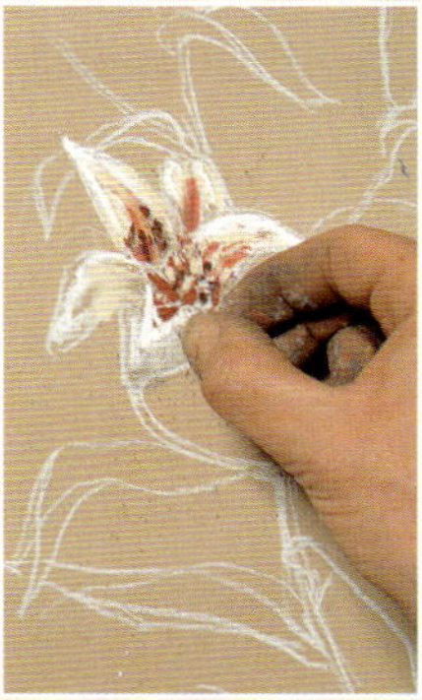

Soft-pastel strokes follow the forms of the petals.

327

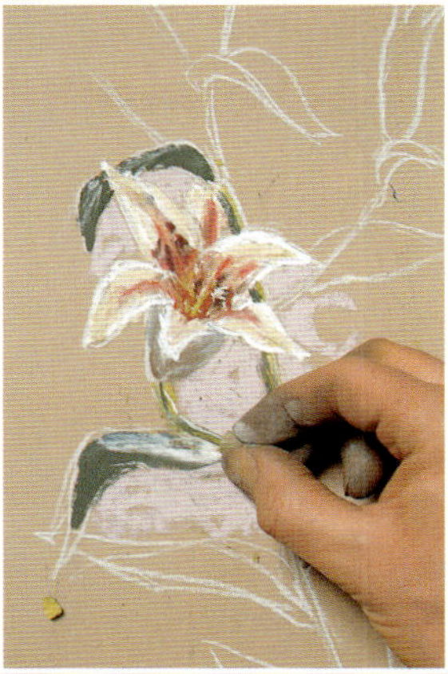

The pale background color is applied.

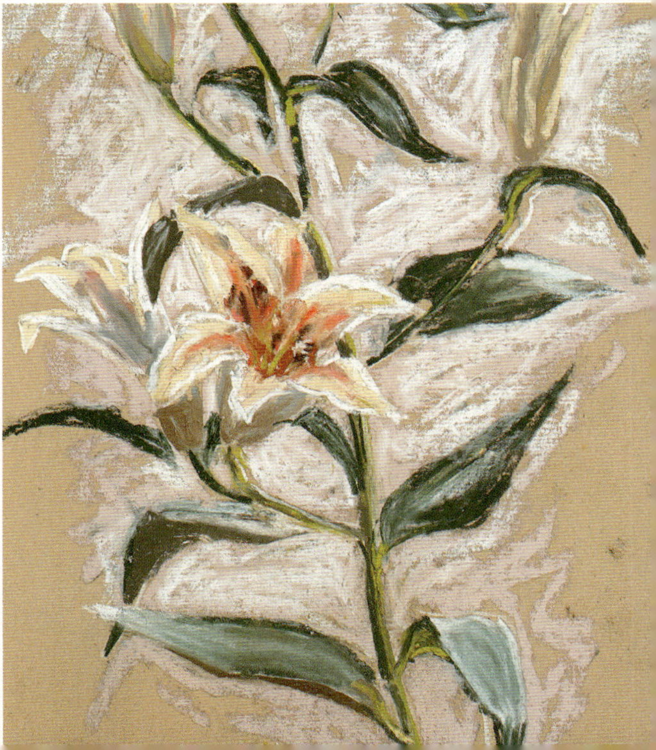

The fine sandpaper used holds the pigment well and encourages firm, positive drawing.

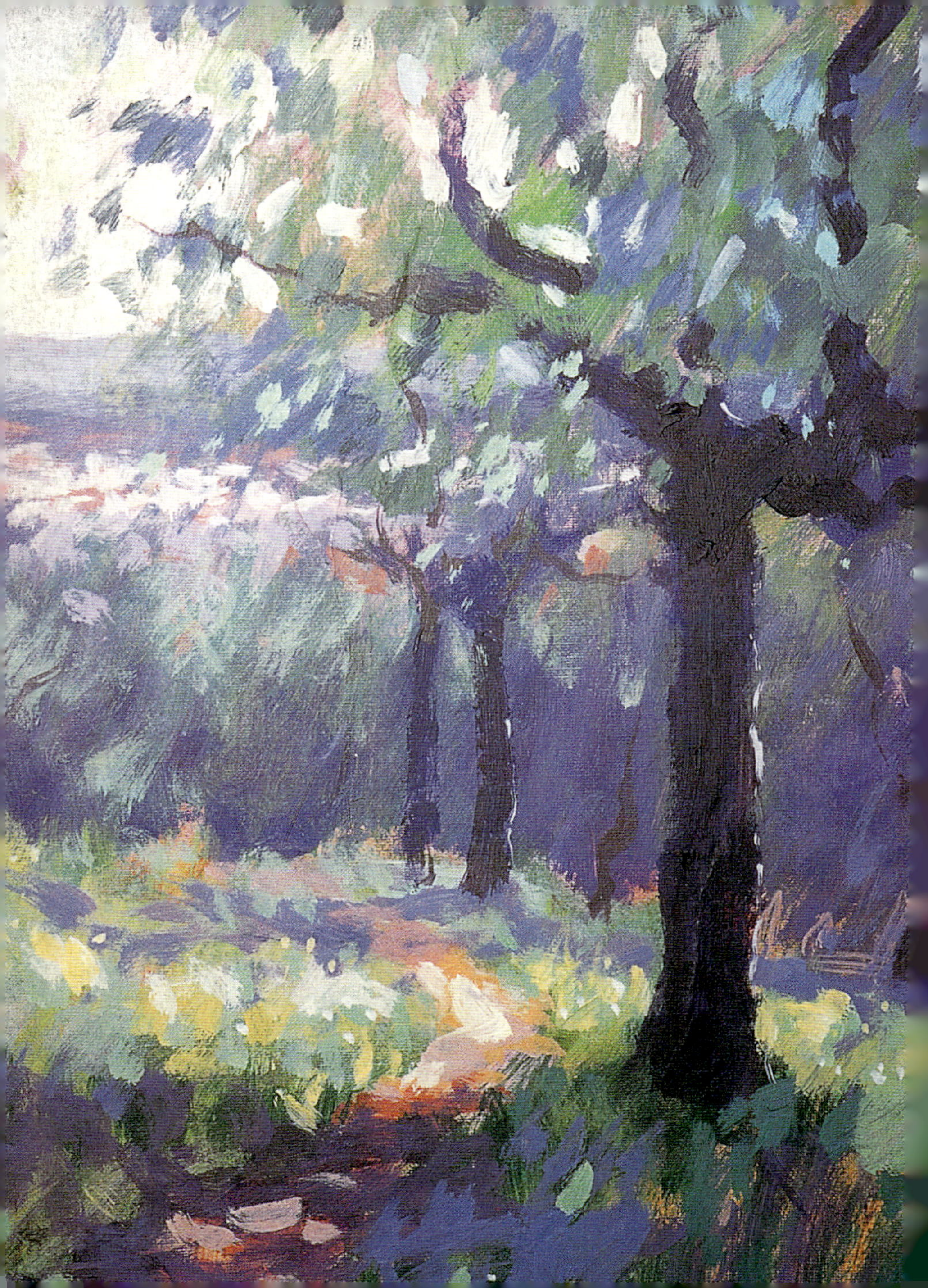

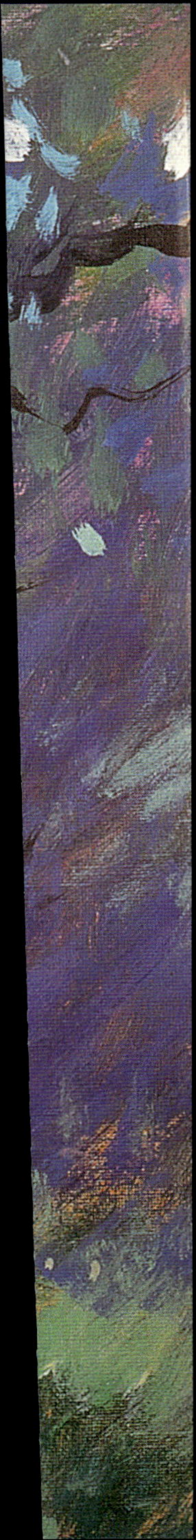

4

ACRYLIC

Acrylics are easy to use and have a wide range of applications, and the wealth of practical advice that follows will enable you to get the most out of this versatile medium. Advice is given on selecting paints, surfaces for painting on, brushes and palettes, on choosing and mixing colors, on the different techniques for creating a range of surface effects, ways of making corrections and alterations, subject-related problems, and ideas for a wide range of craft applications.

Alan Oliver, "Olive Grove Overlooking Florence" (detail).

INTRODUCTION TO ACRYLICS

WHEN YOU look at a finished painting you can nearly always tell whether it has been done in watercolor, pastels, or oils. Acrylic, however, tends to hide its identity simply because it is a medium that can be used in so many different ways. This high degree of versatility is part of its charm, but it can lead to a rather sterile approach, where acrylic is used to imitate oils, watercolors, or gouache paints instead of being appreciated for its own special qualities. Because acrylic is a new medium in art-history terms, having only been around since the mid-20th century, there is no "official" body of techniques associated with it, as there is for the other painting media. And there can never really be one because you can do more or less anything you like with it. You can paint on paper, canvas, or board, use the paint thin or thick, apply it with knives or brushes, combine it with other media, stick pieces of paper into it for collage effects—the list is virtually endless.

Here we do not attempt to provide a full acrylic course, but to open your eyes to just a few of the things you can do. If you go to a painting class, or buy a standard book on acrylic painting, you will learn how one artist goes about using acrylics, but you may never explore the wider possibilities or conduct your own experiments.

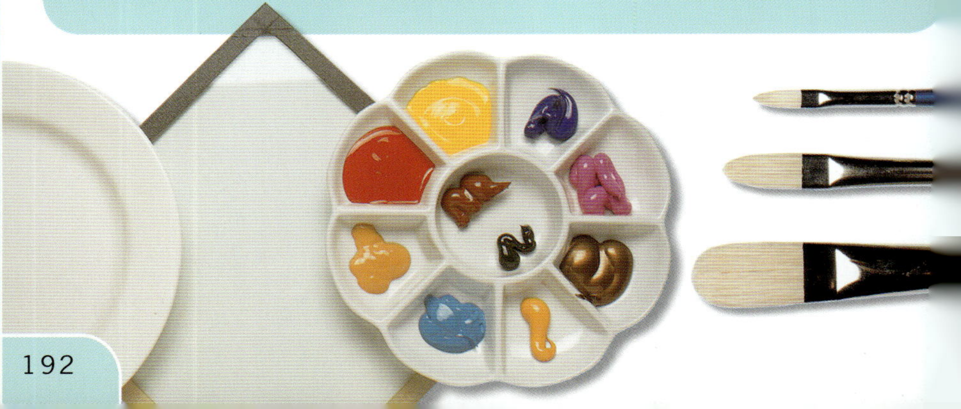

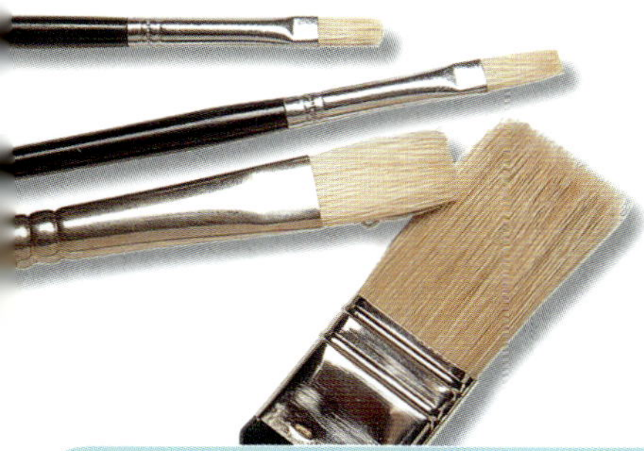

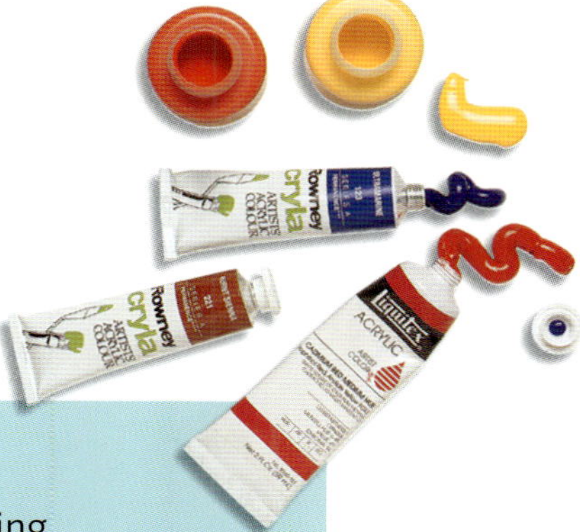

This section contains a wealth of exciting techniques for you to try out at your leisure, but it does not neglect practical advice. As anyone who has used the medium will know, acrylic dries very fast, which can cause you to waste expensive paint and ruin good brushes. But a little know-how, combined with self-discipline, can prevent this, and you can also save money by working on inexpensive surfaces.

Like this book, this section is intended for dipping into rather than reading from cover to cover, and is divided up for easy access to the kind of information you want. For advice on paints, surfaces, brushes, and palettes, and help on choosing and mixing colors, turn to the first sections, and refer to the later ones for inspiration on techniques, special effects, and methods for dealing with subject-related problems. Had you thought, for example, of using masking tape to keep the edges of buildings straight?

There is even a section on making corrections and alterations, so if a painting hasn't quite worked, use it as a learning tool and see if you can improve it by overpainting or laying colored glazes.

PAINTS

Starting out with a new medium can be bewildering; and without any guidance you may have little idea of what to buy. This section provides practical advice that will help the beginner to make wise initial purchases, while some of the hints will give the "old hand" food for thought.

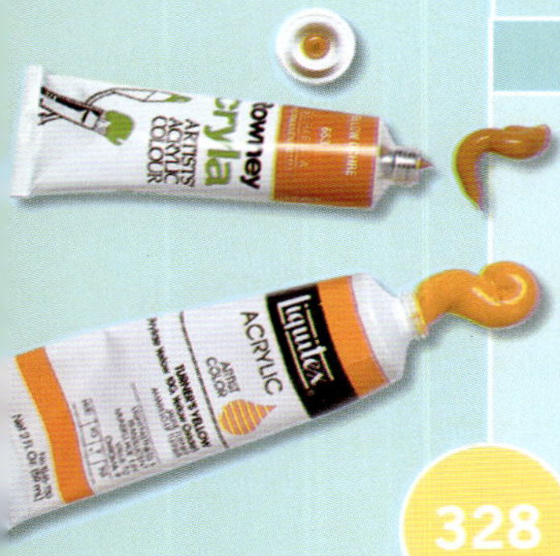

328

PAINT TEXTURE

The different brands of acrylic paints vary in texture, from thick and buttery to smooth and relatively fluid. It is a worthwhile experiment to try two or three brands to see whether one suits your painting methods better than another. You can mix or layer different types to use up any odd tubes you have collected, but it is advisable to do samples to test their compatibility before combining them in a finished painting.

PAINT QUALITY

Acrylics are most widely available in tubes. Free-flow types are also packaged in jars, providing greater quantity but sometimes in a more restricted color range. White is often sold in a large-sized tube in addition to the standard size, because it is used up more quickly than other colors.

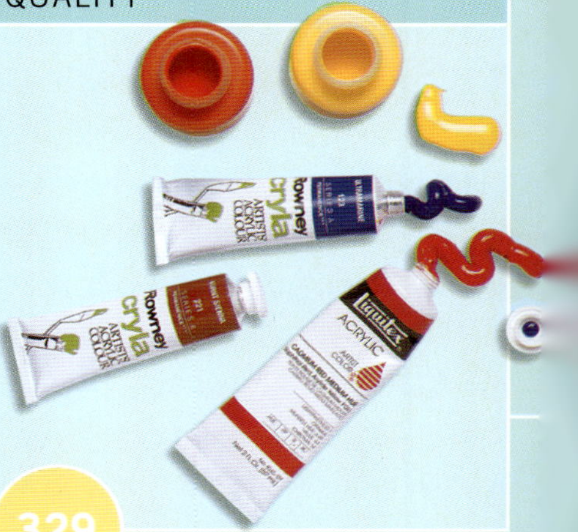

329

DRYING TESTS

330

Acrylics dry much more rapidly than other types of paint, but the drying rate can vary according to the absorbency of the surface you are painting on. Try making some color doodles on a small offcut of paper, board, or canvas, to see how quickly the colors dry. Test the paint in different consistencies, such as straight from the tube, just moistened with water, and brushed out in a wet wash.

MIXABLE PAINTS

331

Some types of acrylic are sold in the form of basic mediums together with liquid pigments or color pastes, which you can use to mix up your own colors. Put them into screw-top jars and they will store well long-term. This is useful if you do large-scale work, or if you are sharing costs between members of a painting class.

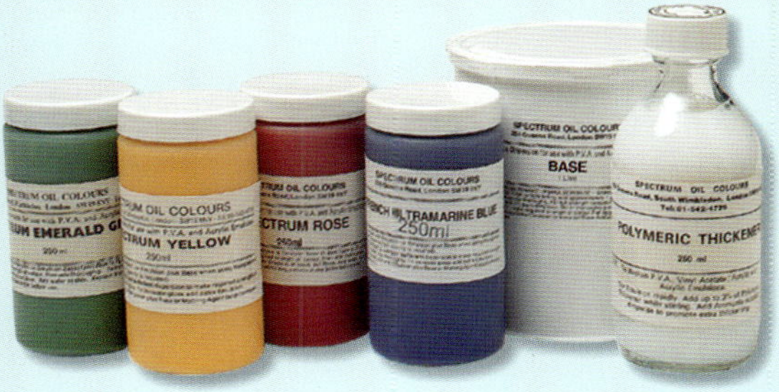

Some established oil paint manufacturers have begun producing acrylic paints like those pictured left.

SURFACES

One of the beauties of acrylics is that you can paint on more or less anything, even newspaper, so you need not spend a great deal of money in the early trying-out stages. If you find you like working on canvas, you can save money by stretching your own, even recycling old sheets by sticking them down on board.

ECONOMY PAPERS

332

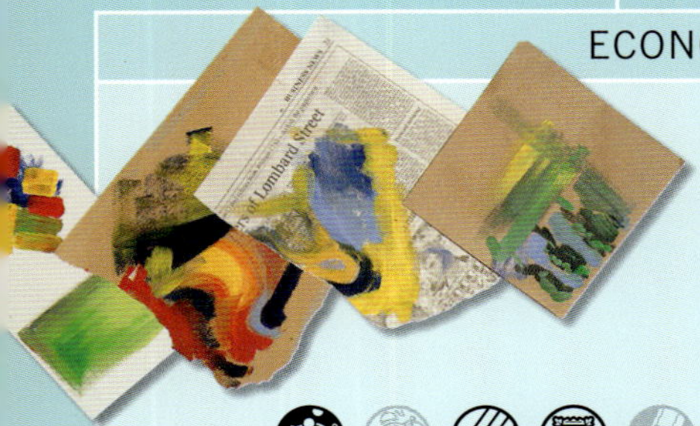

You can paint with acrylics on all kinds of paper. Ordinary brown wrapping paper, writing paper, and even newspaper can be recycled and used for practicing your brushwork or experimenting with color mixes.

PAPER TEXTURE

On a smooth-surfaced support, such as cartridge or coated paper, the paint rapidly seals the surface and "sits" on top. The colors can start to skid around as you add to the layers, making coverage uneven, so you should expect to make use of directional brushmarks. Watercolor papers with a pronounced grain grip the paint more firmly and so the paint texture remains fully workable for longer.

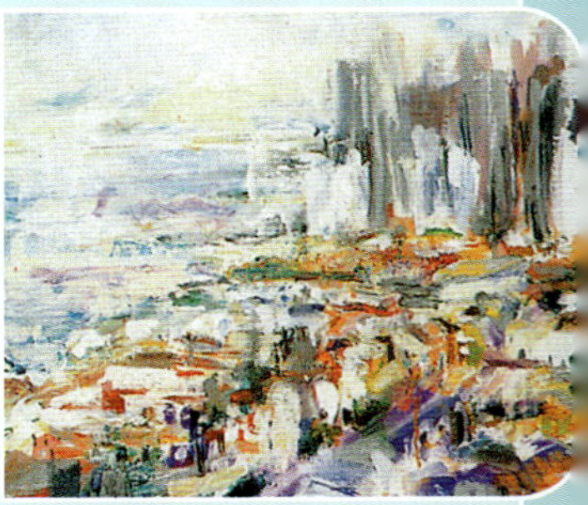

In "View of San Francisco" (detail), Jacquie Turner has used smooth watercolor paper.

333

STRETCHING PAPER

Lightweight watercolor papers buckle when wetted by the paint, but will always dry out flat again if stretched beforehand. Soak the paper either by immersing it in clean water or by sponging on both sides. Lay it on a drawing board and tape down each edge in turn with gummed-paper tape. Leave it to dry naturally on a flat surface. If you leave it propped up, water drains to the lower edge and may loosen the tape.

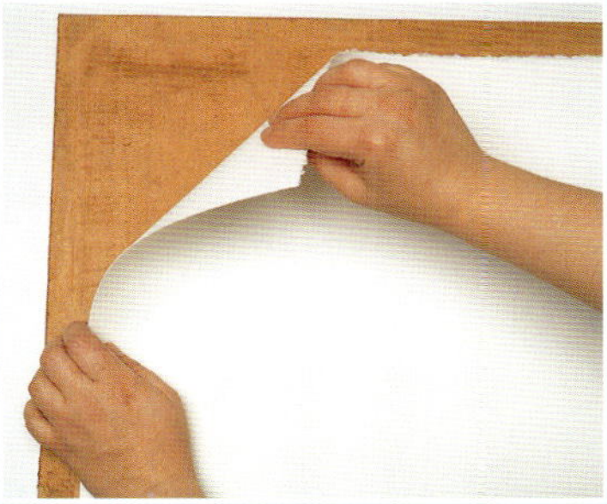

Wet the paper on both sides and place it carefully on the board.

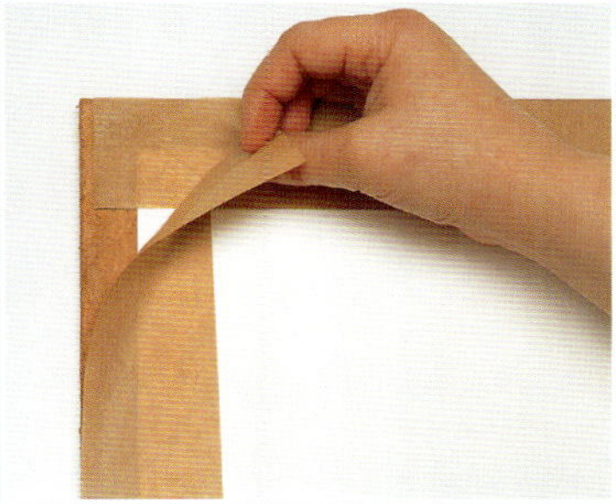

Damp the gummed-paper tape and stick it around the edges, allowing an overlap of at least ½ inch (1.5cm).

334

USING CARDBOARD

Cardboard is a useful surface for acrylic painting, and often available free of charge—you may find pieces from commercial packaging, or the back cover of a used-up paper pad. Look for a firm, fibrous texture rather than cardboard composed of paper layers; the top layer may peel up when wetted by the paint.

335

PREPARED SURFACES

336

Canvas boards are relatively expensive but have the advantages of being lightweight, self-supporting, and easy to frame. Pre-stretched canvases are also available. Check that the type you buy is suitable for acrylics; most are now usable for work in acrylics or oils, but acrylics will not adhere to a surface specially primed for oils.

HARDBOARD

337

This is an inexpensive surface that has the advantage of rigidity. The smooth side is normally used, and can be made less slippery by light sanding followed by a coat of matte medium or acrylic gesso. For a really heavy texture, try using the rough side.

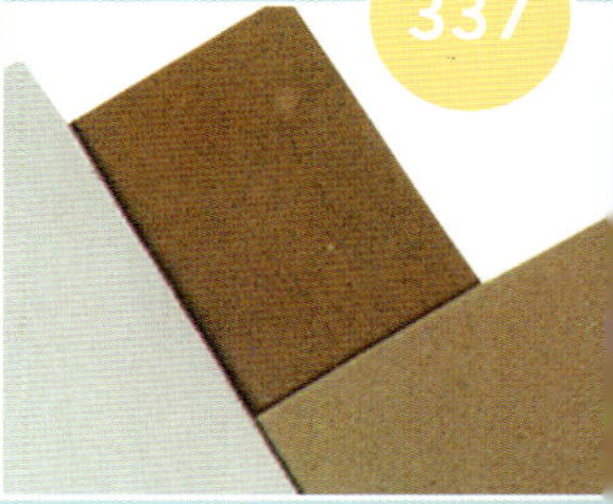

STRETCHING CANVAS

You can buy both prepared and "raw" canvas by the yard (meter). Assemble the stretchers, cut the canvas to size, allowing for a turnover, and tack or staple it to the back of the stretchers, pulling it taut and taking care to keep the grain straight.

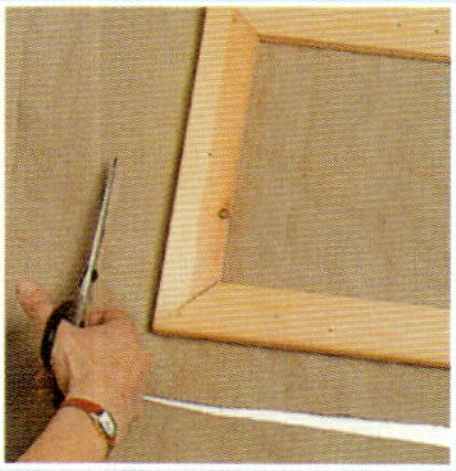

First assemble the stretchers and cut the canvas to size.

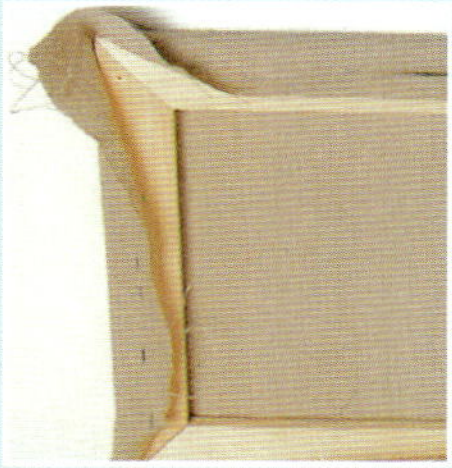

Staple or tack first one long side and then the other.

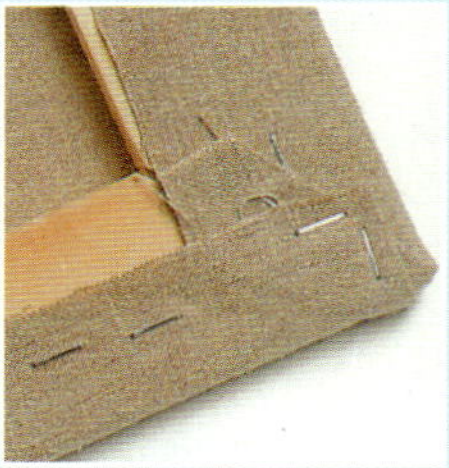

Staple each side before folding the corners over.

338

ECONOMY CANVAS

You can use pieces of an old sheet or pillowcase instead of canvas, "stretching" it by sticking it down on the smooth side of hardboard, with an overlap of about 1 inch (2.5cm) taken around the back. For light fabrics, use acrylic medium, and for heavier ones white glue thinned with water to about half and half.

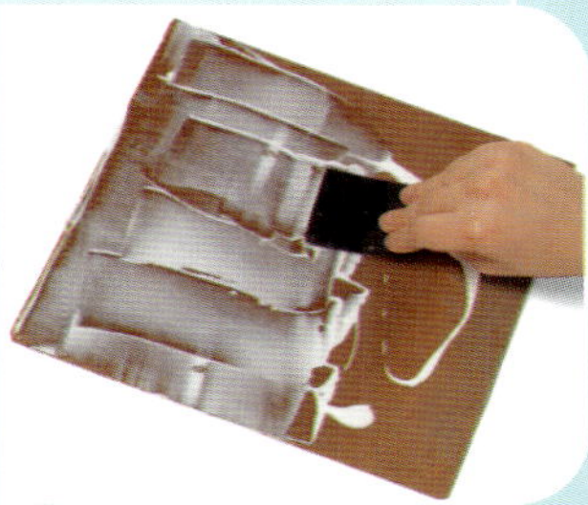

Place the glued side down on the canvas, apply more glue around the back edges then fold over.

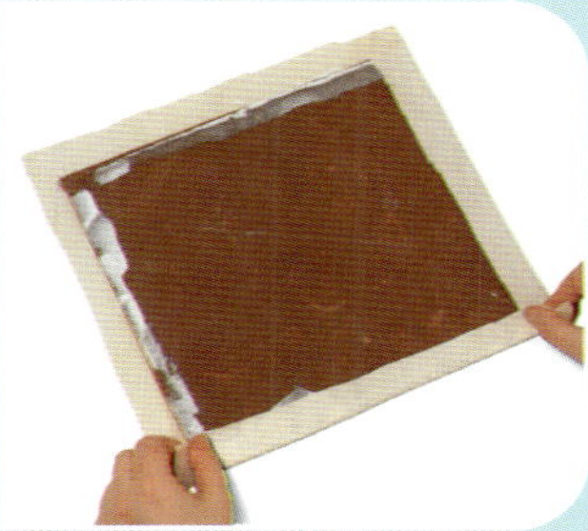

Cover the board with medium. Use a brush, or a spreader to give a thicker application.

339

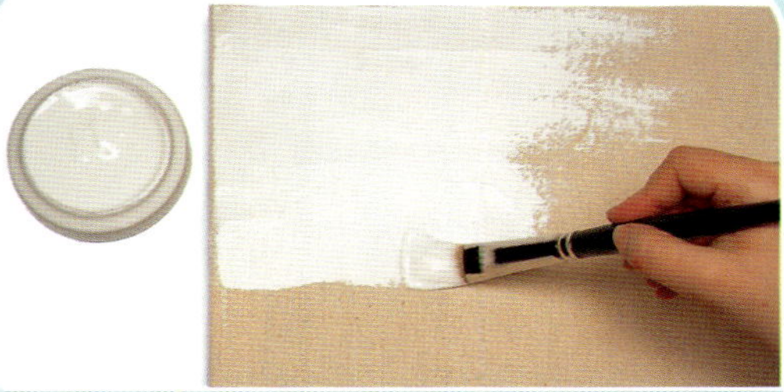

PRIMING

Untreated fabric is absorbent, so canvases are usually primed before use. Give them at least two coats of acrylic gesso, or if you like the natural color of the canvas, seal it with matte medium.

340

COLORED GROUND

Working on a white surface makes it hard to assess the initial colors. Primed canvas or hardboard is often given an overall tint in a mid-toned neutral color such as ocher or gray. You can pre-tint watercolor paper in the same way.

341

BRUSHES AND PALETTES

However much you enjoy working with acrylics you may love them rather less when you find you have ruined expensive brushes or a good wooden oil-painting palette by letting the paint dry on them. This section, which combines advice on the best choices of brushes and palettes with hints on equipment care, will help you to avoid such occurrences.

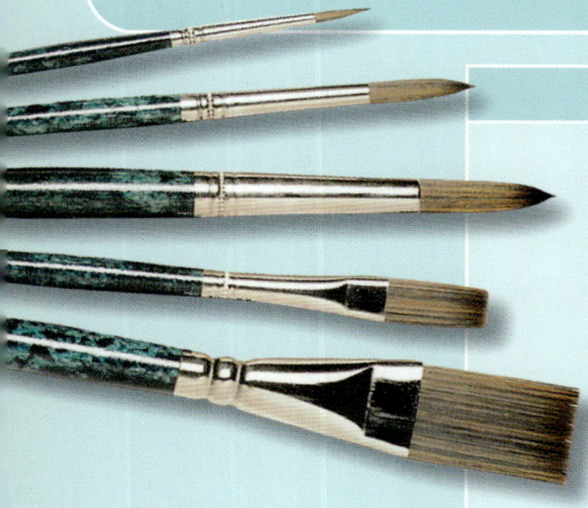

ACRYLIC BRUSHES

342

Manufacturers make brush ranges specially designed for working with acrylic paints. These are made with synthetic rather than animal hairs and are available in round or flat shapes and in varying sizes. The quality of the brush tip is smooth but resilient for manipulating thick and thin paint.

BRUSH ACTION

343

When you buy a brush, test out its versatility with some simple brush sketching. Try variations on using the tip and side, turning a flat brush onto its edges and corners. Apply different pressures and create thick and thin strokes, dashes or dabs and long traveling marks.

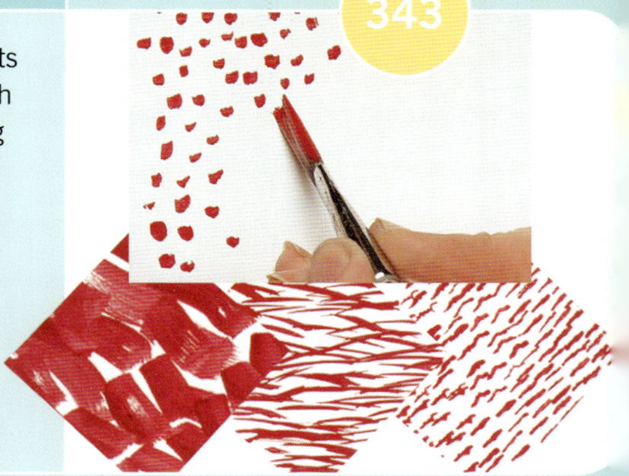

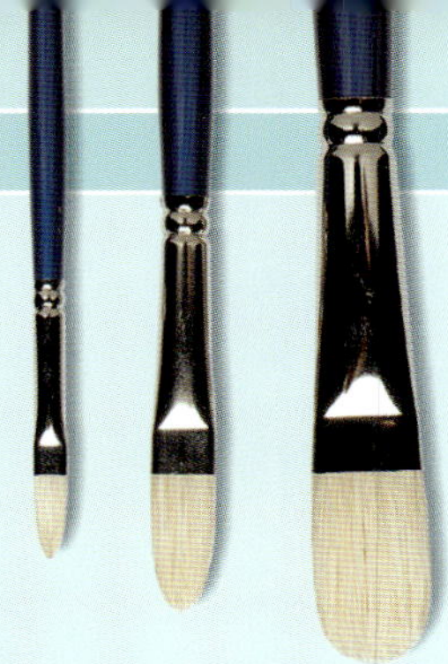

BRISTLE BRUSHES

344

The hoghair brushes traditionally used for oil painting are also suited to acrylics. Their toughness makes them useful for applying rough, heavy, or coarse painting effects, such as dry brushing and impasto.

BOLD STROKES

345

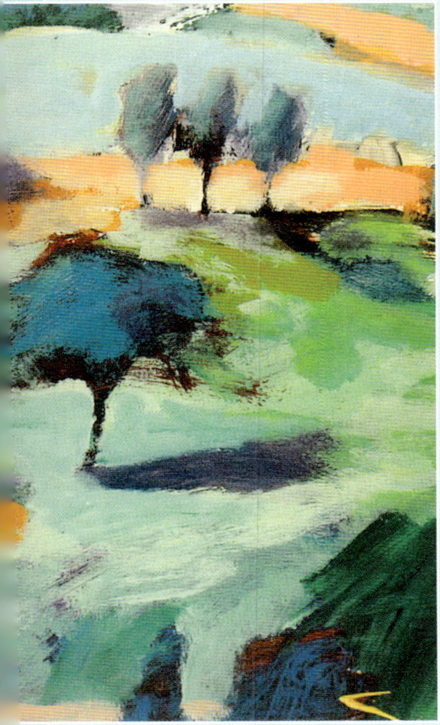

Large-scale decorators' brushes are useful for blocking in the early stages of a painting and for covering broad color areas, such as skies and fields in a landscape. Using a 1 inch (2.5cm) or larger brush can help you to loosen up your technique. By experimenting with pushing and pulling the brush through fluid paint you can discover interesting ways of blending and texturing the color.

In Paul Powls' "Late Afternoon" (detail), the broad brushstrokes, which suggest shapes and forms without literal description, are an important part of the image.

THOROUGH CLEANING

346

Dried acrylic ruins brushes. Be scrupulous about rinsing your brush every time you complete a color application, keep brushes moist throughout a working session, and wash them out well at the end. The most common cause of damage is paint collecting at the heel of the brush above the metal ferrule, causing gradual stiffening, so pay special attention to washing that part right through.

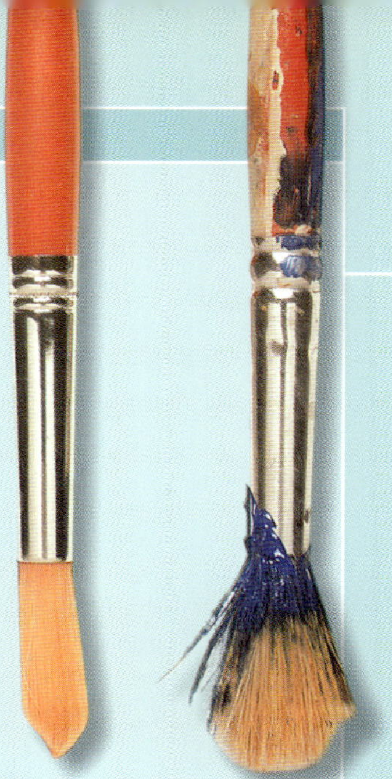

OLD BRUSHES

347

If you have let paint dry in your brush, it can be loosened by soaking in denatured alcohol. The brush shape and texture will be damaged, but many artists like to keep old, worn brushes for creating scrubbed and scumbled textures, saving hard wear on newer brushes.

STRAY BRISTLES

348

A bristle or hair shed into the paint as you work will become firmly trapped as soon as the color begins to dry. Keep an eye out for shed hairs and quickly flick them out of the wet paint with an upward and outward motion of the brush tip.

RESHAPING A BRUSH

If your brush has begun to splay or shed hairs, wash it out thoroughly and shake off excess moisture, then take the tip between your fingers and carefully stroke and press it back into shape, teasing out loose hairs as you do so.

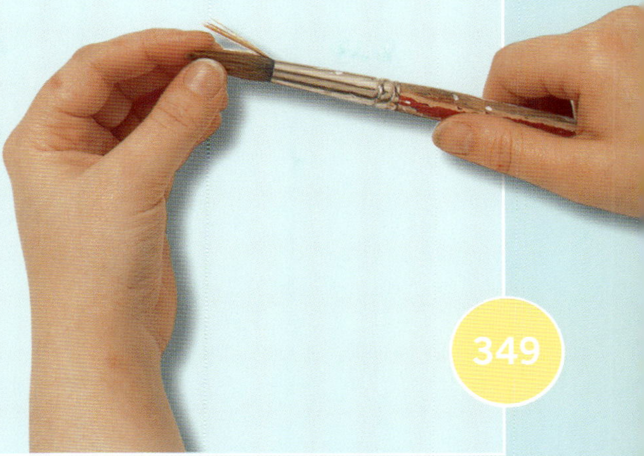

349

KNIFE WORK

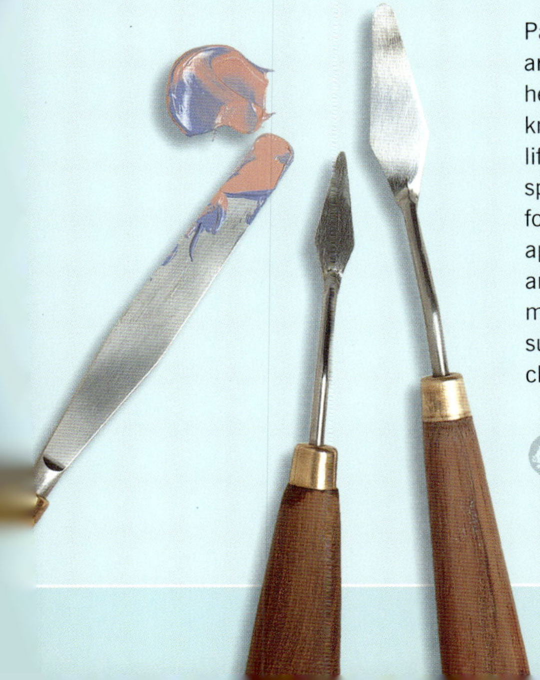

Painting knives and palette knives are invaluable for working into heavy acrylics; making good use of knives can help you to prolong the life of your brushes. A flat, spatulate palette knife is the tool for mixing the colors before you apply them. A painting knife has an angled shaft so you can manipulate the blade on the surface while keeping your hand clear of the painting.

350

SCRAPERS

Save old credit cards or telephone cards—they make very useful paint applicators for scraped and pasted textures, and also provide a clean, broad edge for scraping off wet color when you have made an error.

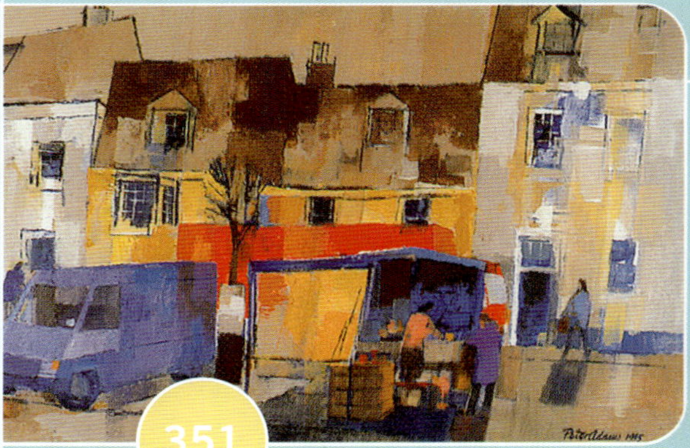

In Peter Adams' "Board Street, Alresford" (detail), paint has been scraped onto hardboard and colors layered over each other.

351

PERMANENT PALETTES

You can use a purpose-made plastic or ceramic palette for acrylic paint, but many artists improvise with cheaper items. For long-term use, the material must be non-absorbent. A piece of plastic-coated wood is fine, as is an old plate or a plain sheet of glass, the thicker the better. Cover the edges of glass with insulating tape to avoid cutting yourself accidentally.

352

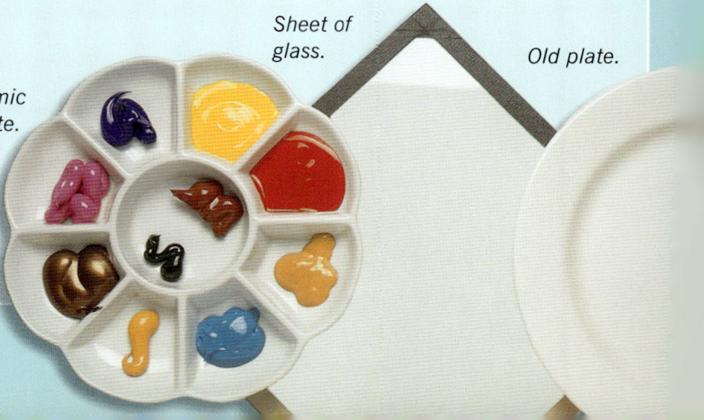

Ceramic palette.

Sheet of glass.

Old plate.

TEAR-OFF PALETTES

Tear-off paper palettes are available to buy, but an old telephone directory provides a cheap alternative for quick painting sessions. Lay out and mix your colors on the top sheet. When the colors get muddy, or you have used up all the paint, tear off the top few pages and start again.

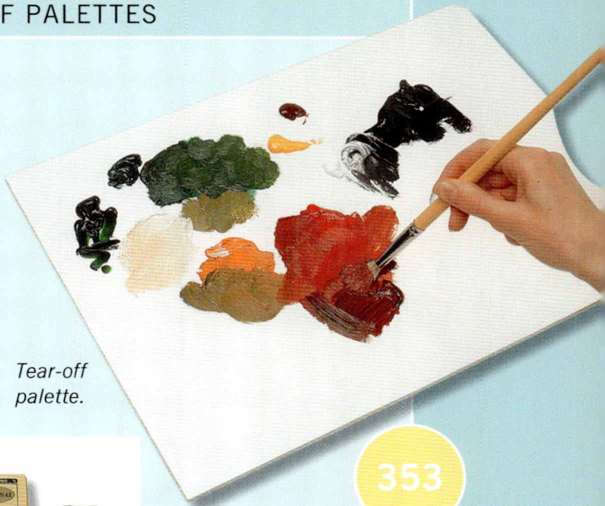

Tear-off palette.

353

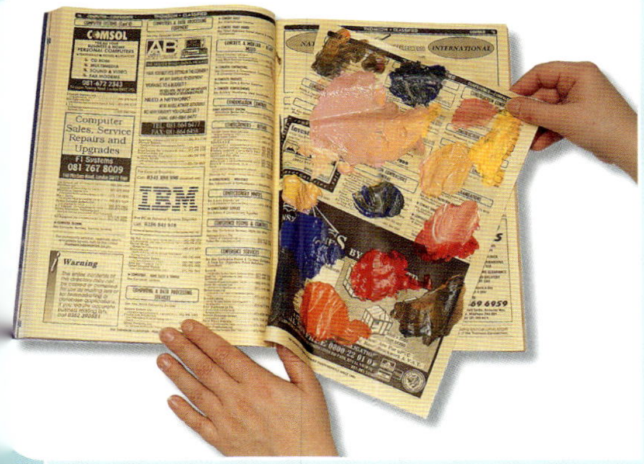

Old telephone directory.

COLOR QUANTITIES

Acrylics start to harden quite fast once exposed to air. To avoid waste, when you put them out on the palette, start with small quantities and add to them as you need. If a blob of paint has started to dry, peel off the rubbery "skin" so you do not brush shreds of it into still-wet colors.

354

MOIST PAINT

355 To keep palette colors moist you can use a specially designed "reservoir" palette, in which a damp underlayer continuously supplies the paint with enough moisture to keep it workable, or you can make your own version. You need a plastic or metal tray, a piece of capillary matting (as used to keep potted plants moist), a piece of absorbent paper, such as cartridge or newspaper, and a same-size piece of greaseproof paper or thin tracing paper. To prime the palette, soak the matting for 15 minutes and squeeze it out so that it is moist, not wet, then put it in the tray base and layer in the absorbent paper and greaseproof or tracing paper.

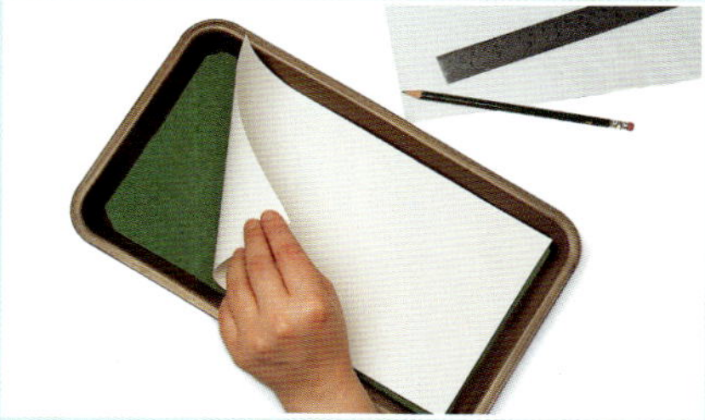

Allow the capillary matting to absorb the water, then lay the cartridge paper on top.

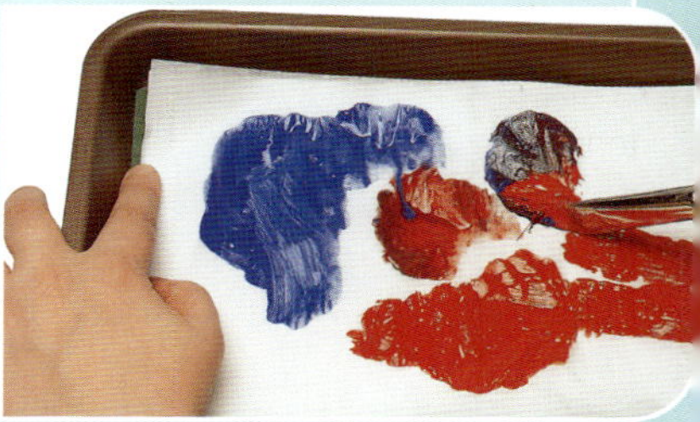

Finally, place the greaseproof or tracing paper on top. To keep moist between working sessions, cover the whole tray with plastic wrap.

AVOID WASTAGE

356 If you are using a conventional palette and have to leave blobs of paint already laid out, for a short time only, thoroughly wet a rag or kitchen cloth, wring it out, and drape it lightly over the palette.

REMOVING DRIED PAINT

357 Dried acrylic on a plastic, glass, or ceramic palette can be loosened by running warm water over it. The paint skin softens and begins to lift, so you can peel or scrape it off.

COLOR

It is wise to begin with a small range of colors, as this helps you build up the skills of identifying the colors you see and mixing them accurately. This section explains which colors you must have, and gives hints on color mixing and on methods of modifying over-bright colors.

WHITE AND BLACK

358

You need to include white in your starter palette for heightening bright colors and mixing pale tints. Black can be used for darkening colors and tones, but is not essential; some artists regard it as a deadening influence and prefer to mix their own "colored blacks." Try this out with varying proportions of red, yellow, and blue.

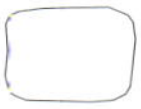

Ultramarine Blue + white

Ultramarine Blue + black

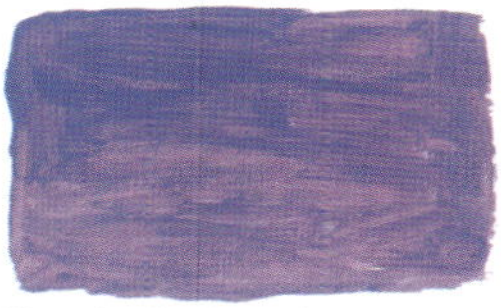

Dioxazine Purple + white

Dioxazine Purple + black

Phthalo Green + white

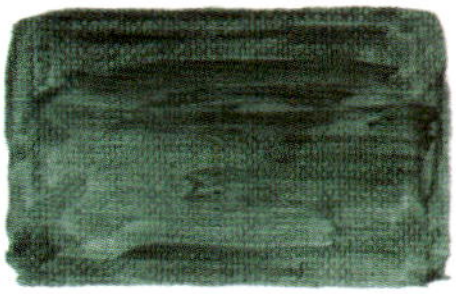

Phthalo Green + black

PRIMARY CHOICE

359

In theory, you can mix all colors from only three—red, yellow, and blue—but in practice it is not quite that simple, because there are different versions of these colors. In a limited palette, select two types of each, for example, Cadmium Red and Crimson; Cadmium Yellow and Lemon Yellow; Ultramarine and Phthalo Blue. Used in pairs, these give you many grades of secondary mixes—oranges, purples, and greens—and by mixing two or more colors you can obtain subtler shades and neutral colors.

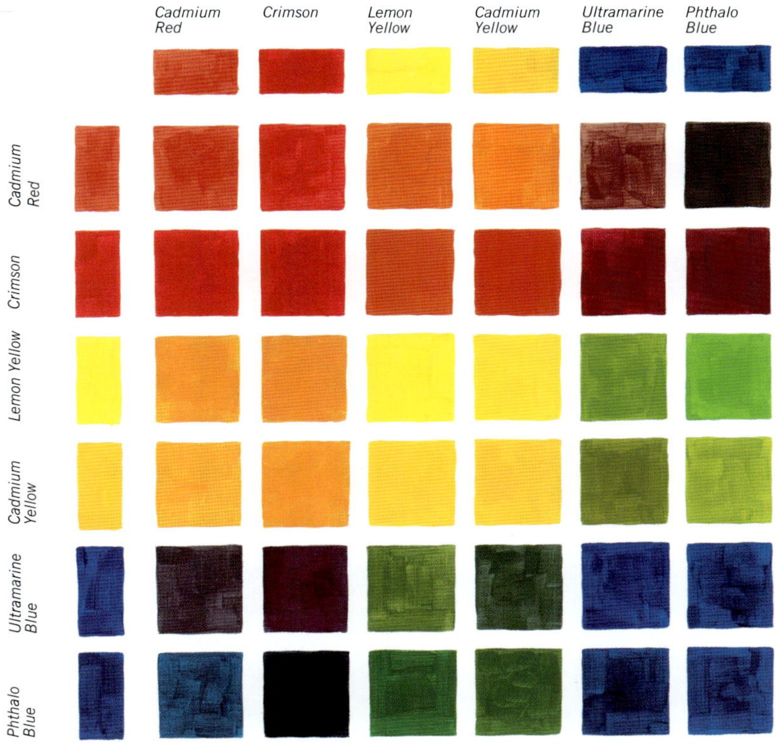

For this chart, the mix is in a ratio of 80% strength to 20% strength.

CHART YOUR MIXES

360

If you buy a manufacturer's starter pack of acrylic colors, take the time to make your own color chart for reference. Mix all of the colors in pairs; try out two of three variants with each pair, using equal and 3:1 proportions. Some results may surprise you, and you will find out whether particular colors can or cannot be mixed from your given range.

EXTRA COLORS

Some colors, notably purples, are virtually impossible to mix satisfactorily. A tube of purple is a useful addition to your palette, both as a color in its own right and as a good mixer. It is ideal for warming up townscape grays and beiges and is a versatile shading color for landscape greens and blues.

Brilliant mauves like the shadows in Gerry Baptist's "Summer Day in Grimaud" (detail) are best achieved with tube purples.

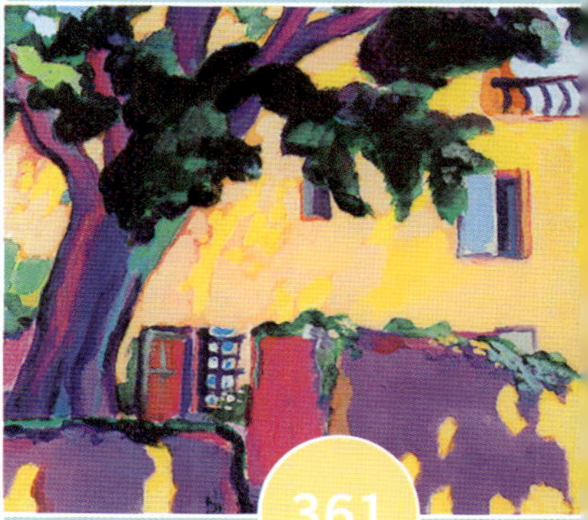

361

362

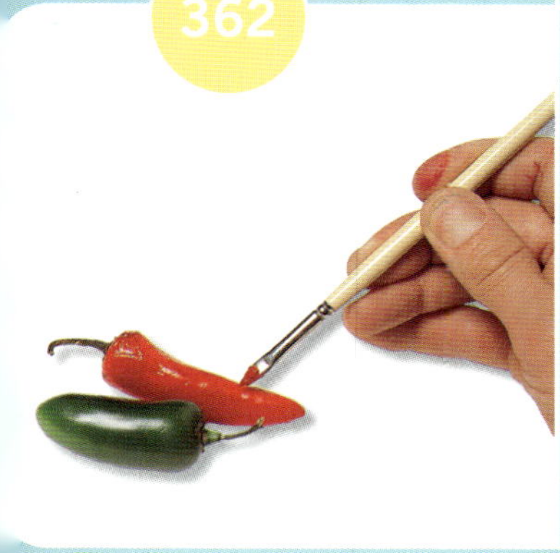

CHECKING A MATCH

When you think you have a correct mix for something in your subject, load the brush thickly with paint and hold it up in front of you against the "real-life" color. This will quickly show you whether the overall character of the color and the level of tone are accurate.

IDENTIFYING COLORS

363

Some colors are more difficult to mix than others, but it can be helpful to think your way through a checklist of points that will give you clues to the ingredients of your mix.

- What kind of color is it?
- Is it light, mid-toned, or dark?
- Which of my tube colors is nearest the main component?
- Does it have a distinct tinge of another color—which of my tube colors is nearest to that?
- Is it warm or cool?
- Is it intense or subdued?

The color swatches below show examples of how these principles can be applied.

Warm

Cadmium Red + black + white

Cool

Phthalo Green + black+ white

Dark

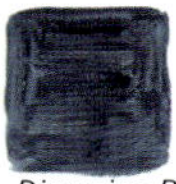

Dioxazine Purple + Phthalo Green

Light

white + Lemon Yellow + black

Color bias

Lemon Yellow (+ Raw Umber + white)

Cadmium Yellow + white + Dioxazine Purple

Dioxazine Purple + Raw Umber + white

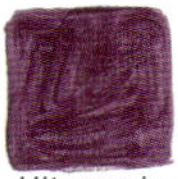

Ultramarine Blue + Naphthol Crimson

white + Dioxazine Purple + Cadmium Yellow

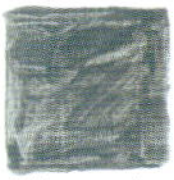

Ultramarine Blue (+ Raw Umber + white)

ORDER OF MIXING

364

When mixing a pale color, start with the weakest ingredient, say, yellow or white. Then add the stronger colors such as red or blue in small quantities, building up gradually to the strength you require. If you start with a strong hue you will have to add much more of the mixer color, wasting a lot of paint.

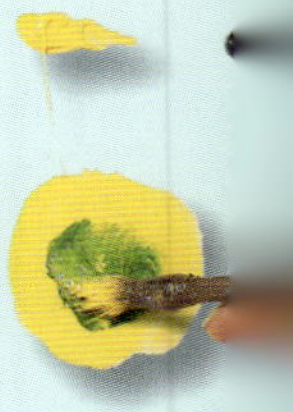

RECORDING MIXES

365

When you have mixed a color that was specially difficult to achieve, take a minute to paint a patch on a spare piece of paper and note down the component colors that you used. Put the color samples into a pocket file or scrapbook for later reference.

Alizarin Crimson + Cobalt Blue + Ivory Black

BRIGHTER COLORS

366

Adding white sometimes deadens the color intensity. Borrow a trick from watercolor painting, and use transparent washes rather than opaque paint to build up the required hue. Thin color allows the underlying white paper (or a ground of clean, fully dry white paint) to shine through, giving luminosity and freshness. This is often specially good for flower colors (pinks, violets, oranges, and deep reds) that have a natural brilliance.

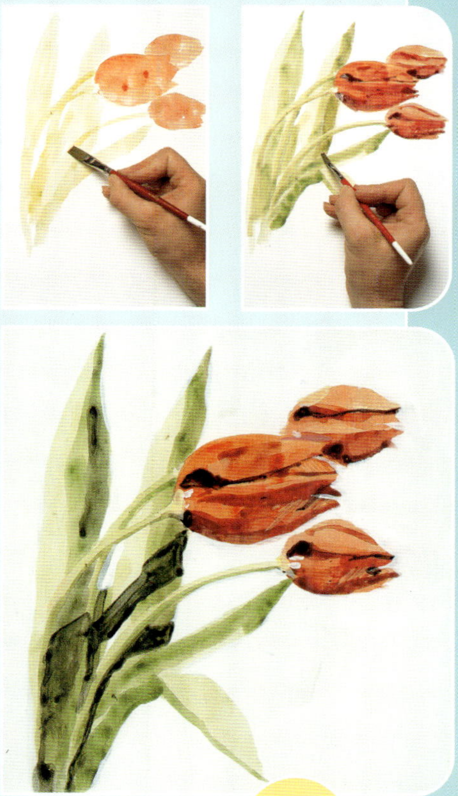

MODIFYING HUES

367

Some acrylic colors are very strong and artificial-looking and are not always suitable for painting natural subjects. If you want to modify a hue quite subtly, try adding small touches of the more subdued earth colors—the muted browns and yellows. For example, mix Burnt Sienna into green, and Yellow Ocher into mauve.

Bright Green | *Bright Green + Burnt Sienna* | *Bright Green + Red Violet*

BEAUTIFUL NEUTRALS

Neutral grays and beiges need not be boring and dull. Try mixing unlike colors that neutralize each other but retain lively undertones. For example, mix Crimson and Hooker's Green; Cadmium Orange and Ultramarine; Cadmium Yellow and Deep Violet. Titanium White is added to heighten and vary the tones.

368

KNOCKING BACK

If one color or area of the painting looks too bright, lay a thick glaze of a neutral color over it. Use a large soft brush and dilute the paint either with plain water or with a mixture of water and acrylic medium, which gives a glossier effect.

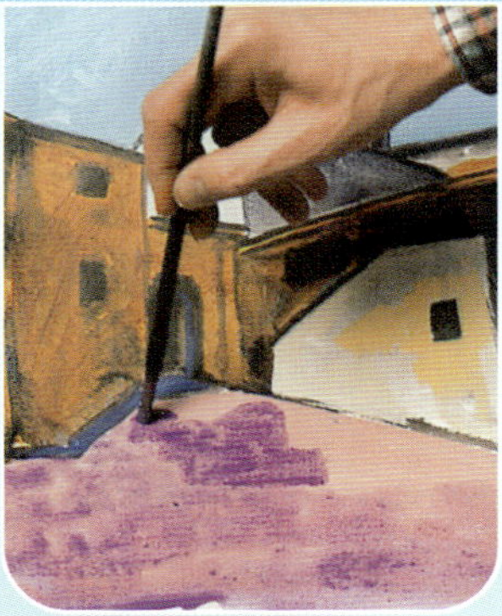

A vivid purple, diluted with water, is laid over dry paint.

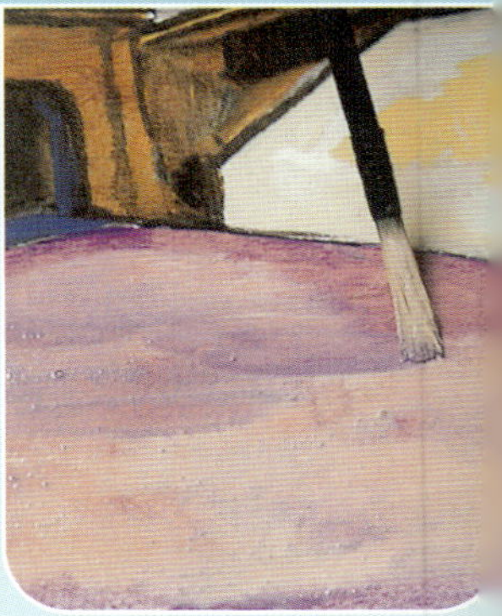

The effect was over-bright, so i modified with glazes of a more muted hue.

369

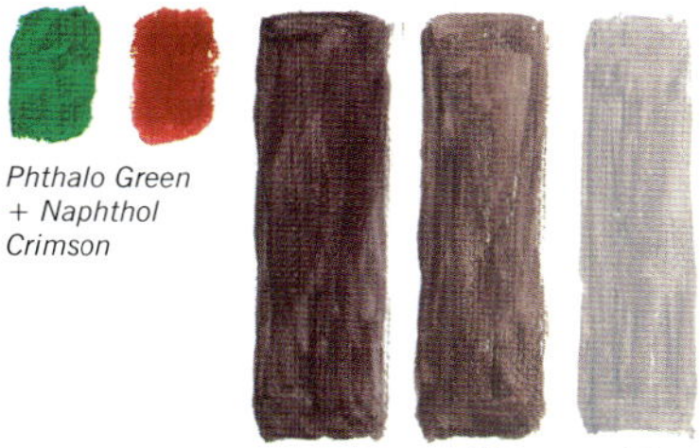

Phthalo Green + Naphthol Crimson

+ white *+ white*

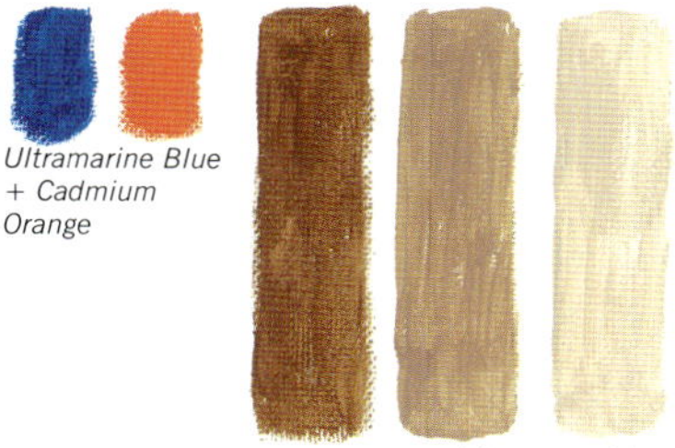

Ultramarine Blue + Cadmium Orange

+ white *+ white*

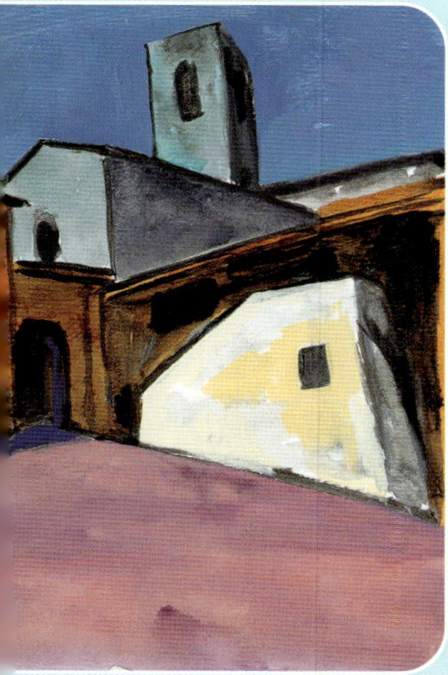

INCREASING OPACITY

370

Some acrylic colors, though deep-toned, are relatively transparent and will not give flat, even coverage in one coat. A little added white increases the opacity without significantly altering the tone or intensity. This also brings out the color of some dark shades of purple, blue, and green, which otherwise become dulled as they dry.

Alizarin Crimson

Ultramarine Blue

Ultramarine Blue + Titanium White

MIXING A WASH

371

When diluting thick color to wash consistency, add the water in small amounts and brush it in thoroughly; keep working in a little more water at a time until you get the fluidity you want. If you add too much water in one go, the paint may separate into tiny blobs and particles that do not all disperse, and your wash will be streaky.

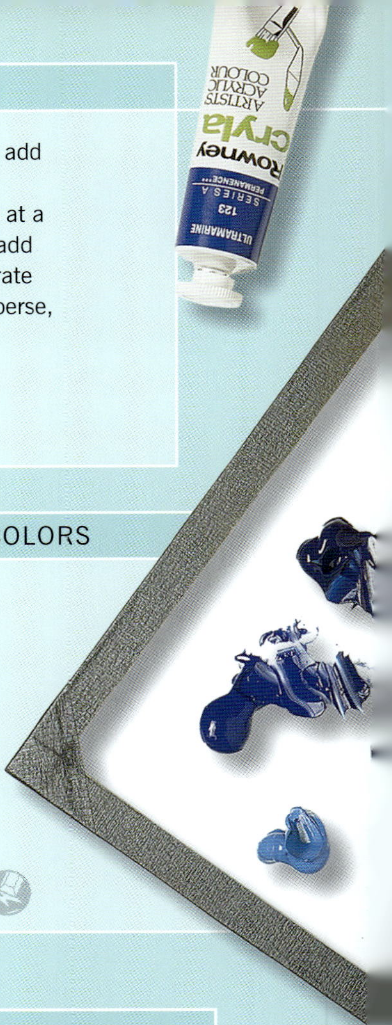

LAYING OUT COLORS

372

Set out your colors in the same order on your palette each time you start to paint. That way you can get used to finding the color you need quickly, making it easier to create your color mixes.

BRUSHING OUT

Thick acrylic can be quite resistant and you may need to brush it out thoroughly on the palette to avoid transferring lumpy-textured color onto the working surface. Use a springy, tough bristle or synthetic-hair brush to work into the paint until it is smooth and malleable.

373

KNIFE MIXING

If you are mixing thick acrylic colors, you may find it easiest to work them together on the palette with a knife. Don't just mash them together, as this can leave them partially unmixed, so the color changes shade as you lay on the paint. Use a palette knife to scoop the colors up together and knead them on the palette; spread the paint to check for unblended streaks.

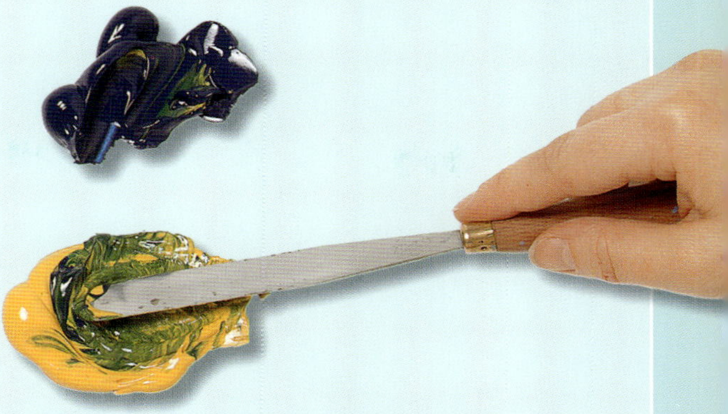

Blend the colors thoroughly together on the palette before transferring to the working surface. Some artists, however, like the effect of partially mixed colors; this can be effective in some cases.

374

BRUSH MIXING

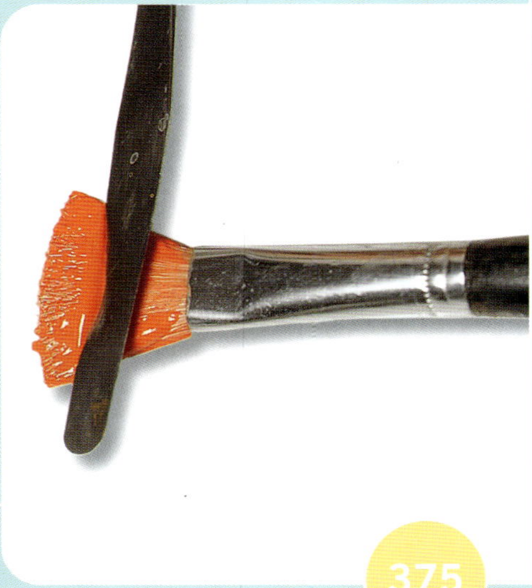

When you mix colors together using a brush, you will find it ends up overloaded with paint. To squeeze out the excess color, put it down flat on the palette and run the edge of a palette knife or plastic card down the bristles from base to tip.

375

METHODS AND MEDIUMS

Acrylic is the most versatile of all the painting media. You do not have to use it at tube consistency—you can thin it so that it resembles watercolor, bulk it out with special mediums for rich impasto effects, or even mix it with sand to produce textured effects. The tips on these pages will help you to experiment and discover your own methods.

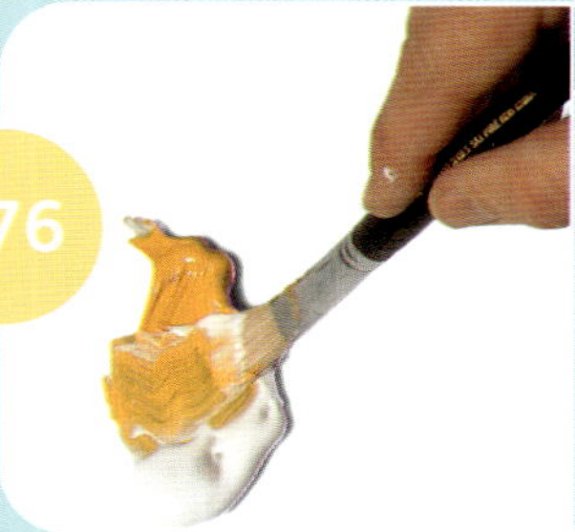

376

THICKENING PAINT

If you like to apply paint very thickly, consider buying one of the special impasto mediums sold for the purpose. These are a good economy measure, as they bulk out the paint without changing the color.

KNIFE PAINTING

Paint well thickened with impasto medium can be applied with painting knives as well as with brushes. Knives create exciting effects; they press the paint onto the surface, creating flat planes and small ridges at the end of each stroke.

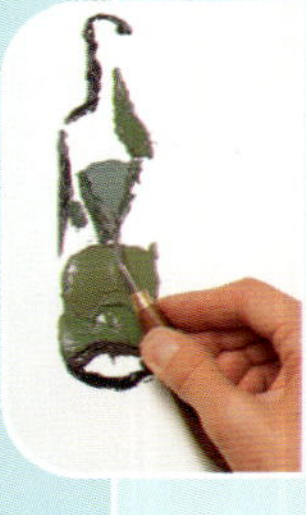

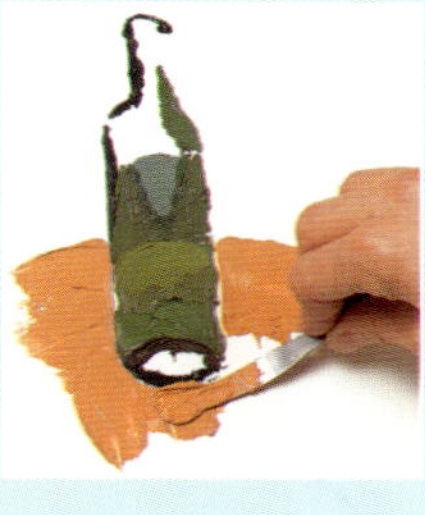

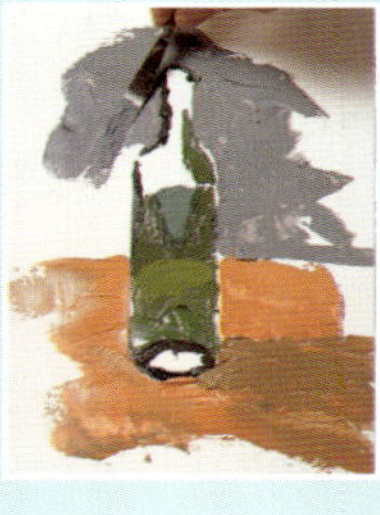

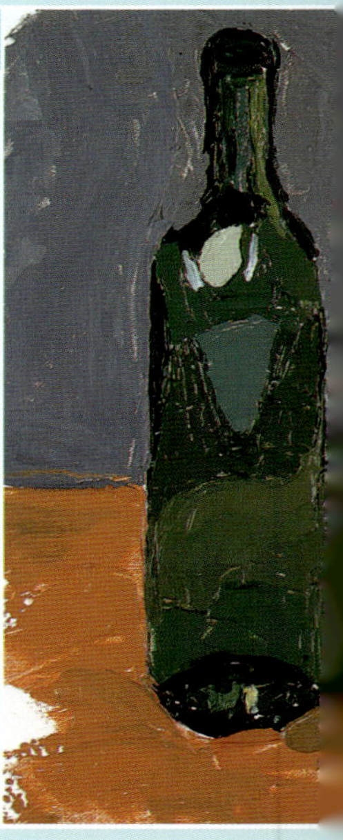

377

RETARDING MEDIUM

Because acrylic dries so quickly it is difficult to blend thick colors wet into wet unless you use retarding medium. This keeps the paint moist for longer so that it remains workable on the surface. It is used with thick paint, not washes, as water affects its action.

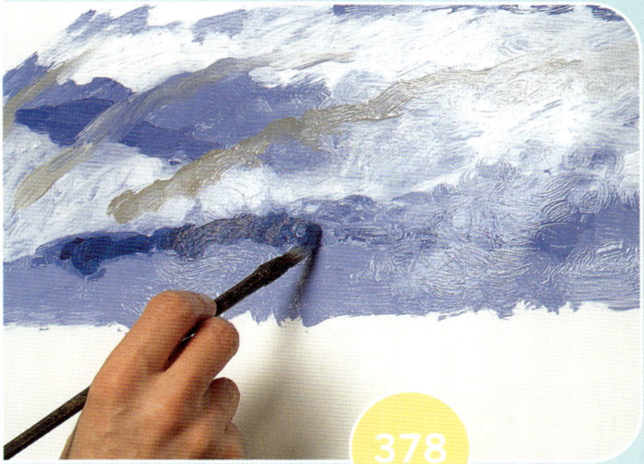

378

PAINT TEXTURE

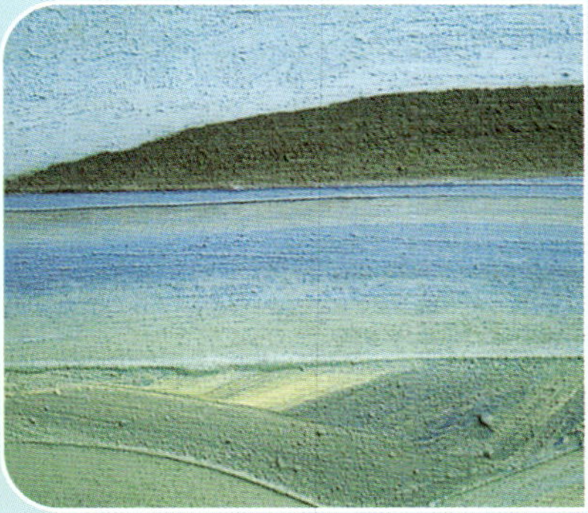

In his painting "Winter Headland" (detail), Robert Tilling has achieved a variety of textures by mixing his paint with sand.

Acrylic can be given different textures by mixing it with any one of various special texture mediums. A less costly alternative is to mix it with natural substances, such as sand or sawdust.

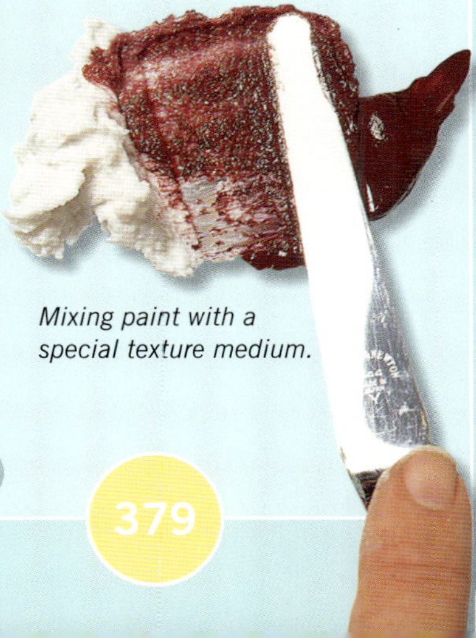

Mixing paint with a special texture medium.

379

TEXTURED GROUNDS

Interesting effects can also be achieved by texturing the ground, using acrylic modeling paste. You must use a rigid surface for this. Lay the paste on with a knife to create a random rough surface, or press crumpled kitchen foil or relief-patterned objects into it while wet.

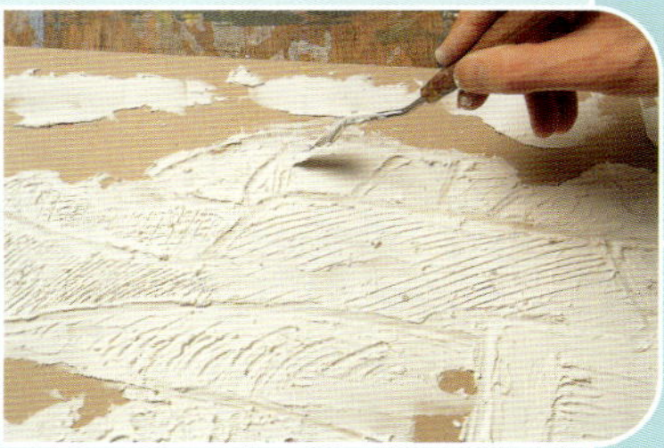

Intricate patterns can be built up by scratching into the wet modeling paste.

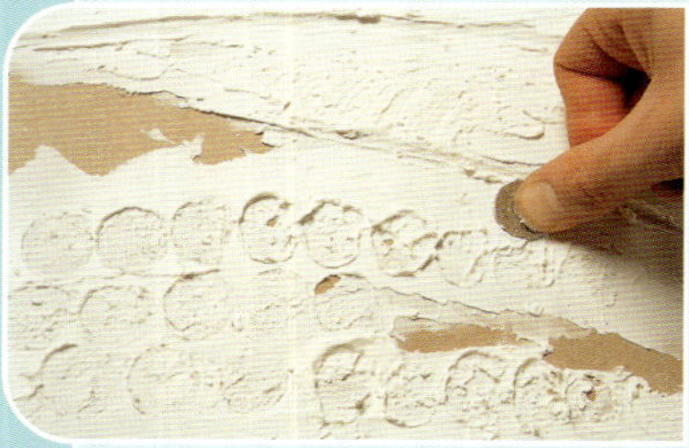

Pressing any relief-patterned object into the surface leaves an imprint.

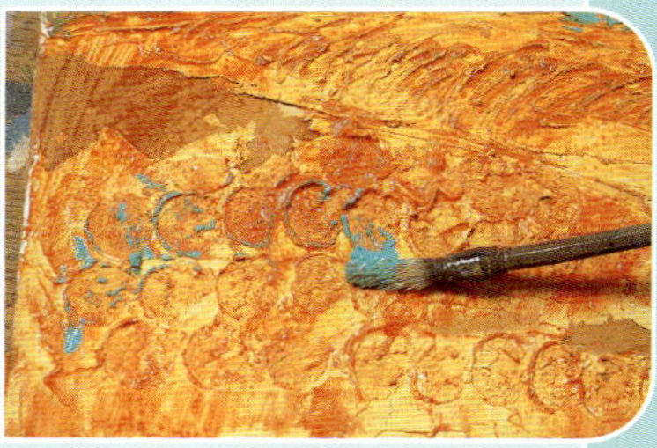

The thick paint catches on the raised ridges, while the diluted yellow-red has collected in the "valleys."

380

The best effects come from varying the paint's consistency so that the underlying pattern shows more in some places than others.

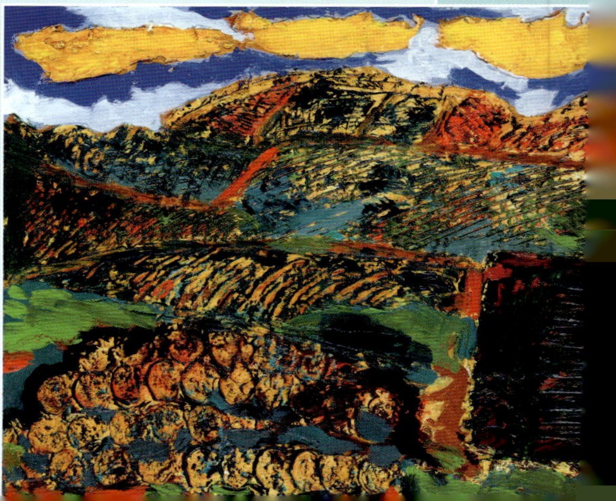

EVEN WASHES

381

Acrylics can be thinned and used like watercolors. To lay a flat wash, choose a large brush and load it as fully as possible with wet paint. Work in even stokes from one side of the paper the other, making sure that you pick up the wet edge of the previous stroke each time. If you have a large area to blend, such as a sky getting lighter toward the horizon, try working flat and adding more water to the paint. Use a broad brush to "flow" the colors into each other with rapid, bold strokes.

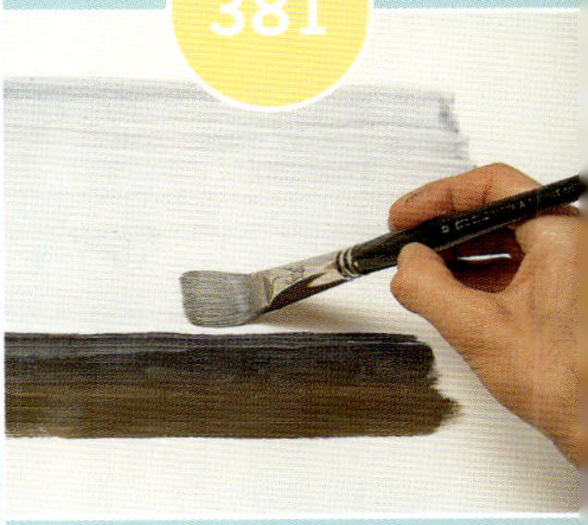

LINE AND WASH

382

The density of acrylic paint may lead you to overlook its potential for very delicate effects. Used in small quantities and smoothly diluted, it works excellently for the watercolor technique of tinting a pencil or ink drawing.

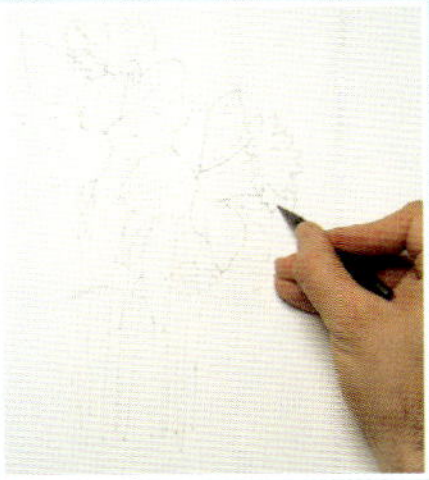

A line drawing is made first, using a fine pen.

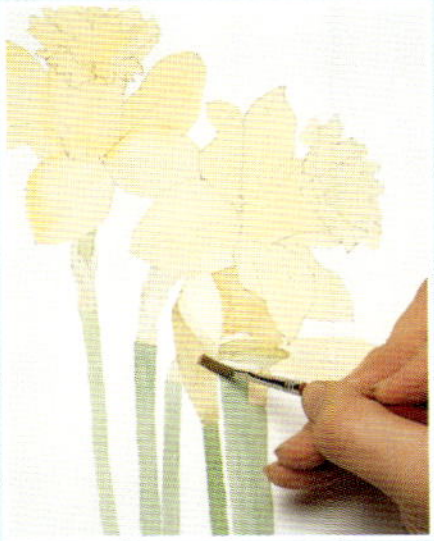

Diluted color is then brushed in carefully within the pen lines.

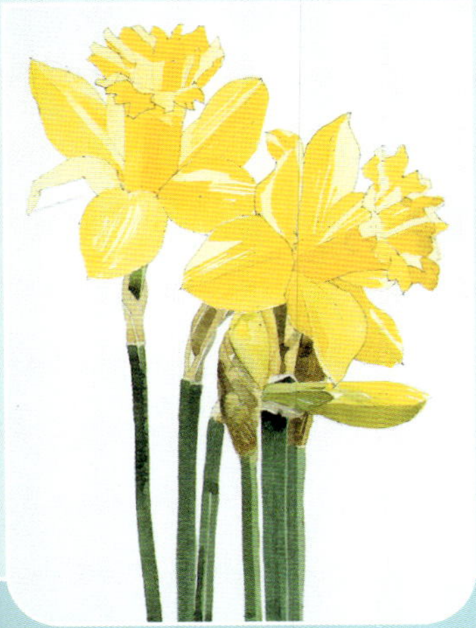

The effect is as delicate as watercolor, with the fine pen lines adding a touch of crisp definition.

STAINING

383 Diluted color can be applied to primed or raw canvas, with the picture built up in layers of transparent stains. To help the paint adhere and help to eliminate brushmarks, you can either mix the paint with a water-tension breaker or dampen the canvas with a solution of water and washing-up liquid.

UNDERPAINTING

384 Understanding the basic tonal pattern of your painting helps you to key in the colors effectively. Underpainting, in monochrome, using a restricted range of tonal values, gives you this important plan. Sketch your subject lightly with the brush, then block in the shadows and mid-tones with thinned paint. You can either retain the key of the picture by then overpainting with washes and glazes, or start to build opaque color on the underpainted image.

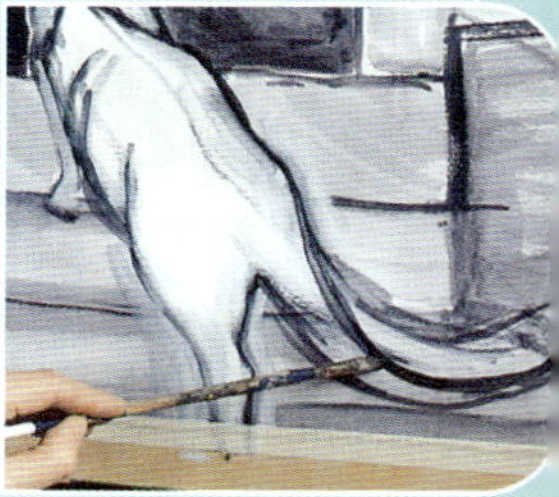

Sketch in your subject using monochrome colors.

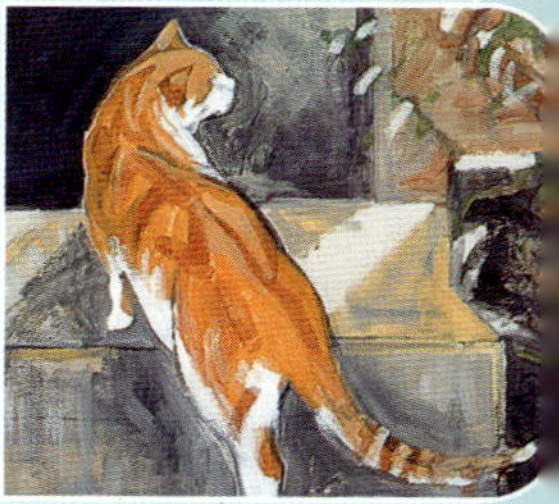

The artist has retained the tones in the finished picture.

POINTILLISM

385 If you have tried the pointillist technique and the colors don't seem to be mixing, it could be because they vary too much in tone. To work effectively, the colors used should be the same tone. Use dryish paint, and apply it in short strokes, making sure that the brushstrokes don't blend together.

SURFACE EFFECTS

More than any other paint, acrylic is capable of achieving rich textures that give your painting a lively surface quality. Here you will find some exciting ideas and unconventional methods such as scraping paint onto the surface and mixing acrylic with other media for mixed-media and collage work.

DRY-BRUSH TECHNIQUES

386

Dry brushing, with either thick or thin paint, creates a broken dragged texture that is useful for rough or linear textures such as stonework, grass, hair, or animal fur. Load the brush with paint, then blot off the excess onto kitchen paper or a rag. Spread the brush bristles and stroke them gently over the working surface.

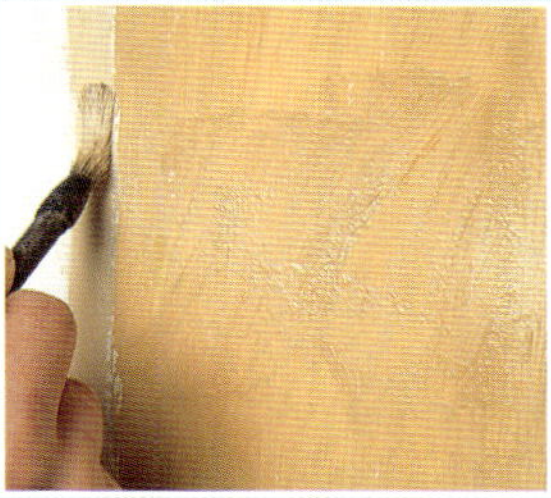

A base color is laid thickly, letting the brushmarks show.

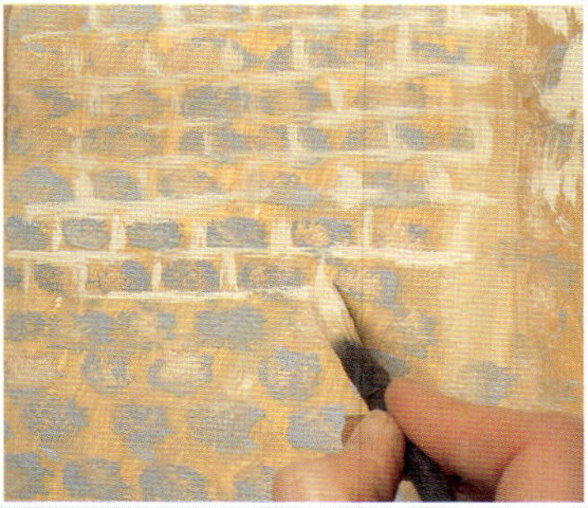

Paint is dragged lightly over the surface.

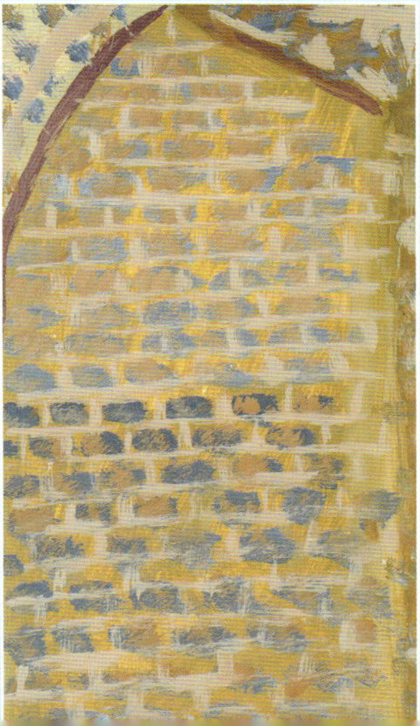

With further layers of color applied, the texture and pattern are rendered convincingly.

SPLATTERING

387

Flicked and spattered paint can suggest a specific texture, or simply create contrast for areas of flat color. For a coarse spatter, load a bristle brush with wet paint and draw your thumb along the top of it. For a fine spray, mix watered paint in a jar and blow it onto the surface with a mouth diffuser. These are made for spraying fixative onto pastel work, and are available in art shops.

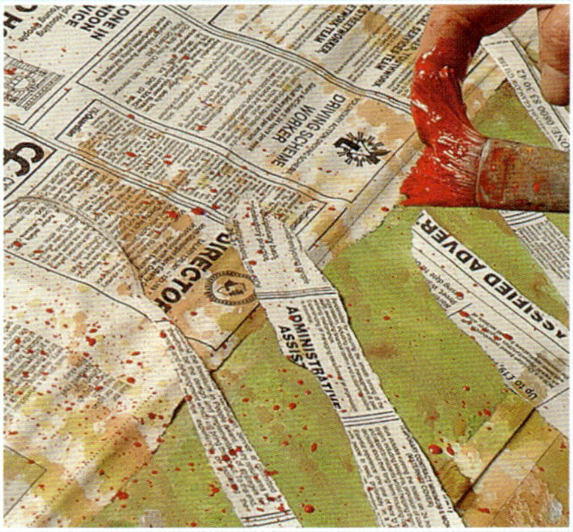

Mask out areas not to be spattered.

THIN AND THICK

Whole pictures can be built up with layers of transparent glazes, or you can vary the surface by glazing over thick impastos. The thin paint slides off the raised areas but runs into the crevices between brush-and-knife strokes to heighten the three-dimensional effect.

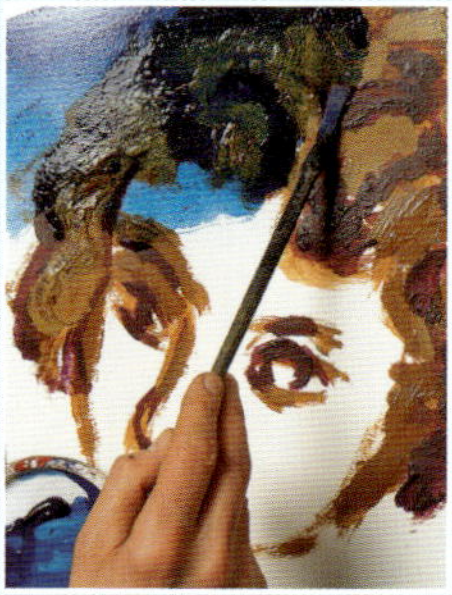

Thick paint was used for the hair and allowed to dry. A transparent glaze, made by mixing paint with water and medium, is applied on top. The effect can be seen in the finished picture (right).

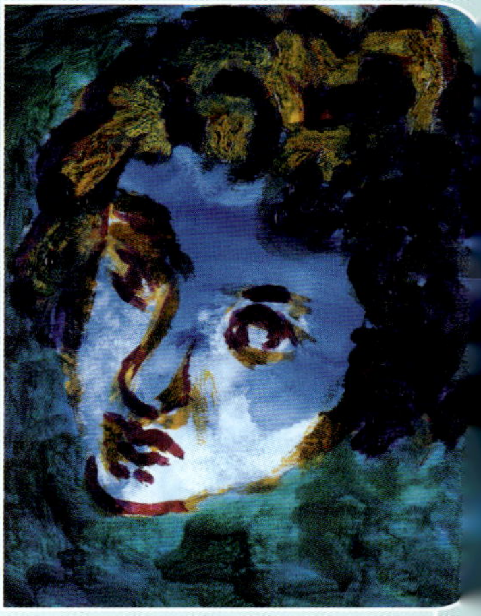

388

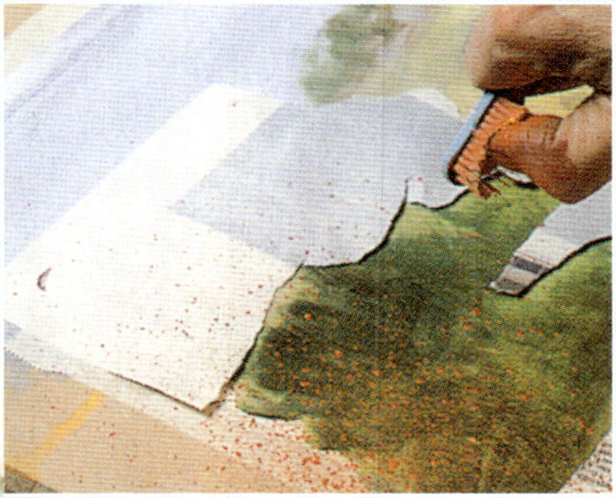

A toothbrush gives a fine splatter.

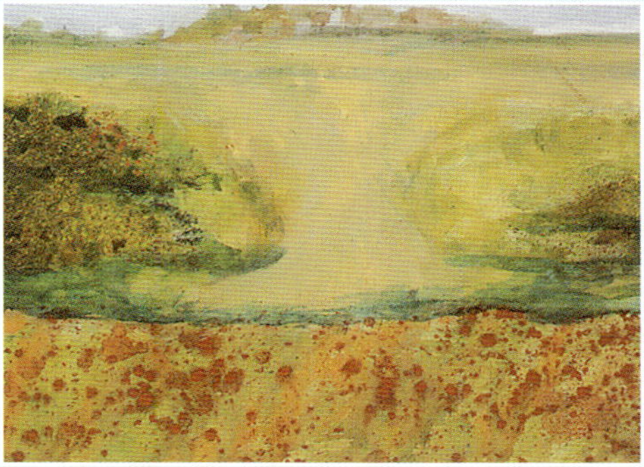

Paper has been used to merge the splatter drops.

SCRAPING

Scraping paint onto and across the surface produces thin layers of color that only partially cover those below. The effect is a little like glazing, but with a livelier surface texture. There are no implements sold for this method, but you can use improvised ones, such as plastic cards.

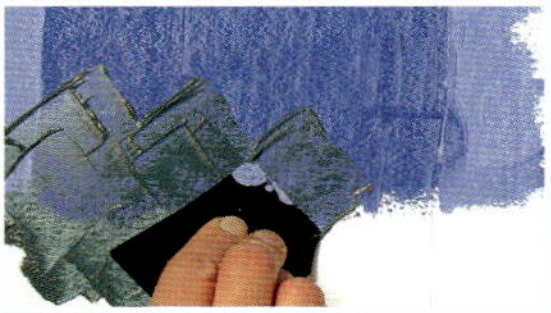

Using a plastic card, the artist scrapes paint onto the paper.

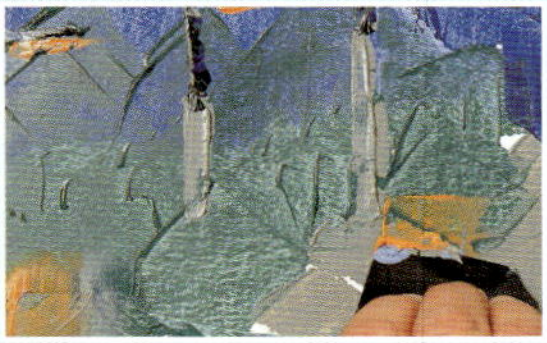

Successive applications build up colors and textures.

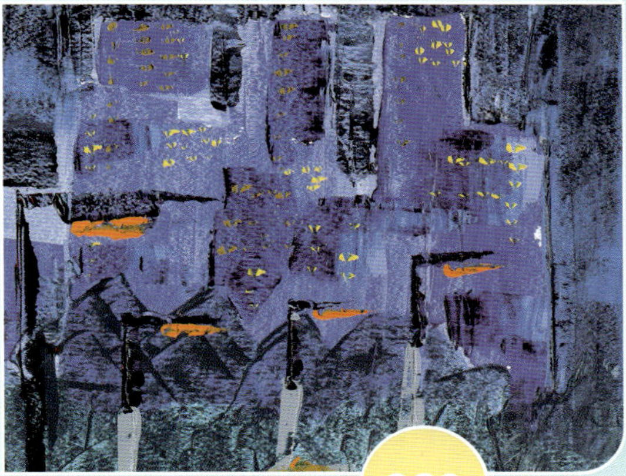

389

COMBING

390

Thick paint remains workable for some time, allowing you to work into it to create texture effects. Try dragging a comb through wet color, or drawing patterns into it with a knife point. Bear in mind, though, that such approaches are best suited to abstract or semi-abstract work.

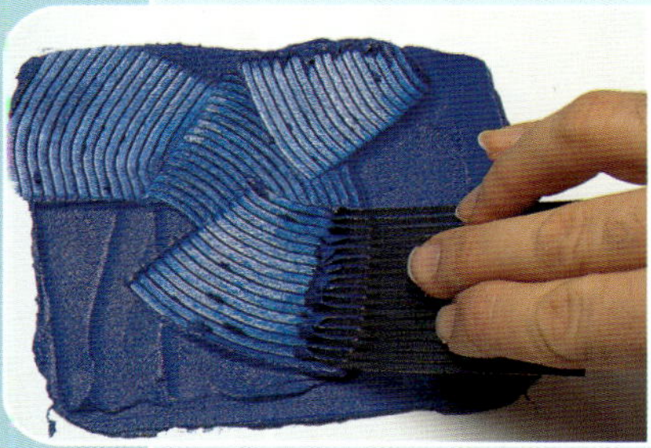

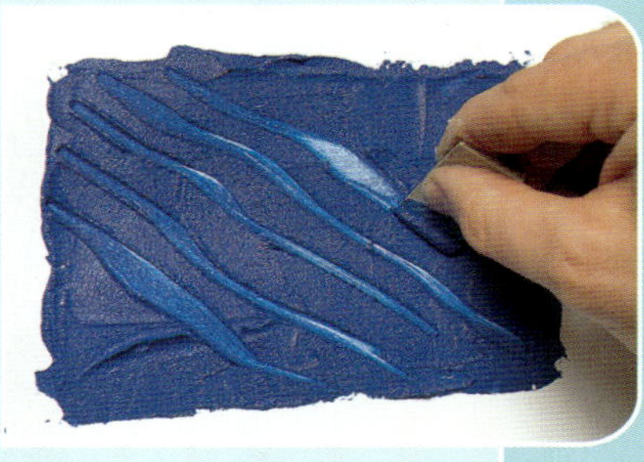

PAINTS AND MEDIUMS

391

At least one manufacturer now produces metallic and iridescent paints and special mediums that help you give excitement and variety to your work. These are worth experimenting with, particularly for collage and mixed-media work.

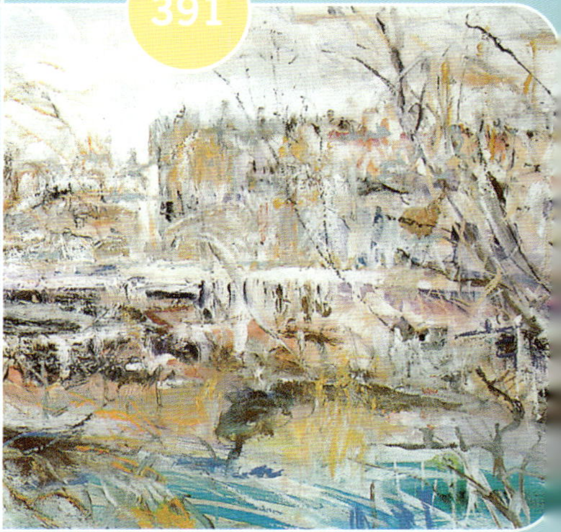

"Birthday in Edinburgh" by Jacquie Turner.

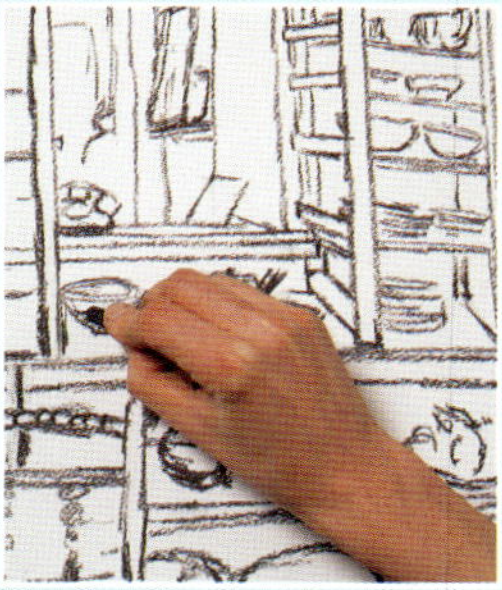

A drawing is made in charcoal.

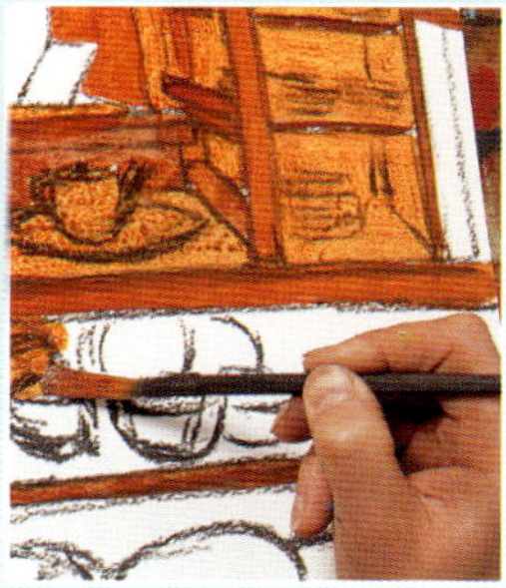

Thin paint is used, so the charcoal shows through.

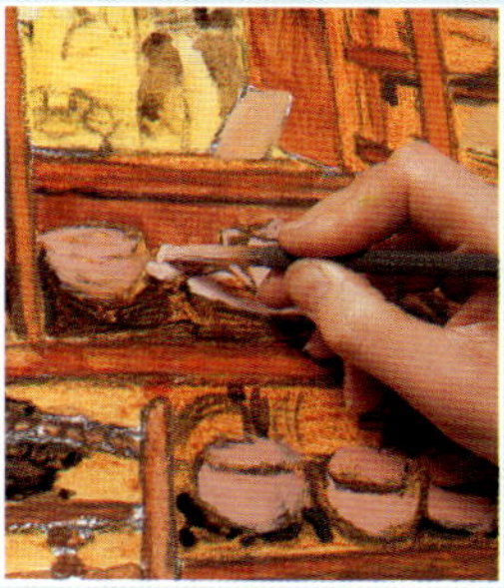

Thicker paint is applied in places.

Charcoal lines give a crisp edge to acrylic painting, but be sure to blow away excess charcoal dust that can contaminate the paint color. A thin wash of acrylic seals the line drawing onto the surface of canvas or paper.

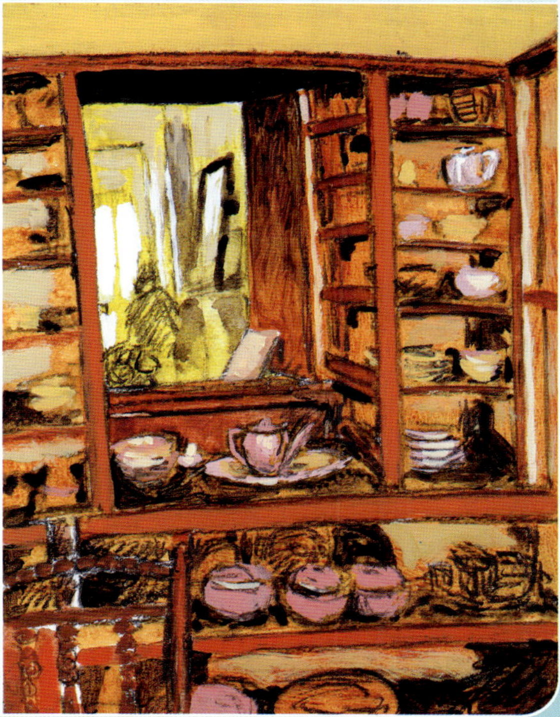

By varying the consistency of the paint, and drawing with charcoal both under and over the color, the artist has achieved a lively surface.

392

WAX RESIST

Because of its very regular consistency, even thinned acrylic color may adhere to and cover a drawing in wax crayon, not giving the resist effect you want. Make a quick test patch and if the paint sticks, add more water.

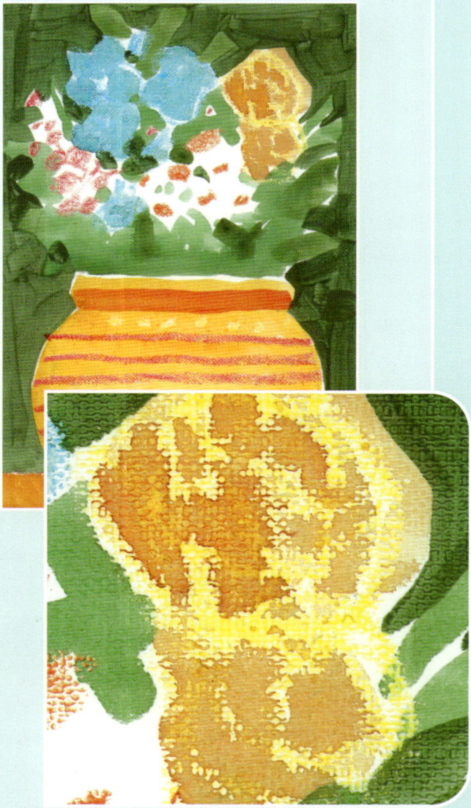

The detail shows where the paint has slid off the waxed areas.

393

COLLAGE OPTIONS

Because acrylic paints are themselves adhesive, you can add all sorts of collage elements directly to the paint, such as paper scraps, images or textures taken from magazine tear-sheets, or lightweight fabrics, strings, and yarns. These can be painted over with thin glazes, if you so wish.

USING PASTEL

Acrylic can be combined with pastel to exploit the different textures; linear strokes or scumbles of pastel contrasting with smoother applications of paint. Soft pastel can be "fixed" with a light application of acrylic medium so that you can build up a painting in layers. Or, use oil pastel, which has better qualities of adherence.

Collage can be used on its own, but is more often combined with paint, as in Mike Bernard's "Road to the Sea." In places, patterned or printed paper has been stuck down and left as it is, while in others (the road in the foreground), thinner paper has been collaged and painted over to create texture.

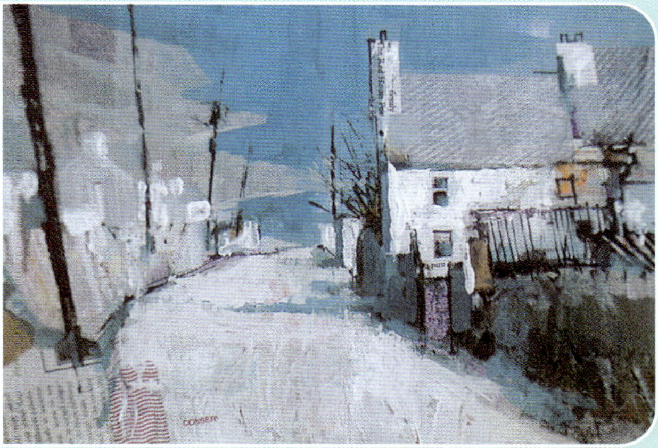

394

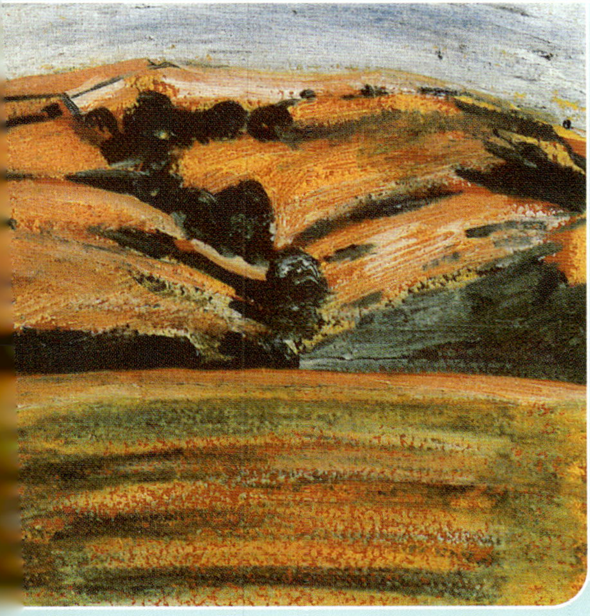

Oil pastel, used in Helena Greene's "Exmoor," can create exciting resist effects when combined with thinned acrylic.

395

SUBJECTS

Although there are no "special" ways of painting particular subjects—a landscape and a still life by the same artist will not differ much in style and technique—there are a few subject-related problems, and this section shows you some useful "tricks of the trade" for solving them. Rulers and masking tape, for example, are invaluable for helping you achieve straight edges on buildings.

VARIED GREENS

396

If you have trouble getting variety into your landscape greens, try creating much more distinct color contrasts in highlights and shadows. Vibrant yellow, pink, or orange can help to light the greens, while true blues and blue-mauves are good shadowing colors. Add them in small touches, and they will "read" as green variations.

In Gerry Baptist's "Life Goes on in Provence" (detail), the overall effect is of rich, varied greens, but in fact there are relatively small areas of pure green, enhanced by the rich, singing blues, oranges, and yellows.

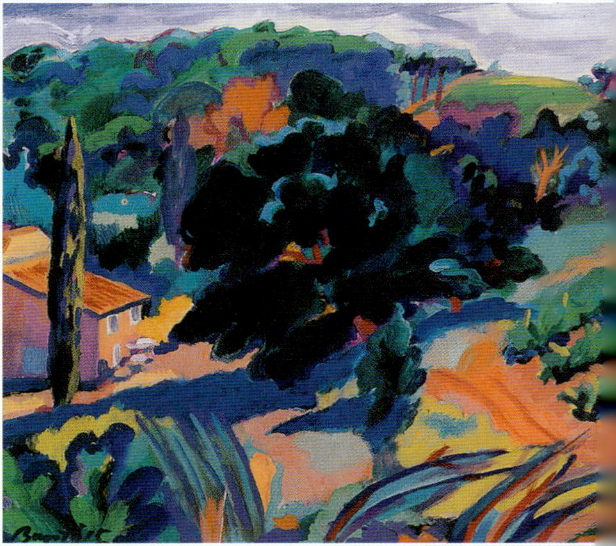

QUIETER GREENS

Artificial paint colors don't directly match the subtlety of natural greens. If your tube colors look too garish, try mixing in touches of red, red-purple, or red-brown. Red is the opposite color to green and has a subduing influence.

Oxide of Chromium

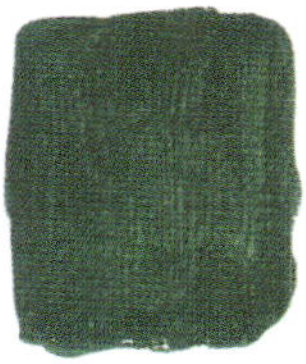

Oxide of Chromium + Deep Violet

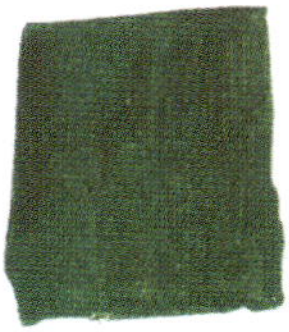

Oxide of Chromium + Raw Sienna

397

BRUSHWORK

When you are painting trees, look carefully at the growth pattern of branches and leaves and let them guide the direction of your brushwork. Notice whether the foliage canopy sweeps down or fans outward, whether leaves hang from the twigs or push up.

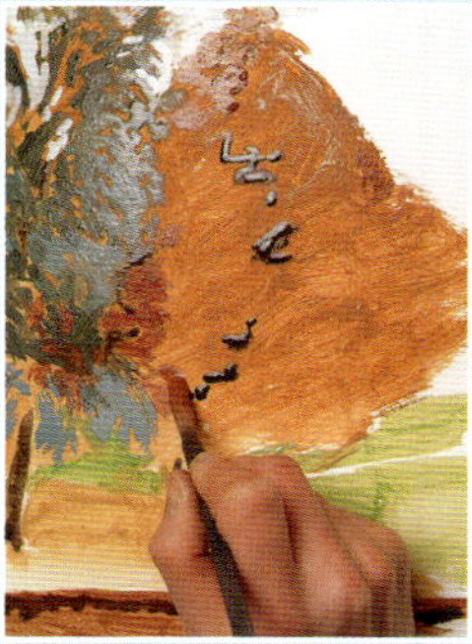

The shapes of the brushmarks describe the foliage on the left.

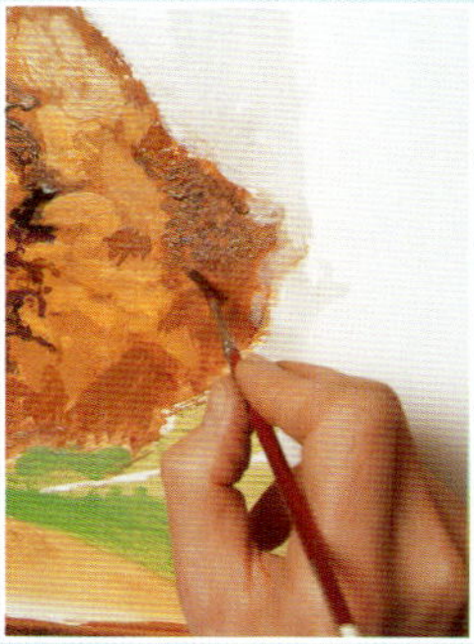

After blocking in the main shape, the artist begins to define the clumps of foliage.

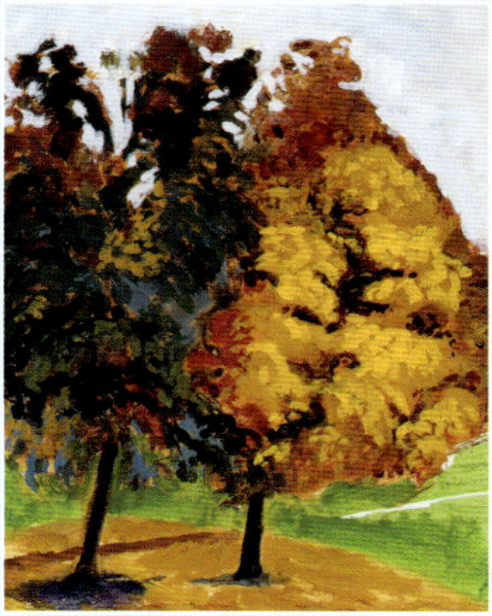

Notice how the artist established the main shape and slanting thrust of the right-hand tree before dealing with specific areas of foliage. On both trees, the brushmarks follow the directions of the foliage clumps.

398

LETTING IN LIGHT

If you have made tree foliage look too heavy and solid, insert some patches, dabs, and trails of sky color among the greens to open up the shapes. It is easiest to identify these "sky holes" when you have established the main shape of the tree, and because acrylics are opaque, it is no problem to overpaint them over darker colors.

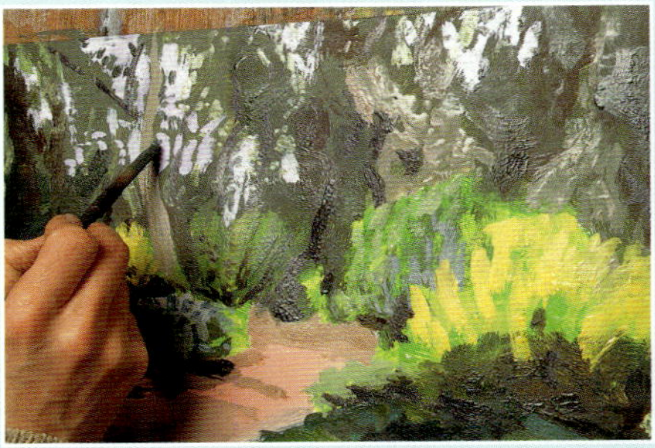

The main areas of background foliage are painted initially as solid color.

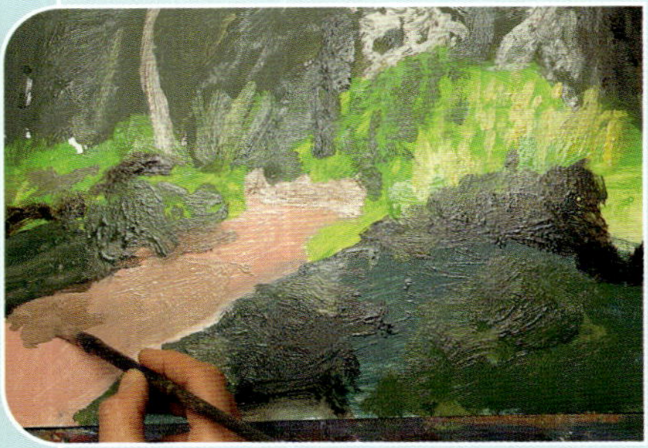

Trunks and branches are defined by painting light colors around and between the shapes.

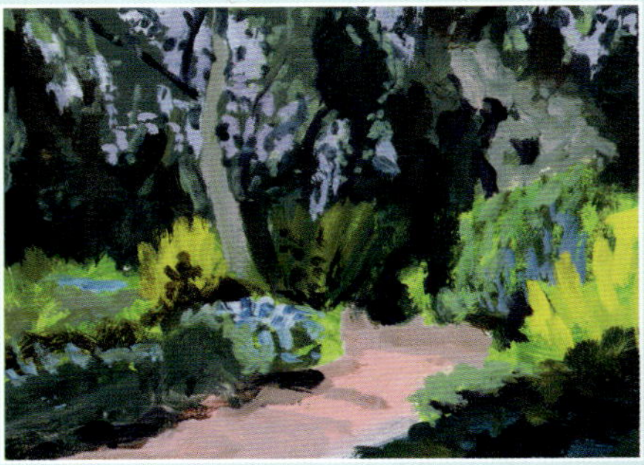

Finally, the colors were deepened and enriched with glazes.

REGULAR PATTERNS

On buildings, use a flat brush to create the patterns of brickwork or roof tiles—choose one that is the right width to paint each rectangle boldly in one stroke. Use shorter strokes to add shading or highlighting to the shapes.

Precisely placed rows of diagonal brushmarks build up the chevron-patterned wall.

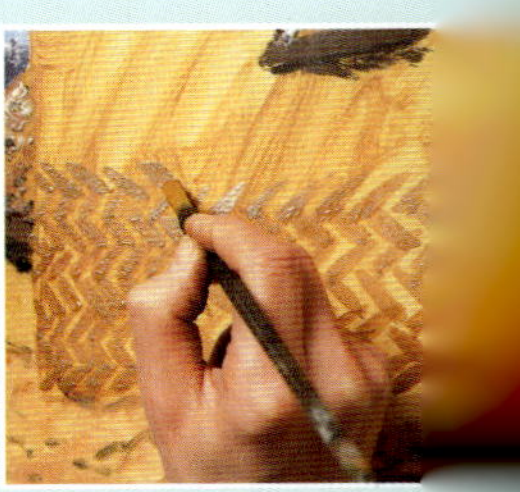

400

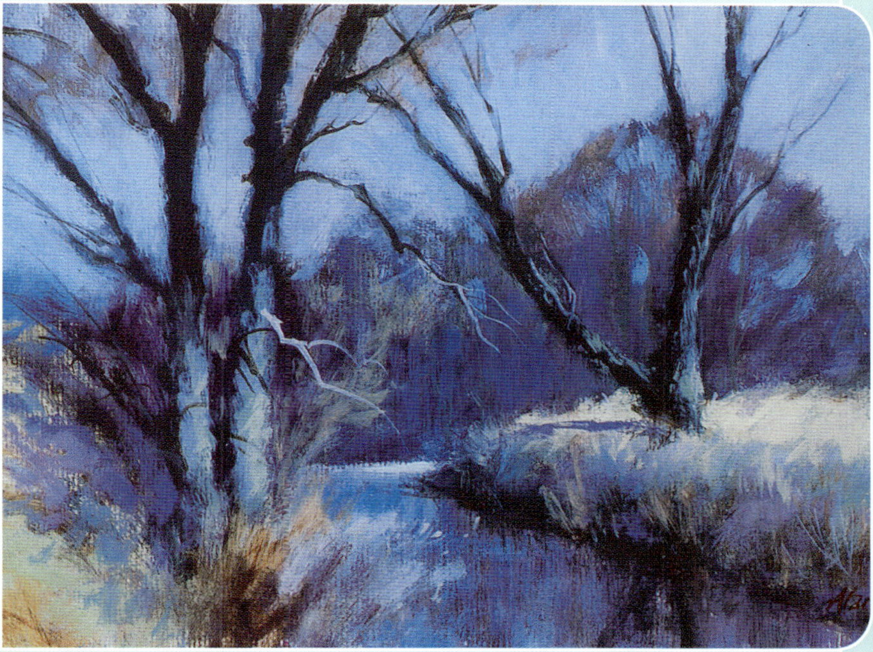

Alan Oliver has used a similar technique in his "Winter's Morning," painting sky color lightly over the colors used for the background trees.

399

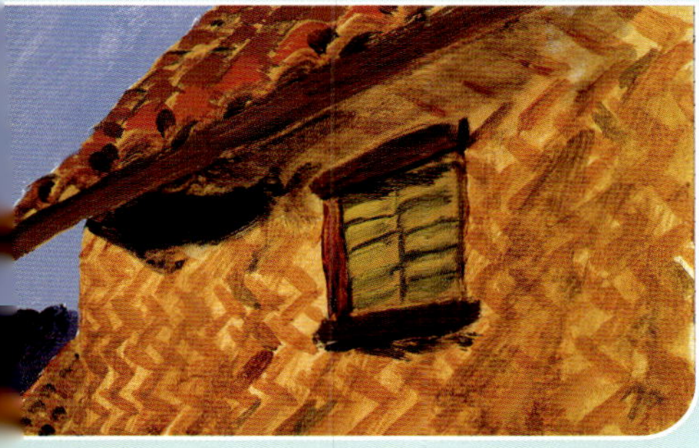

On the wall, care was taken to gradually reduce the size of the brushmarks, creating the effect of the receding plane.

MASKING

A wobbly or tilting edge on the walls or windows of a building can spoil the effect, so if clean straight lines are important to your painting, use masking tape to harden the edges of the main shapes and brush ruling for straight-line details.

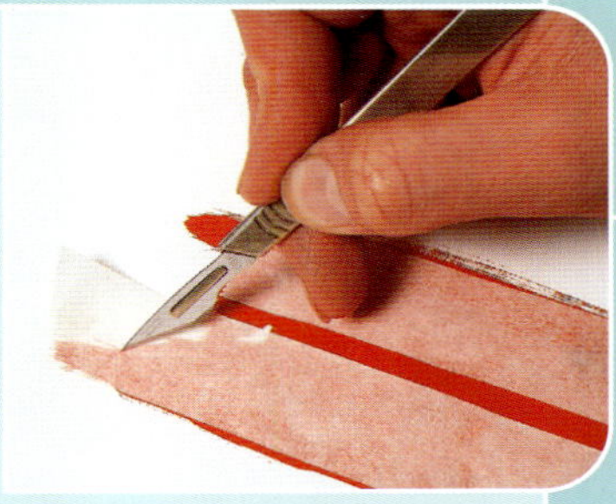

Put masking tape on the area to be masked.

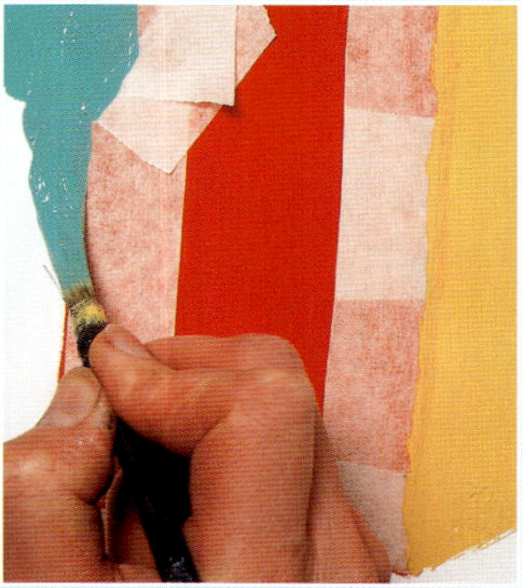

Apply paint along edge of the tape.

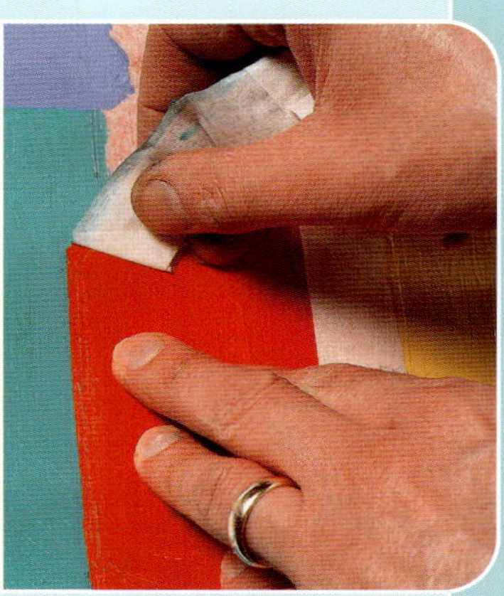

Peel off masking tape to reveal a straight edge.

401

ONE-STROKE TOUCHES

Distant houses or cottages in landscapes can be simply touched in using a flat brush in one decisive stroke.

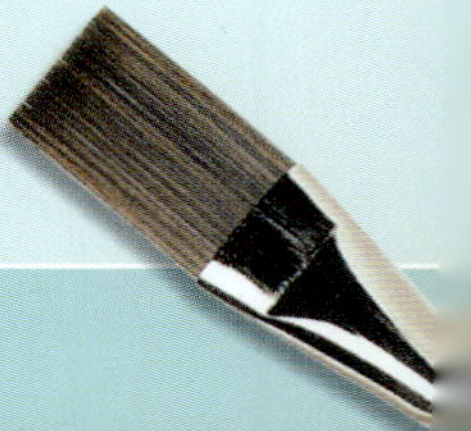

402

CHECKING ACCURACY

403

When painting an architectural subject that has straight lines and hard angles, stand back from the painting frequently to check that the verticals and horizontals are accurate. Hold up a ruler with your arm out straight and align it to the painted shapes. If you keep working close to the image, wrongly angled brushstrokes can push parts of the subject out of line.

EDGE QUALITIES

In still-life painting, bear in mind that objects do not really have outlines, we perceive a line where one surface overlaps or turns against another. The edge quality may be indistinct in parts, for example if the color or tone is similar, so it should not be painted as a hard divide. By contrast, another part may appear sharply defined. The contrast of "lost-and-found" edges gives a sense of reality.

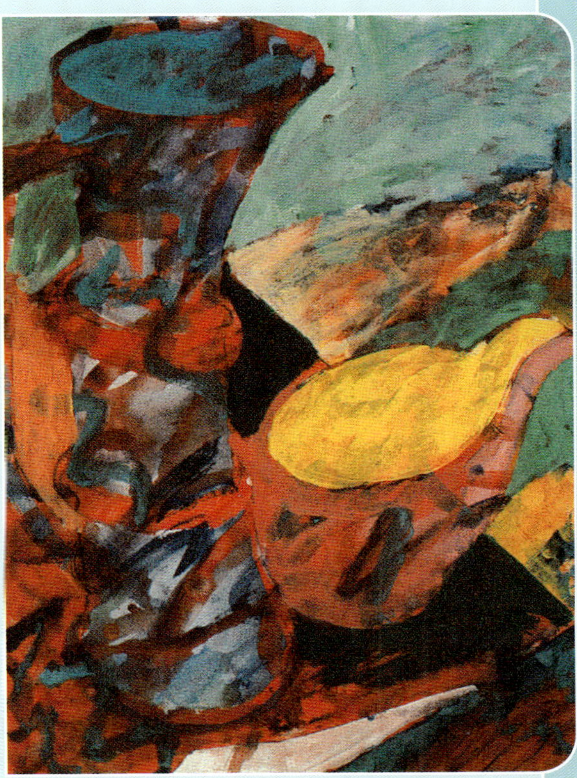

In Paul Powis' "Jugs," the two vessels on the left merge into one another, while in the center—also the picture's center of interest—the edges are sharp and clear.

404

405

HIGHLIGHTS

The shinier a surface is, the more intense its highlights. If you are painting a glass or white-metal object, don't be afraid to make strong highlights really dazzling—apply thick, opaque, pure white paint.

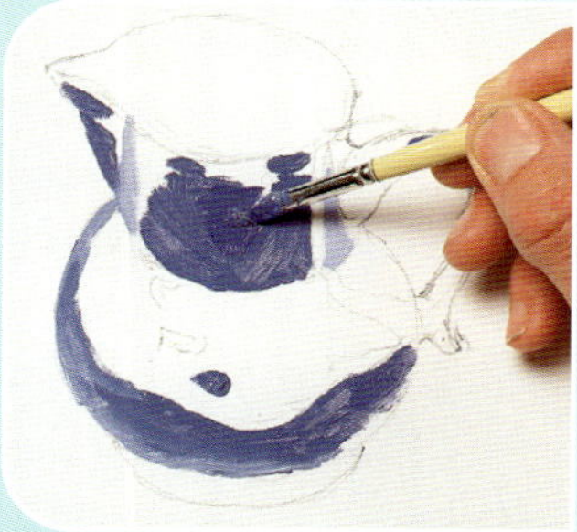

Begin with a mid-blue, to which the darker and lighter colors will be added.

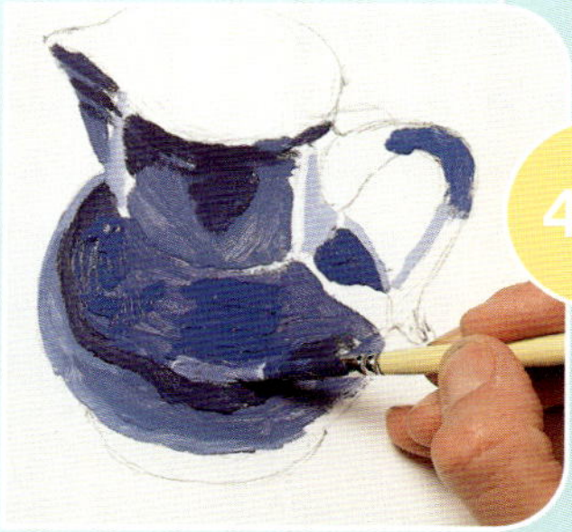

This curving highlight is put on after the band of shadow beneath, using thick paint.

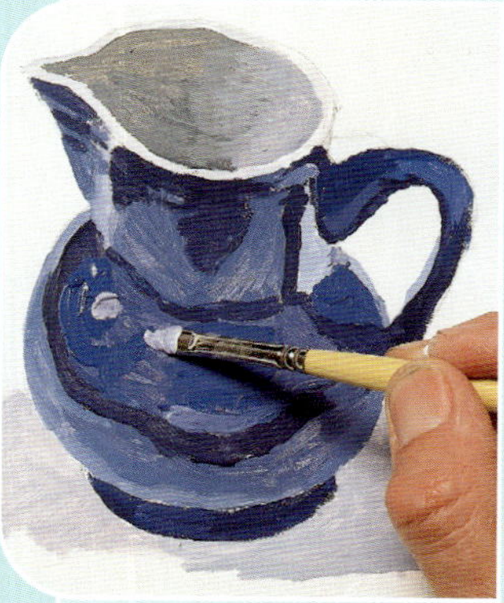

On a shiny, rounded surface the pattern of highlights can be quite intricate, resulting in a wide variety of colors.

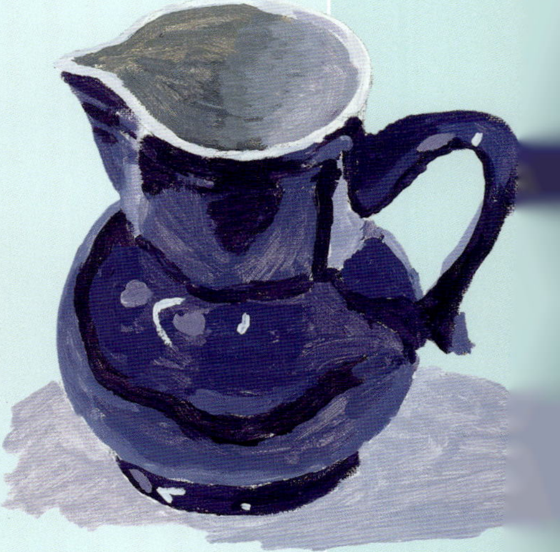

The small highlights where the jug catches direct light are almost pure white. These were added last.

Because glass is both transparent and reflective, it often presents confusing layers of information that are difficult to sort out. Try first looking through the glass to see shapes created by the background colors, and block them in quite broadly. Then, look for highlights and dark tones that define the form of the object itself; these typically fall on edges, angles, and curves, giving definition to the shapes.

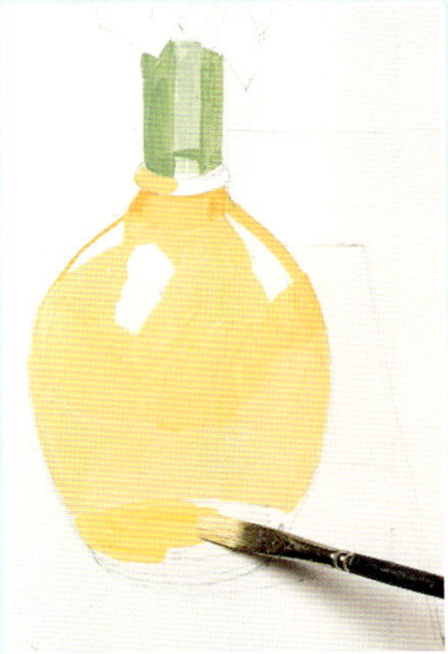

Main shape blocked in.

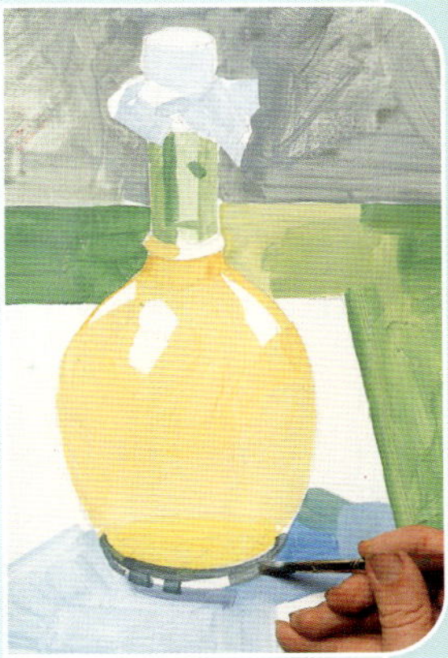

Dark tone added to edges.

406

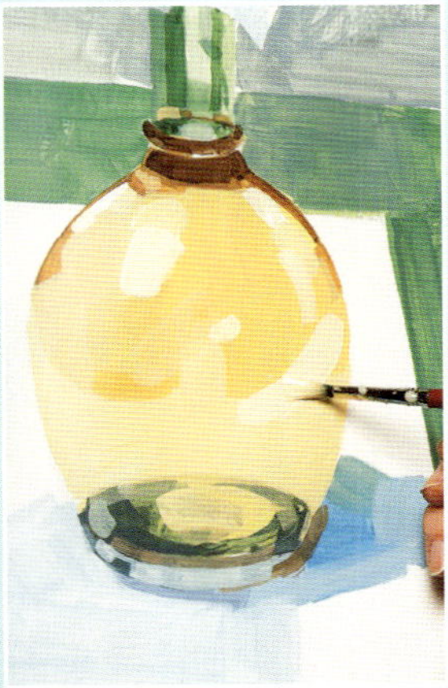

Highlights added.

The foot of the bottle reflects darker color, with little of the yellow visible.

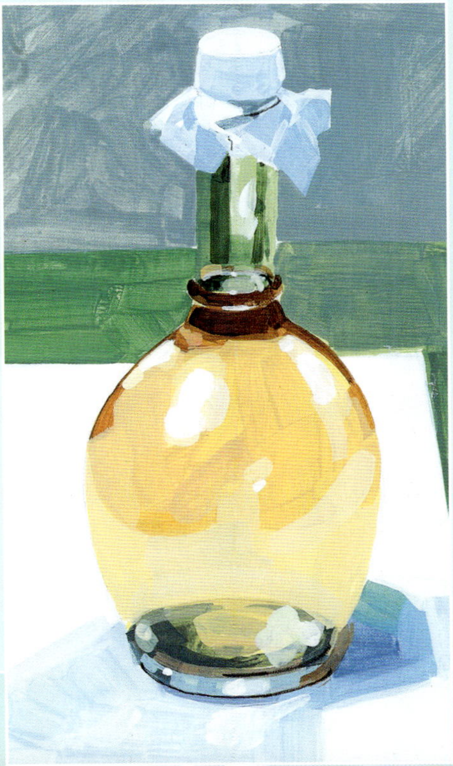

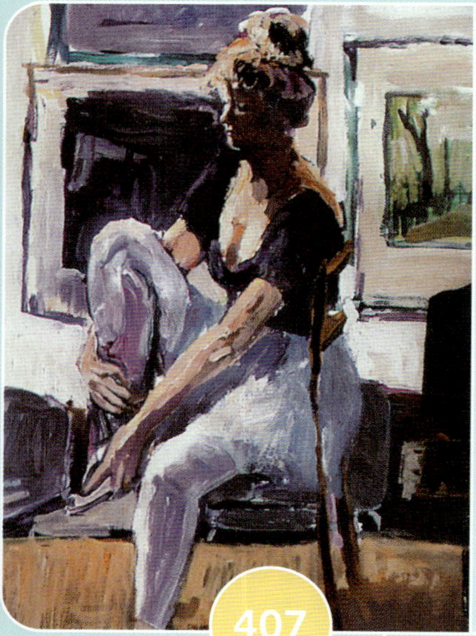

407

HIGHLIGHT COLORS

A common mistake when painting pale skin is to make the highlights too light, resulting in a painting that is too high in "key." You can check the tone of highlights by holding up a piece of white card in front of the subject; this will show you that they are nowhere near white.

In Daniel Stedman's "Fleur, Dancer Backlit," the highlights on face and chest stand out dramatically against the dark tones, but are nowhere near pure white.

DIRECTIONAL BRUSHWORK

Look for the main forms when you are painting a figure and let your brushstrokes follow them, using long strokes for legs, arms, and the folds of clothing or drapery, and shorter curves for rounded forms.

In Daniel Stedman's "Julie," brushwork plays a vital role in describing the shapes and forms.

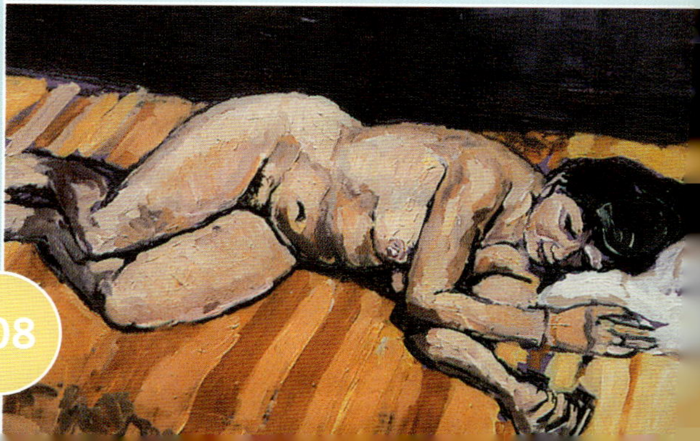

408

409

Dry brushing is an excellent technique for painting animal hair or fur. Use a strong bristle brush for coarse hair and a nylon brush for a softer effect. Paint the texture over a base coat of flat color. If you want to add fine lines representing individual hairs or whiskers, use a narrow, round brush and paint with the tip.

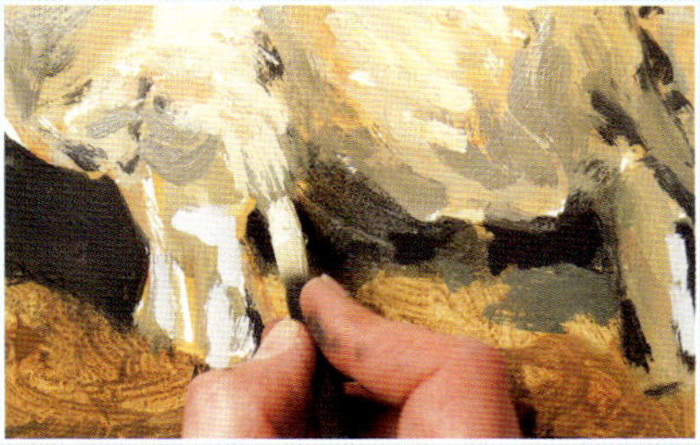

A soft brush is used to drag thick color over a dry underlayer.

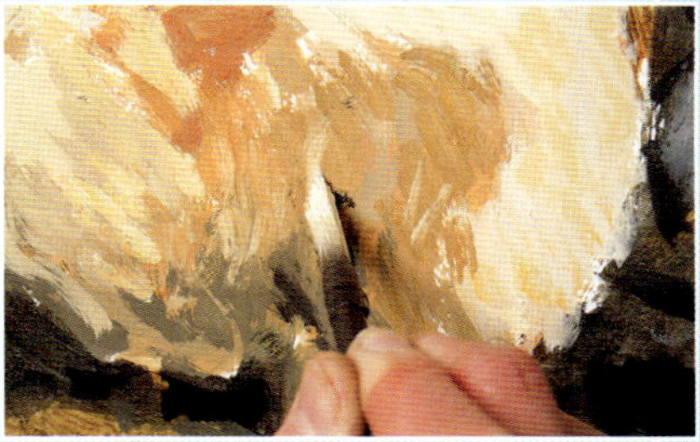

The effect of the long, shaggy coat is built up with brushmarks in different directions.

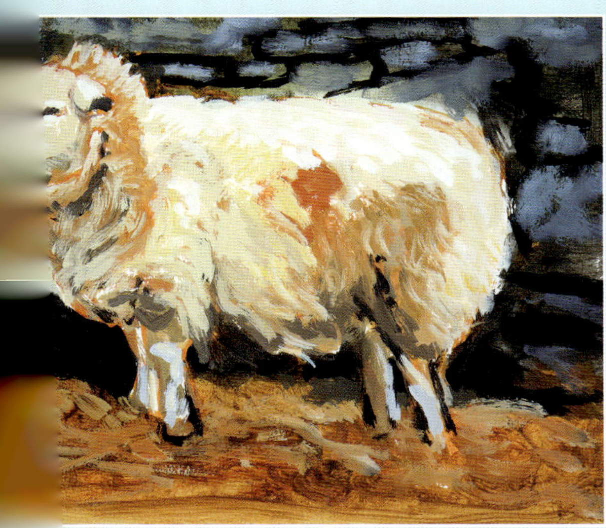

You can see the dry-brush effect clearly around the neck and haunches; the paint does not completely cover the colors beneath.

REMEDIAL METHODS

One of the great attractions of acrylic is that you can make corrections in a number of ways without damaging the picture surface; this makes it the ideal medium for the beginner. If you are using thick, opaque paint you can simply overpaint any mistakes, while colors can be amended by glazing over them.

CLEAN EDGES

410

When you are trying to paint to an outline and your brush wobbles over the edge, use the side of your thumb to gently "push" the color back into place.

While still wet, the paint can be moved around with fingers or thumbs, but do not attempt this if it has begun to dry.

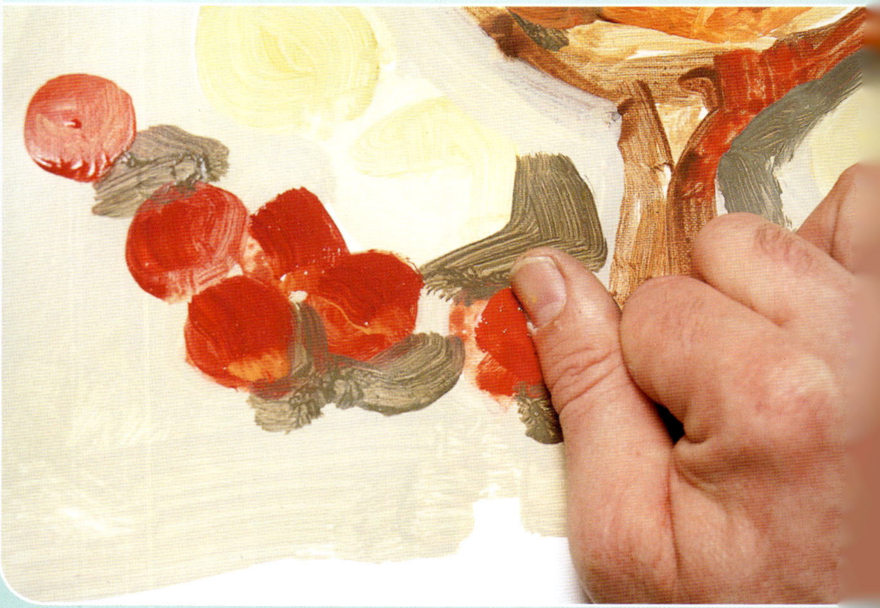

Avoid overworking your colors when making corrections. If you make successive, rapid changes working wet into wet, you will start to get a smeared, muddy surface. At this point, it is best to leave the painting to dry. When you come back to it, you can overpaint cleanly on the sealed surface. Bringing a fresh eye to your work may also suggest a different solution.

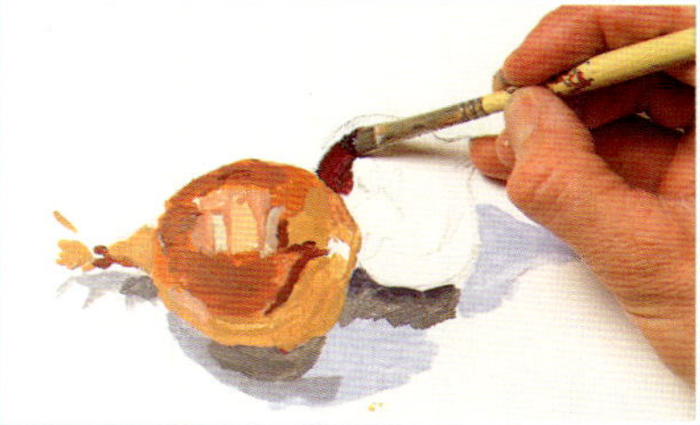

The onions are painted wet into wet to create soft blends.

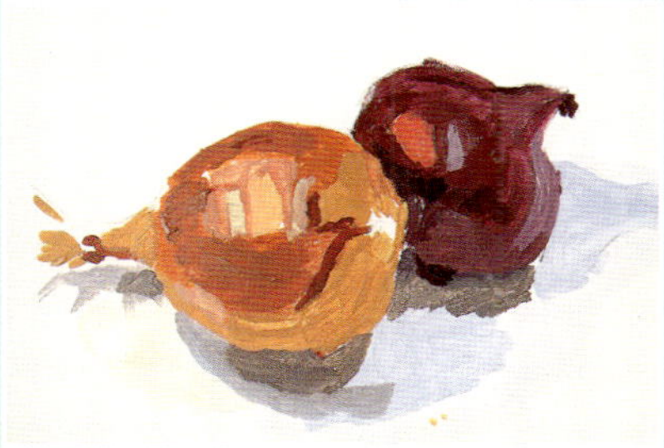

The work is assessed.

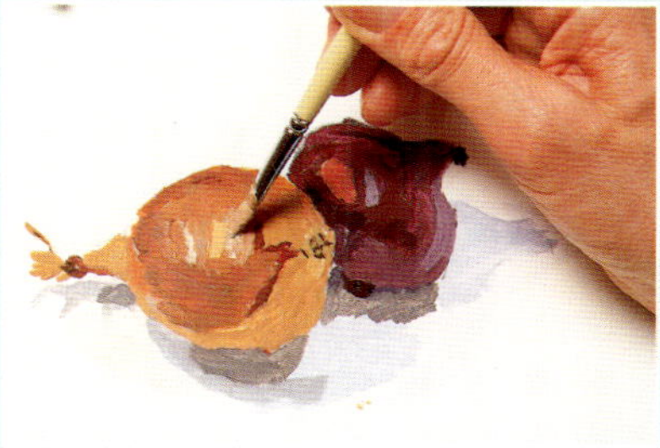

When the painting is dry, the highlights are overpainted.

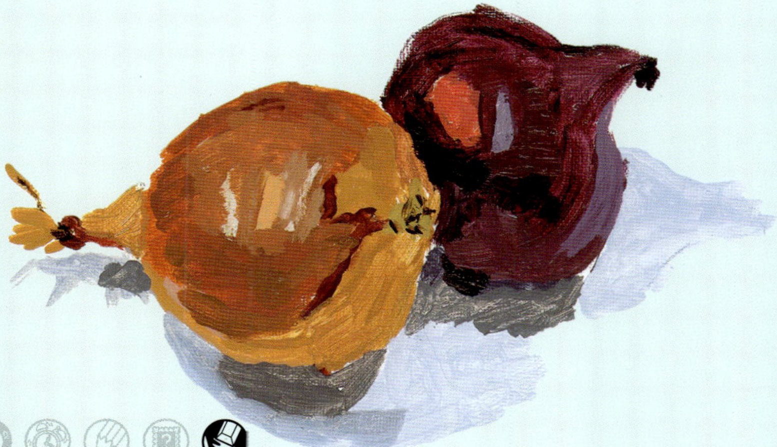

BLOCKING OUT

412

To rework individual shapes and details, simply block them out with a layer of opaque white paint, giving yourself a clean ground for the revision. This method can also help you to make bold decisions about color changes that might lift a dull picture.

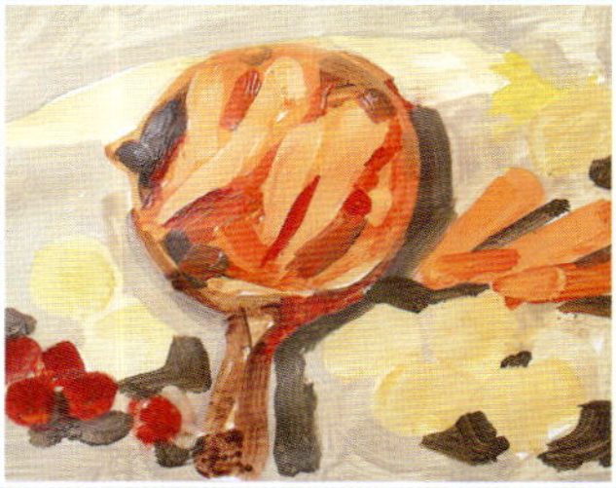

A yellow shape was tried out in the background to balance the foreground fruit.

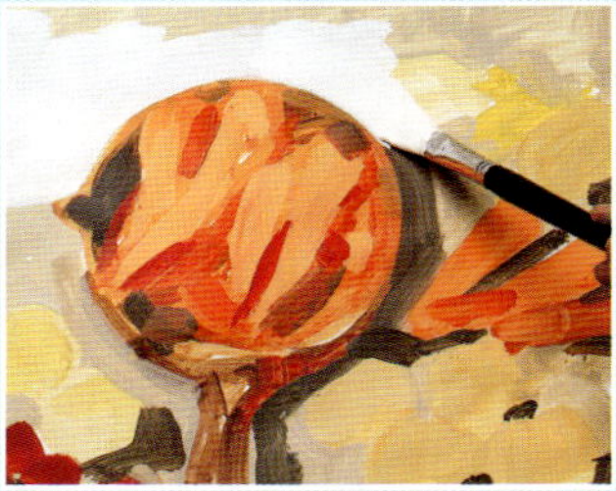

However, the artist decided against this, and so overpaints the area with thick white paint before proceeding further

PATCHING

413

If you want to use a palette knife to scrape back an error or remove some too-thick paint, make your decision quickly before it really starts to dry. Once the plastic skin has formed, the paint will peel away raggedly and may form a rough edge that cannot be overpainted cleanly.

REMOVING PAINT

414

If a particular area of your painting has gone disastrously wrong but you are pleased with the rest, you can stick on a patch of clean paper using an acrylic-based adhesive. Redraw that part of your subject and build up the colors gradually, taking the fresh paint over the edges of the patch to fill the join.

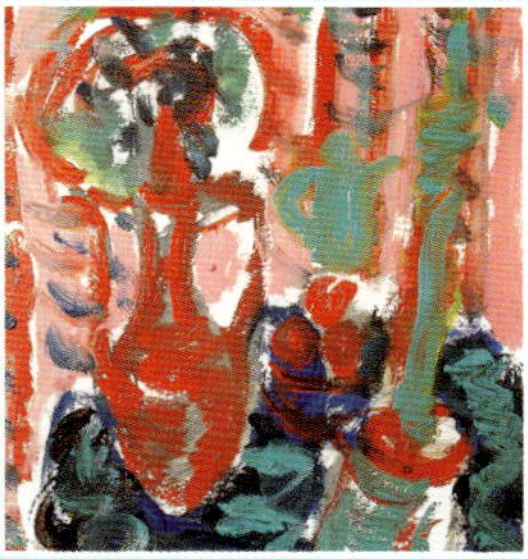

The original choice of color scheme is blue-green and pink.

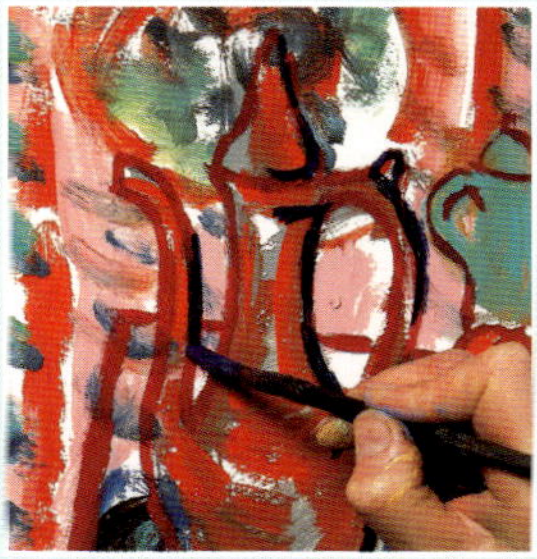

The jug's shape is strengthened with dark outlines.

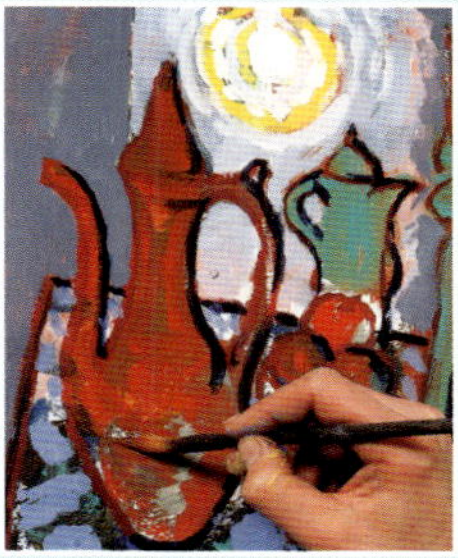

Having added the light, the artist works on the jug.

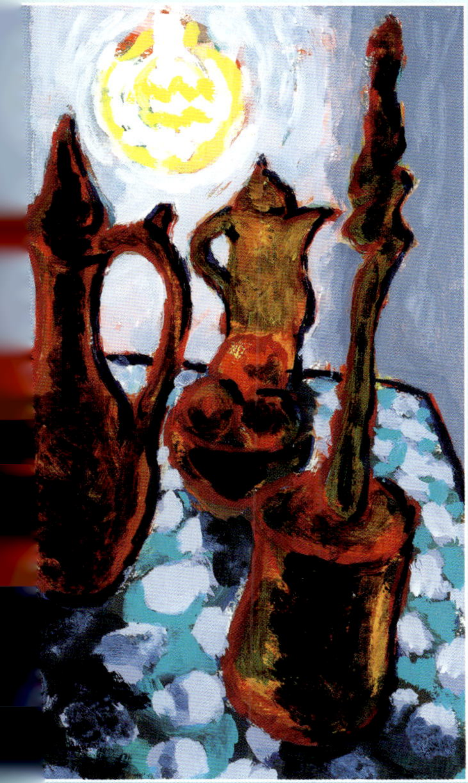

415

Don't throw away a composition that has gone wrong—use it as a learning tool to help you get it right on a second try. Draw with a brush over the shapes and colors that you previously put down, using them as your guide for improving the image. If you always start from scratch, it's easy to repeat the same kind of errors.

In the final stages the picture was radically changed, with the objects now appearing in dark semi-silhouette against the glowing light.

COLOR BALANCE

You can heighten the overall mood of a painting by putting on a final color glaze. For example, a landscape that is not sufficiently sunny can be glazed over thinly with bright yellow; a cozy interior can be bathed in a red glow. Lay the painting flat while you brush on the thinned paint, and let it dry flat to avoid runs and dribbles.

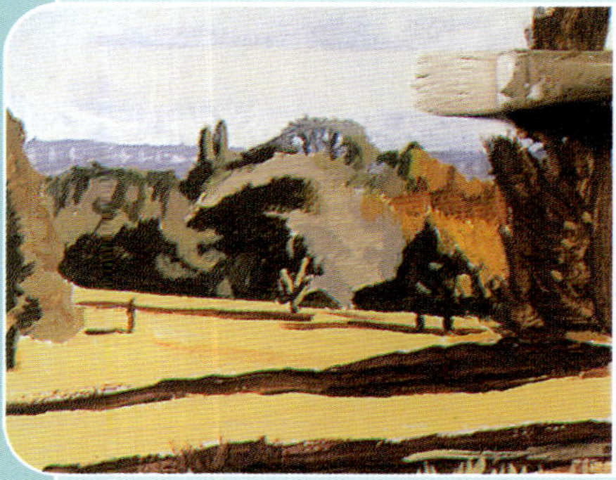

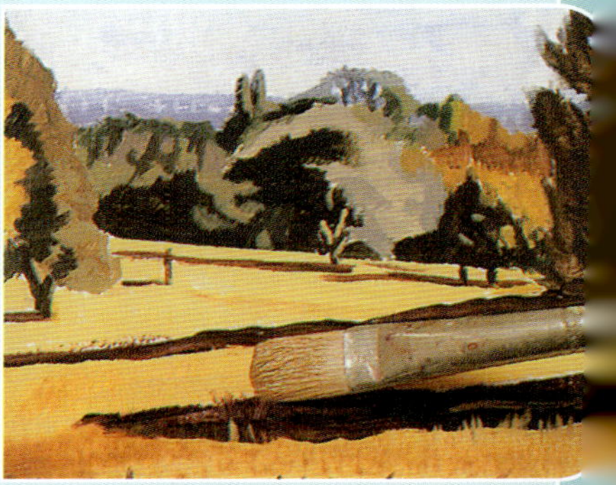

Water-diluted paint is glazed over the foreground.

416

(Below) The foreground glaze has strengthened the color as well as softening the boundaries between sunlight and shadows.

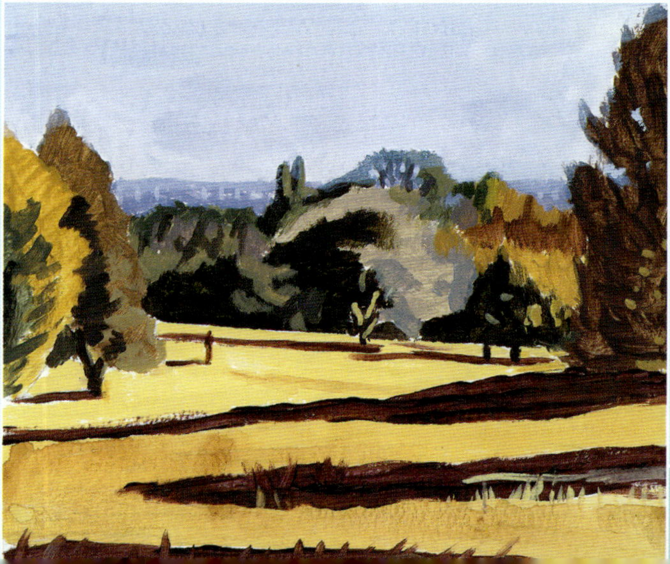

CRAFT APPLICATIONS

Acrylics are tough and highly versatile, and can be used on a wide variety of surfaces, which makes them ideal for decorating a range of household objects, clothing, and children's toys. For shiny surfaces such as glass, you may need to buy a special type of paint, as the normal acrylics are not designed for this purpose, and will not adhere well. Ask for information in your art or craft shop.

CRAFT ACRYLICS

417

For craft projects such as decorative painting and stenciling onto wood, fabrics, paper, cardboard, plastic, papier mâché, or ceramics, special acrylic craft paints are available. These work on all surfaces. Normal artists' acrylics can be used in some craft work though they are not advised for use on non-absorbent surfaces, like ceramics, nor highly absorbent ones. If you're using artists' acrylics on wood, seal the wood first.

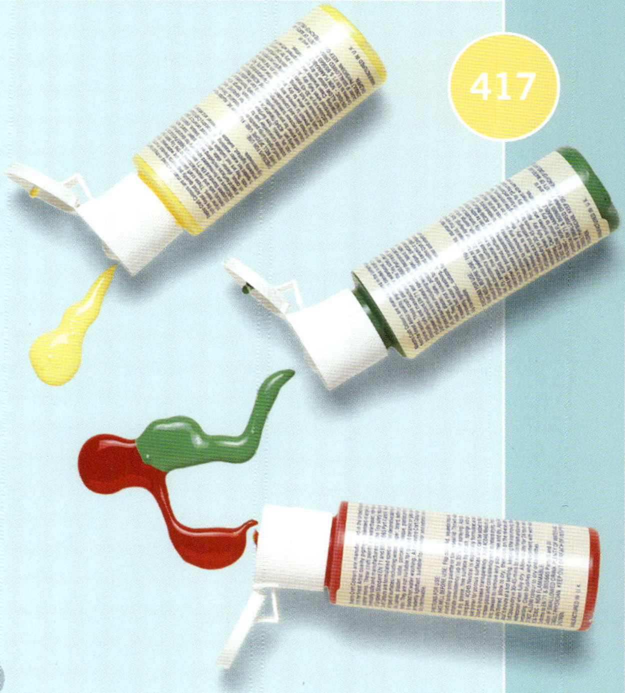

WOODEN TOYS

Simple wooden toys can be easily colored with acrylic paints, but make sure the paints are non-toxic—check the tube or bottle labels or ask for paint information sheets. Use the paint fairly thickly to build up an opaque surface and add details when the paint is dry. When complete, the toy can be varnished to protect the paint.

418

PICTURE FRAMES

Acrylics can be used to give old picture frame a new lease of life or new ones a different surface color. First sand the frame lightly to help the paint adhere to the surface, and ther apply a layer of acrylic gesso and allow to dry Work each side separately, covering the corners with masking tape along the mitered joint before you begin on a section. The paint should be thinned and put on with a wide brush to give a dragged-paint effect. To highlight parts of the frame, wipe carefully with a rag while the paint is still wet. Remov the tape and allow to dry thoroughly before treating the remaining sides.

419

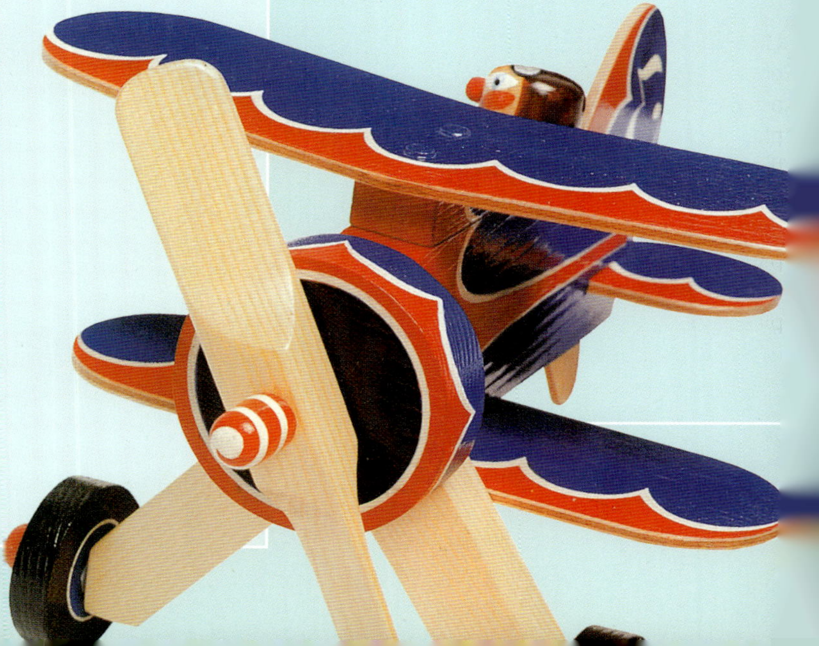

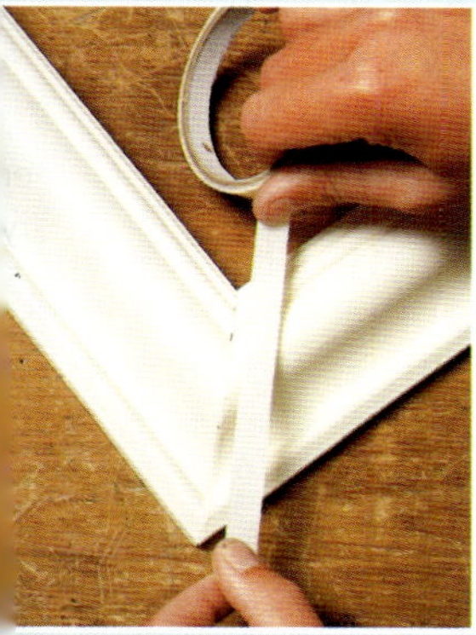

Apply gesso glaze and leave to dry, then stick masking tape over one of the miters.

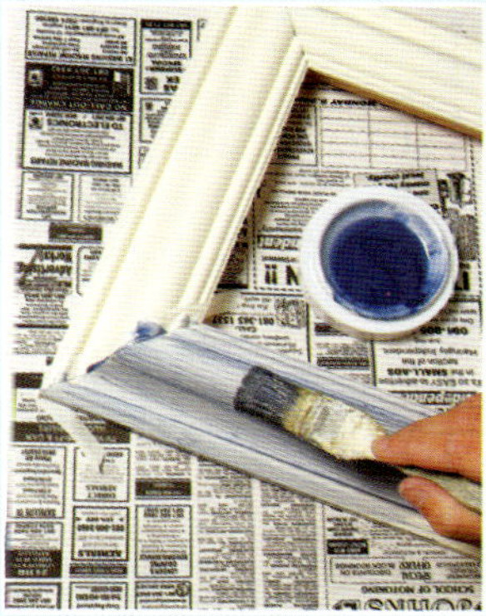

Apply acrylic paint, using long strokes to "drag" the surface evenly.

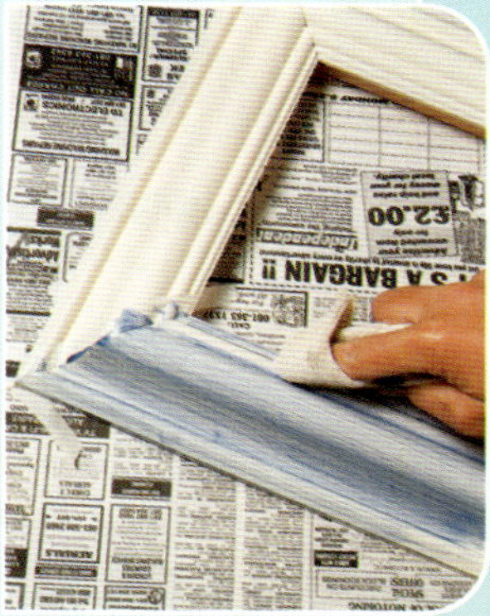

Wipe paint from some of the moldings. Leave to dry. Repeat for remaining sides.

DECORATIVE TERRA COTTA

Liven up an old plant pot by decorating it with acrylic paints. If you plan to grow plants in the pots, leave some of the surface area unpainted, otherwise the painted surface will deteriorate when the plant is watered.

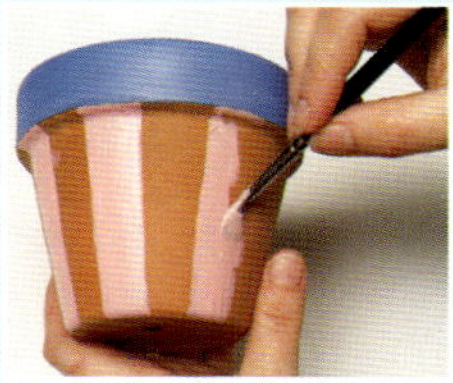

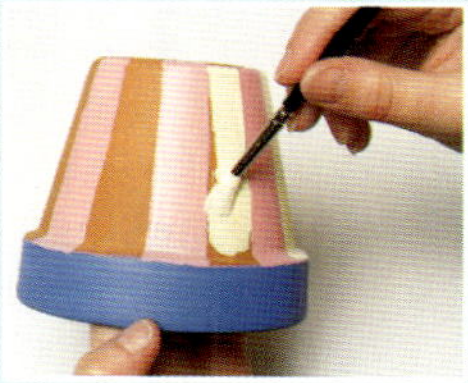

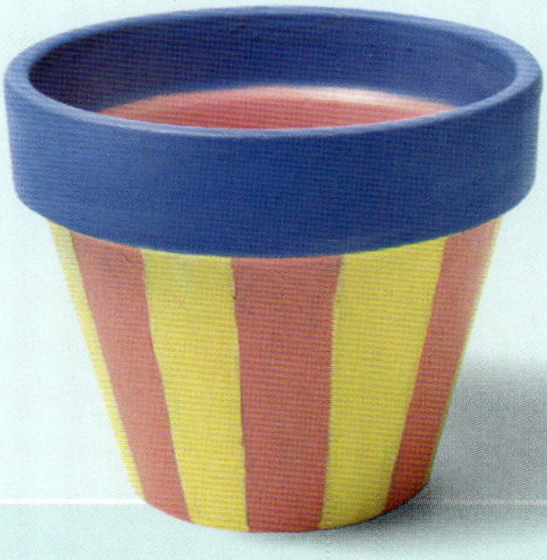

420

PEARLIZED ACRYLIC INKS

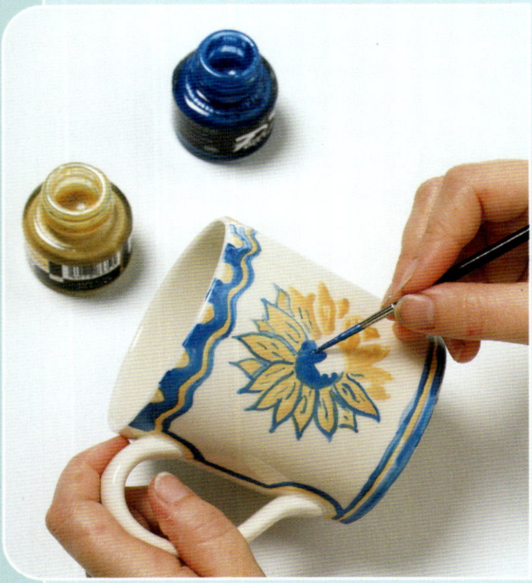

These shimmering colors can be used on glass, ceramic, wood, paper, and board. They are water resistant, though if you have painted a ceramic item you should wash it by hand.

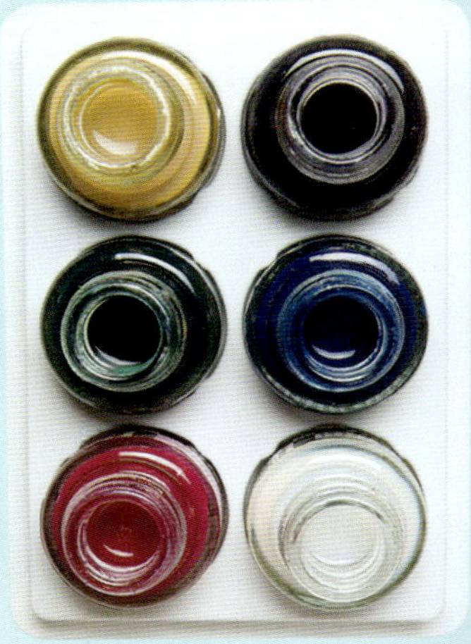

421

THIN FABRICS

422

Acrylic paint can come through a thin fabric, so, if you are painting a garment such as a T-shirt, place a piece of clean card between the two layers so that the paint is only absorbed by the layer on which you are working. The card will also provide a firm surface on which to paint.

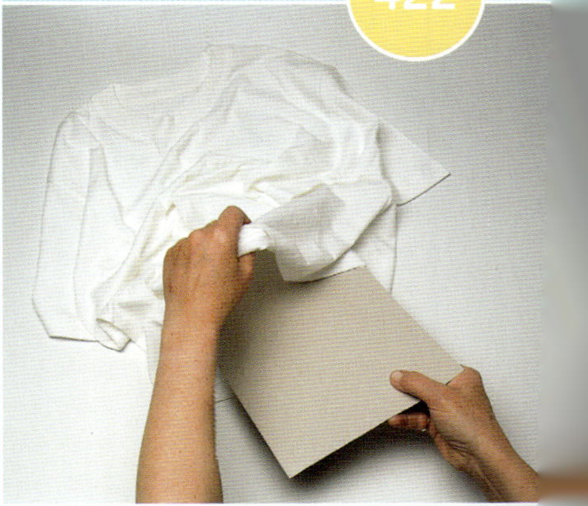

423

Whether stenciling or painting fabrics, such as canvas, it is important to wash the fabric first so that any size is removed, since this may hinder paint absorption. If the fabric becomes too soft, it can be starched when the decoration is completed. If you are decorating a large area, such as a pair of curtains, before starting test the paint on the wrong side of the fabric or on a spare piece.

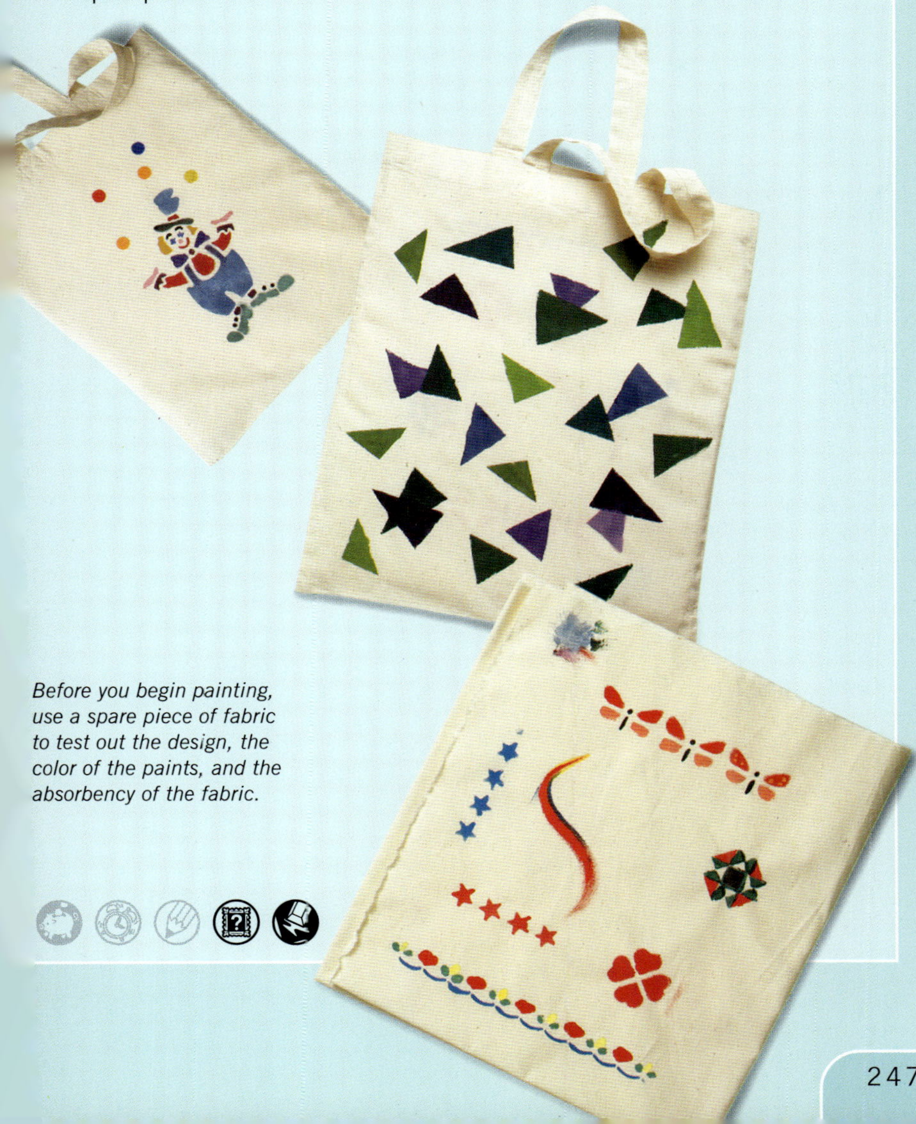

Before you begin painting, use a spare piece of fabric to test out the design, the color of the paints, and the absorbency of the fabric.

PAINTING PAPIER MÂCHÉ

Acrylic paints give a strong, solid flat finish to papier mâché, which can then be varnished. If using a light base color, cover the papier mâché with a coat of white latex paint or gesso to prevent the newsprint showing through. The design details here have been added with a black fine-pointed permanent marker.

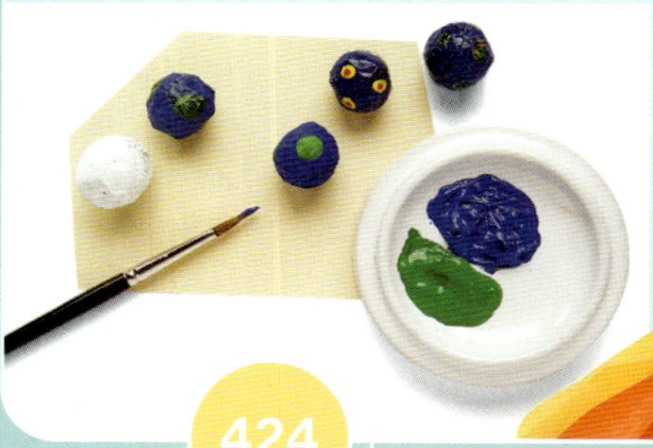

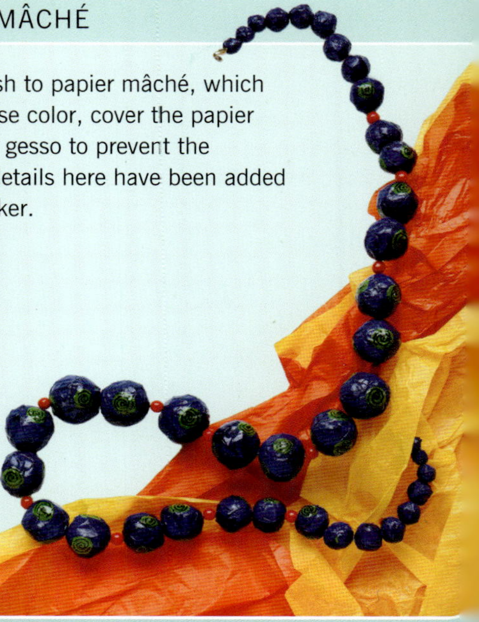

424

PAINT AND GLITTER

This shell has been decorated with a combination of pearlized paint, glitter, and gilt. You can buy ready-made blank plaster casts from craft shops. You could try making a set of shells, pearlized in different colors using the gilded finish to link them as a set.

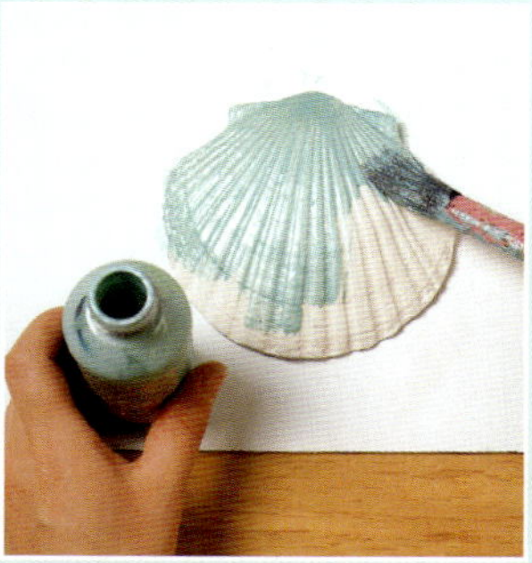

Brush on the pearlized paint.

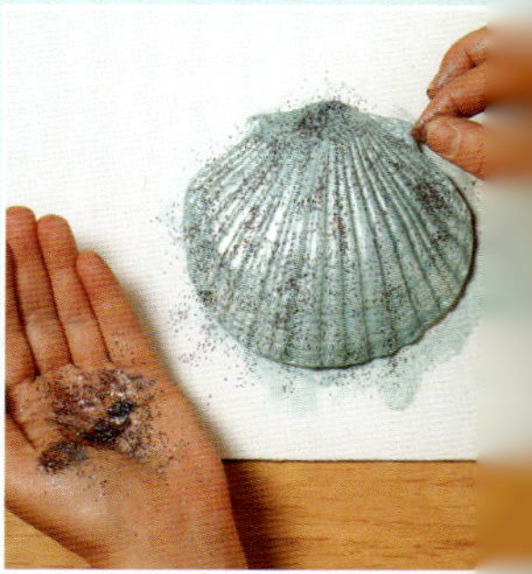

Before the paint dries, sprin on the glitter.

425

PAINTED GLASS

426

You can make an art object out of a plain glass bottle or storage container by painting a design on the outside. Cut a piece of paper that will fit inside the container and draw the design on it. Stick the paper firmly to the inside of the container to act as a guide.

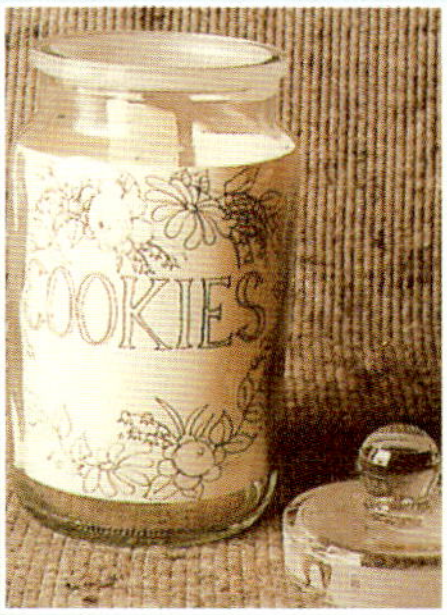

Draw your design on a piece of paper and put it inside the jar.

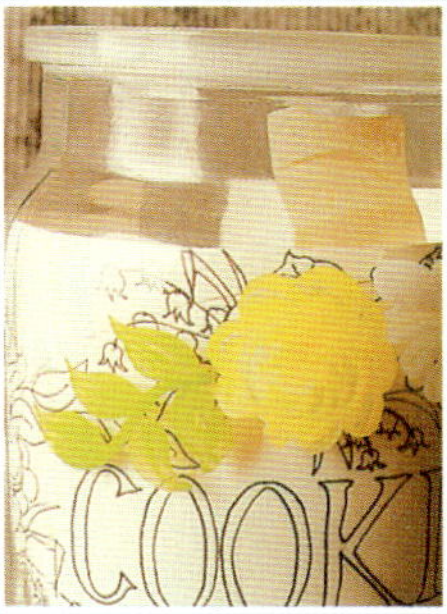

Paint onto the glass following the paper pattern.

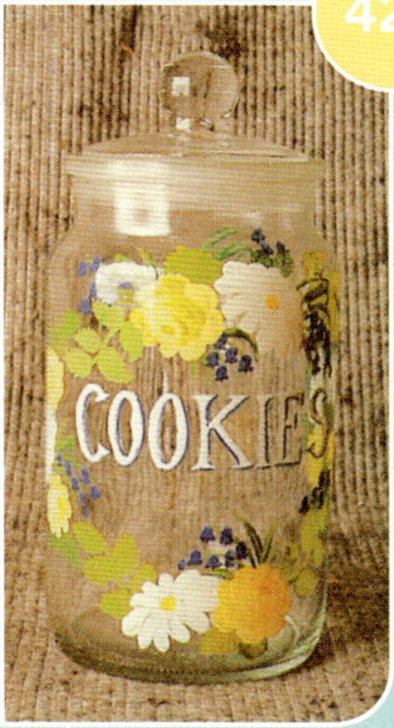

The finished cookie jar.

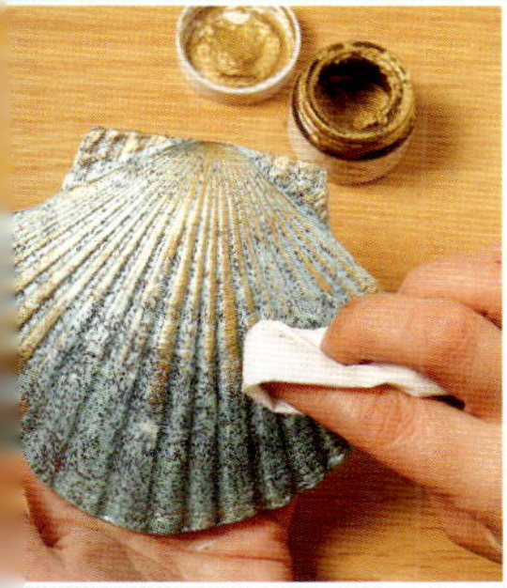

y highlights of gold gilding along the shell's ridges.

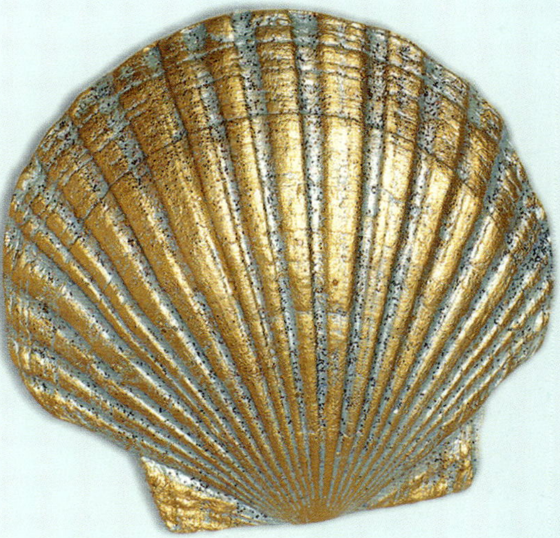

GLOSSARY

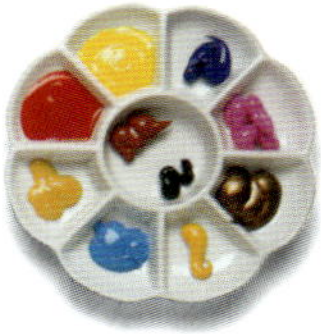

Backrun The ragged-edged blotch that occurs when new paint comes into contact with paint that is not quite dry.

Blocking in The first stage of a painting: the main areas are roughly put in as broad, flat areas of *tone* and color.

Broken color Dabs and specks of different colors combine and mix in the viewer's eye.

Complementary colors The pairs of colors that are opposite each other on the color wheel: red and green, blue and orange, and yellow and violet.

Dry brush Dryish paint is pulled across the surface of the painting. The paint is picked up by ridges in the surface that are caused by the texture of the canvas, paper, or paint surface. It creates a *broken color* effect.

Earth colors A range of colors made from pigments containing metal oxides (naturally occurring substances in soil and rock). They include the ochers, siennas, and umbers.

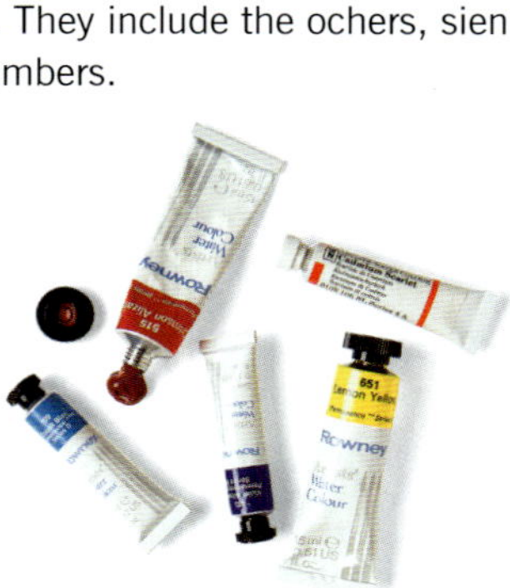

Fat over lean Applies to oil painting done in layers. The oil content of the paint is increased for each successive layer. This helps to prevent cracking as the paint dries out.

Fixative A thin varnish sprayed onto pastel or charcoal drawings to prevent smudging.

Form The three-dimensional quality of objects. An object's form is revealed by light and shadow.

Glaze A layer of thin, transparent paint applied over an opaque layer altering or modifying the underlying color.

Ground A preparatory coating of paint (primer) given to the support. A ground can be white or colored.

Impasto Paint is applied thickly so that it stands out from the surface of the painting.

Lifting out In watercolor, paint is removed with a wet brush or sponge.

Lost and found Refers to painted edges that alternate between sharp and broken, to imitate the way edges betw objects are visible in lit areas and disappear in shadow.

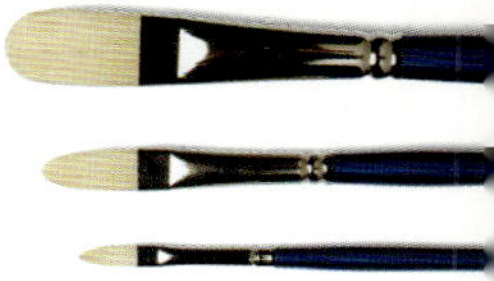

Medium 1. The type of paint or other material from which any artwork is made. 2. The substance with which pigment is mixed to make paint. 3. The substances added to paint to change its consistency or appearance.

Palette 1. The flat surface on which paints are laid out and mixed. 2. The range of colors used in a work, or the characteristic range used by an individual artist.

igment The substance that provides olor in paints.

lane A flat surface. An object is ade up of many planes facing in fferent directions.

ointillism Pure colors are applied in y specks that combine and mix to eate other colors. See *broken color*.

imary colors The only colors that nnot be made by mixing other colors: l, yellow, and blue.

iming Applying one or two coats of mer—oil, acrylic, or acrylic gesso—to upport to make the support less sorbent or easier to paint on.

umbling Opaque or semi-nsparent thick or dry paint is pulled oss another color so that flecks of the erlying color can still be seen.

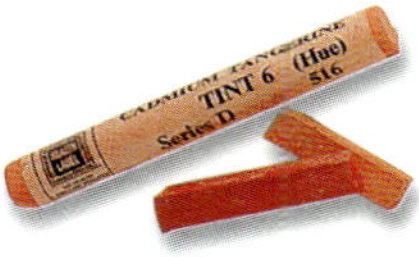

Secondary colors The colors that are obtained by mixing two *primaries*.

Sgraffito A way of drawing by scratching or scraping through the top layer of a painting to reveal a different color or tone beneath.

Shade A darkened version of a color, made by adding black.

Staining A very thin, transparent layer of color applied to a *ground*.

Support The surface—canvas, wood, board, or paper—on which a painting is made.

Tint A lightened version of a color, made by adding white.

Tone, also value The lightness or darkness of a color. Every color has a natural tone.

Wash A very diluted, transparent paint mixture that is applied broadly over large areas in watercolor and acrylics.

Wet into wet The addition of wet paint into or over an area of paint that has not dried, in order to blend or modify colors and tones already on the canvas.

Wet over dry The application of wet paint over an area of dry paint.

INDEX

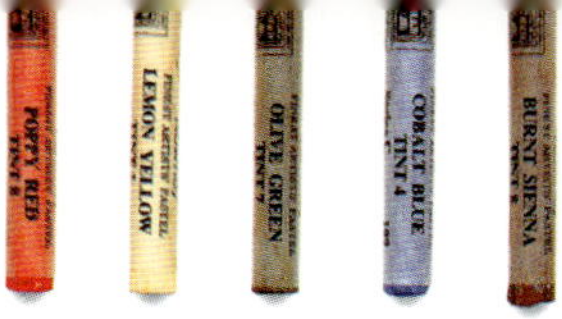
POPPY RED
LEMON YELLOW
OLIVE GREEN
COBALT BLUE
TINT 4
BURNT SIENNA

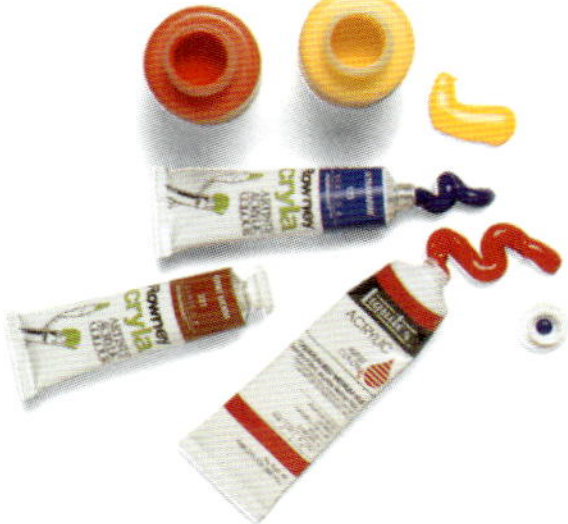

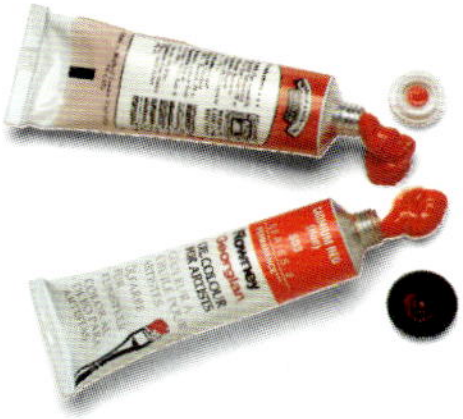

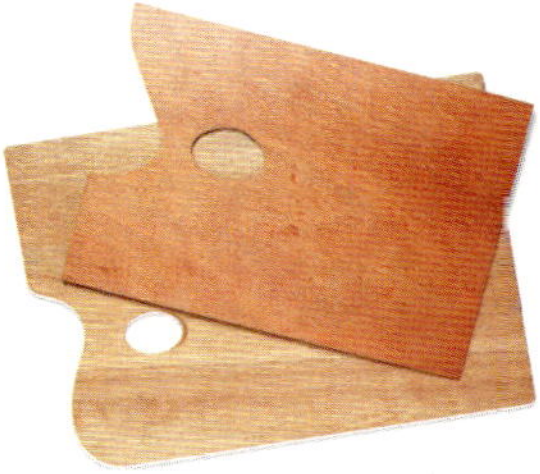

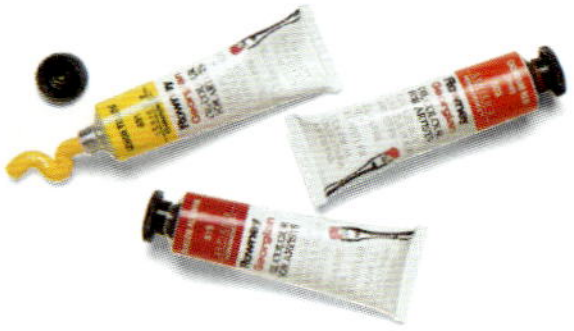

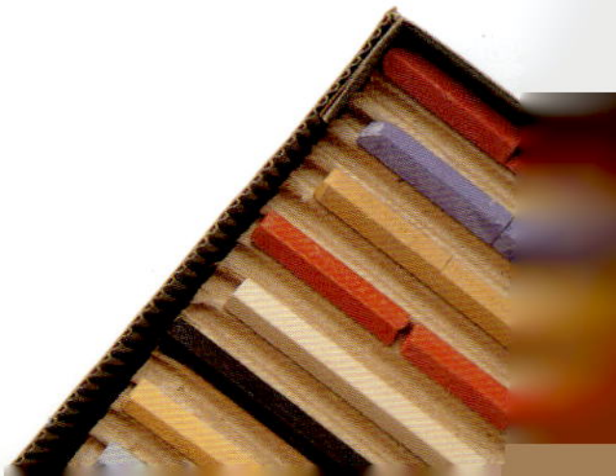

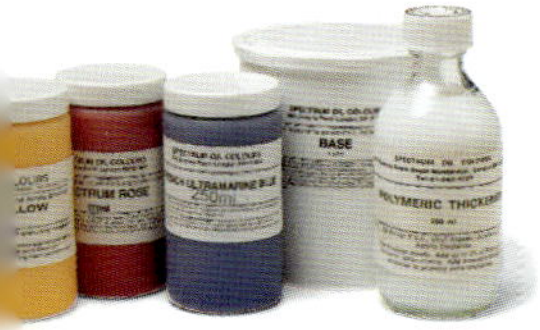

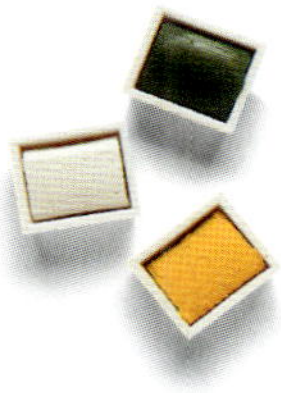

CREDITS

Quarto would like to thank the following:

Mrs. G. Barwick; Gordana Bjelic-Rados; John S. Bowman; Rosalind Cuthbert; Jean Canter; Moira Clinch; Miranda Creswell; Brian Dunce; Vivien Frank; Charles Glover; Hazel Harrison; Sally Launder; J. Lockheart Davidson; Emma Pearce (Technical Advisor, Winsor & Newton), Jackie Simmonds; Hazel Soan and Frances Treanor for invaluable hints and tips given while researching this book.

George Cayford; Patrick Cullen; Sarah Doe; Ron Fuller; Jeremy Galton; Debra Manifold; Karen Rainey; Ian Sidaway; Jackie Schou; Jane Strother and Mark Topham for demonstrating the techniques.

Daler-Rowney and Langford & Hill for the artist's materials.

Maestro Craft Colours Ltd. for the craft paints.

Spectrum Oil Colours, London, SW19, for pigments for mixing your own paints.

Peter Russel of P.R. Art, Stevenage, Herts, who supplied the pochade box.

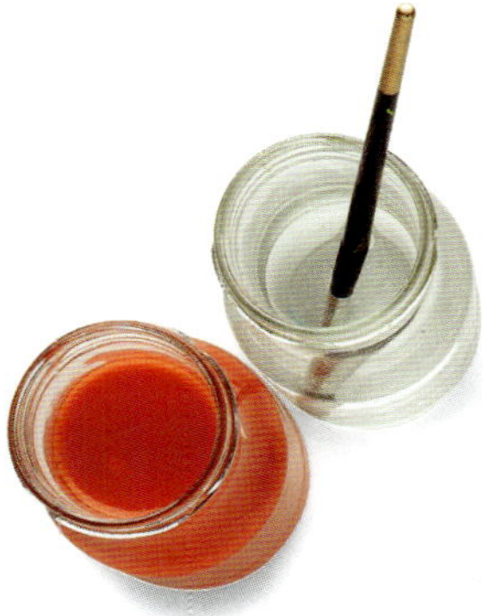

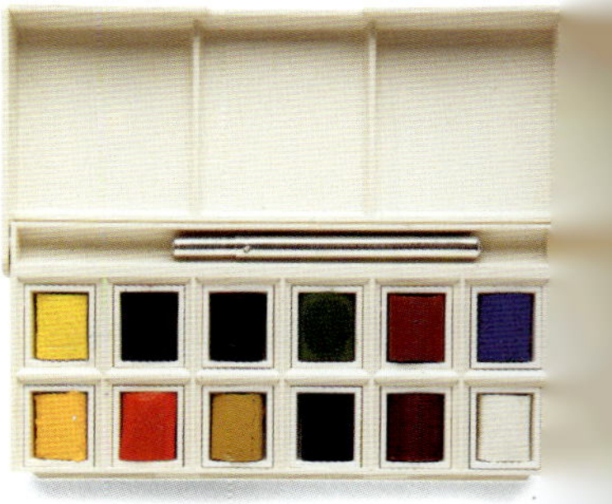

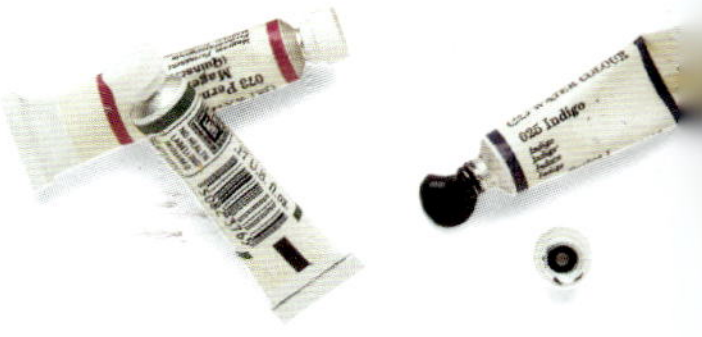